The Oxford Book of
Twentieth-Century
English Verse

The Oxford Book of Twentieth-Century English Verse

Chosen by
Philip Larkin

Clarendon Press · Oxford
1973

Oxford University Press, Ely House, London W. 1

GLASGOW NEW YORK TORONTO MELBOURNE WELLINGTON
CAPE TOWN IBADAN NAIROBI DAR ES SALAAM LUSAKA ADDIS ABABA
DELHI BOMBAY CALCUTTA MADRAS KARACHI LAHORE DACCA
KUALA LUMPUR SINGAPORE HONG KONG TOKYO

PRINTED IN GREAT BRITAIN BY
RICHARD CLAY (THE CHAUCER PRESS), LTD.
BUNGAY, SUFFOLK

PREFACE

I have taken 'twentieth-century English verse' to mean verse written in English by writers born in these islands (or resident here for an appreciable time) who were alive during the twentieth century and during it made or added to their reputations. At first I made the further qualification that such writers must also have published at least one collection of poems under their own names by the end of 1965, but ultimately I relaxed this ruling in a few cases.

These terms of reference mean that I have not included poems by American or Commonwealth writers, nor poems requiring a glossary for their full understanding. Nor have I included translations, as distinct from poems based on other poems. No doubt in making up the collection I have unwittingly broken most of these self-imposed limitations at one time or another, but this is where I meant to draw the line.

In textual matters I have tried to use the latest version that the author may be supposed to have approved, but in some instances I have accepted the text that came readiest to hand. The table of contents, at any rate, supplies my sources. Many people have helped me in my choice of poems, sometimes unconsciously, but I must record my indebtedness to Miss M. M. B. Jones for her constant encouragement and for many valuable suggestions for the book's improvement. I am grateful, too, to Mr. Anthony Thwaite who unselfishly allowed me to draw on his superior knowledge of present-day literature. Without the generosity of the Warden and Fellows of All Souls College, Oxford, in offering me a Visiting Fellowship for two terms in 1970/1 I do not think I should ever have completed my task, and similar acknowledgement must be made to the University of Hull for granting me concurrent study leave. My work in Oxford, finally, was immeasurably facilitated by the kind help of Bodley's Librarian and his staff, and in particular that of Mr. I. G. Philip, Keeper of Printed Books.

In making my selection I have striven to hold a balance between all the different considerations that press on anyone undertaking a book of this kind. At first I thought I would let the century choose the poets while I chose the poems, but outside two or three dozen names this did not really work. In the end I found that my material fell into three groups: poems representing aspects of the talents of poets judged either by the age or by myself to be worthy of inclusion, poems judged by me to be worthy of inclusion without reference to their authors, and

v

poems judged by me to carry with them something of the century in which they were written. Needless to say, the three groups are not equal in size, nor are they mutually exclusive. Looking at what I have chosen, I see that it represents a much greater number of poets than are to be found in the volumes corresponding to this one for the nineteenth and eighteenth centuries. To some extent this is due to the kind of book I wanted to produce, but it also prompts the conclusion that once the anthologist has to deal with poets born after 1914 his loyalty turns perforce to poems rather than to individuals. The consequence of this is wide rather than deep representation, and in accepting it I have acted not so much critically, or even historically, but as someone wanting to bring together poems that will give pleasure to their readers both separately and as a collection.

PHILIP LARKIN

University of Hull,
1971

ACKNOWLEDGEMENTS

The editor and publishers gratefully acknowledge permission to reproduce copyright poems in this book.

Drummond Allison: from *The Yellow Night*. Reprinted by permission of the Fortune Press.

Kenneth Allott: from *Poems* (The Hogarth Press, 1938). Reprinted by permission of the author.

Kingsley Amis: from *A Look Round the Estate : Poems 1957–67*. Copyright © 1962, 1967 by Kingsley Amis. Reprinted by permission of Jonathan Cape Ltd. and Harcourt Brace Jovanovich, Inc.; from *A Case of Samples*. Reprinted by permission of Victor Gollancz Ltd. and Curtis Brown Ltd.

Herbert Asquith: from *The Volunteer*. Reprinted by permission of Sidgwick & Jackson Ltd.

W. H. Auden: 'In memory of W. B. Yeats', 'Brussels in Winter', 'Lullaby', 'Miss Gee' (Copyright 1940 and renewed 1968 by W. H. Auden); 'That night when joy began' (Copyright 1937 and renewed 1965 by W. H. Auden); 'The Exiles', 'This Lunar Beauty', 'Missing', 'No Change of Place' (Copyright 1934 and renewed 1962 by W. H. Auden); 'Goodbye to the Mezzogiorno' (Copyright 1958 by W. H. Auden); 'The Fall of Rome' (Copyright 1947 by W. H. Auden); 'Night Mail'. All from *Collected Shorter Poems 1927–1957*. 'You are the Town and we are the Clock' (Copyright 1945 by W. H. Auden) and 'The summer holds: upon its glittering lake' from *The Dog Beneath the Skin* (Copyright 1935 and renewed 1963 by W. H. Auden and Christopher Isherwood). 'On the Circuit' and 'Up There' from *About the House* (Copyright 1965 by W. H. Auden. Reprinted by permission of Faber and Faber Ltd. and Random House, Inc.).

Gavin Bantock: from *A New Thing Breathing*. Reprinted by permission of Anvil Press Poetry.

George Barker: from *Collected Poems 1930–1955*. Copyright 1957, 1962, and 1965 by George Granville Barker. Reprinted by permission of Faber and Faber Ltd. and October House Inc.; from *Dreams of a Summer Night*. Reprinted by permission of Faber and Faber Ltd. and John Johnson.

Joan Barton: from *Listen*, 1960. Reprinted by permission of the author and The Marvell Press.

Patricia Beer: from *Just Like the Resurrection*. Reprinted by permission of Macmillan London and Basingstoke.

Sir Max Beerbohm: from *Max in Verse*, ed. J. G. Riewald. Reprinted by permission of William Heinemann Ltd. and The Stephen Greene Press.

Martin Bell: from *Collected Poems 1937–1966*. Reprinted by permission of Macmillan London and Basingstoke.

Hilaire Belloc: from *Sonnets and Verse* (Gerald Duckworth & Co. Ltd.). Reprinted by permission of A. D. Peters and Company.

vii

ACKNOWLEDGEMENTS

Arnold Bennett: from *Journals 1896–1910*. Reprinted by permission of A. P. Watt & Son on behalf of Mrs. Dorothy Cheston Bennett and Penguin Books Ltd.

Stella Benson: from *Poems*. Reprinted by permission of Curtis Brown Ltd. on behalf of the Estate of Stella Benson.

Sir John Betjeman: from *Collected Poems* and from *Summoned by Bells* (Copyright © 1960 by John Betjeman). Reprinted by permission of John Murray (Publishers) Ltd. and Houghton Mifflin Company.

Laurence Binyon: from *Collected Poems*, *The Four Years*, and *The Burning of the Leaves*. Reprinted by permission of Mrs. Nicolete Gray and The Society of Authors on behalf of the Laurence Binyon Estate.

Thomas Blackburn: from *The Next Word*. Reprinted by permission of the author; from *A Smell of Burning*. Reprinted by permission of Putnam & Company.

Edmund Blunden: from *Collected Poems*. Reprinted by permission of Gerald Duckworth & Co. Ltd.

Wilfrid S. Blunt: from *The Poetry of Wilfrid Blunt*. Reprinted by permission of the Fitzwilliam Museum, Cambridge.

Robert Bridges: from *The Poetical Works with the Testament of Beauty*. Reprinted by permission of the Clarendon Press, Oxford.

Alan Brownjohn: from *The Lion's Mouth*. Reprinted by permission of Macmillan London and Basingstoke; from *The Railings*. Reprinted by permission of the author.

Basil Bunting: from *Collected Poems*. Copyright © Basil Bunting 1968. Reprinted by permission of the Fulcrum Press.

Norman Cameron: from *Collected Poems*. Reprinted by permission of The Hogarth Press on behalf of the Author's Literary Estate.

Joseph Campbell: from *Poems* (Figgis & Co. Ltd.). Reprinted by permission of Simon Campbell.

Roy Campbell: 'Heartbreak Camp', 'The Georgiad' and 'The Golden Shower' from *Collected Poems 1949–1960*. Reprinted by permission of The Bodley Head and of Henry Regnery Co. for 'The Georgiad'; 'Autumn', 'On Some South African Novelists' and 'On the Same' from *Adamastor* (Faber and Faber Ltd.). Reprinted by permission of Curtis Brown Ltd. on behalf of the Estate of Roy Campbell.

May Wedderburn Cannan: from *In War Time* (Basil Blackwell Ltd.). Reprinted by permission of the author.

Christopher Caudwell: from *Poems*. Reprinted by permission of Lawrence & Wishart Ltd.

Charles Causley: 'Chief Petty Officer', 'Recruiting Drive' and 'Betjeman, 1984' from *Union Street* (Hart-Davis). Reprinted by permission of David Higham Associates Ltd.; from *Underneath the Water*. Reprinted by permission of Macmillan London and Basingstoke.

G. K. Chesterton: from *The Collected Poems of G. K. Chesterton*. Reprinted by permission of A. P. Watt & Son on behalf of Miss D. E. Collins and Methuen & Co. Ltd.

Richard Church: from *Collected Poems* (William Heinemann Ltd.) Reprinted

ACKNOWLEDGEMENTS

by permission of Laurence Pollinger Ltd. on behalf of the Estate of the late Richard Church.

Austin Clarke: from *Collected Poems*. Reprinted by permission of George Allen & Unwin Ltd.

Barry Cole: from *The Visitors*. Reprinted by permission of Methuen & Co. Ltd.

G. D. H. Cole: from *The Crooked World* (Victor Gollancz Ltd.). Reprinted by permission of Mrs. G. D. H. Cole.

Padraic Colum: from *Poems* (The Macmillan Company). Reprinted by permission of Emmet M. Greene, Executor of the Estate of Padraic Colum.

Alex Comfort and George Orwell: from *The Collected Essays, Journalism and Letters of George Orwell*. (Secker & Warburg, Ltd.). Reprinted by permission of Dr. A. Comfort. A. M. Heath & Co. Ltd. and Harcourt Brace Jovanovich, Inc.

Tony Connor: from *Lodgers*. © Oxford University Press 1965. Reprinted by permission of Oxford University Press, London.

Robert Conquest: from *Between Mars and Venus*. Reprinted by permission of Curtis Brown Ltd. on behalf of Robert Conquest.

Frances Cornford: from *Collected Poems*. Reprinted by permission of Barrie and Jenkins Ltd.

John Cornford: from *John Cornford: A Memoir*, edited by Pat Sloan. Reprinted by permission of Jonathan Cape Ltd. on behalf of Pat Sloan.

Sir Noel Coward: from *Not Yet the Dodo*. Copyright © 1967 by Sir Noel Coward. Reprinted by permission of Curtis Brown Ltd. and Doubleday & Co. Inc.

R. N. Currey: from *This Other Planet*. Reprinted by permission of Routledge & Kegan Paul Ltd; from *Tiresias*. Reprinted by permission of the author.

Donald Davie: from *The Forests of Lithuania*. Reprinted by permission of The Marvell Press; from *A Winter Talent* and *Essex Poems*. Reprinted by permission of Routledge & Kegan Paul Ltd.; from *Brides of Reason*. Reprinted by permission of the author.

Idris Davies: from *Tonypandy* and *Selected Poems* (Faber and Faber Ltd.). Reprinted by permission of Mrs. D. Morris.

W. H. Davies: from *Complete Poems*. Reprinted by permission of Mrs. H. M. Davies, Jonathan Cape Ltd. and Wesleyan University Press.

C. Day-Lewis: from *Collected Poems*. (Copyright 1954 by C. Day-Lewis); from *The Room and Other Poems* and *The Gate* (Copyright by C. Day-Lewis). Reprinted by permission of Jonathan Cape Ltd. and the Harold Matson Company, Inc.

Paul Dehn: from *The Fern on the Rock*. Copyright © 1965 by Paul Dehn. Reprinted by permission of Hamish Hamilton Ltd.

Walter de la Mare: from *Complete Poems*. Reprinted by permission of the Literary Trustees of Walter de la Mare and The Society of Authors as their representative.

Keith Douglas: from *Collected Poems*. Reprinted by permission of Faber and Faber Ltd. and Chilmark Press.

John Drinkwater: from *Collected Poems*. Reprinted by permission of the author's representatives and Sidgwick & Jackson Ltd.

ACKNOWLEDGEMENTS

Douglas Dunn: from *Terry Street*. Reprinted by permission of Faber and Faber Ltd. and Chilmark Press.

Lawrence Durrell: from *Collected Poems*. Copyright © 1956, 1960 by Lawrence Durrell. Reprinted by permission of Faber and Faber Ltd. and E. P. Dutton & Co., Inc.

Clifford Dyment: from *Collected Poems*. Reprinted by permission of J. M. Dent & Sons Ltd.

T. S. Eliot: from *The Complete Poems and Plays of T. S. Eliot*. Reprinted by permission of Faber and Faber Ltd. In the U.S. 'Gus: The Theatre Cat' is reprinted from *Old Possum's Book of Practical Cats*. Copyright 1939 by T. S. Eliot, copyright 1967 by Esmé Valerie Eliot, by permission of Harcourt Brace Jovanovich. All other poems are reprinted by permission of Harcourt Brace Jovanovich, Inc. from *Collected Poems 1909-1962*, copyright 1936 by Harcourt Brace Jovanovich, Inc.; copyright © 1943, 1963, 1964 by T. S. Eliot, and from *Murder in the Cathedral*, copyright 1935 by Harcourt Brace Jovanovich, Inc.; copyright 1963 by T. S. Eliot.

Colin Ellis: from *Mournful Numbers*. Reprinted by permission of Macmillan London and Basingstoke.

William Empson: from *Collected Poems*. Copyright 1949 by William Empson. Reprinted by permission of the author, Chatto and Windus Ltd. and Harcourt Brace Jovanovich, Inc.

D. J. Enright: from *The Laughing Hyena* (Routledge & Kegan Paul Ltd.), *Unlawful Assembly* and *Selected Poems* (Chatto & Windus Ltd.). Copyright © D. J. Enright. Reprinted by permission of Bolt & Watson Ltd.

Gavin Ewart: from *The Poetry of War 1939-45*, ed. Ian Hamilton and from *The Deceptive Grin of the Gravel Porters*. Reprinted by permission of The London Magazine.

Gilbert Frankau: from *Selected Verses*. Reprinted by permission of A. P. Watt & Son on behalf of the Estate of the late Gilbert Frankau.

G. S. Fraser: from *Home Town Elegy*. Reprinted by permission of the author.

Roy Fuller: from *Collected Poems 1936-1961* and from *New Poems*. Reprinted by permission of André Deutsch Ltd.

Robert Garioch: from *Selected Poems*. Reprinted by permission of the author.

David Gascoyne: from *Collected Poems*, edited by Robin Skelton. Reprinted by permission of Oxford University Press, London.

Wilfrid Gibson: from *Collected Poems*. Reprinted by permission of Mr. M. Gibson, The Macmillan Company of Canada and Macmillan London and Basingstoke.

Robert Gittings: from *This Tower my Prison*. Reprinted by permission of the author.

Oliver St. John Gogarty: from *Collected Poems*. Copyright 1954 by Oliver St. John Gogarty. Reprinted by permission of Constable Publishers and The Devin-Adair Company.

W. S. Graham: from *The Nightfishing*. Reprinted by permission of Faber and Faber Ltd.

K. W. Gransden: from *Any Day*. Copyright © 1960. Reprinted by permission of Abelard-Schuman Ltd.

ACKNOWLEDGEMENTS

Robert Graves: from *Collected Poems 1965* and *Over the Brazier*. Reprinted by permission of A. P. Watt & Son on behalf of Mr. Robert Graves.

F. Pratt Green: from *New Poems 1965* (Hutchinson). Originally published in *The Listener*, 27 April, 1964. Reprinted by permission of the author.

Julian Grenfell: from *Men Who March Away*, ed. I. M. Parsons. Reprinted by permission of Burns & Oates Ltd.

Geoffrey Grigson: from *Collected Poems*. Reprinted by permission of the author.

Thom Gunn: from *The Sense of Movement*. Reprinted by permission of Faber and Faber Ltd.; from *My Sad Captains* © 1961 by Thom Gunn and *Touch*. Copyright 1967 by Thom Gunn. Reprinted by permission of the author, Faber and Faber Ltd. and The University of Chicago Press.

Ivor Gurney: from *Poems*. Reprinted by permission of Hutchinson Publishing Group.

J. B. S. Haldane: from *Writing in England Today*, ed. Karl Miller (Penguin, 1968). Reprinted by permission of The Government of Orissa.

Michael Hamburger: from *Travelling*. Copyright © Michael Hamburger 1969. Reprinted by permission of Fulcrum Press.

Thomas Hardy: 'She to Him', 'Thoughts of Phena', 'I Need Not Go', 'The Ruined Maid', 'In Tenebris', 'On the Departure Platform', 'A Church Romance', 'Channel Firing', 'The Convergence of the Twain', 'The Year's Awakening', 'After a Journey', 'Where the Picnic Was', 'The Newcomer's Wife', 'The Oxen', 'An Anniversary', 'Old Furniture', 'The Sunshade', 'During Wind and Rain', 'If It's Ever Spring Again', 'Voices from Things Growing in a Churchyard', 'An Ancient to Ancients' (Copyright 1925 by The Macmillan Company); 'Snow in the Suburbs', 'When Oats Were Reaped', 'This Summer and Last' (Copyright 1925 by The Macmillan Company, renewed 1953 by Lloyds Bank, Ltd.); 'I Am the One', 'The Mound', 'He Never Expected Much' (Copyright 1928 by Florence E. Hardy and Sydney E. Cockerell, renewed 1956 by Lloyds Bank, Ltd.). All from *Collected Poems*. Reprinted by permission of the Trustees of the Hardy Estate, The Macmillan Company of Canada, The Macmillan Company of New York and Macmillan London and Basingstoke.

F. W. Harvey: from *Gloucestershire* (Oliver & Boyd). Reprinted by permission of P. W. H. Harvey, Executor of Copyright.

Christopher Hassall: from *The Red Leaf* (Oxford University Press). Reprinted by permission of J. B. Marks & Co. on behalf of the Administrators of the author's estate.

John Heath-Stubbs: from *Beauty and the Beast*, *Selected Poems*, and *A Charm Against the Toothache*. Reprinted by permission of David Higham Associates Ltd.

Adrian Henri: from *Tonight at Noon*. Copyright © 1968 by Adrian Henri. Published by Rapp & Whiting. Reprinted by permission of Deborah Rogers Ltd., London.

Sir Alan Herbert: from *Less Nonsense* (Methuen & Co. Ltd.). Reprinted by permission of A. P. Watt & Son on behalf of the Estate of the late Sir Alan Herbert.

ACKNOWLEDGEMENTS

John Hewitt: from *Collected Poems 1930–1963*. Reprinted by permission of MacGibbon & Kee Ltd.

Brian Higgins: from *The Northern Fiddler*. Reprinted by permission of Methuen & Co. Ltd.

Geoffrey Hill: from *For the Unfallen*. Reprinted by permission of André Deutsch Ltd.

Philip Hobsbaum: from *Coming Out Fighting*. Reprinted by permission of Macmillan London and Basingstoke.

Ralph Hodgson: from *Collected Poems*. Reprinted by permission of Mrs. Hodgson, St. Martin's Press, Inc., The Macmillan Company of Canada and Macmillan London and Basingstoke.

David Holbrook: from *Against the Cruel Frost*. Reprinted by permission of Putnam & Co. Ltd.; from *Object Relations*. Reprinted by permission of Methuen & Co. Ltd.

Molly Holden: from *To Make Me Grieve*. Reprinted by permission of the author and Chatto & Windus Ltd. and Wesleyan University Press.

A. E. Housman: 'Epitaph on an Army of Mercenaries', 'Tell me not here, it needs not saying', 'Because I liked you better' from *The Collected Poems of A. E. Housman*. Copyright 1922 by Holt, Rinehart and Winston, Inc. Copyright 1936, 1950 by Barclays Bank Ltd. Copyright © 1964 by Robert E. Symons. All other poems from 'A Shropshire Lad'—Authorized Edition—from *The Collected Poems of A. E. Housman*. Copyright 1939, 1940, © 1965 by Holt, Rinehart and Winston, Inc. Copyright © 1967, 1968 by Robert E. Symons. Reprinted by permission of Holt, Rinehart and Winston, Inc. The poems are also reprinted from *Collected Poems* by permission of The Society of Authors as the literary representative of the Estate of A. E. Housman, and Jonathan Cape Ltd.

Ted Hughes: 'Hawk Roosting' and 'Pike' from *Lupercal*. Copyright © 1959 by Ted Hughes; 'View of a Pig' from *Lupercal*, copyright © 1960 by Ted Hughes; 'Thistles' from *Wodwo*, copyright © 1961 by Ted Hughes; 'The Howling of Wolves' from *Wodwo*, copyright © 1965 by Ted Hughes. Reprinted by permission of Faber and Faber Ltd. and Harper & Row, Publishers, Inc.

T. E. Hulme: from A. R. Jones: *T. E. Hulme*. Copyright © 1960 by Alun R. Jones. Reprinted by permission of Victor Gollancz Ltd. and the Beacon Press.

Valentin Iremonger: from *Horan's Field and Other Reservations*. Reprinted by permission of The Dolmen Press Ltd.

Christopher Isherwood: from *Exhumations*. Copyright 1966 by Christopher Isherwood. Reprinted by permission of Methuen & Co. Ltd. and Simon & Schuster, Inc.

Michael Ivens: from *Private and Public*. Reprinted by permission of the author and Villiers Publications Ltd.

Elizabeth Jennings: from *Collected Poems*. Reprinted by permission of The Macmillan Company of Canada, Macmillan London and Basingstoke and David Higham Associates, Ltd.

Jenny Joseph: from *New Poems, 1963*. Reprinted by permission of the author.

ACKNOWLEDGEMENTS

James Joyce: from 'The Holy Office' from *The Critical Writings of James Joyce*, ed. Ellsworth Mason and Richard Ellman. Copyright © 1959 by Harriet Weaver and F. Lionel Monro as administrators of the Estate of James Joyce. Reprinted by permission of The Viking Press and The Society of Authors as the literary representative of the Estate of James Joyce; 'I hear an army charging upon the land' from *Collected Poems*. Copyright 1918 by B. W. Huebsch, Inc., renewed 1946 by Nora Joyce. Reprinted by permission of The Viking Press Inc., The Society of Authors as the Literary representative of the Estate of James Joyce and Jonathan Cape Ltd.

Patrick Kavanagh: from *A Soul for Sale* (Macmillan). Reprinted by permission of Mrs. P. Kavanagh.

P. J. Kavanagh: from *On the Way to the Depot*. Reprinted by permission of the author and Chatto & Windus Ltd.

Sidney Keyes: from *Collected Poems*. Reprinted by permission of Routledge & Kegan Paul Ltd.

Thomas Kinsella: from *Downstream*. Reprinted by permission of The Dolmen Press Ltd.

Rudyard Kipling: from *The Definitive Edition of Rudyard Kipling's Verse*. Reprinted by permission of A. P. Watt on behalf of Mrs. George Bambridge, Methuen & Co. Ltd., and Macmillan & Co. Ltd., and Doubleday & Company, Inc.

James Kirkup: from *A Correct Compassion* (Oxford University Press). Reprinted by permission of the author.

Philip Larkin: from *The Whitsun Weddings*. Copyright © 1964 by Philip Larkin. Reprinted by permission of Faber and Faber Ltd. and Random House, Inc.; from *The Less Deceived*. Copyright © The Marvell Press 1955, 1973. Reprinted by permission of The Marvell Press, England.

D. H. Lawrence: from *The Complete Poems of D. H. Lawrence*, ed. Vivian de Sola Pinto and F. Warren Roberts. Copyright © 1964, 1971 by Angelo Ravagli and C. M. Weekley. Reprinted by permission of Laurence Pollinger Ltd. on behalf of the Estate of the late Mrs. Frieda Lawrence, and The Viking Press, Inc.

John Lehmann: from *Collected Poems 1930–1963* (Eyre & Spottiswoode). Reprinted by permission of David Higham Associates Ltd.

Laurence Lerner: from *Selves*. Reprinted by permission of Routledge & Kegan Paul Ltd.

Alun Lewis: 'All Day it has Rained' from *Raider's Dawn* and 'Goodbye' from *Ha Ha Among the Trumpets*. Reprinted by permission of George Allen & Unwin Ltd.

C. S. Lewis: from *Poems*, ed. Walter Hooper, © 1964 by the Executors of the Estate of C. S. Lewis. Reprinted by permission of Collins Publishers and Harcourt Brace Jovanovich, Inc.

Wyndham Lewis: from *One-Way Song*. Reprinted by permission of Methuen & Co. Ltd.

Christopher Logue: from *New Numbers*. Copyright © 1970 by Christopher

ACKNOWLEDGEMENTS

Logue. Reprinted by permission of Jonathan Cape Ltd. and Alfred A. Knopf, Inc.; from *Songs*. Reprinted by permission of the author.

Malcolm Lowry: from *Selected Poems*. Copyright © 1962 by Marjorie Lowry. Reprinted by permission of City Lights Books.

Edward Lucie-Smith: from *A Tropical Childhood and Other Poems*. © Oxford University Press 1961. Reprinted by permission of Oxford University Press, London.

Lilian Bowes Lyon: from *Collected Poems*. Copyright 1948 by Lilian Bowes Lyon. Reprinted by permission of Jonathan Cape Ltd. on behalf of the Lilian Bowes Lyon Estate, and E. P. Dutton & Co., Inc.

George MacBeth: from *The Broken Places* and *The Doomsday Book*. Reprinted by permission of the author.

Norman MacCaig: from *Riding Lights*, *A Round of Applause*, *A Man in my Position*. Reprinted by permission of the Hogarth Press and also of the Wesleyan University Press for *A Man in My Position*.

Hugh MacDiarmid: from *Collected Poems*. Reprinted by permission of MacGibbon and Kee Ltd.

Donagh MacDonagh: from *The Hungry Grass*. Reprinted by permission of Faber and Faber Ltd.

Roger McGough: from *Watchwords*. © 1969 by Roger McGough. Reprinted by permission of Jonathan Cape Ltd. and Hope Leresche & Steele.

Louis MacNeice: from *The Collected Poems*, ed. E. R. Dodds. Copyright © The Estate of Louis MacNeice 1966. Reprinted by permission of Faber and Faber Ltd. and Oxford University Press, Inc.

Charles Madge: from *The Disappearing Castle*. Reprinted by permission of Faber and Faber Ltd.

John Masefield: 'Biography', 'Sea Fever', 'Twilight' and 'C.L.M.' (Copyright 1912 by The Macmillan Company, renewed 1940 by John Masefield); 'Reynard the Fox, Or, the Ghost Heath Run' (Copyright 1919 by John Masefield, renewed 1947 by John Masefield); 'The Crowd' (Copyright 1930 by John Masefield, renewed 1958 by John Masefield); 'An Epilogue' (Copyright 1932 by John Masefield, renewed 1960 by John Masefield); 'Partridges' (Copyright 1936 by John Masefield, renewed 1964 by John Masefield) from *Poems*. Reprinted by permission of The Macmillan Company of New York and The Society of Authors as the literary representative of the Estate of John Masefield.

Charlotte Mew: from *Collected Poems*. Reprinted by permission of Gerald Duckworth & Co. Ltd.

Alice Meynell: from *Poems 1847–1943*. Reprinted by permission of Miss Sylvia Mulvey on behalf of Meynell Family Properties Ltd.

James Michie: from *Possible Laughter* (Hart–Davis). Reprinted by permission of David Higham Associates, Ltd.

Susan Miles: from *Little Mirrors* (Basil Blackwell Ltd.). Reprinted by permission of the author.

Adrian Mitchell: from *Poems*. Reprinted by permission of Jonathan Cape Ltd.

Matthew Mitchell: from *Guinness Book of Poetry 1958–59*. Reprinted by permission of Guinness Superlatives Ltd.

ACKNOWLEDGEMENTS

Harold Munro: from *Collected Poems*. Reprinted by permission of Gerald Duckworth & Co. Ltd.

T. Sturge Moore: from *Selected Poems*. Reprinted by permission of Macmillan London and Basingstoke.

Edwin Muir: from *Collected Poems 1921–1958*. Copyright © 1960 by Willa Muir. Reprinted by permission of Faber and Faber Ltd. and Oxford University Press, Inc.

E. Nesbit: from *The Rainbow and the Rose* (Longman). Reprinted by permission of John Farquharson Ltd.

Sir Henry Newbolt: from *Poems New and Old* (John Murray Ltd.). Reprinted by permission of A. P. Watt & Son on behalf of the Estate of the late Sir Henry Newbolt.

Alfred Noyes: from *Collected Poems*. Copyright © 1913, renewed 1941 by Alfred Noyes. Reprinted by permission of John Murray (Publishers) Ltd. and J. B. Lippincott Company.

Philip O'Connor: from *Selected Poems 1936–1966*. Reprinted by permission of Jonathan Cape Ltd. on behalf of the author.

Moira O'Neill: from *Collected Poems* (Blackwood & Sons Ltd.). Reprinted by permission of Miss S. Skrine.

George Orwell and Alex Comfort: from *The Collected Essays, Journalism and Letters of George Orwell*. (Secker and Warburg, Ltd.). Reprinted by permission of Dr. A. Comfort, A. M. Heath & Co. Ltd. and Harcourt Brace Jovanovich, Inc.

Wilfred Owen: from *Collected Poems*. Copyright Chatto & Windus Ltd. 1946, © 1963. Reprinted by permission of the Estate of Harold Owen, Chatto & Windus Ltd. and New Directions Publishing Corporation.

Brian Patten: from *Notes to the Hurrying Man*, © Brian Patten, 1969. Reprinted by permission of George Allen & Unwin Ltd. and Hill and Wang, a division of Farrar, Straus & Giroux.

Eden Phillpotts: from *Wild Fruit*. Reprinted by permission of The Bodley Head; from *Cherry-Stones*. Reprinted by permission of The Royal Literary Fund.

Ruth Pitter: from *Poems 1926–66*. Reprinted by permission of Barrie & Jenkins Ltd.

William Plomer: from *Collected Poems*. Reprinted by permission of Jonathan Cape Ltd. on behalf of the author.

Hugh Popham: from *Against the Lightning* (The Bodley Head). Reprinted by permission of the author.

Peter Porter: from *Once Bitten, Twice Bitten*, and 'Your Attention Please' from *Poems of the Sixties*, ed. F. E. S. Finn (John Murray). Reprinted by permission of the Scorpion Press.

John Cowper Powys: from *A Selection of his Poems* (Macdonald & Co. Ltd.). Reprinted by permission of Laurence Pollinger Ltd. on behalf of the Estate of the late John Cowper Powys.

F. T. Prince: from *The Doors of Stone*. Reprinted by permission of Rupert Hart-Davis Ltd.

ACKNOWLEDGEMENTS

John Pudney: from *Collected Poems.* © 1957 by John Pudney. Reprinted by permission of David Higham Associates, Ltd. and A. Watkins, Inc.

Kathleen Raine: from *Collected Poems.* Copyright © 1956 by Kathleen Raine. Reprinted by permission of Hamish Hamilton Ltd.

Sir Herbert Read: from *Collected Poems.* Copyright 1966. Reprinted by permission of Faber and Faber Ltd. and Horizon Press, New York.

Peter Redgrove: from *The Nature of Cold Weather and Other Poems.* Reprinted by permission of Routledge & Kegan Paul Ltd.

Henry Reed: from *A Map of Verona.* Reprinted by permission of Jonathan Cape Ltd.

James Reeves: from *Collected Poems.* Reprinted by permission of William Heinemann Ltd.

Robert Rendall: from *Shore Poems* (Kirkwall Press). Reprinted by permission of R. P. Rendall.

Edgell Rickword: from *Collected Poems.* Reprinted by permission of the author, c/o Lloyds Bank, 263 Tottenham Court Rd., W.I.

Michael Roberts: from *Collected Poems.* Reprinted by permission of Faber and Faber Ltd.

Isaac Rosenberg: from *Complete Works.* Copyright © 1949 by Schocken Books Inc. Reprinted by permission of the Author's Literary Estate, Chatto & Windus and Schocken Books Inc.

Alan Ross: from *Poems 1942–67.* Reprinted by permission of Eyre & Spottiswoode (Publishers) Ltd.

A. L. Rowse: from *Poems of Cornwall and America.* Reprinted by permission of Faber and Faber Ltd.

V. Sackville-West: from *The Land.* Reprinted by permission of Nigel Nicolson, Executor of the Estate of V. Sackville-West.

'Sagittarius': from *Sagittarius Rhyming.* Reprinted by permission of Jonathan Cape Ltd. on behalf of the author.

Siegfried Sassoon: from *Collected Poems 1908–1956.* Reprinted by permission of G. T. Sassoon.

Vernon Scannell: from *Epithets of War.* Reprinted by permission of Eyre & Spottiswoode (Publishers) Ltd.; from *Walking Wounded.* Reprinted by permission of the author.

E. J. Scovell: from *The River Steamer.* Reprinted by permission of Barrie & Jenkins Ltd.

Martin Seymour-Smith: from *New Poems 1958.* Reprinted by permission of the author.

Edward Shanks: from *Poems.* Reprinted by permission of Sidgwick & Jackson Ltd.

Jon Silkin: from *Poems New and Selected.* Reprinted by permission of the author, Chatto & Windus and Wesleyan University Press.

Alan Sillitoe: from *The Rats.* Reprinted by permission of W. H. Allen & Co. Ltd.

C. H. Sisson: from *Numbers.* Reprinted by permission of Methuen & Co. Ltd.

Edith Sitwell: from *Collected Poems* (Macmillan). Reprinted by permission of David Higham Associates Ltd.

ACKNOWLEDGEMENTS

Sir Osbert Sitwell: from *Poems about People* (Hutchinson). Reprinted by permission of David Higham Associates Ltd.

Iain Crichton Smith: from *Thistles and Roses* (Eyre and Spottiswoode Ltd.). Reprinted by permission of the author.

Stevie Smith: from *Selected Poems*. Copyright © Stevie Smith 1962. Copyright © 1964 by Stevie Smith. Reprinted by permission of Longman Group Ltd. and New Directions Publishing Corporation; from *The Frog Prince and Other Poems*. Reprinted by permission of Longman Group Ltd.

Bernard Spencer: from *With Luck Lasting*. Copyright by Hodder & Stoughton. Reprinted by permission of Hodder & Stoughton.

Stephen Spender: 'I think continually of those' and 'The Landscape near an Aerodrome' (Copyright 1934 and renewed 1962 by Stephen Spender); 'Beethoven's Death Mask', 'Acts passed beyond the boundary of mere wishing' (Copyright 1934 and renewed 1961 by Stephen Spender); 'Two Armies' (Copyright 1942 by Stephen Spender). Reprinted by permission of Faber and Faber Ltd. and Random House, Inc.

Sir John Squire: from *Collected Poems*. Reprinted by permission of Macmillan London and Basingstoke.

James Stephens: 'Seamus Beg' (Copyright 1909 by The Macmillan Company); 'A Glass of Beer' (Copyright 1918 by The Macmillan Company, renewed 1946 by James Stephens) from *Collected Poems*. Reprinted by permission of Mrs. Iris Wise, the Trustees of the Hardy Estate, The Macmillan Company of Canada Ltd., The Macmillan Company of New York, and Macmillan London and Basingstoke; 'The Cage' from *Songs from the Clay*. Reprinted by permission of The Society of Authors as the literary representative of the Estate of James Stephens.

L. A. G. Strong: from *The Body's Imperfection*. Reprinted by permission of Methuen & Co. Ltd.

Muriel Stuart: from *Poems*. Reprinted by permission of Jonathan Cape Ltd. on behalf of the Executors of the Muriel Stuart Estate.

Hal Summers: from *The Listener*, 24 March, 1960. Reprinted by permission of the author.

A. S. J. Tessimond: from *Selection* (Putnam). Reprinted by permission of Herbert Nicholson for the Estate of A. S. J. Tessimond.

Dylan Thomas: from *The Collected Poems*. Copyright 1939, 1946 by New Directions Publishing Corporation. Copyright 1952 by Dylan Thomas; from *Letters to Vernon Watkins*. Copyright © 1957 by New Directions Publishing Corporation. Reprinted by permission of J. M. Dent & Sons Ltd, the Trustees for the copyrights of the late Dylan Thomas and New Directions Publishing Corporation.

Edward Thomas: from *Collected Poems* (Faber and Faber). Reprinted by permission of Miss Myfanwy Thomas.

R. S. Thomas: from *Poetry for Supper*, *Bread of Truth*, and *Not that He Brought Flowers*. Reprinted by permission of Rupert Hart-Davis Ltd.

Anthony Thwaite: from *The Owl in the Tree*. © Oxford University Press 1963; from *The Stones of Emptiness*. © Oxford University Press 1967. Reprinted by permission of Oxford University Press, London.

ACKNOWLEDGEMENTS

Charles Tomlinson: from *Seeing is Believing*. Reprinted by permission of the author and of Oxford University Press, London.

Rosemary Tonks: from *Iliad of Broken Sentences*. Reprinted by permission of The Bodley Head; from *Notes on Cafés and Bedrooms* (Putnam). Reprinted by permission of Miss Tonks.

John Wain: from *Weep before God*. Reprinted by permission of Macmillan London and Basingstoke and Curtis Brown Ltd. on behalf of John Wain; from *Guinness Book of Poetry 1960/61*. Reprinted by permission of Guinness Superlatives Ltd.

Dereck Walcott: from *In a Green Night*. Reprinted by permission of Jonathan Cape Ltd. In the U.S. from *Selected Poems*, copyright © 1962, 1963, 1964 by permission of Farrar, Straus & Giroux, Inc.

Arthur Waley: from *The Secret History of the Mongols*. Reprinted by permission of George Allen & Unwin Ltd. and Barnes and Noble, Inc.

Vernon Watkins: from *The Ballad of the Mari Lwyd* (Copyright © 1962 by Vernon Watkins); from *Cypress and Acacia* (copyright © 1959 by Vernon Watkins); from *Fidelities* (copyright © 1969 by Gwendolyn Watkins). Reprinted by permission of Faber and Faber Ltd. and New Directions Publishing Corporation; from *The Lady with the Unicorn*. Reprinted by permission of Faber and Faber Ltd.

Dorothy Wellesley: from *Selections from the Poems*. Reprinted by permission of Macmillan London and Basingstoke.

Anna Wickham: from *Selected Poems*. Reprinted by permission of Mr James Hepburn and Chatto & Windus Ltd.

Hugo Williams: from *Symptoms of Loss*. © Oxford University Press 1965. Reprinted by permission of Oxford University Press, London.

Humbert Wolfe: from *The Uncelestial City* (Victor Gollancz) and from *Early Poems* (Basil Blackwell). Reprinted by permission of Miss E. A. Wolfe.

W. B. Yeats: 'The Lake Isle of Innisfree', 'He Hears the Cry of the Sedge', 'When You are Old' (© 1906 by The Macmillan Company, renewed 1934 by W. B. Yeats); 'No Second Troy' (© 1912 by The Macmillan Company, renewed 1940 by Bertha Georgie Yeats); 'The Collar-Bone of a Hare' (© 1919 by the Macmillan Company, renewed 1947 by Bertha Georgie Yeats); 'The Second Coming', 'Easter 1916', 'A Prayer for my Daughter' (© 1924 by The Macmillan Company, renewed 1952 by Bertha Georgie Yeats); 'Sailing to Byzantium', 'Among School Children' (© 1928 by The Macmillan Company, renewed 1956 by Georgie Yeats); 'In Memory of Eva Gore-Booth and Con Markiewicz', 'Byzantium', 'The Choice', 'Crazy Jane on God' (© 1933 by The Macmillan Company, renewed 1961 by Bertha Georgie Yeats); 'The Municipal Gallery Revisited', 'The Circus Animals' Desertion', 'Under Ben Bulben', 'The Statesman's Holiday', 'Politics' (© 1940 by Georgie Yeats, renewed 1968 by Bertha Georgie Yeats, Michael Butler Yeats and Anne Yeats). Reprinted from *Collected Poems* by permission of A. P. Watt on behalf of Mr. M. B. Yeats and Macmillan & Co. Ltd., and The Macmillan Company of New York.

Andrew Young: from *Collected Poems* (Hart-Davis). Reprinted by permission of Leonard Clark, Literary Executor of the Estate.

ACKNOWLEDGEMENTS

Francis Brett Young: from *Selections from Modern Poets.* ed. J. C. Squire (Secker & Warburg). Reprinted by permission of David Higham Associates, Ltd.

While every effort has been made to secure permission, it has in a few cases proved impossible to trace the author or his executor. We apologize for our apparent negligence.

CONTENTS

CONTENTS

CONTENTS

CONTENTS

CONTENTS

CONTENTS

xxvi

CONTENTS

CONTENTS

CONTENTS

CONTENTS

CONTENTS

CONTENTS

CONTENTS

CONTENTS

CONTENTS

CONTENTS

CONTENTS

CONTENTS

CONTENTS

CONTENTS

CONTENTS

xli

CONTENTS

CONTENTS

CONTENTS

CONTENTS

CONTENTS

CONTENTS

CONTENTS

CONTENTS

CONTENTS

NOTE

The Editor regrets that he was unable to obtain permission
to include W. H. Auden's *Spain 1937*.

1

WILFRID SCAWEN BLUNT
1840–1922

FROM *Love Sonnets of Proteus*

I SEE you, Juliet, still, with your straw hat
Loaded with vines, and with your dear pale face,
On which those thirty years so lightly sat,
And the white outline of your muslin dress.
You wore a little *fichu* trimmed with lace
And crossed in front, as was the fashion then,
Bound at your waist with a broad band or sash,
All white and fresh and virginally plain.
There was a sound of shouting far away
Down in the valley, as they called to us,
And you, with hands clasped seeming still to pray
Patience of fate, stood listening to me thus
With heaving bosom. There a rose lay curled.
It was the reddest rose in all the world.

THOMAS HARDY
1840–1928

2

She, to Him

WHEN you shall see me in the toils of Time,
My lauded beauties carried off from me,
My eyes no longer stars as in their prime,
My name forgot of Maiden Fair and Free;

When, in your being, heart concedes to mind,
And judgment, though you scarce its process know,
Recalls the excellencies I once enshrined,
And you are irked that they have withered so:

Remembering mine the loss is, not the blame,
That Sportsman Time but rears his brood to kill,
Knowing me in my soul the very same—
One who would die to spare you touch of ill!—
Will you not grant to old affection's claim
The hand of friendship down Life's sunless hill?

3 *Thoughts of Phena*

At News of Her Death

NOT a line of her writing have I,
    Not a thread of her hair,
No mark of her late time as dame in her dwelling, whereby
    I may picture her there;
  And in vain do I urge my unsight
    To conceive my lost prize
At her close, whom I knew when her dreams were upbrimming
        with light,
    And with laughter her eyes.

What scenes spread around her last days,
    Sad, shining, or dim?
Did her gifts and compassions enray and enarch her sweet ways
    With an aureate nimb?
  Or did life-light decline from her years,
    And mischances control
Her full day-star; unease, or regret, or forebodings, or fears
    Disennoble her soul?

  Thus I do but the phantom retain
    Of the maiden of yore
As my relic; yet haply the best of her—fined in my brain
    It may be the more
  That no line of her writing have I,
    Nor a thread of her hair,
No mark of her late time as dame in her dwelling, whereby
    I may picture her there.

'*I Need Not Go*'

I NEED not go
Through sleet and snow
To where I know
She waits for me;
She will tarry me there
Till I find it fair,
And have time to spare
From company.

When I've overgot
The world somewhat,
When things cost not
Such stress and strain,
Is soon enough
By cypress sough
To tell my Love
I am come again.

And if some day,
When none cries nay,
I still delay
To seek her side,
(Though ample measure
Of fitting leisure
Await my pleasure)
She will not chide.

What—not upbraid me
That I delayed me,
Nor ask what stayed me
So long? Ah, no!—
New cares may claim me,
New loves inflame me,
She will not blame me,
But suffer it so.

5 *The Ruined Maid*

'O 'MELIA, my dear, this does everything crown!
Who could have supposed I should meet you in Town?
And whence such fair garments, such prosperi-ty?'—
'O didn't you know I'd been ruined?' said she.

—'You left us in tatters, without shoes or socks,
Tired of digging potatoes, and spudding up docks;
And now you've gay bracelets and bright feathers three!'—
'Yes: that's how we dress when we're ruined,' said she.

—'At home in the barton you said "thee" and "thou,"
And "thik oon," and "theäs oon," and "t'other"; but now
Your talking quite fits 'ee for high compa-ny!'—
'Some polish is gained with one's ruin,' said she.

—'Your hands were like paws then, your face blue and bleak
But now I'm bewitched by your delicate cheek,
And your little gloves fit as on any la-dy!'—
'We never do work when we're ruined,' said she.

—'You used to call home-life a hag-ridden dream,
And you'd sigh, and you'd sock; but at present you seem
To know not of megrims or melancho-ly!'—
'True. One's pretty lively when ruined,' said she.

—'I wish I had feathers, a fine sweeping gown,
And a delicate face, and could strut about Town!'—
'My dear—a raw country girl, such as you be,
Cannot quite expect that. You ain't ruined,' said she.

6   *In Tenebris*

II

'Considerabam ad dexteram, et videbam; et non erat qui cognosceret
me. . . . Non est qui requirat animam meam.'—Psalm 141.

WHEN the clouds' swoln bosoms echo back the shouts of the many
    and strong
That things are all as they best may be, save a few to be right ere long,
And my eyes have not the vision in them to discern what to these is so
    clear,
The blot seems straightway in me alone; one better he were not here.

The stout upstanders say, All's well with us: ruers have nought to rue!
And what the potent say so oft, can it fail to be somewhat true?
Breezily go they, breezily come; their dust smokes around their career,
Till I think I am one born out of due time, who has no calling here.

Their dawns bring lusty joys, it seems; their evenings all that is sweet;
Our times are blessed times, they cry: Life shapes it as is most meet,
And nothing is much the matter; there are many smiles to a tear;
Then what is the matter is I, I say. Why should such an one be
    here? . . .

Let him in whose ears the low-voiced Best is killed by the clash of the
    First,
Who holds that if way to the Better there be, it exacts a full look at the
    Worst,
Who feels that delight is a delicate growth cramped by crookedness,
    custom, and fear,
Get him up and be gone as one shaped awry; he disturbs the order
    here.

7   *On the Departure Platform*

WE kissed at the barrier; and passing through
She left me, and moment by moment got
Smaller and smaller, until to my view
    She was but a spot;

A wee white spot of muslin fluff
That down the diminishing platform bore
Through hustling crowds of gentle and rough
    To the carriage door.

Under the lamplight's fitful glowers,
Behind dark groups from far and near,
Whose interests were apart from ours,
    She would disappear,

Then show again, till I ceased to see
That flexible form, that nebulous white;
And she who was more than my life to me
    Had vanished quite. . . .

We have penned new plans since that fair fond day,
And in season she will appear again—
Perhaps in the same soft white array—
    But never as then!

—'And why, young man, must eternally fly
A joy you'll repeat, if you love her well?'
—O friend, nought happens twice thus; why,
    I cannot tell!

8   *A Church Romance*
(*Mellstock: circa* 1835)

SHE turned in the high pew, until her sight
Swept the west gallery, and caught its row
Of music-men with viol, book, and bow
Against the sinking sad tower-window light.

She turned again; and in her pride's despite
One strenuous viol's inspirer seemed to throw
A message from his string to her below,
Which said: 'I claim thee as my own forthright!'

Thus their hearts' bond began, in due time signed.
And long years thence, when Age had scared Romance,
At some old attitude of his or glance
That gallery-scene would break upon her mind,
With him as minstrel, ardent, young, and trim,
Bowing 'New Sabbath' or 'Mount Ephraim.'

9   *Channel Firing*

THAT night your great guns, unawares,
Shook all our coffins as we lay,
And broke the chancel window-squares,
We thought it was the Judgment-day

And sat upright. While drearisome
Arose the howl of wakened hounds:
The mouse let fall the altar-crumb,
The worms drew back into the mounds,

The glebe cow drooled. Till God called, 'No;
It's gunnery practice out at sea
Just as before you went below;
The world is as it used to be:

'All nations striving strong to make
Red war yet redder. Mad as hatters
They do no more for Christés sake
Than you who are helpless in such matters.

'That this is not the judgment-hour
For some of them's a blessed thing,
For if it were they'd have to scour
Hell's floor for so much threatening. . . .

'Ha, ha. It will be warmer when
I blow the trumpet (if indeed
I ever do; for you are men,
And rest eternal sorely need).'

So down we lay again. 'I wonder,
Will the world ever saner be,'
Said one, 'than when He sent us under
In our indifferent century!'

And many a skeleton shook his head.
'Instead of preaching forty year,'
My neighbour Parson Thirdly said,
'I wish I had stuck to pipes and beer.'

Again the guns disturbed the hour,
Roaring their readiness to avenge,
As far inland as Stourton Tower,
And Camelot, and starlit Stonehenge.

10   *The Convergence of the Twain*

(*Lines on the loss of the* Titanic)

I

IN a solitude of the sea
Deep from human vanity,
And the Pride of Life that planned her, stilly couches she.

II

Steel chambers, late the pyres
Of her salamandrine fires,
Cold currents thrid, and turn to rhythmic tidal lyres.

III

Over the mirrors meant
To glass the opulent
The sea-worm crawls—grotesque, slimed, dumb, indifferent.

IV

Jewels in joy designed
To ravish the sensuous mind
Lie lightless, all their sparkles bleared and black and blind.

8

V

Dim moon-eyed fishes near
Gaze at the gilded gear
And query: 'What does this vaingloriousness down here?'

VI

Well: while was fashioning
This creature of cleaving wing,
The Immanent Will that stirs and urges everything

VII

Prepared a sinister mate
For her—so gaily great—
A Shape of Ice, for the time far and dissociate.

VIII

And as the smart ship grew
In stature, grace, and hue,
In shadowy silent distance grew the Iceberg too.

IX

Alien they seemed to be:
No mortal eye could see
The intimate welding of their later history,

X

Or sign that they were bent
By paths coincident
On being anon twin halves of one august event.

XI

Till the Spinner of the Years
Said 'Now!' And each one hears,
And consummation comes, and jars two hemispheres.

11 *The Year's Awakening*

How do you know that the pilgrim track
Along the belting zodiac
Swept by the sun in his seeming rounds
Is traced by now to the Fishes' bounds
And into the Ram, when weeks of cloud
Have wrapt the sky in a clammy shroud,
And never as yet a tinct of spring
Has shown in the Earth's apparelling;
　　　O vespering bird, how do you know,
　　　How do you know?

How do you know, deep underground,
Hid in your bed from sight and sound,
Without a turn in temperature,
With weather life can scarce endure,
That light has won a fraction's strength,
And day put on some moments' length,
Whereof in merest rote will come,
Weeks hence, mild airs that do not numb;
　　　O crocus root, how do you know,
　　　How do you know?

12 *After a Journey*

HERETO I come to view a voiceless ghost;
　　Whither, O whither will its whim now draw me?
Up the cliff, down, till I'm lonely, lost,
　　And the unseen waters' ejaculations awe me.
Where you will next be there's no knowing,
　　Facing round about me everywhere,
　　　　With your nut-coloured hair,
And gray eyes, and rose-flush coming and going.

Yes: I have re-entered your olden haunts at last;
　　Through the years, through the dead scenes I have tracked you;
What have you now found to say of our past—
　　Scanned across the dark space wherein I have lacked you?
Summer gave us sweets, but autumn wrought division?
　　Things were not lastly as firstly well
　　　　With us twain, you tell?
But all's closed now, despite Time's derision.

I see what you are doing: you are leading me on
　　To the spots we knew when we haunted here together,
The waterfall, above which the mist-bow shone
　　At the then fair hour in the then fair weather,
And the cave just under, with a voice still so hollow
　　That it seems to call out to me from forty years ago,
　　　　When you were all aglow,
And not the thin ghost that I now fraily follow!

Ignorant of what there is flitting here to see,
　　The waked birds preen and the seals flop lazily;
Soon you will have, Dear, to vanish from me,
　　For the stars close their shutters and the dawn whitens hazily.
Trust me, I mind not, though Life lours,
　　The bringing me here; nay, bring me here again!
　　　　I am just the same as when
Our days were a joy, and our paths through flowers.

13　　　　　　*Where the Picnic Was*

　　　　　　　WHERE we made the fire
　　　　　　　In the summer time
　　　　　　　Of branch and briar
　　　　　　　On the hill to the sea,
　　　　　　　I slowly climb
　　　　　　　Through winter mire,
　　　　　　　And scan and trace
　　　　　　　The forsaken place
　　　　　　　Quite readily.

Now a cold wind blows,
And the grass is gray,
But the spot still shows
As a burnt circle—aye,
And stick-ends, charred,
Still strew the sward
Whereon I stand,
Last relic of the band
Who came that day!

Yes, I am here
Just as last year,
And the sea breathes brine
From its strange straight line
Up hither, the same
As when we four came.
—But two have wandered far
From this grassy rise
Into urban roar
Where no picnics are,
And one—has shut her eyes
For evermore.

14   *The Newcomer's Wife*

HE paused on the sill of a door ajar
That screened a lively liquor-bar,
For the name had reached him through the door
Of her he had married the week before.

'We called her the Hack of the Parade;
But she was discreet in the games she played;
If slightly worn, she's pretty yet,
And gossips, after all, forget:

'And he knows nothing of her past;
I am glad the girl's in luck at last;
Such ones, though stale to native eyes,
Newcomers snatch at as a prize.'

'Yes, being a stranger he sees her blent
Of all that's fresh and innocent,
Nor dreams how many a love-campaign
She had enjoyed before his reign!'

That night there was the splash of a fall
Over the slimy harbour-wall:
They searched, and at the deepest place
Found him with crabs upon his face.

15 *The Oxen*

CHRISTMAS EVE, and twelve of the clock.
  'Now they are all on their knees,'
An elder said as we sat in a flock
  By the embers in hearthside ease.

We pictured the meek mild creatures where
  They dwelt in their strawy pen,
Nor did it occur to one of us there
  To doubt they were kneeling then.

So fair a fancy few would weave
  In these years! Yet, I feel,
If someone said on Christmas Eve,
  'Come; see the oxen kneel

'In the lonely barton by yonder coomb
  Our childhood used to know,'
I should go with him in the gloom,
  Hoping it might be so.

16   *An Anniversary*

IT was at the very date to which we have come,
  In the month of the matching name,
When, at a like minute, the sun had upswum,
  Its couch-time at night being the same.
And the same path stretched here that people now follow,
  And the same stile crossed their way,
And beyond the same green hillock and hollow
  The same horizon lay;
And the same man pilgrims now hereby who pilgrimed here that day.

Let so much be said of the date-day's sameness;
  But the tree that neighbours the track,
And stoops like a pedlar afflicted with lameness,
  Knew of no sogged wound or wind-crack.
And the joints of that wall were not enshrouded
  With mosses of many tones,
And the garth up afar was not overcrowded
  With a multitude of white stones,
And the man's eyes then were not so sunk that you saw the socket-
  bones.

17   *Old Furniture*

I KNOW not how it may be with others
    Who sit amid relics of householdry
That date from the days of their mothers' mothers,
    But well I know how it is with me
      Continually.

I see the hands of the generations
    That owned each shiny familiar thing
In play on its knobs and indentations,
    And with its ancient fashioning
      Still dallying:

Hands behind hands, growing paler and paler,
    As in a mirror a candle-flame
Shows images of itself, each frailer
    As it recedes, though the eye may frame
        Its shape the same.

On the clock's dull dial a foggy finger,
    Moving to set the minutes right
With tentative touches that lift and linger
    In the wont of a moth on a summer night,
        Creeps to my sight.

On this old viol, too, fingers are dancing—-
    As whilom—just over the strings by the nut,
The tip of a bow receding, advancing
    In airy quivers, as if it would cut
        The plaintive gut.

And I see a face by that box for tinder,
    Glowing forth in fits from the dark,
And fading again, as the linten cinder
    Kindles to red at the flinty spark,
        Or goes out stark.

Well, well. It is best to be up and doing,
    The world has no use for one to-day
Who eyes things thus—no aim pursuing!
    He should not continue in this stay,
        But sink away.

18   *The Sunshade*

AH—it's the skeleton of a lady's sunshade,
    Here at my feet in the hard rock's chink,
    Merely a naked sheaf of wires!—
    Twenty years have gone with their livers and diers
    Since it was silked in its white or pink.

Noonshine riddles the ribs of the sunshade,
  No more a screen from the weakest ray;
  Nothing to tell us the hue of its dyes,
  Nothing but rusty bones as it lies
  In its coffin of stone, unseen till to-day.

Where is the woman who carried that sunshade
  Up and down this seaside place?—
  Little thumb standing against its stem,
  Thoughts perhaps bent on a love-stratagem,
  Softening yet more the already soft face!

Is the fair woman who carried that sunshade
  A skeleton just as her property is,
  Laid in the chink that none may scan?
  And does she regret—if regret dust can—
  The vain things thought when she flourished this?

19   *During Wind and Rain*

THEY sing their dearest songs—
He, she, all of them—yea,
Treble and tenor and bass,
    And one to play;
With the candles mooning each face. . . .
    Ah, no; the years O!
How the sick leaves reel down in throngs!

They clear the creeping moss—
Elders and juniors—aye,
Making the pathways neat
    And the garden gay;
And they build a shady seat. . . .
    Ah, no; the years, the years;
See, the white storm-birds wing across!

They are blithely breakfasting all—
Men and maidens—yea,
Under the summer tree,
   With a glimpse of the bay,
While pet fowl come to the knee. . . .
    Ah, no; the years O!
And the rotten rose is ript from the wall.

They change to a high new house,
He, she, all of them—aye,
Clocks and carpets and chairs
   On the lawn all day,
And brightest things that are theirs. . . .
    Ah, no; the years, the years;
Down their carved names the rain-drop ploughs.

20   *'If It's Ever Spring Again'*

IF it's ever spring again,
    Spring again,
I shall go where went I when
Down the moor-cock splashed, and hen,
Seeing me not, amid their flounder,
Standing with my arm around her;
If it's ever spring again,
    Spring again,
I shall go where went I then.

If it's ever summer-time,
    Summer-time,
With the hay crop at the prime,
And the cuckoos—two—in rhyme,
As they used to be, or seemed to,
We shall do as long we've dreamed to,
If it's ever summer-time,
    Summer-time,
With the hay, and bees achime.

21   *Voices from Things Growing in a Churchyard*

THESE flowers are I, poor Fanny Hurd,
       Sir or Madam,
A little girl here sepultured.
Once I flit-fluttered like a bird
Above the grass, as now I wave
In daisy shapes above my grave,
       All day cheerily,
       All night eerily!

—I am one Bachelor Bowring, 'Gent,'
       Sir or Madam;
In shingled oak my bones were pent;
Hence more than a hundred years I spent
In my feat of change from a coffin-thrall
To a dancer in green as leaves on a wall,
       All day cheerily,
       All night eerily!

—I, these berries of juice and gloss,
       Sir or Madam,
Am clean forgotten as Thomas Voss;
Thin-urned, I have burrowed away from the moss
That covers my sod, and have entered this yew,
And turned to clusters ruddy of view,
       All day cheerily,
       All night eerily!

—The Lady Gertrude, proud, high-bred,
       Sir or Madam,
Am I—this laurel that shades your head;
Into its veins I have stilly sped,
And made them of me; and my leaves now shine,
As did my satins superfine,
       All day cheerily,
       All night eerily!

—I, who as innocent withwind climb,
       Sir or Madam,
Am one Eve Greensleeves, in olden time
Kissed by men from many a clime,

Beneath sun, stars, in blaze, in breeze,
As now by glowworms and by bees,
    All day cheerily,
    All night eerily!

—I'm old Squire Audeley Grey, who grew,
    Sir or Madam,
Aweary of life, and in scorn withdrew;
Till anon I clambered up anew
As ivy-green, when my ache was stayed,
And in that attire I have longtime gayed
    All day cheerily,
    All night eerily!

—And so these maskers breathe to each
    Sir or Madam
Who lingers there, and their lively speech
Affords an interpreter much to teach,
As their murmurous accents seem to come
Thence hitheraround in a radiant hum,
    All day cheerily,
    All night eerily!

22   *An Ancient to Ancients*

WHERE once we danced, where once we sang,
    Gentlemen,
The floors are sunken, cobwebs hang,
And cracks creep; worms have fed upon
The doors. Yea, sprightlier times were then
Than now, with harps and tabrets gone,
    Gentlemen!

Where once we rowed, where once we sailed,
    Gentlemen,
And damsels took the tiller, veiled
Against too strong a stare (God wot
    Their fancy, then or anywhen!)
Upon that shore we are clean forgot,
    Gentlemen!

We have lost somewhat, afar and near,
      Gentlemen,
The thinning of our ranks each year
Affords a hint we are nigh undone,
That we shall not be ever again
The marked of many, loved of one,
      Gentlemen.

In dance the polka hit our wish,
      Gentlemen,
The paced quadrille, the spry schottische,
'Sir Roger.'—And in opera spheres
The 'Girl' (the famed 'Bohemian'),
And 'Trovatore,' held the ears,
      Gentlemen.

This season's paintings do not please,
      Gentlemen,
Like Etty, Mulready, Maclise;
Throbbing romance has waned and wanned;
No wizard wields the witching pen
Of Bulwer, Scott, Dumas, and Sand,
      Gentlemen.

The bower we shrined to Tennyson,
      Gentlemen,
Is roof-wrecked; damps there drip upon
Sagged seats, the creeper-nails are rust,
The spider is sole denizen;
Even she who voiced those rhymes is dust,
      Gentlemen!

We who met sunrise sanguine-souled,
      Gentlemen,
Are wearing weary. We are old;
These younger press; we feel our rout
Is imminent to Aïdes' den,—
That evening shades are stretching out,
      Gentlemen!

And yet, though ours be failing frames,
    Gentlemen,
So were some others' history names,
Who trode their track light-limbed and fast
As these youth, and not alien
From enterprise, to their long last,
    Gentlemen.

Sophocles, Plato, Socrates,
    Gentlemen,
Pythagoras, Thucydides,
Herodotus, and Homer,—yea,
Clement, Augustin, Origen,
Burnt brightlier towards their setting-day,
    Gentlemen.

And ye, red-lipped and smooth-browed; list,
    Gentlemen;
Much is there waits you we have missed;
Much lore we leave you worth the knowing,
Much, much has lain outside our ken:
Nay, rush not: time serves: we are going,
    Gentlemen.

23   *Snow in the Suburbs*

EVERY branch big with it,
  Bent every twig with it;
Every fork like a white web-foot;
Every street and pavement mute:
Some flakes have lost their way, and grope back upward, when
Meeting those meandering down they turn and descend again.
  The palings are glued together like a wall,
  And there is no waft of wind with the fleecy fall.

A sparrow enters the tree,
  Whereon immediately
A snow-lump thrice his own slight size
Descends on him and showers his head and eyes,

And overturns him,
And near inurns him,
And lights on a nether twig, when its brush
Starts off a volley of other lodging lumps with a rush.

The steps are a blanched slope,
Up which, with feeble hope,
A black cat comes, wide-eyed and thin;
And we take him in.

24   *When Oats Were Reaped*

THAT day when oats were reaped, and wheat was ripe, and barley
    ripening,
  The road-dust hot, and the bleaching grasses dry,
    I walked along and said,
While looking just ahead to where some silent people lie:

'I wounded one who's there, and now know well I wounded her;
  But, ah, she does not know that she wounded me!'
    And not an air stirred,
Nor a bill of any bird; and no response accorded she.

25   *This Summer and Last*

UNHAPPY summer you,
    Who do not see
What your yester-summer saw!
Never, never will you be
    Its match to me,
  Never, never draw
Smiles your forerunner drew,
  Know what it knew!

Divine things done and said
Illumined it,
Whose rays crept into corn-brown curls,
Whose breezes heard a humorous wit
Of fancy flit.—
Still the alert brook purls,
Though feet that there would tread
Elsewhere have sped.

So, bran-new summer, you
Will never see
All that yester-summer saw!
Never, never will you be
In memory
Its rival, never draw
Smiles your forerunner drew,
Know what it knew!

26   *'I Am the One'*

I AM the one whom ringdoves see
Through chinks in boughs
When they do not rouse
In sudden dread,
But stay on cooing, as if they said:
'Oh; it's only he.'

I am the passer when up-eared hares,
Stirred as they eat
The new-sprung wheat,
Their munch resume
As if they thought: 'He is one for whom
Nobody cares.'

Wet-eyed mourners glance at me
As in train they pass
Along the grass
To a hollowed spot,
And think: 'No matter; he quizzes not
Our misery.'

I hear above: 'We stars must lend
    No fierce regard
    To his gaze, so hard
    Bent on us thus,—
Must scathe him not. He is one with us
    Beginning and end.'

27   *The Mound*

      FOR a moment pause:—
      Just here it was;
And through the thin thorn hedge, by the rays of the moon,
I can see the tree in the field, and beside it the mound—
Now sheeted with snow—whereon we sat that June
    When it was green and round,
And she crazed my mind by what she coolly told—
    The history of her undoing,
(As I saw it), but she called 'comradeship,'
    That bred in her no rueing:
    And saying she'd not be bound
For life to one man, young, ripe-yeared, or old,
Left me—an innocent simpleton to her viewing;
For, though my accompt of years outscored her own,
    Hers had more hotly flown. . . .
We never met again by this green mound,
To press as once so often lip on lip,
    And palter, and pause:—
    Yes; here it was!

28

He Never Expected Much
[or]
A CONSIDERATION
[*A reflection*] ON MY EIGHTY-SIXTH BIRTHDAY

WELL, World, you have kept faith with me,
     Kept faith with me;
Upon the whole you have proved to be
     Much as you said you were.
Since as a child I used to lie
Upon the leaze and watch the sky,
Never, I own, expected I
     That life would all be fair.

'Twas then you said, and since have said,
     Times since have said,
In that mysterious voice you shed
     From clouds and hills around:
'Many have loved me desperately,
Many with smooth serenity,
While some have shown contempt of me
     Till they dropped underground.

'I do not promise overmuch,
     Child; overmuch;
Just neutral-tinted haps and such,'
     You said to minds like mine.
Wise warning for your credit's sake!
Which I for one failed not to take,
And hence could stem such strain and ache
     As each year might assign.

ELIZABETH WORDSWORTH
1840–1932

29 *Good and Clever*

IF all the good people were clever,
    And all clever people were good,
The world would be nicer than ever
    We thought that it possibly could.

But somehow 'tis seldom or never
    The two hit it off as they should,
The good are so harsh to the clever,
    The clever, so rude to the good!

So friends, let it be our endeavour
    To make each by each understood;
For few can be good, like the clever,
    Or clever, so well as the good.

ROBERT BRIDGES
1844–1930

30 *A Passer-By*

WHITHER, O splendid ship, thy white sails crowding,
    Leaning across the bosom of the urgent West,
That fearest nor sea rising, nor sky clouding,
    Whither away, fair rover, and what thy quest?
    Ah! soon, when Winter has all our vales opprest,
When skies are cold and misty, and hail is hurling,
    Wilt thou glide on the blue Pacific, or rest
In a summer haven asleep, thy white sails furling.

I there before thee, in the country that well thou knowest,
    Already arrived am inhaling the odorous air:
I watch thee enter unerringly where thou goest,
    And anchor queen of the strange shipping there,

Thy sails for awnings spread, thy masts bare;
Nor is aught from the foaming reef to the snow-capped, grandest
    Peak, that is over the feathery palms more fair
Than thou, so upright, so stately, and still thou standest.

And yet, O splendid ship, unhailed and nameless,
    I know not if, aiming a fancy, I rightly divine
That thou hast a purpose joyful, a courage blameless,
    Thy port assured in a happier land than mine.
    But for all I have given thee, beauty enough is thine,
As thou, aslant with trim tackle and shrouding,
    From the proud nostril curve of a prow's line
In the offing scatterest foam, thy white sails crowding.

31   *London Snow*

WHEN men were all asleep the snow came flying,
In large white flakes falling on the city brown,
Stealthily and perpetually settling and loosely lying,
    Hushing the latest traffic of the drowsy town;
Deadening, muffling, stifling its murmurs failing;
Lazily and incessantly floating down and down:
    Silently sifting and veiling road, roof and railing;
Hiding difference, making unevenness even,
Into angles and crevices softly drifting and sailing.
    All night it fell, and when full inches seven
It lay in the depth of its uncompacted lightness,
The clouds blew off from a high and frosty heaven;
    And all woke earlier for the unaccustomed brightness
Of the winter dawning, the strange unheavenly glare:
The eye marvelled—marvelled at the dazzling whiteness;
    The ear hearkened to the stillness of the solemn air;
No sound of wheel rumbling nor of foot falling,
And the busy morning cries came thin and spare.
    Then boys I heard, as they went to school, calling,
They gathered up the crystal manna to freeze
Their tongues with tasting, their hands with snowballing;
    Or rioted in a drift, plunging up to the knees;
Or peering up from under the white-mossed wonder,
'O look at the trees!' they cried, 'O look at the trees!'

With lessened load a few carts creak and blunder,
Following along the white deserted way,
A country company long dispersed asunder:
   When now already the sun, in pale display
Standing by Paul's high dome, spread forth below
His sparkling beams, and awoke the stir of the day.
   For now doors open, and war is waged with the snow;
And trains of sombre men, past tale of number,
Tread long brown paths, as toward their toil they go:
   But even for them awhile no cares encumber
Their minds diverted; the daily word is unspoken,
The daily thoughts of labour and sorrow slumber
At the sight of the beauty that greets them, for the charm they have
    broken.

32   *April 1885*

WANTON with long delay the gay spring leaping cometh;
The blackthorn starreth now his bough on the eve of May:
All day in the sweet box-tree the bee for pleasure hummeth:
The cuckoo sends afloat his note on the air all day.

Now dewy nights again and rain in gentle shower
At root of tree and flower have quenched the winter's drouth:
On high the hot sun smiles, and banks of cloud uptower
In bulging heads that crowd for miles the dazzling south.

33   *Poor Poll*

I SAW it all, Polly, how when you had call'd for sop
and your good friend the cook came & fill'd up your pan
you yerk'd it out deftly by beakfuls scattering it
away far as you might upon the sunny lawn
then summon'd with loud cry the little garden birds
to take their feast. Quickly came they flustering around

Ruddock & Merle & Finch squabbling among themselves
nor gave you thanks nor heed while you sat silently
watching, and I beside you in perplexity
lost in the maze of all mystery and all knowledge
felt how deep lieth the fount of man's benevolence
if a bird can share it & take pleasure in it.
  If you, my bird, I thought, had a philosophy
it might be a sounder scheme than what our moralists
propound: because thou, Poll, livest ín the darkness
which human Reason searching from outside would pierce,
but, being of so feeble a candle-power, can only
show up to view the cloud that it illuminates.
Thus reason'd I: then marvell'd how you can adapt
your wild bird-mood to endure your tame environment
the domesticities of English household life
and your small brass-wire cabin, who sh^{dst} live on wing
harrying the tropical branch-flowering wilderness:
Yet Nature gave you a gift of easy mimicry
whereby you have come to win uncanny sympathies
and morsell'd utterance of our Germanic talk
as schoolmasters in Greek will flaunt their hackney'd tags
φωνᾶντα συνετοῖσιν and κτῆμα ἐς ἀεὶ,
ἡ γλῶσσ' ὀμώμοχ, ἡ δὲ φρὴν ἀνώμοτος
tho' you with a better ear copy ús more perfectly
nor without connotation as when you call'd for sop
all with that stumpy wooden tongue & vicious beak
that dry whistling shrieking tearing cutting pincer
now eagerly subservient to your cautious claws
exploring all varieties of attitude
in irrepressible blind groping for escape
—a very figure & image of man's soul on earth
the almighty cosmic Will fidgeting in a trap—
in your quenchless unknown desire for the unknown life
of which some homely British sailor robb'd you, alas!
'Tis all that doth your silly thoughts so busy keep
the while you sit moping like Patience on a perch
——*Wie viele Tag' und Nächte bist du geblieben!*
La possa delle gambe posta in tregue—
the impeccable spruceness of your grey-feather'd pôll
a model in hairdressing for the dandiest old Duke
enough to qualify you for the House of Lords
or the Athenaeum Club, to poke among the nobs
great intellectual nobs and literary nobs

scientific nobs and Bishops *ex officio*:
nor lack you simulation of profoundest wisdom
such as men's features oft acquire in very old age
by mere cooling of passion & decay of muscle
by faint renunciation even of untold regrets;
who seeing themselves a picture of that wh: man should-be
learn almost what it were to be what they-are-not.
But you can never have cherish'd a determined hope
consciously to renounce or lose it, you will live
your threescore years & ten idle and puzzle-headed
as any mumping monk in his unfurnish'd cell
in peace that, poor Polly, passeth Understanding—
merely because you lack what we men understand
by Understanding. Well! well! that's the difference
C'est la seule différence, mais c'est important.
Ah! your pale sedentary life! but would you change?
exchange it for one crowded hour of glorious life,
one blind furious tussle with a madden'd monkey
who would throttle you and throw your crude fragments away
shreds unintelligible of an unmeaning act
dans la profonde horreur de l'éternelle nuit?
Why ask? You cannot know. 'Twas by no choice of yours
that you mischanged for monkeys' man's society,
'twas that British sailor drove you from Paradise—
Εἴθ' ὤφελ' Ἀργοῦς μὴ διαπτάσθαι σκύφος!
I'd hold embargoes on such a ghastly traffic.
    I am writing verses to you & grieve that you sh^d be
absolument incapable de les comprendre,
Tu, Polle, nescis ista nec potes scire:—
Alas! Iambic, scazon and alexandrine,
spondee or choriamb, all is alike to you—
my well-continued fanciful experiment
wherein so many strange verses amalgamate
on the secure bedrock of Milton's prosody:
not but that when I speak you will incline an ear
in critical attention lest by chánce I míght
póssibly say sómething that was worth repeating:
I am adding (do you think?) pages to literature
that gouty excrement of human intellect
accumulating slowly & everlastingly
depositing, like guano on the Peruvian shore,
to be perhaps exhumed in some remotest age
(*piis secunda, vate me, detur fuga*)

to fertilize the scanty dwarf'd intelligence
of a new race of beings the unhallow'd offspring
of them who shall have quite dismember'd & destroy'd
our temple of Christian faith & fair Hellenic art
just as that monkey would, poor Polly, have done for you.

34   FROM *The Testament of Beauty*

IV: ETHICK

AND yet hath PRAYER, the heav'n-breathing foliage of faith,
found never a place in ethick: for Philosophy
filtering out delusions from her theory of life,
in dread of superstition gave religion away
to priests and monks, who rich in their monopoly
furbish and trim the old idols, that they dare not break,
for fear of the folk and need of good disciplin.
But since all men alike, in any strain of heart
or great emotion of soul, credulous or sceptic, fall
instinctively to prayer for thatt solace and strength
which they who use the habit may be seen to hav found—
nay, had Prayer no effect other than reverence
for the self-knowledge, which the Greek enjoin'd, whereby
'tis sovran to bind character, concentrate Will,
and purify intention—nay, ev'n so 'twould claim
a place among the causes of determin'd flux.
    Ah! tho' it may be a simple thing in reach of all,
Best ever is rare, a toilsome guerdon; and prayer is like
those bodily exercises that athletes wil use,
which each must humbly learn, and ere he win to power
so diligently practise, and in such strict course
as wil encroach unkindly on the agreements of life:
whence men slouch in the laxity that they call ease,
rather than rouse to acquiring thatt strength, without which
the body cannot know the pleasur of its full ease,
    the leisur of strength in the hard labor of life.

Now every emotion hath the bodily expression
beseeming each; and since the body cannot be
without some attitude, so Prayer wil hav its own:
and here just as in any athletic exercise

ther be postures and motions foolish in themselves
and often undignified, so too the postur of prayer
may shame our pride of spirit, which would grudge the limbs
warrant of entry upon her sacred solitudes;
albeit the body come there in full abject guize
to do submission and pay fealty to the soul:
And since our speech, in its mere vocal cries and calls,
hath less natural beauty and true significance
than the bodily gestures which convey our desires,
so ev'n the words of prayer wil lack in dignity
and seem impertinent; as full often they be,
and ever had been, unless man's language had upgrown
from makeshift unto mastery of his thought, and learn'd
by its fine musing art to redeem for his soul
the beauty of holiness, marrrying creativly
his best earthly delight with his heav'nliest desire,
when he calleth on God, *Send forth thy light and truth
that they may lead me and bring me unto thy Holy Hill,
to thatt fair place* which is *the joy of the whole earth.*

   See! ther is never dignity in a concourse of men,
save only as some spiritual gleam hearteneth the herd.
Any idea whatsoe'er new-born to consciousness,
if it infect the folk, taketh repetend life
and exuberant difformity of disorder'd growth
from physical communion of emotion and thought;
and of its nascent appetency 'twil embrace
affinity in its host, to stagger and eliminate
all other ideas, thus improportionably
surmounting its own province in Nature's order;
so that unless itself it be a thing of Beauty,
insurmountable of kind, more beauteous in excess—
as when the glow reverberating in a golden cup
multiplyeth the splendour,—it cometh that the herd,
being in its empassionment ever irrational,
wil even of harmless enthusiasm breed disgrace.
   Thus in our English sport, the spectacular games,
where tens of thousands flock throttling the entrance-gates
like sheep to th' pen, wherein they sit huddled to watch
the fortune o' the football, ther is often here and there
mid the seething glomeration of thatt ugly embankment
of gazing faces, one that came to enjoy the sight
knowingly, and yet looketh little on the contest: to him
the crowd is the spectacle; its wrestle and agony

is more than the actors, and its contagion so thick
and irresistible, that ere he feel surprise
he too may find himself, yea philosophy and all,
carried away – as when a strong swimmer in the sea
who would regain the shore, is by the headlong surf
toss'd out of action, and like a drifted log roll'd up
breathless and unresisting on the roaring beach.
   But if he join the folk, when at the cloze of Lent
they kneel in the vast dimness of a city church,
while on the dense silence the lector's chant treadeth
from cadence to cadence the long dolorous way
of the great passion of Christ,—or anon when they rise
to free their mortal craving in the exultant hymn
that ringeth with far promise of eternal peace . . .
or should it happen to him, in strange lands far from home,
to watch the Moslem host, when at their hour of prayer
they troop in wild accoutrement their long-drill'd line
motionless neath the sun upon the Arabian sands,
hush'd to th' Imám's solemnel invocation of God,
as their proud tribal faith savagely draweth strength
from the well-spring of life,—then at the full Amen
of their deep-throated respond he wil feel his spirit
drawn into kinship and their exaltation his own;
the more that he himself can be no part thereof,
incomprehensible because comprehending:
—and they be muddied pools whereat the herd water.
   Such is the dignity of prayer in the common folk;
and its humility is the robe of intellect.
So whenever it hath been by some mystics renounced
in sanctuary of their sublime abstraction—as if
utter abnegation had left no manners else to abjure,—
they appear to lack in use and duty of fellowship.
Yet in such solitaries, pallid clerks of heaven,
souls blanch'd for lack of sunjoys (as 'twould seem to hav been),
their contemplation (it may be) of very intensity
generateth ideas of higher irradiance;
for ideas born to human personality,
having their proper attractions like as atom or cell,
from soul to soul pass freely; and 'twas this mystery,
whereof they kenn'd the need who set that clause i' the creed,
which, compelling belief in the COMMUNION OF SAINTS,
foldeth the sheep in pastures of eternal life.

ALICE MEYNELL
1847–1922

35   *The Rainy Summer*

THERE'S much afoot in heaven and earth this year;
    The winds hunt up the sun, hunt up the moon,
Trouble the dubious dawn, hasten the drear
    Height of a threatening noon.

No breath of boughs, no breath of leaves, of fronds,
    May linger or grow warm; the trees are loud;
The forest, rooted, tosses in her bonds,
    And strains against the cloud.

No scents may pause within the garden-fold;
    The rifled flowers are cold as ocean-shells;
Bees, humming in the storm, carry their cold
    Wild honey to cold cells.

JOHN DAVIDSON
1857–1909

36   *Thirty Bob a Week*

I COULDN'T touch a stop and turn a screw,
    And set the blooming world a-work for me,
Like such as cut their teeth—I hope, like you—
    On the handle of a skeleton gold key;
I cut mine on a leek, which I eat it every week:
    I'm a clerk at thirty bob as you can see.

But I don't allow it's luck and all a toss;
    There's no such thing as being starred and crossed;
It's just the power of some to be a boss,
    And the bally power of others to be bossed:
I face the music, sir; you bet I ain't a cur;
    Strike me lucky if I don't believe I'm lost!

For like a mole I journey in the dark,
    A-travelling along the underground
From my Pillar'd Halls and broad Suburbean Park,
    To come the daily dull official round;
And home again at night with my pipe all alight,
    A-scheming how to count ten bob a pound.

And it's often very cold and very wet,
    And my missis stitches towels for a hunks;
And the Pillar'd Halls is half of it to let—
    Three rooms about the size of travelling trunks.
And we cough, my wife and I, to dislocate a sigh,
    When the noisy little kids are in their bunks.

But you never hear her do a growl or whine,
    For she's made of flint and roses, very odd;
And I've got to cut my meaning rather fine,
    Or I'd blubber, for I'm made of greens and sod:
So p'r'aps we are in Hell for all that I can tell,
    And lost and damn'd and served up hot to God.

I ain't blaspheming, Mr. Silver-tongue;
    I'm saying things a bit beyond your art:
Of all the rummy starts you ever sprung,
    Thirty bob a week's the rummiest start!
With your science and your books and your the'ries about spooks,
    Did you ever hear of looking in your heart?

I didn't mean your pocket, Mr., no:
    I mean that having children and a wife,
With thirty bob on which to come and go,
    Isn't dancing to the tabor and the fife:
When it doesn't make you drink, by Heaven! it makes you think,
    And notice curious items about life.

I step into my heart and there I meet
    A god-almighty devil singing small,
Who would like to shout and whistle in the street,
    And squelch the passers flat against the wall;
If the whole world was a cake he had the power to take,
    He would take it, ask for more, and eat it all.

And I meet a sort of simpleton beside,
  The kind that life is always giving beans;
With thirty bob a week to keep a bride
  He fell in love and married in his teens:
At thirty bob he stuck; but he knows it isn't luck:
  He knows the seas are deeper than tureens.

And the god-almighty devil and the fool
  That meet me in the High Street on the strike,
When I walk about my heart a-gathering wool,
  Are my good and evil angels if you like.
And both of them together in every kind of weather
  Ride me like a double-seated bike.

That's rough a bit and needs its meaning curled.
  But I have a high old hot un in my mind—
A most engrugious notion of the world,
  That leaves your lightning 'rithmetic behind:
I give it at a glance when I say 'There ain't no chance,
  Nor nothing of the lucky-lottery kind.'

And it's this way that I make it out to be:
  No fathers, mothers, countries, climates—none;
Not Adam was responsible for me,
  Nor society, nor systems, nary one:
A little sleeping seed, I woke—I did, indeed—
  A million years before the blooming sun.

I woke because I thought the time had come;
  Beyond my will there was no other cause;
And everywhere I found myself at home,
  Because I chose to be the thing I was;
And in whatever shape of mollusc or of ape
  I always went according to the laws.

I was the love that chose my mother out;
  I joined two lives and from the union burst;
My weakness and my strength without a doubt
  Are mine alone for ever from the first:
It's just the very same with a difference in the name
  As 'Thy will be done.' You say it if you durst!

They say it daily up and down the land
    As easy as you take a drink, it's true;
But the difficultest go to understand,
    And the difficultest job a man can do,
Is to come it brave and meek with thirty bob a week,
    And feel that that's the proper thing for you.

It's a naked child against a hungry wolf;
    It's playing bowls upon a splitting wreck;
It's walking on a string across a gulf
    With millstones fore-and-aft about your neck;
But the thing is daily done by many and many a one;
    And we fall, face forward, fighting, on the deck.

37   *In Romney Marsh*

As I went down to Dymchurch Wall,
    I heard the South sing o'er the land;
I saw the yellow sunlight fall
    On knolls where Norman churches stand.

And ringing shrilly, taut and lithe,
    Within the wind a core of sound,
The wire from Romney town to Hythe
    Alone its airy journey wound.

A veil of purple vapour flowed
    And trailed its fringe along the Straits;
The upper air like sapphire glowed;
    And roses filled Heaven's central gates.

Masts in the offing wagged their tops;
    The swinging waves pealed on the shore;
The saffron beach, all diamond drops
    And beads of surge, prolonged the roar.

As I came up from Dymchurch Wall,
    I saw above the Downs' low crest
The crimson brands of sunset fall,
    Flicker and fade from out the west.

Night sank: like flakes of silver fire
    The stars in one great shower came down;
Shrill blew the wind; and shrill the wire
    Rang out from Hythe to Romney town.

The darkly shining salt sea drops
    Streamed as the waves clashed on the shore;
The beach, with all its organ stops
    Pealing again, prolonged the roar.

38   *A Runnable Stag*

WHEN the pods went pop on the broom, green broom,
    And apples began to be golden-skinned,
We harboured a stag in the Priory coomb,
    And we feathered his trail up-wind, up-wind,
    We feathered his trail up-wind—
        A stag of warrant, a stag, a stag,
        A runnable stag, a kingly crop,
        Brow, bay and tray and three on top,
        A stag, a runnable stag.

Then the huntsman's horn rang yap, yap, yap,
    And 'Forwards' we heard the harbourer shout;
But 'twas only a brocket that broke a gap
    In the beechen underwood, driven out,
    From the underwood antlered out
        By warrant and might of the stag, the stag,
        The runnable stag, whose lordly mind
        Was bent on sleep, though beamed and tined
        He stood, a runnable stag.

So we tufted the covert till afternoon
    With Tinkerman's Pup and Bell-of-the-North;
And hunters were sulky and hounds out of tune
    Before we tufted the right stag forth,
    Before we tufted him forth,
        The stag of warrant, the wily stag,
        The runnable stag with his kingly crop,
        Brow, bay and tray and three on top,
        The royal and runnable stag.

It was Bell-of-the-North and Tinkerman's Pup
  That stuck to the scent till the copse was drawn.
'Tally ho! tally ho!' and the hunt was up,
  The tufters whipped and the pack laid on,
  The resolute pack laid on,
    And the stag of warrant away at last,
    The runnable stag, the same, the same,
    His hoofs on fire, his horns like flame,
    A stag, a runnable stag.

'Let your gelding be: if you check or chide
  He stumbles at once and you're out of the hunt;
For three hundred gentlemen, able to ride,
  On hunters accustomed to bear the brunt,
  Accustomed to bear the brunt,
    Are after the runnable stag, the stag,
    The runnable stag with his kingly crop,
    Brow, bay and tray and three on top,
    The right, the runnable stag.'

By perilous paths in coomb and dell,
  The heather, the rocks, and the river-bed,
The pace grew hot, for the scent lay well,
  And a runnable stag goes right ahead,
  The quarry went right ahead—
    Ahead, ahead, and fast and far;
    His antlered crest, his cloven hoof,
    Brow, bay and tray and three aloof,
    The stag, the runnable stag.

For a matter of twenty miles and more,
  By the densest hedge and the highest wall,
Through herds of bullocks he baffled the lore
  Of harbourer, huntsman, hounds and all,
  Of harbourer hounds and all—
    The stag of warrant, the wily stag,
    For twenty miles, and five and five,
    He ran, and he never was caught alive,
    This stag, this runnable stag.

When he turned at bay in the leafy gloom,
    In the emerald gloom where the brook ran deep,
He heard in the distance the rollers boom,
    And he saw in a vision of peaceful sleep,
    In a wonderful vision of sleep,
        A stag of warrant, a stag, a stag,
        A runnable stag in a jewelled bed,
        Under the sheltering ocean dead,
        A stag, a runnable stag.

So a fateful hope lit up his eye,
    And he opened his nostrils wide again,
And he tossed his branching antlers high
    As he headed the hunt down the Charlock glen,
    As he raced down the echoing glen
        For five miles more, the stag, the stag,
        For twenty miles, and five and five,
        Not to be caught now, dead or alive,
        The stag, the runnable stag.

Three hundred gentlemen, able to ride,
    Three hundred horses as gallant and free,
Beheld him escape on the evening tide,
    Far out till he sank in the Severn Sea,
    Till he sank in the depths of the sea—
        The stag, the buoyant stag, the stag
        That slept at last in a jewelled bed
        Under the sheltering ocean spread,
        The stag, the runnable stag.

JOHN MEADE FALKNER

1858–1922

39   *After Trinity*

WE have done with dogma and divinity
    Easter and Whitsun past,
The long, long Sundays after Trinity
    Are with us at last;
The passionless Sundays after Trinity,
    Neither feast-day nor fast.

Christmas comes with plenty,
    Lent spreads out its pall,
But these are five and twenty,
    The longest Sundays of all;
The placid Sundays after Trinity,
Wheat-harvest, fruit-harvest, Fall.

Spring with its burst is over,
    Summer has had its day,
The scented grasses and clover
    Are cut, and dried into hay;
The singing-birds are silent,
    And the swallows flown away.

Post pugnam pausa fiet;
    Lord, we have made our choice;
In the stillness of autumn quiet,
    We have heard the still, small voice.
We have sung *Oh where shall Wisdom?*
Thick paper, folio, Boyce.

Let it not all be sadness,
    Not *omnia vanitas,*
Stir up a little gladness
    To lighten the *Tibi cras;*
Send us that little summer.
    That comes with Martinmas.

When still the cloudlet dapples
    The windless cobalt-blue,
And the scent of gathered apples
    Fills all the store-rooms through,
The gossamer silvers the bramble,
    The lawns are gemmed with dew.

An end of tombstone Latinity,
    Stir up sober mirth,
Twenty-fifth after Trinity,
    Kneel with the listening earth,
Behind the Advent trumpets
    They are singing Emmanuel's birth.

40 *Christmas Day*
The Family Sitting

IN the days of Cæsar Augustus
    There went forth this decree:
Si quis rectus et justus
    Liveth in Galilee,
Let him go up to Jerusalem
    And pay his scot to me.

There are passed one after the other
    Christmases fifty-three,
Since I sat here with my mother
    And heard the great decree:
How they went up to Jerusalem
    Out of Galilee.

They have passed one after the other;
    Father and mother died,
Brother and sister and brother
    Taken and sanctified.
I am left alone in the sitting,
    With none to sit beside.

On the fly-leaves of these old prayer-books
    The childish writings fade,
Which show that once they were their books
    In the days when prayer was made
For other kings and princesses,
    William and Adelaide.

The pillars are twisted with holly,
    And the font is wreathed with yew
Christ forgive me for folly,
    Youth's lapses—not a few,
For the hardness of my middle life,
    For age's fretful view.

Cotton-wool letters on scarlet,
    All the ancient lore,
Tell how the chieftains starlit
    To Bethlehem came to adore;
To hail Him King in the manger,
    Wonderful, Counsellor.

42

The bells ring out in the steeple
   The gladness of erstwhile,
And the children of other people
   Are walking up the aisle;
They brush my elbow in passing,
   Some turn to give me a smile.

Is the almond-blossom bitter?
   Is the grasshopper heavy to bear?
Christ make me happier, fitter
   To go to my own over there:
Jerusalem the Golden,
   What bliss beyond compare!

My Lord, where I have offended
   Do Thou forgive it me.
That so, when all being ended,
   I hear Thy last decree,
I may go up to Jerusalem
   Out of Galilee.

41
Arabia
Hogarth's Penetration of Arabia

Who are these from the strange, ineffable places,
   From the Topaze Mountain and Desert of Doubt,
With the glow of the Yemen full on their faces,
   And a breath from the spices of Hadramaut?

Travel-apprentices, travel-indenturers,
   Young men, old men, black hair, white,
Names to conjure with, wild adventurers,
   From the noonday furnace and purple night.

Burckhardt, Halévy, Niebuhr, Slater,
   Seventeenth, eighteenth-century bays,
Seetzen, Sadleir, Struys, and later
   Down to the long Victorian days.

A thousand miles at the back of Aden,
   There they had time to think of things;
In the outer silence and burnt air laden
   With the shadow of death and a vulture's wings.

There they remembered the last house in Samna,
   Last of the plane-trees, last shepherd and flock,
Prayed for the heavens to rain down manna,
   Prayed for a Moses to strike the rock.

Famine and fever flagged their forces
   Till they died in a dream of ice and fruit,
In the long-forgotten watercourses
   By the edge of Queen Zobëide's route.

They have left the hope of the green oases,
   The fear of the bleaching bones and the pest,
They have found the more ineffable places—
   Allah has given them rest.

E. NESBIT

1858–1924

42   *The Things That Matter*

Now that I've nearly done my days,
   And grown too stiff to sweep or sew,
I sit and think, till I'm amaze,
   About what lots of things I know:
Things as I've found out one by one—
   And when I'm fast down in the clay,
My knowing things and how they're done
   Will all be lost and thrown away.

There's things, I know, as won't be lost,
   Things as folks write and talk about:
The way to keep your roots from frost,
   And how to get your ink spots out.
What medicine's good for sores and sprains,
   What way to salt your butter down,
What charms will cure your different pains,
   And what will bright your faded gown.

But more important things than these,
　　They can't be written in a book:
How fast to boil your greens and peas,
　　And how good bacon ought to look;
The feel of real good wearing stuff,
　　The kind of apple as will keep,
The look of bread that's rose enough,
　　And how to get a child asleep.

Whether the jam is fit to pot,
　　Whether the milk is going to turn,
Whether a hen will lay or not,
　　Is things as some folks never learn.
I know the weather by the sky,
　　I know what herbs grow in what lane;
And if sick men are going to die,
　　Or if they'll get about again.

Young wives come in, a-smiling, grave,
　　With secrets that they itch to tell:
I know what sort of times they'll have,
　　And if they'll have a boy or gell.
And if a lad is ill to bind,
　　Or some young maid is hard to lead,
I know when you should speak 'em kind,
　　And when it's scolding as they need.

I used to know where birds ud set,
　　And likely spots for trout or hare,
And God may want me to forget
　　The way to set a line or snare;
But not the way to truss a chick,
　　To fry a fish, or baste a roast,
Nor how to tell, when folks are sick,
　　What kind of herb will ease them most!

Forgetting seems such silly waste!
　　I know so many little things,
And now the Angels will make haste
　　To dust it all away with wings!
O God, you made me like to know,
　　You kept the things straight in my head,
Please God, if you can make it so,
　　Let me know *something* when I'm dead.

A. E. HOUSMAN
1859–1936

43

LOVELIEST of trees, the cherry now
Is hung with bloom along the bough,
And stands about the woodland ride
Wearing white for Eastertide.

Now, of my threescore years and ten,
Twenty will not come again,
And take from seventy springs a score,
It only leaves me fifty more.

And since to look at things in bloom
Fifty springs are little room,
About the woodlands I will go
To see the cherry hung with snow.

44

THE lads in their hundreds to Ludlow come in for the fair,
    There's men from the barn and the forge and the mill and the fold,
The lads for the girls and the lads for the liquor are there,
    And there with the rest are the lads that will never be old.

There's chaps from the town and the field and the till and the cart,
    And many to count are the stalwart, and many the brave,
And many the handsome of face and the handsome of heart,
    And few that will carry their looks or their truth to the grave.

I wish one could know them, I wish there were tokens to tell
    The fortunate fellows that now you can never discern;
And then one could talk with them friendly and wish them farewell
    And watch them depart on the way that they will not return.

But now you may stare as you like and there's nothing to scan;
    And brushing your elbow unguessed-at and not to be told
They carry back bright to the coiner the mintage of man,
    The lads that will die in their glory and never be old.

45

OTHERS, I am not the first,
Have willed more mischief than they durst:
If in the breathless night I too
Shiver now, 'tis nothing new.

More than I, if truth were told,
Have stood and sweated hot and cold,
And through their reins in ice and fire
Fear contended with desire.

Agued once like me were they,
But I like them shall win my way
Lastly to the bed of mould
Where there's neither heat nor cold.

But from my grave across my brow
Plays no wind of healing now,
And fire and ice within me fight
Beneath the suffocating night.

46

ON Wenlock Edge the wood's in trouble;
    His forest fleece the Wrekin heaves;
The gale, it plies the saplings double,
    And thick on Severn snow the leaves.

'Twould blow like this through holt and hanger
    When Uricon the city stood:
'Tis the old wind in the old anger,
    But then it threshed another wood.

Then, 'twas before my time, the Roman
    At yonder heaving hill would stare:
The blood that warms an English yeoman,
    The thoughts that hurt him, they were there.

There, like the wind through woods in riot,
   Through him the gale of life blew high;
The tree of man was never quiet:
   Then 'twas the Roman, now 'tis I.

The gale, it plies the saplings double,
   It blows so hard, 'twill soon be gone:
To-day the Roman and his trouble
   Are ashes under Uricon.

47

INTO my heart an air that kills
   From yon far country blows:
What are those blue remembered hills,
   What spires, what farms are those?

That is the land of lost content,
   I see it shining plain,
The happy highways where I went
   And cannot come again.

48   *Epitaph on an Army of Mercenaries*

THESE, in the day when heaven was falling,
   The hour when earth's foundations fled,
Followed their mercenary calling
   And took their wages and are dead.

Their shoulders held the sky suspended;
   They stood, and earth's foundations stay;
What God abandoned, these defended,
   And saved the sum of things for pay.

49

TELL me not here, it needs not saying,
  What tune the enchantress plays
In aftermaths of soft September
  Or under blanching mays,
For she and I were long acquainted
  And I knew all her ways.

On russet floors, by waters idle,
  The pine lets fall its cone;
The cuckoo shouts all day at nothing
  In leafy dells alone;
And traveller's joy beguiles in autumn
  Hearts that have lost their own.

On acres of the seeded grasses
  The changing burnish heaves;
Or marshalled under moons of harvest
  Stand still all night the sheaves;
Or beeches strip in storms for winter
  And stain the wind with leaves.

Possess, as I possessed a season,
  The countries I resign,
Where over elmy plains the highway
  Would mount the hills and shine,
And full of shade the pillared forest
  Would murmur and be mine.

For nature, heartless, witless nature,
  Will neither care nor know
What stranger's feet may find the meadow
  And trespass there and go,
Nor ask amid the dews of morning
  If they are mine or no.

50

BECAUSE I liked you better
　Than suits a man to say,
It irked you, and I promised
　To throw the thought away.

To put the world between us
　We parted, stiff and dry;
'Good-bye', said you, 'forget me.'
　'I will, no fear', said I.

If here, where clover whitens
　The dead man's knoll, you pass,
And no tall flower to meet you
　Starts in the trefoiled grass,

Halt by the headstone naming
　The heart no longer stirred,
And say the lad that loved you
　Was one that kept his word.

SIR HENRY NEWBOLT

1862–1938

51　*Master and Man*

Do ye ken hoo to fush for the salmon?
　If ye'll listen I'll tell ye.
Dinna trust to the books and their gammon,
　They're but tryin' to sell ye.
Leave professors to read their ain cackle
　And fush their ain style;
Come awa', sir, we'll oot wi' oor tackle
　And be busy the while.

'Tis a wee bit ower bright, ye were thinkin'?
　Aw, ye'll no be the loser;
'Tis better ten baskin' and blinkin'
　Than ane that's a cruiser.

If ye're bent, as I tak it, on slatter,
   Ye should pray for the droot,
For the salmon's her ain when there's watter,
   But she's oors when it's oot.

Ye may just put your flee-book behind ye,
   Ane hook wull be plenty;
If they'll no come for this, my man, mind ye,
   They'll no come for twenty.
Ay, a rod; but the shorter the stranger
   And the nearer to strike;
For myself I prefare it nae langer
   Than a yard or the like.

Noo, ye'll stand awa' back while I'm creepin'
   Wi' my snoot i' the gowans;
There's a bonny twalve-poonder a-sleepin'
   I' the shade o' yon rowans.
Man, man! I was fearin' I'd stirred her,
   But I've got her the noo!
Hoot! fushin's as easy as murrder
   When ye ken what to do.

Na, na, sir, I doot na ye're willin',
   But I canna permit ye;
For I'm thinkin' that yon kind o' killin'
   Wad hardly befit ye.
And some work is deefficult hushin',
   There'd be havers and chaff:
'Twull be best, sir, for you to be fushin'
   And me wi' the gaff.

52   *He Fell Among Thieves*

'YE have robbed,' said he, 'ye have slaughtered and made an end,
   Take your ill-got plunder, and bury the dead:
What will ye more of your guest and sometime friend?'
   'Blood for our blood,' they said.

He laughed: 'If one may settle the score for five,
    I am ready; but let the reckoning stand till day:
I have loved the sunlight as dearly as any alive.'
    'You shall die at dawn,' said they.

He flung his empty revolver down the slope,
    He climbed alone to the Eastward edge of the trees;
All night long in a dream untroubled of hope
    He brooded, clasping his knees.

He did not hear the monotonous roar that fills
    The ravine where the Yassin river sullenly flows;
He did not see the starlight on the Laspur hills,
    Or the far Afghan snows.

He saw the April noon on his books aglow,
    The wistaria trailing in at the window wide;
He heard his father's voice from the terrace below
    Calling him down to ride.

He saw the gray little church across the park,
    The mounds that hide the loved and honoured dead;
The Norman arch, the chancel softly dark,
    The brasses black and red.

He saw the School Close, sunny and green,
    The runner beside him, the stand by the parapet wall,
The distant tape, and the crowd roaring between
    His own name over all.

He saw the dark wainscot and timbered roof,
    The long tables, and the faces merry and keen;
The College Eight and their trainer dining aloof,
    The Dons on the daïs serene.

He watched the liner's stem ploughing the foam,
    He felt her trembling speed and the thrash of her screw;
He heard her passengers' voices talking of home,
    He saw the flag she flew.

And now it was dawn. He rose strong on his feet,
    And strode to his ruined camp below the wood;
He drank the breath of the morning cool and sweet;
    His murderers round him stood.

Light on the Laspur hills was broadening fast,
  The blood-red snow-peaks chilled to a dazzling white:
He turned, and saw the golden circle at last,
  Cut by the Eastern height.

'O glorious Life, Who dwellest in earth and sun,
  I have lived, I praise and adore Thee."
                              A sword swept.
Over the pass the voices one by one
  Faded, and the hill slept.

EDEN PHILLPOTTS

1862–1960

53   *Man's Days*

A SUDDEN wakin', a sudden weepin';
A li'l suckin', a li'l sleepin';
A cheel's full joys an' a cheel's short sorrows,
Wi' a power o' faith in gert to-morrows.

Young blood red hot an' the love of a maid;
Wan glorious hour as'll never fade;
Some shadows, some sunshine, some triumphs, some tears;
An' a gatherin' weight o' the flyin' years.

Then auld man's talk o' the days behind 'e;
Your darter's youngest darter to mind 'e;
A li'l dreamin', a li'l dyin',
A li'l lew corner o' airth to lie in.

54   *The Houses*

FORLORN and glum the couples go
While Capital and Labour fight.
For lack of homes they can't unite
And love says 'Yes,' the builders, 'No.'

Yet, troubling not for time nor rest,
The courting rooks be flying thick,
And not a beak wi'out a stick
And not an elm wi'out a nest.

It do cast down my ancient mind
How senseless fowls can run their show,
Marry and help their childer grow,
And not us clever human kind.

Lords of creation we may be,
Though what the mischief we creates
But trouble, taxes, higher rates,
Be damned to us if I can see.

MOIRA O'NEILL

1864–1955

55   *Her Sister*

'BRIGID is a Caution, sure!'—What's that ye say?
Is it my sister then, Brigid MacIlray?
Caution or no Caution, listen what I'm tellin' ye . . .
Childer, hould yer noise there, faix! there's no quellin' ye! . . .
Och, well, I've said it now this many a long day,
'Tis the quare pity o' Brigid MacIlray.

An' she that was the beauty, an' never married yet!
An' fifty years gone over her, but do ye think she'll fret?
Sorra one o' Brigid then, that's not the sort of her,
Ne'er a *hate* would *she* care though not a man had thought of her.
Heaps o' men she might 'a had. . . . *Here, get out o' that,*
Mick, ye rogue! desthroyin' o' the poor ould cat!

Ah, no use o' talkin'! Sure a woman's born to wed,
An' not go wastin' all her life by waitin' till she's dead.
Haven't we the men to mind, that couldn't for the lives o' them
Keep their right end uppermost, only for the wives o' them?—
Stick to yer pipe, Tim, an' give me no talk now!
There's the door fore'nenst ye, man! out ye can walk now.

Brigid, poor Brigid will never have a child,
An' she you'd think a mother born, so gentle an' so mild. . . .
Danny, is it puttin' little Biddy's eyes out ye're after,
Swishin' wid yer rod there, an' splittin' wid yer laughter?
Come along the whole o' yez, in out o' the wet,
Or may I never but ye'll soon see what ye'll get!

She to have no man at all. . . . *Musha, look at Tim!*
Off an' up the road he is, an' wet enough to swim,
An' his tea sittin' waitin' on him, there he'll sthreel about now,—
Amn't I the heart-scalded woman out an' out now?
Here I've lived an' wrought for him all the ways I can,
But the Goodness grant me patience, for I'd need it wid that man!

What was I sayin' then? Brigid lives her lone,
Ne'er a one about the house, quiet as a stone. . . .
Lave a-go the pig's tail, boys, an' quet the squealin' now,
Mind! I've got a sally switch that only wants the peelin' now. . . .
Ah, just to think of her, 'deed an' well-a-day!
'Tis the quare pity o' Brigid MacIlray.

RUDYARD KIPLING

1865–1936

56   *Tommy*

I WENT into a public-'ouse to get a pint o' beer,
The publican 'e up an' sez, 'We serve no red-coats here.'
The girls be'ind the bar they laughed an' giggled fit to die,
I outs into the street again an' to myself sez I:
    O it's Tommy this, an' Tommy that, an' 'Tommy, go away';
    But it's 'Thank you, Mister Atkins,' when the band begins to
      play—
    The band begins to play, my boys, the band begins to play,
    O it's 'Thank you, Mister Atkins,' when the band begins to play.

I went into a theatre as sober as could be,
They gave a drunk civilian room, but 'adn't none for me;
They sent me to the gallery or round the music-'alls,
But when it comes to fightin', Lord! they'll shove me in the stalls!
    For it's Tommy this, an' Tommy that, an' 'Tommy, wait outside';
    But it's 'Special train for Atkins' when the trooper's on the tide—
    The troopship's on the tide, my boys, the troopship's on the tide,
    O it's 'Special train for Atkins' when the trooper's on the tide.

Yes, makin' mock o' uniforms that guard you while you sleep
Is cheaper than them uniforms, an' they're starvation cheap;
An' hustlin' drunken soldiers when they're goin' large a bit
Is five times better business than paradin' in full kit.
    Then it's Tommy this, an' Tommy that, an' 'Tommy, 'ow's yer
      soul?'
    But it's 'Thin red line of 'eroes' when the drums begin to roll—
    The drums begin to roll, my boys, the drums begin to roll,
    O it's 'Thin red line of 'eroes' when the drums begin to roll.

We aren't no thin red 'eroes, nor we aren't no blackguards too,
But single men in barricks, most remarkable like you;
An' if sometimes our conduck isn't all your fancy paints,
Why, single men in barricks don't grow into plaster saints;
    While it's Tommy this, an' Tommy that, an' 'Tommy, fall be'ind,'
    But it's 'Please to walk in front, sir,' when there's trouble in the
      wind—
    There's trouble in the wind, my boys, there's trouble in the wind,
    O it's 'Please to walk in front, sir,' when there's trouble in the
      wind.

You talk o' better food for us, an' schools, an' fires, an' all:
We'll wait for extry rations if you treat us rational.
Don't mess about the cook-room slops, but prove it to our face
The Widow's Uniform is not the soldier-man's disgrace.
    For it's Tommy this, an' Tommy that, an' 'Chuck him out, the
      brute!'
    But it's 'Saviour of 'is country' when the guns begin to shoot;
    An' it's Tommy this, an' Tommy that, an' anything you please;
    An' Tommy ain't a bloomin' fool—you bet that Tommy sees!

57 *My Rival*

I GO to concert, party, ball—
    What profit is in these?
I sit alone against the wall
    And strive to look at ease.
The incense that is mine by right
    They burn before Her shrine;
And that's because I'm seventeen
    And She is forty-nine.

I cannot check my girlish blush,
    My colour comes and goes.
I redden to my finger-tips,
    And sometimes to my nose.
But She is white where white should be,
    And red where red should shine.
The blush that flies at seventeen
    Is fixed at forty-nine.

I wish *I* had Her constant cheek;
    I wish that I could sing
All sorts of funny little songs,
    Not quite the proper thing.
I'm very *gauche* and very shy,
    Her jokes aren't in my line;
And, worst of all, I'm seventeen
    While She is forty-nine.

The young men come, the young men go,
    Each pink and white and neat,
She's older than their mothers, but
    They grovel at Her feet.
They walk beside Her '*rickshaw*-wheels—
    None ever walk by mine;
And that's because I'm seventeen
    And She is forty-nine.

She rides with half a dozen men
    (She calls them 'boys' and 'mashes'),
I trot along the Mall alone;
    My prettiest frocks and sashes

Don't help to fill my programme-card,
 And vainly I repine
From ten to two A.M. Ah me!
 Would I were forty-nine.

She calls me 'darling,' 'pet,' and 'dear,'
 And 'sweet retiring maid.'
I'm always at the back, I know—
 She puts me in the shade.
She introduces me to men—
 'Cast' lovers, I opine;
For sixty takes to seventeen,
 Nineteen to forty-nine.

But even She must older grow
 And end Her dancing days,
She can't go on for ever so
 At concerts, balls, and plays.
One ray of priceless hope I see
 Before my footsteps shine;
Just think, that She'll be eighty-one
 When I am forty-nine!

58   *McAndrew's Hymn*

LORD, Thou hast made this world below the shadow of a dream,
An', taught by time, I tak' it so—exceptin' always Steam.
From coupler-flange to spindle-guide I see Thy Hand, O God—
Predestination in the stride o' yon connectin'-rod.
John Calvin might ha' forged the same—enorrmous, certain, slow—
Ay, wrought it in the furnace-flame—*my* 'Institutio.'
I cannot get my sleep to-night; old bones are hard to please;
I'll stand the middle watch up here—alone wi' God an' these
My engines, after ninety days o' race an' rack an' strain
Through all the seas of all Thy world, slam-bangin' home again.
Slam-bang too much—they knock a wee—the crosshead-gibs are loose,
But thirty thousand mile o' sea has gied them fair excuse. . . .
Fine, clear an' dark—a full-draught breeze, wi' Ushant out o' sight,
An' Ferguson relievin' Hay. Old girl, ye'll walk to-night!

His wife's at Plymouth. . . . Seventy—One—Two—Three since he
    began—
Three turns for Mistress Ferguson . . . and who's to blame the man?
There's none at any port for me, by drivin' fast or slow,
Since Elsie Campbell went to Thee, Lord, thirty years ago.
(The year the *Sarah Sands* was burned. Oh, roads we used to tread,
Fra' Maryhill to Pollokshaws—fra' Govan to Parkhead!)
Not but they're ceevil on the Board. Ye'll hear Sir Kenneth say:
'Good morrn, McAndrew! Back again? An' how's your bilge to-day?'
Miscallin' technicalities but handin' me my chair
To drink Madeira wi' three Earls—the auld Fleet Engineer
That started as a boiler-whelp—when steam and he were low.
I mind the time we used to serve a broken pipe wi' tow!
Ten pound was all the pressure then—Eh! Eh!—a man wad drive;
An' here, our workin' gauges give one hunder sixty-five!
We're creepin' on wi' each new rig—less weight an' larger power;
There'll be the loco-boiler next an' thirty mile an hour!
Thirty an' more. What I ha' seen since ocean-steam began
Leaves me na doot for the machine: but what about the man?
The man that counts, wi' all his runs, one million mile o' sea:
Four time the span from earth to moon. . . . How far, O Lord, from
    Thee
That wast beside him night an' day? Ye mind my first typhoon?
It scoughed the skipper on his way to jock wi' the saloon.
Three feet were on the stokehold-floor—just slappin' to an' fro—
An' cast me on a furnace-door. I have the marks to show.
Marks! I ha' marks o' more than burns—deep in my soul an' black,
An' times like this, when things go smooth, my wickudness comes
    back.
The sins o' four an' forty years, all up an' down the seas,
Clack an' repeat like valves half-fed. . . . Forgie's our trespasses!
Nights when I'd come on deck to mark, wi' envy in my gaze,
The couples kittlin' in the dark between the funnel-stays;
Years when I raked the Ports wi' pride to fill my cup o' wrong—
Judge not, O Lord, my steps aside at Gay Street in Hong-Kong!
Blot out the wastrel hours of mine in sin when I abode—
Jane Harrigan's an' Number Nine, The Reddick an' Grant Road!
An' waur than all—my crownin' sin—rank blasphemy an' wild.
I was not four and twenty then—Ye wadna judge a child?
I'd seen the Tropics first that run—new fruit, new smells, new air—
How could I tell—blind-fou wi' sun—the Deil was lurkin' there?
By day like playhouse-scenes the shore slid past our sleepy eyes;
By night those soft, lasceevious stars leered from those velvet skies,

In port (we used no cargo-steam) I'd daunder down the streets—
An ijjit grinnin' in a dream—for shells an' parrakeets,
An' walkin'-sticks o' carved bamboo an' blowfish stuffed an' dried—
Fillin' my bunk wi' rubbishry the Chief put overside.
Till, off Sambawa Head, Ye mind, I heard a land-breeze ca',
Milk-warm wi' breath o' spice an' bloom: 'McAndrew, come awa'!'
Firm, clear an' low—no haste, no hate—the ghostly whisper went,
Just statin' eevidential facts beyon' all argument:
'Your mither's God's a graspin' deil, the shadow o' yoursel',
'Got out o' books by meenisters clean daft on Heaven an' Hell.
'They mak' him in the Broomielaw, o' Glasgie cold an' dirt,
'A jealous, pridefu' fetich, lad, that's only strong to hurt
'Ye'll not go back to Him again an' kiss His red-hot rod,
'But come wi' Us' (Now, who were *They*?) 'an' know the Leevin' God,
'That does not kipper souls for sport or break a life in jest,
'But swells the ripenin' cocoanuts an' ripes the woman's breast.'
An' there it stopped—cut off—no more—that quiet, certain voice—
For me, six months o' twenty-four, to leave or take at choice.
'Twas on me like a thunderclap—it racked me through an' through—
Temptation past the show o' speech, unnameable an' new—
The Sin against the Holy Ghost? . . . An' under all, our screw.

That storm blew by but left behind her anchor-shiftin' swell.
Thou knowest all my heart an' mind, Thou knowest, Lord, I fell—
Third on the *Mary Gloster* then, and first that night in Hell!
Yet was Thy Hand beneath my head, about my feet Thy Care—
Fra' Deli clear to Torres Strait, the trial o' despair,
But when we touched the Barrier Reef Thy answer to my prayer! . . .
We dared na run that sea by night but lay an' held our fire,
An' I was drowsin' on the hatch—sick—sick wi' doubt an' tire:
'*Better the sight of eyes that see than wanderin' o' desire!*'
Ye mind that word? Clear as our gongs—again, an' once again,
When rippin' down through coral-trash ran out our moorin'-chain:
An', by Thy Grace, I had the Light to see my duty plain.
Light on the engine-room—no more—bright as our carbons burn.
I've lost it since a thousand times, but never past return!

Obsairve! Per annum we'll have here two thousand souls aboard—
Think not I dare to justify myself before the Lord,
But—average fifteen hunder souls safe-borne fra' port to port—
I *am* o' service to my kind. Ye wadna blame the thought?
Maybe they steam from Grace to Wrath—to sin by folly led—
It isna mine to judge their path—their lives are on my head.

Mine at the last—when all is done it all comes back to me,
The fault that leaves six thousand ton a log upon the sea.
We'll tak' one stretch—three weeks an' odd by ony road ye steer—
Fra' Cape Town east to Wellington—ye need an engineer.
Fail there—ye've time to weld your shaft—ay, eat it, ere ye're spoke;
Or make Kerguelen under sail—three jiggers burned wi' smoke!
An' home again—the Rio run: it's no child's play to go
Steamin' to bell for fourteen days o' snow an' floe an' blow.
The bergs like kelpies overside that girn an' turn an' shift
Whaur, grindin' like the Mills o' God, goes by the big South drift.
(Hail, Snow and Ice that praise the Lord. I've met them at their work,
An' wished we had anither route or they anither kirk.)
Yon's strain, hard strain, o' head an' hand, for though Thy Power
    brings
All skill to naught, Ye'll understand a man must think o' things.
Then, at the last, we'll get to port an' hoist their baggage clear—
The passengers, wi' gloves an' canes—an' this is what I'll hear:
'Well, thank ye for a pleasant voyage. The tender's comin' now.'
While I go testin' follower-bolts an' watch the skipper bow.
They've words for every one but me—shake hands wi' half the crew,
Except the dour Scots engineer, the man they never knew.
An' yet I like the wark for all we've dam'-few pickin's here—
No pension, an' the most we'll earn's four hunder pound a year.
Better myself abroad? Maybe. *I'd* sooner starve than sail
Wi' such as call a snifter-rod *ross*. . . . French for nightingale.
Commeesion on my stores? Some do; but I cannot afford
To lie like stewards wi' patty-pans. I'm older than the Board.
A bonus on the coal I save? Ou ay, the Scots are close,
But when I grudge the strength Ye gave I'll grudge their food to *those*.
(There's bricks that I might recommend—an' clink the fire-bars cruel.
No! Welsh—Wangarti at the worst—an' damn all patent fuel!)
Inventions? Ye must stay in port to mak' a patent pay.
My Deeferential Valve-Gear taught me how that business lay.
I blame no chaps wi' clearer heads for aught they make or sell.
I found that I could not invent an' look to these as well.
So, wrestled wi' Apollyon—Nah! fretted like a bairn—
But burned the workin'-plans last run, wi' all I hoped to earn.
Ye know how hard an Idol dies, an' what that meant to me—
E'en tak' it for a sacrifice acceptable to Thee. . . .
Below there! Oiler! What's your wark? Ye find it runnin' hard?
Ye needn't swill the cup wi' oil—this isn't the Cunard!
Ye thought? Ye are not paid to think. Go, sweat that off again!
Tck! Tck! It's deeficult to sweer nor tak' The Name in vain!

Men, ay, an' women, call me stern. Wi' these to oversee,
Ye'll note I've little time to burn on social repartee.
The bairns see what their elders miss; they'll hunt me to an' fro,
Till for the sake of—well, a kiss—I tak' 'em down below.
That minds me of our Viscount loon—Sir Kenneth's kin—the chap
Wi' Russia-leather tennis-shoon an' spar-decked yachtin'-cap.
I showed him round last week, o'er all—an' at the last says he:
'Mister McAndrew, don't you think steam spoils romance at sea?'
Damned ijjit! I'd been doon that morn to see what ailed the throws,
Manholin', on my back—the cranks three inches off my nose.
Romance! Those first-class passengers they like it very well,
Printed an' bound in little books; but why don't poets tell?
I'm sick of all their quirks an' turns—the loves an' doves they dream—
Lord, send a man like Robbie Burns to sing the Song o' Steam!
To match wi' Scotia's noblest speech yon orchestra sublime
Whaurto—uplifted like the Just—the tail-rods mark the time.
The crank-throws give the double-bass, the feed-pump sobs an' heaves,
An' now the main eccentrics start their quarrel on the sheaves:
Her time, her own appointed time, the rocking link-head bides,
Till—hear that note?—the rod's return whings glimmerin' through the
    guides.
They're all awa'! True beat, full power, the clangin' chorus goes
Clear to the tunnel where they sit, my purrin' dynamoes.
Interdependence absolute, foreseen, ordained, decreed,
To work, Ye'll note, at ony tilt an' every rate o' speed.
Fra' skylight-lift to furnace-bars, backed, bolted, braced an' stayed,
An' singin' like the Mornin' Stars for joy that they are made;
While, out o' touch o' vanity, the sweatin' thrust-block says:
'Not unto us the praise, or man—not unto us the praise!'
Now, a' together, hear them lift their lesson—theirs an' mine:
'Law, Orrder, Duty an' Restraint, Obedience, Discipline!'
Mill, forge an' try-pit taught them that when roarin' they arose,
An' whiles I wonder if a soul was gied them wi' the blows.
O for a man to weld it then, in one trip-hammer strain,
Till even first-class passengers could tell the meanin' plain!
But no one cares except mysel' that serve an' understand
My seven thousand horse-power here. Eh, Lord! They're grand—
    they're grand!
Uplift am I? When first in store the new-made beasties stood,
Were Ye cast down that breathed the Word declarin' all things good?
Not so! O' that warld-liftin' joy no after-fall could vex,
Ye've left a glimmer still to cheer the Man—the Arrtifex!

That holds, in spite o' knock and scale, o' friction, waste an' slip,
An' by that light—now, mark my word—we'll build the Perfect Ship.
I'll never last to judge her lines or take her curve—not I.
But I ha' lived an' I ha' worked. Be thanks to Thee, Most High!
An' I ha' done what I ha' done—judge Thou if ill or well—
Always Thy Grace preventin' me. . . .
                                        Losh! Yon's the 'Stand-by' bell.
Pilot so soon? His flare it is. The mornin'-watch is set.
Well, God be thanked, as I was sayin', I'm no Pelagian yet.
Now I'll tak' on. . . .
    'Morrn, Ferguson. Man, have ye ever thought
What your good leddy costs in coal? . . . I'll burn 'em down to port.

59   *Danny Deever*

'WHAT are the bugles blowin' for?' said Files-on-Parade.
'To turn you out, to turn you out,' the Colour-Sergeant said.
'What makes you look so white, so white?' said Files-on-Parade.
'I'm dreadin' what I've got to watch,' the Colour-Sergeant said.
    For they're hangin' Danny Deever, you can hear the Dead March
        play,
    The Regiment's in 'ollow square—they're hangin' him to-day;
    They've taken of his buttons off an' cut his stripes away,
    An' they're hangin' Danny Deever in the mornin'.

'What makes the rear-rank breathe so 'ard?' said Files-on-Parade.
'It's bitter cold, it's bitter cold,' the Colour-Sergeant said.
'What makes that front-rank man fall down?' said Files-on-Parade.
'A touch o' sun, a touch o' sun,' the Colour-Sergeant said.
    They are hangin' Danny Deever, they are marchin' of 'im round,
    They 'ave 'alted Danny Deever by 'is coffin on the ground;
    An' 'e'll swing in 'arf a minute for a sneakin shootin' hound—
    O they're hangin' Danny Deever in the mornin'!

' 'Is cot was right-'and cot to mine,' said Files-on-Parade.
' 'E's sleepin' out an' far to-night,' the Colour-Sergeant said.
'I've drunk 'is beer a score o' times,' said Files-on-Parade.
' 'E's drinkin' bitter beer alone,' the Colour-Sergeant said.
    They are hangin' Danny Deever, you must mark 'im to 'is place,
    For 'e shot a comrade sleepin'—you must look 'im in the face;
    Nine 'undred of 'is county an' the Regiment's disgrace,
    While they're hangin' Danny Deever in the mornin'.

'What's that so black agin the sun?' said Files-on-Parade.
'It's Danny fightin' 'ard for life,' the Colour-Sergeant said.
'What's that that whimpers over'ead?' said Files-on-Parade.
'It's Danny's soul that's passin' now,' the Colour-Sergeant said.

    For they've done with Danny Deever, you can 'ear the quickstep
      play,
    The Regiment's in column, an' they're marchin' us away;
    Ho! the young recruits are shakin', an' they'll want their beer
      to-day,
    After hangin' Danny Deever in the mornin'!

60   *The Sergeant's Weddin'*

'E WAS warned agin 'er—
   That's what made 'im look;
She was warned agin' 'im—
   That is why she took.
Wouldn't 'ear no reason,
   Went an' done it blind;
We know all about 'em,
   They've got all to find!

Cheer for the Sergeant's weddin'—
   Give 'em one cheer more!
Grey gun-'orses in the lando,
   An' a rogue is married to, etc.

What's the use o' tellin'
   'Arf the lot she's been?
'E's a bloomin' robber,
   An' 'e keeps canteen.
'Ow did 'e get 'is buggy?
   Gawd, you needn't ask!
'Made 'is forty gallon
   Out of every cask!

Watch 'im, with 'is 'air cut,
   Count us filin' by—
Won't the Colonel praise 'is
   Pop—u—lar—i—ty!

We 'ave scores to settle—
    Scores for more than beer;
She's the girl to pay 'em—
    That is why we're 'ere!

See the Chaplain thinkin'?
    See the women smile?
Twig the married winkin'
    As they take the aisle?
Keep your side-arms quiet,
    Dressin' by the Band.
Ho! You 'oly beggars,
    Cough be'ind your 'and!

Now it's done an' over,
    'Ear the organ squeak,
' *'Voice that breathed o'er Eden'*—
    Ain't she got the cheek!
White an' laylock ribbons,
    'Think yourself so fine!
I'd pray Gawd to take yer
    'Fore I made yer mine!

Escort to the kerridge,
    Wish 'im luck, the brute!
Chuck the slippers after—
    (Pity 'tain't a boot!)
Bowin' like a lady,
    Blushin' like a lad—
'Oo would say to see 'em
    Both is rotten bad?

Cheer for the Sergeant's weddin'—
    Give 'em one cheer more!
Grey gun-'orses in the lando,
    An' a rogue is married to, etc.

61 *The 'Eathen*

THE 'eathen in 'is blindness bows down to wood an' stone;
'E don't obey no orders unless they is 'is own;
'E keeps 'is side-arms awful: 'e leaves 'em all about,
An' then comes up the Regiment an' pokes the 'eathen out.

> *All along o' dirtiness, all along o' mess,*
> *All along o' doin' things rather-more-or-less,*
> *All along of abby-nay,[1] kul,[2] an' hazar-ho,[3]*
> *Mind you keep your rifle an' yourself jus' so!*

The young recruit is 'aughty—'e draf's from Gawd knows where;
They bid 'im show 'is stockin's an' lay 'is mattress square;
'E calls it bloomin' nonsense—'e doesn't know, no more—
An' then up comes 'is Company an' kicks 'im round the floor!

The young recruit is 'ammered—'e takes it very hard;
'E 'angs 'is 'ead an' mutters—'e sulks about the yard;
'E talks o' 'cruel tyrants' which 'e'll swing for by-an'-by,
An' the others 'ears an' mocks 'im, an' the boy goes orf to cry.

The young recruit is silly—'e thinks o' suicide.
'E's lost 'is gutter-devil; 'e 'asn't got 'is pride;
But day by day they kicks 'im, which 'elps 'im on a bit,
Till 'e finds 'isself one mornin' with a full an' proper kit.

> *Gettin' clear o' dirtiness, gettin' done with mess,*
> *Gettin' shut o' doin' things rather-more-or-less;*
> *Not so fond of abby-nay, kul, nor hazar-ho,*
> *Learns to keep 'is rifle an' 'isself jus' so!*

The young recruit is 'appy—'e throws a chest to suit;
You see 'im grow mustaches; you 'ear 'im slap 'is boot.
'E learns to drop the 'bloodies' from every word 'e slings,
An' 'e shows an 'ealthy brisket when 'e strips for bars an' rings.

The cruel-tyrant-sergeants they watch 'im 'arf a year;
They watch 'im with 'is comrades, they watch 'im with 'is beer;
They watch 'im with the women at the regimental dance,
And the cruel-tyrant-sergeants send 'is name along for 'Lance.'

---

[1] Not now.   [2] To-morrow.   [3] Wait a bit.

An' now 'e's 'arf o' nothin', an' all a private yet,
'Is room they up an' rags 'im to see what they will get.
They rags 'im low an' cunnin', each dirty trick they can,
But 'e learns to sweat 'is temper an' 'e learns to sweat 'is man.

An', last, a Colour-Sergeant, as such to be obeyed,
'E schools 'is men at cricket, 'e tells 'em on parade;
They sees 'im quick an' 'andy, uncommon set an' smart,
An' so 'e talks to orficers which 'ave the Core at 'eart.

'E learns to do 'is watchin' without it showin' plain;
'E learns to save a dummy, an' shove 'im straight again;
'E learns to check a ranker that's buyin' leave to shirk;
An' 'e learns to make men like 'im so they'll learn to like their work.

An' when it comes to marchin' he'll see their socks are right,
An' when it comes to action 'e shows 'em how to sight.
'E knows their ways of thinkin' and just what's in their mind;
'E knows when they are takin' on an' when they've fell be'ind.

'E knows each talkin' corp'ral that leads a squad astray;
'E feels 'is innards 'eavin', 'is bowels givin' way;
'E sees the blue-white faces all tryin' 'ard to grin,
An' 'e stands an' awaits an' suffers till it's time to cap 'em in.

An' now the hugly bullets come peckin' through the dust,
An' no one wants to face 'em, but every beggar must;
So, like a man in irons, which isn't glad to go,
They moves 'em off by companies uncommon stiff an' slow.

Of all 'is five years' schoolin' they don't remember much
Excep' the not retreatin', the step an' keepin' touch.
It looks like teachin' wasted when they duck an' spread an' 'op—
But if 'e 'adn't learned 'em they'd be all about the shop.

An' now it's ' 'Oo goes backward?' an' now it's ' 'Oo comes on?'
And now it's 'Get the doolies,' an' now the Captain's gone;
An' now it's bloody murder, but all the while they 'ear
'Is voice, the same as barrick-drill, a-shepherdin' the rear.

'E's just as sick as they are, 'is 'eart is like to split,
But 'e works 'em, works 'em, works 'em till he feels 'em take the bit;
The rest is 'oldin' steady till the watchful bugles play,
An' 'e lifts 'em, lifts 'em, lifts 'em through the charge that wins the day!

The 'eathen in 'is blindness bows down to wood an' stone;
'E don't obey no orders unless they is 'is own.
The 'eathen in 'is blindness must end where 'e began,
But the backbone of the Army is the Non-commissioned Man!

Keep away from dirtiness—keep away from mess,
Don't get into doin' things rather-more-or-less!
Let's ha' done with abby-nay, kul, and hazar-ho;
Mind you keep your rifle an' yourself jus' so!

62   *'Cities and Thrones and Powers'*

CITIES and Thrones and Powers
   Stand in Time's eye,
Almost as long as flowers,
   Which daily die:
But, as new buds put forth
   To glad new men,
Out of the spent and unconsidered Earth
   The Cities rise again.

This season's Daffodil,
   She never hears
What change, what chance, what chill,
   Cut down last year's;
But with bold countenance,
   And knowledge small,
Esteems her seven days' continuance
   To be perpetual.

So Time that is o'er-kind
   To all that be,
Ordains us e'en as blind,
   As bold as she:
That in our very death,
   And burial sure,
Shadow to shadow, well persuaded, saith,
   'See how our works endure!'

63   *The Way Through the Woods*

THEY shut the road through the woods
Seventy years ago.
Weather and rain have undone it again,
And now you would never know
There was once a road through the woods
Before they planted the trees.
It is underneath the coppice and heath
And the thin anemones.
Only the keeper sees
That, where the ring-dove broods,
And the badgers roll at ease,
There was once a road through the woods.

Yet, if you enter the woods
Of a summer evening late,
When the night-air cools on the trout-ringed pools
Where the otter whistles his mate,
(They fear not men in the woods,
Because they see so few)
You will hear the beat of a horse's feet,
And the swish of a skirt in the dew,
Steadily cantering through
The misty solitudes,
As though they perfectly knew
The old lost road through the woods. . . .
But there is no road through the woods.

64   *If—*

IF you can keep your head when all about you
    Are losing theirs and blaming it on you,
If you can trust yourself when all men doubt you,
    But make allowance for their doubting too;
If you can wait and not be tired by waiting,
    Or being lied about, don't deal in lies,
Or being hated, don't give way to hating,
    And yet don't look too good, nor talk too wise:

If you can dream—and not make dreams your master;
   If you can think—and not make thoughts your aim;
If you can meet with Triumph and Disaster
   And treat those two impostors just the same;
If you can bear to hear the truth you've spoken
   Twisted by knaves to make a trap for fools,
Or watch the things you gave your life to, broken,
   And stoop and build 'em up with worn-out tools:

If you can make one heap of all your winnings
   And risk it on one turn of pitch-and-toss,
And lose, and start again at your beginnings
   And never breathe a word about your loss;
If you can force your heart and nerve and sinew
   To serve your turn long after they are gone,
And so hold on when there is nothing in you
   Except the Will which says to them: 'Hold on!'

If you can talk with crowds and keep your virtue,
   Or walk with Kings—nor lose the common touch,
If neither foes nor loving friends can hurt you,
   If all men count with you, but none too much;
If you can fill the unforgiving minute
   With sixty seconds' worth of distance run,
Yours is the Earth and everything that's in it,
   And—which is more—you'll be a Man, my son!

65 *Dane-Geld*

A.D. 980–1016

IT is always a temptation to an armed and agile nation,
   To call upon a neighbour and to say:—
'We invaded you last night—we are quite prepared to fight,
   Unless you pay us cash to go away.'

   And that is called asking for Dane-geld,
     And the people who ask it explain
   That you've only to pay 'em the Dane-geld
     And then you'll get rid of the Dane!

It is always a temptation to a rich and lazy nation,
  To puff and look important and to say:—
'Though we know we should defeat you, we have not the time to meet
    you.
  We will therefore pay you cash to go away.'

And that is called paying the Dane-geld;
  But we've proved it again and again,
That if once you have paid him the Dane-geld
  You never get rid of the Dane.

It is wrong to put temptation in the path of any nation,
  For fear they should succumb and go astray;
So when you are requested to pay up or be molested,
  You will find it better policy to say:—

'We never pay *any*-one Dane-geld,
  No matter how trifling the cost;
For the end of that game is oppression and shame,
  And the nation that plays it is lost!'

66   *The Gods of the Copybook Headings*

As I pass through my incarnations in every age and race,
I make my proper prostrations to the Gods of the Market-Place.
Peering through reverent fingers I watch them flourish and fall,
And the Gods of the Copybook Headings, I notice, outlast them all.

We were living in trees when they met us. They showed us each in turn
That Water would certainly wet us, as Fire would certainly burn:
But we found them lacking in Uplift, Vision and Breadth of Mind,
So we left them to teach the Gorillas while we followed the March of
  Mankind.

We moved as the Spirit listed. *They* never altered their pace,
Being neither cloud nor wind-borne like the Gods of the Market-
  Place;
But they always caught up with our progress, and presently word
  would come
That a tribe had been wiped off its icefield, or the lights had gone out
  in Rome.

With the Hopes that our World is built on they were utterly out of touch,
They denied that the Moon was Stilton; they denied she was even Dutch.
They denied that Wishes were Horses; they denied that a Pig had Wings.
So we worshipped the Gods of the Market Who promised these beautiful things.

When the Cambrian measures were forming, They promised perpetual peace.
They swore, if we gave them our weapons, that the wars of the tribes would cease.
But when we disarmed They sold us and delivered us bound to our foe,
And the Gods of the Copybook Headings said: '*Stick to the Devil you know.*'

On the first Feminian Sandstones we were promised the Fuller Life
(Which started by loving our neighbour and ended by loving his wife)
Till our women had no more children and the men lost reason and faith,
And the Gods of the Copybook Headings said: '*The Wages of Sin is Death.*'

In the Carboniferous Epoch we were promised abundance for all,
By robbing selected Peter to pay for collective Paul;
But, though we had plenty of money, there was nothing our money could buy,
And the Gods of the Copybook Headings said: '*If you don't work you die.*'

Then the Gods of the Market tumbled, and their smooth-tongued wizards withdrew,
And the hearts of the meanest were humbled and began to believe it was true
That All is not Gold that Glitters, and Two and Two make Four—
And the Gods of the Copybook Headings limped up to explain it once more.

.   .   .   .

As it will be in the future, it was at the birth of Man—
There are only four things certain since Social Progress began:
That the Dog returns to his Vomit and the Sow returns to her Mire,
And the burnt Fool's bandaged finger goes wabbling back to the Fire;

And that after this is accomplished, and the brave new world begins
When all men are paid for existing and no man must pay for his sins,
As surely as Water will wet us, as surely as Fire will burn,
The Gods of the Copybook Headings with terror and slaughter return!

67   *The Last Lap*

HOW do we know, by the bank-high river,
   Where the mired and sulky oxen wait,
And it looks as though we might wait for ever,
   How do we know that the floods abate?
There is no change in the current's brawling—
   Louder and harsher the freshet scolds;
Yet we can feel she is falling, falling,
   And the more she threatens the less she holds.
Down to the drift, with no word spoken,
   The wheel-chained wagons slither and slue. . . .
Achtung! The back of the worst is broken!
   And—lash your leaders!—we're through—we're through!

How do we know, when the port-fog holds us
   Moored and helpless, a mile from the pier,
And the week-long summer smother enfolds us—
   How do we know it is going to clear?
There is no break in the blindfold weather,
   But, one and another, about the bay,
The unseen capstans clink together,
   Getting ready to up and away.
A pennon whimpers—the breeze has found us—
   A headsail jumps through the thinning haze.
The whole hull follows, till—broad around us—
   The clean-swept ocean says: 'Go your ways!'

How do we know, when the long fight rages,
   On the old, stale front that we cannot shake,
And it looks as though we were locked for ages,
   How do we know they are going to break?

There is no lull in the level firing,
   Nothing has shifted except the sun.
Yet we can feel they are tiring, tiring—
   Yet we can tell they are ripe to run.
Something wavers, and, while we wonder,
   Their centre-trenches are emptying out,
And, before their useless flanks go under,
   Our guns have pounded retreat to rout!

68   *The Storm Cone*

THIS is the midnight—let no star
Delude us—dawn is very far.
This is the tempest long foretold—
Slow to make head but sure to hold.

Stand by! The lull 'twixt blast and blast
Signals the storm is near, not past;
And worse than present jeopardy
May our forlorn to-morrow be.

If we have cleared the expectant reef,
Let no man look for his relief.
Only the darkness hides the shape
Of further peril to escape.

It is decreed that we abide
The weight of gale against the tide
And those huge waves the outer main
Sends in to set us back again.

They fall and whelm. We strain to hear
The pulses of her labouring gear,
Till the deep throb beneath us proves,
After each shudder and check, she moves!

She moves, with all save purpose lost,
To make her offing from the coast;
But, till she fetches open sea,
Let no man deem that he is free!

W. B. YEATS
1865–1939

69   *The Lake Isle of Innisfree*

I WILL arise and go now, and go to Innisfree,
And a small cabin build there, of clay and wattles made:
Nine bean-rows will I have there, a hive for the honey-bee,
And live alone in the bee-loud glade.

And I shall have some peace there, for peace comes dropping slow,
Dropping from the veils of the morning to where the cricket sings;
There midnight's all a glimmer, and noon a purple glow,
And evening full of the linnet's wings.

I will arise and go now, for always night and day
I hear lake water lapping with low sounds by the shore;
While I stand on the roadway, or on the pavements grey,
I hear it in the deep heart's core.

70   *When You Are Old*

WHEN you are old and grey and full of sleep,
And nodding by the fire, take down this book,
And slowly read, and dream of the soft look
Your eyes had once, and of their shadows deep;

How many loved your moments of glad grace,
And loved your beauty with love false or true,
But one man loved the pilgrim soul in you,
And loved the sorrows of your changing face;

And bending down beside the glowing bars,
Murmur, a little sadly, how Love fled
And paced upon the mountains overhead
And hid his face amid a crowd of stars.

71 *He Hears the Cry of the Sedge*

I WANDER by the edge
Of this desolate lake
Where wind cries in the sedge:
Until the axle break
That keeps the stars in their round,
And hands hurl in the deep
The banners of East and West,
And the girdle of light is unbound,
Your breast will not lie by the breast
Of your beloved in sleep.

72 *No Second Troy*

WHY should I blame her that she filled my days
With misery, or that she would of late
Have taught to ignorant men most violent ways,
Or hurled the little streets upon the great,
Had they but courage equal to desire?
What could have made her peaceful with a mind
That nobleness made simple as a fire,
With beauty like a tightened bow, a kind
That is not natural in an age like this,
Being high and solitary and most stern?
Why, what could she have done, being what she is?
Was there another Troy for her to burn?

73 *The Collar-Bone of a Hare*

WOULD I could cast a sail on the water
Where many a king has gone
And many a king's daughter,
And alight at the comely trees and the lawn,
The playing upon pipes and the dancing,
And learn that the best thing is
To change my loves while dancing
And pay but a kiss for a kiss.

I would find by the edge of that water
The collar-bone of a hare
Worn thin by the lapping of water,
And pierce it through with a gimlet, and stare
At the old bitter world where they marry in churches,
And laugh over the untroubled water
At all who marry in churches,
Through the white thin bone of a hare.

74

Easter 1916

I HAVE met them at close of day
Coming with vivid faces
From counter or desk among grey
Eighteenth-century houses.
I have passed with a nod of the head
Or polite meaningless words,
Or have lingered awhile and said
Polite meaningless words,
And thought before I had done
Of a mocking tale or a gibe
To please a companion
Around the fire at the club,
Being certain that they and I
But lived where motley is worn:
All changed, changed utterly:
A terrible beauty is born.

That woman's days were spent
In ignorant good-will,
Her nights in argument
Until her voice grew shrill.
What voice more sweet than hers
When, young and beautiful,
She rode to harriers?
This man had kept a school
And rode our wingèd horse;
This other his helper and friend
Was coming into his force;
He might have won fame in the end,

So sensitive his nature seemed,
So daring and sweet his thought.
This other man I had dreamed
A drunken, vainglorious lout.
He had done most bitter wrong
To some who are near my heart,
Yet I number him in the song;
He, too, has resigned his part
In the casual comedy;
He, too, has been changed in his turn,
Transformed utterly:
A terrible beauty is born.

Hearts with one purpose alone
Through summer and winter seem
Enchanted to a stone
To trouble the living stream.
The horse that comes from the road,
The rider, the birds that range
From cloud to tumbling cloud,
Minute by minute they change;
A shadow of cloud on the stream
Changes minute by minute;
A horse-hoof slides on the brim,
And a horse plashes within it;
The long-legged moor-hens dive,
And hens to moor-cocks call;
Minute by minute they live:
The stone's in the midst of all.

Too long a sacrifice
Can make a stone of the heart.
O when may it suffice?
That is Heaven's part, our part
To murmur name upon name,
As a mother names her child
When sleep at last has come
On limbs that had run wild.
What is it but nightfall?
No, no, not night but death;
Was it needless death after all?
For England may keep faith

For all that is done and said.
We know their dream; enough
To know they dreamed and are dead;
And what if excess of love
Bewildered them till they died?
I write it out in a verse—
MacDonagh and MacBride
And Connolly and Pearse
Now and in time to be,
Wherever green is worn,
Are changed, changed utterly:
A terrible beauty is born.

75   *The Second Coming*

TURNING and turning in the widening gyre
The falcon cannot hear the falconer;
Things fall apart; the centre cannot hold;
Mere anarchy is loosed upon the world,
The blood-dimmed tide is loosed, and everywhere
The ceremony of innocence is drowned;
The best lack all conviction, while the worst
Are full of passionate intensity.

Surely some revelation is at hand;
Surely the Second Coming is at hand.
The Second Coming! Hardly are those words out
When a vast image out of *Spiritus Mundi*
Troubles my sight: somewhere in sands of the desert
A shape with lion body and the head of a man,
A gaze blank and pitiless as the sun,
Is moving its slow thighs, while all about it
Reel shadows of the indignant desert birds.
The darkness drops again; but now I know
That twenty centuries of stony sleep
Were vexed to nightmare by a rocking cradle,
And what rough beast, its hour come round at last,
Slouches towards Bethlehem to be born?

76   *A Prayer for My Daughter*

ONCE more the storm is howling, and half hid
Under this cradle-hood and coverlid
My child sleeps on. There is no obstacle
But Gregory's wood and one bare hill
Whereby the haystack- and roof-levelling wind,
Bred on the Atlantic, can be stayed;
And for an hour I have walked and prayed
Because of the great gloom that is in my mind.

I have walked and prayed for this young child an hour
And heard the sea-wind scream upon the tower,
And under the arches of the bridge, and scream
In the elms above the flooded stream;
Imagining in excited reverie
That the future years had come,
Dancing to a frenzied drum,
Out of the murderous innocence of the sea.

May she be granted beauty and yet not
Beauty to make a stranger's eye distraught,
Or hers before a looking-glass, for such,
Being made beautiful overmuch,
Consider beauty a sufficient end,
Lose natural kindness and maybe
The heart-revealing intimacy
That chooses right, and never find a friend.

Helen being chosen found life flat and dull
And later had much trouble from a fool,
While that great Queen, that rose out of the spray,
Being fatherless could have her way
Yet chose a bandy-leggèd smith for man.
It's certain that fine women eat
A crazy salad with their meat
Whereby the Horn of Plenty is undone.

In courtesy I'd have her chiefly learned;
Hearts are not had as a gift but hearts are earned
By those that are not entirely beautiful;
Yet many, that have played the fool
For beauty's very self, has charm made wise,
And many a poor man that has roved,
Loved and thought himself beloved,
From a glad kindness cannot take his eyes.

May she become a flourishing hidden tree
That all her thoughts may like the linnet be,
And have no business but dispensing round
Their magnanimities of sound,
Nor but in merriment begin a chase,
Nor but in merriment a quarrel.
O may she live like some green laurel
Rooted in one dear perpetual place.

My mind, because the minds that I have loved,
The sort of beauty that I have approved,
Prosper but little, has dried up of late,
Yet knows that to be choked with hate
May well be of all evil chances chief.
If there's no hatred in a mind
Assault and battery of the wind
Can never tear the linnet from the leaf.

An intellectual hatred is the worst,
So let her think opinions are accursed.
Have I not seen the loveliest woman born
Out of the mouth of Plenty's horn,
Because of her opinionated mind
Barter that horn and every good
By quiet natures understood
For an old bellows full of angry wind?

Considering that, all hatred driven hence,
The soul recovers radical innocence
And learns at last that it is self-delighting,
Self-appeasing, self-affrighting,
And that its own sweet will is Heaven's will;
She can, though every face should scowl
And every windy quarter howl
Or every bellows burst, be happy still.

And may her bridegroom bring her to a house
Where all's accustomed, ceremonious;
For arrogance and hatred are the wares
Peddled in the thoroughfares.
How but in custom and in ceremony
Are innocence and beauty born?
Ceremony's a name for the rich horn,
And custom for the spreading laurel tree.

77 *Sailing to Byzantium*

I

THAT is no country for old men. The young
In one another's arms, birds in the trees
—Those dying generations—at their song,
The salmon-falls, the mackerel-crowded seas,
Fish, flesh, or fowl, commend all summer long
Whatever is begotten, born, and dies.
Caught in that sensual music all neglect
Monuments of unageing intellect.

II

An aged man is but a paltry thing,
A tattered coat upon a stick, unless
Soul clap its hands and sing, and louder sing
For every tatter in its mortal dress,
Nor is there singing school but studying
Monuments of its own magnificence;
And therefore I have sailed the seas and come
To the holy city of Byzantium.

III

O sages standing in God's holy fire
As in the gold mosaic of a wall,
Come from the holy fire, perne in a gyre,
And be the singing-masters of my soul.
Consume my heart away; sick with desire
And fastened to a dying animal
It knows not what it is; and gather me
Into the artifice of eternity.

IV

Once out of nature I shall never take
My bodily form from any natural thing,
But such a form as Grecian goldsmiths make
Of hammered gold and gold enamelling
To keep a drowsy Emperor awake;
Or set upon a golden bough to sing
To lords and ladies of Byzantium
Of what is past, or passing, or to come.

78 *Among School Children*

I

I WALK through the long schoolroom questioning;
A kind old nun in a white hood replies;
The children learn to cipher and to sing,
To study reading-books and histories,
To cut and sew, be neat in everything
In the best modern way—the children's eyes
In momentary wonder stare upon
A sixty-year-old smiling public man.

II

I dream of a Ledaean body, bent
Above a sinking fire, a tale that she
Told of a harsh reproof, or trivial event
That changed some childish day to tragedy—
Told, and it seemed that our two natures blent
Into a sphere from youthful sympathy,
Or else, to alter Plato's parable,
Into the yolk and white of the one shell.

III

And thinking of that fit of grief or rage
I look upon one child or t'other there
And wonder if she stood so at that age—
For even daughters of the swan can share
Something of every paddler's heritage—
And had that colour upon cheek or hair,
And thereupon my heart is driven wild:
She stands before me as a living child.

IV

Her present image floats into the mind—
Did Quattrocento finger fashion it
Hollow of cheek as though it drank the wind
And took a mess of shadows for its meat?
And I though never of Ledaean kind
Had pretty plumage once—enough of that,
Better to smile on all that smile, and show
There is a comfortable kind of old scarecrow.

V

What youthful mother, a shape upon her lap
Honey of generation had betrayed,
And that must sleep, shriek, struggle to escape
As recollection or the drug decide,
Would think her son, did she but see that shape
With sixty or more winters on its head,
A compensation for the pang of his birth,
Or the uncertainty of his setting forth?

VI

Plato thought nature but a spume that plays
Upon a ghostly paradigm of things;
Solider Aristotle played the taws
Upon the bottom of a king of kings;
World-famous golden-thighed Pythagoras
Fingered upon a fiddle-stick or strings
What a star sang and careless Muses heard:
Old clothes upon old sticks to scare a bird.

VII

Both nuns and mothers worship images,
But those the candles light are not as those
That animate a mother's reveries,
But keep a marble or a bronze repose.
And yet they too break hearts—O Presences
That passion, piety or affection knows,
And that all heavenly glory symbolise—
O self-born mockers of man's enterprise;

VIII

Labour is blossoming or dancing where
The body is not bruised to pleasure soul,
Nor beauty born out of its own despair,
Nor blear-eyed wisdom out of midnight oil.
O chestnut-tree, great-rooted blossomer,
Are you the leaf, the blossom or the bole?
O body swayed to music, O brightening glance,
How can we know the dancer from the dance?

79 *In Memory of Eva Gore-Booth and Con Markiewicz*

THE light of evening, Lissadell,
Great windows open to the south,
Two girls in silk kimonos, both
Beautiful, one a gazelle.
But a raving autumn shears
Blossom from the summer's wreath;
The older is condemned to death,
Pardoned, drags out lonely years
Conspiring among the ignorant.
I know not what the younger dreams—
Some vague Utopia—and she seems,
When withered old and skeleton-gaunt,
An image of such politics.
Many a time I think to seek
One or the other out and speak
Of that old Georgian mansion, mix

Pictures of the mind, recall
That table and the talk of youth,
Two girls in silk kimonos, both
Beautiful, one a gazelle.

Dear shadows, now you know it all,
All the folly of a fight
With a common wrong or right.
The innocent and the beautiful
Have no enemy but time;
Arise and bid me strike a match
And strike another till time catch;
Should the conflagration climb,
Run till all the sages know.
We the great gazebo built,
They convicted us of guilt;
Bid me strike a match and blow.

80   *The Choice*

THE intellect of man is forced to choose
Perfection of the life, or of the work,
And if it take the second must refuse
A heavenly mansion, raging in the dark.

When all that story's finished, what's the news?
In luck or out the toil has left its mark:
That old perplexity an empty purse,
Or the day's vanity, the night's remorse.

81   *Byzantium*

THE unpurged images of day recede;
The Emperor's drunken soldiery are abed;
Night resonance recedes, night-walkers' song
After great cathedral gong;

A starlit or a moonlit dome disdains
All that man is,
All mere complexities,
The fury and the mire of human veins.

Before me floats an image, man or shade,
Shade more than man, more image than a shade;
For Hades' bobbin bound in mummy-cloth
May unwind the winding path;
A mouth that has no moisture and no breath
Breathless mouths may summon;
I hail the superhuman;
I call it death-in-life and life-in-death.

Miracle, bird or golden handiwork,
More miracle than bird or handiwork,
Planted on the star-lit golden bough,
Can like the cocks of Hades crow,
Or, by the moon embittered, scorn aloud
In glory of changeless metal
Common bird or petal
And all complexities of mire or blood.

At midnight on the Emperor's pavement flit
Flames that no faggot feeds, nor steel has lit,
Nor storm disturbs, flames begotten of flame,
Where blood-begotten spirits come
And all complexities of fury leave,
Dying into a dance,
An agony of trance,
An agony of flame that cannot singe a sleeve.

Astraddle on the dolphin's mire and blood,
Spirit after spirit! The smithies break the flood,
The golden smithies of the Emperor!
Marbles of the dancing floor
Break bitter furies of complexity,
Those images that yet
Fresh images beget,
That dolphin-torn, that gong-tormented sea.

82 *Crazy Jane on God*

THAT lover of a night
Came when he would,
Went in the dawning light
Whether I would or no;
Men come, men go;
All things remain in God.

Banners choke the sky;
Men-at-arms tread;
Armoured horses neigh
Where the great battle was
In the narrow pass:
All things remain in God.

Before their eyes a house
That from childhood stood
Uninhabited, ruinous,
Suddenly lit up
From door to top:
All things remain in God.

I had wild Jack for a lover;
Though like a road
That men pass over
My body makes no moan
But sings on:
All things remain in God.

83 *The Municipal Gallery Revisited*

I

AROUND me the images of thirty years:
An ambush; pilgrims at the water-side;
Casement upon trial, half hidden by the bars,
Guarded; Griffith staring in hysterical pride;
Kevin O'Higgins' countenance that wears
A gentle questioning look that cannot hide
A soul incapable of remorse or rest;
A revolutionary soldier kneeling to be blessed;

II

An Abbot or Archbishop with an upraised hand
Blessing the Tricolour. 'This is not,' I say,
'The dead Ireland of my youth, but an Ireland
The poets have imagined, terrible and gay.'
Before a woman's portrait suddenly I stand,
Beautiful and gentle in her Venetian way.
I met her all but fifty years ago
For twenty minutes in some studio.

III

Heart-smitten with emotion I sink down,
My heart recovering with covered eyes;
Wherever I had looked I had looked upon
My permanent or impermanent images:
Augusta Gregory's son; her sister's son,
Hugh Lane, 'onlie begetter' of all these;
Hazel Lavery living and dying, that tale
As though some ballad-singer had sung it all;

IV

Mancini's portrait of Augusta Gregory,
'Greatest since Rembrandt,' according to John Synge;
A great ebullient portrait certainly;
But where is the brush that could show anything
Of all that pride and that humility?
And I am in despair that time may bring
Approved patterns of women or of men
But not that selfsame excellence again.

V

My mediaeval knees lack health until they bend,
But in that woman, in that household where
Honour had lived so long, all lacking found.
Childless I thought, 'My children may find here
Deep-rooted things,' but never foresaw its end,
And now that end has come I have not wept;
No fox can foul the lair the badger swept—

VI

(An image out of Spenser and the common tongue).
John Synge, I and Augusta Gregory, thought
All that we did, all that we said or sang
Must come from contact with the soil, from that
Contact everything Antaeus-like grew strong.
We three alone in modern times had brought
Everything down to that sole test again,
Dream of the noble and the beggar-man.

VII

And here's John Synge himself, that rooted man,
'Forgetting human words,' a grave deep face.
You that would judge me, do not judge alone
This book or that, come to this hallowed place
Where my friends' portraits hang and look thereon;
Ireland's history in their lineaments trace;
Think where man's glory most begins and ends,
And say my glory was I had such friends.

84   *The Statesman's Holiday*

I LIVED among great houses,
Riches drove out rank,
Base drove out the better blood,
And mind and body shrank.
No Oscar ruled the table,
But I'd a troop of friends
That knowing better talk had gone
Talked of odds and ends.
Some knew what ailed the world
But never said a thing,
So I have picked a better trade
And night and morning sing:
Tall dames go walking in grass-green Avalon.

Am I a great Lord Chancellor
That slept upon the Sack?
Commanding officer that tore
The khaki from his back?
Or am I de Valéra,
Or the King of Greece,
Or the man that made the motors?
Ach, call me what you please!
Here's a Montenegrin lute,
And its old sole string
Makes me sweet music
And I delight to sing:
Tall dames go walking in grass-green Avalon.

With boys and girls about him,
With any sort of clothes,
With a hat out of fashion,
With old patched shoes,
With a ragged bandit cloak,
With an eye like a hawk,
With a stiff straight back,
With a strutting turkey walk,
With a bag full of pennies,
With a monkey on a chain,
With a great cock's feather,
With an old foul tune.
Tall dames go walking in grass-green Avalon.

The Circus Animals' Desertion

85

I

I SOUGHT a theme and sought for it in vain,
I sought it daily for six weeks or so.
Maybe at last, being but a broken man,
I must be satisfied with my heart, although
Winter and summer till old age began
My circus animals were all on show,
Those stilted boys, that burnished chariot,
Lion and woman and the Lord knows what.

II

What can I but enumerate old themes?
First that sea-rider Oisin led by the nose
Through three enchanted islands, allegorical dreams,
Vain gaiety, vain battle, vain repose,
Themes of the embittered heart, or so it seems,
That might adorn old songs or courtly shows;
But what cared I that set him on to ride,
I, starved for the bosom of his faery bride?

And then a counter-truth filled out its play,
The Countess Cathleen was the name I gave it;
She, pity-crazed, had given her soul away,
But masterful Heaven had intervened to save it.
I thought my dear must her own soul destroy,
So did fanaticism and hate enslave it,
And this brought forth a dream and soon enough
This dream itself had all my thought and love.

And when the Fool and Blind Man stole the bread
Cuchulain fought the ungovernable sea;
Heart-mysteries there, and yet when all is said
It was the dream itself enchanted me:
Character isolated by a deed
To engross the present and dominate memory.
Players and painted stage took all my love,
And not those things that they were emblems of.

III

Those masterful images because complete
Grew in pure mind, but out of what began?
A mound of refuse or the sweepings of a street,
Old kettles, old bottles, and a broken can,
Old iron, old bones, old rags, that raving slut
Who keeps the till. Now that my ladder's gone,
I must lie down where all the ladders start,
In the foul rag-and-bone shop of the heart.

86 *Politics*

'In our time the destiny of man presents its meaning in
political terms.'—Thomas Mann

How can I, that girl standing there,
My attention fix
On Roman or on Russian
Or on Spanish politics?
Yet here's a travelled man that knows
What he talks about,
And there's a politician
That has read and thought,
And maybe what they say is true
Of war and war's alarms,
But O that I were young again
And held her in my arms!

87 *Under Ben Bulben*

I

SWEAR by what the sages spoke
Round the Mareotic Lake
That the Witch of Atlas knew,
Spoke and set the cocks a-crow.

Swear by those horsemen, by those women
Complexion and form prove superhuman,
That pale, long-visaged company
That air in immortality
Completeness of their passions won;
Now they ride the wintry dawn
Where Ben Bulben sets the scene.

Here's the gist of what they mean.

93

II

Many times man lives and dies
Between his two eternities,
That of race and that of soul,
And ancient Ireland knew it all.
Whether man die in his bed
Or the rifle knocks him dead,
A brief parting from those dear
Is the worst man has to fear.
Though grave-diggers' toil is long,
Sharp their spades, their muscles strong,
They but thrust their buried men
Back in the human mind again.

III

You that Mitchel's prayer have heard,
'Send war in our time, O Lord!'
Know that when all words are said
And a man is fighting mad,
Something drops from eyes long blind,
He completes his partial mind,
For an instant stands at ease,
Laughs aloud, his heart at peace.
Even the wisest man grows tense
With some sort of violence
Before he can accomplish fate,
Know his work or choose his mate.

IV

Poet and sculptor, do the work,
Nor let the modish painter shirk
What his great forefathers did,
Bring the soul of man to God,
Make him fill the cradles right.

Measurement began our might:
Forms a stark Egyptian thought,
Forms that gentler Phidias wrought.
Michael Angelo left a proof
On the Sistine Chapel roof,

Where but half-awakened Adam
Can disturb globe-trotting Madam
Till her bowels are in heat,
Proof that there's a purpose set
Before the secret working mind:
Profane perfection of mankind.

Quattrocento put in paint
On backgrounds for a God or Saint
Gardens where a soul's at ease;
Where everything that meets the eye,
Flowers and grass and cloudless sky,
Resemble forms that are or seem
When sleepers wake and yet still dream,
And when it's vanished still declare,
With only bed and bedstead there,
That heavens had opened.
                              Gyres run on;
When that greater dream had gone
Calvert and Wilson, Blake and Claude,
Prepared a rest for the people of God,
Palmer's phrase, but after that
Confusion fell upon our thought.

V

Irish poets, learn your trade,
Sing whatever is well made,
Scorn the sort now growing up
All out of shape from toe to top,
Their unremembering hearts and heads
Base-born products of base beds.
Sing the peasantry, and then
Hard-riding country gentlemen,
The holiness of monks, and after
Porter-drinkers' randy laughter;
Sing the lords and ladies gay
That were beaten into the clay
Through seven heroic centuries;
Cast your mind on other days
That we in coming days may be
Still the indomitable Irishry.

VI

Under bare Ben Bulben's head
In Drumcliff churchyard Yeats is laid.
An ancestor was rector there
Long years ago, a church stands near,
By the road an ancient cross.
No marble, no conventional phrase;
On limestone quarried near the spot
By his command these words are cut:

> *Cast a cold eye*
> *On life, on death.*
> *Horseman, pass by!*

ARNOLD BENNETT

1867–1931

88   *A Love Affair*

DOWN flew the shaft of the god,
Barbed with miraculous change.
Struck—and a woman emerged from a clod.
This was strange.

Eyes and a mouth it had owned,
Movable head that would nod,
Waist and a bosom agreeably zoned—
But a clod.

Now when her eyes met the male's,
Flame from them wrapped him in fire;
Breath of that bosom o'erwhelmed him in gales
Of desire.

Stung by the flattering wave,
Proudly his manhood he spent.
Rare was the gift of her soul—for she gave,
But he lent.

Wit she had none to amuse,
Knew not the trade of a wife,
Heard not the voice of the muse. Now the muse
Was his life.

Weary, he called on his God:
'Quench me this woman I've kissed!'
Lo! In due time she returned to the clod.
She was missed.

CHARLOTTE MEW

1869–1928

89 *Sea Love*

TIDE be runnin' the great world over:
    'Twas only last June month I mind that we
Was thinkin' the toss and the call in the breast of the lover
    So everlastin' as the sea.

Heer's the same little fishes that sputter and swim,
    Wi' the moon's old glim on the grey, wet sand;
An' him no more to me nor me to him
    Than the wind goin' over my hand.

90 *I so liked Spring*

I so liked Spring last year
    Because you were here;—
        The thrushes too—
Because it was these you so liked to hear—
    I so liked you.

    This year's a different thing,—
        I'll not think of you.
But I'll like Spring because it is simply Spring
    As the thrushes do.

91 *The Farmer's Bride*

THREE Summers since I chose a maid,
Too young maybe—but more's to do
At harvest-time than bide and woo.
　　When us was wed she turned afraid
Of love and me and all things human;
Like the shut of a winter's day
Her smile went out, and 'twadn't a woman—
　　More like a little frightened fay.
　　One night, in the Fall, she runned away.

'Out 'mong the sheep, her be,' they said,
'Should properly have been abed;
But sure enough she wadn't there
Lying awake with her wide brown stare.
So over seven-acre field and up-along across the down
　　We chased her, flying like a hare
Before our lanterns. To Church-Town
　　All in a shiver and a scare
We caught her, fetched her home at last
　　And turned the key upon her, fast.

She does the work about the house
As well as most, but like a mouse:
　　Happy enough to chat and play
　　With birds and rabbits and such as they,
　　So long as men-folk keep away.

'Not near, not near!' her eyes beseech
When one of us comes within reach.
　　The women say that beasts in stall
　　Look round like children at her call.
　　I've hardly heard her speak at all.

Shy as a leveret, swift as he,
Straight and slight as a young larch tree,
Sweet as the first wild violets, she,
To her wild self. But what to me?

The short days shorten and the oaks are brown,
 The blue smoke rises to the low grey sky,
One leaf in the still air falls slowly down,
 A magpie's spotted feathers lie
On the black earth spread white with rime,
The berries redden up to Christmas-time.
  What's Christmas-time without there be
  Some other in the house than we!

  She sleeps up in the attic there
  Alone, poor maid. 'Tis but a stair
Betwixt us. Oh! my God! the down,
The soft young down of her, the brown,
The brown of her—her eyes, her hair, her hair!

92   *A Quoi Bon Dire*

SEVENTEEN years ago you said
  Something that sounded like Good-bye;
 And everybody thinks that you are dead,
   But I.

 So I, as I grow stiff and cold
 To this and that say Good-bye too;
  And everybody sees that I am old
   But you.

 And one fine morning in a sunny lane
Some boy and girl will meet and kiss and swear
 That nobody can love their way again
   While over there
You will have smiled, I shall have tossed your hair.

93   *Old Shepherd's Prayer*

UP to the bed by the window, where I be lyin',
Comes bells and bleat of the flock wi' they two children's clack.
Over, from under the eaves there's the starlings flyin',
And down in yard, fit to burst his chain, yapping out at Sue I do hear
     young Mac.

Turning around like a falled-over sack
I can see team ploughin' in Whithy-bush field and meal carts startin'
     up road to Church-Town;
Saturday arternoon the men goin' back
And the women from market, trapin' home over the down.

Heavenly Master, I wud like to wake to they same green places
Where I know'd for breakin' dogs and follerin' sheep.
And if I may not walk in th' old ways and look on th' old faces
I wud sooner sleep.

LAURENCE BINYON
1869–1943

94   *Hunger*

I COME among the peoples like a shadow.
I sit down by each man's side.

None sees me, but they look on one another,
And know that I am there.

My silence is like the silence of the tide
That buries the playground of children;

Like the deepening of frost in the slow night,
When birds are dead in the morning.

Armies trample, invade, destroy,
With guns roaring from earth and air.

I am more terrible than armies,
I am more feared than the cannon.

Kings and chancellors give commands;
I give no command to any;

But I am listened to more than kings
And more than passionate orators.

I unswear words, and undo deeds.
Naked things know me.

I am first and last to be felt of the living.
I am Hunger.

95   *The Little Dancers*

LONELY, save for a few faint stars, the sky
Dreams; and lonely, below, the little street
Into its gloom retires, secluded and shy.
Scarcely the dumb roar enters this soft retreat;
And all is dark, save where come flooding rays
From a tavern-window; there, to the brisk measure
Of an organ that down in an alley merrily plays,
Two children, all alone and no one by,
Holding their tattered frocks, thro' an airy maze
Of motion lightly threaded with nimble feet
Dance sedately; face to face they gaze,
Their eyes shining, grave with a perfect pleasure.

96   *For the Fallen*

WITH proud thanksgiving, a mother for her children,
England mourns for her dead across the sea.
Flesh of her flesh they were, spirit of her spirit,
Fallen in the cause of the free.

Solemn the drums thrill: Death august and royal
Sings sorrow up into immortal spheres.
There is music in the midst of desolation
And a glory that shines upon our tears.

They went with songs to the battle, they were young,
Straight of limb, true of eye, steady and aglow.
They were staunch to the end against odds uncounted,
They fell with their faces to the foe.

They shall grow not old, as we that are left grow old:
Age shall not weary them, nor the years condemn.
At the going down of the sun and in the morning
We will remember them.

They mingle not with their laughing comrades again;
They sit no more at familiar tables of home;
They have no lot in our labour of the day-time;
They sleep beyond England's foam.

But where our desires are and our hopes profound,
Felt as a well-spring that is hidden from sight,
To the innermost heart of their own land they are known
As the stars are known to the Night;

As the stars that shall be bright when we are dust,
Moving in marches upon the heavenly plain,
As the stars that are starry in the time of our darkness,
To the end, to the end, they remain.

97   *The Burning of the Leaves*

Now is the time for the burning of the leaves.
They go to the fire; the nostril pricks with smoke
Wandering slowly into a weeping mist.
Brittle and blotched, ragged and rotten sheaves!
A flame seizes the smouldering ruin and bites
On stubborn stalks that crackle as they resist.

The last hollyhock's fallen tower is dust;
All the spices of June are a bitter reek,
All the extravagant riches spent and mean.
All burns! The reddest rose is a ghost;
Sparks whirl up, to expire in the mist: the wild
Fingers of fire are making corruption clean.

Now is the time for stripping the spirit bare,
Time for the burning of days ended and done,
Idle solace of things that have gone before:
Rootless hopes and fruitless desire are there;
Let them go to the fire, with never a look behind.
The world that was ours is a world that is ours no more.

They will come again, the leaf and the flower, to arise
From squalor of rottenness into the old splendour,
And magical scents to a wondering memory bring;
The same glory, to shine upon different eyes.
Earth cares for her own ruins, naught for ours.
Nothing is certain, only the certain spring.

T. STURGE MOORE

1870–1944

98 *On Harting Down*

ONCE, when their hearts were wild with joy,
They bedded on the downs:
Hours drifted past, the dawn grew ghast,
Their polls wore dewy crowns.

While the stars paled, she, first, awoke
And saw, no more alone,
They kernel were to a herd of deer,
Come round them all unknown.

A dun buck couched upon the left,
A white doe to their right,
An hundred others, like watching mothers,
Loomed peacefully out of night.

Ere she could wake him, they rose and were shaking
Small droplets from cold thighs;
Proudly the leader then streamed them afar
To where the sun would rise.

Till, dot by dot, they threaded the arch
His lifting forehead raised,
And, sublimed to light, were lost to sight,
Though still enthralled she gazed.

Her lover rose and, leaning close,
Through to her mind he peered;
Parked therein, numerous, timid, dumb
Musings retired or neared.

HILAIRE BELLOC

1870–1953

99

THE world's a stage. The trifling entrance fee
Is paid (by proxy) to the registrar.
The Orchestra is very loud and free
But plays no music in particular.
They do not print a programme, that I know.
The cast is large. There isn't any plot.
The acting of the piece is far below
The very worst of modernistic rot.

The only part about it I enjoy
Is what was called in English the Foyay.
There will I stand apart awhile and toy
With thought, and set my cigarette alight;
And then—without returning to the play—
On with my coat and out into the night.

100 *Ha'nacker Mill*

SALLY is gone that was so kindly
　　Sally is gone from Ha'nacker Hill.
And the Briar grows ever since then so blindly
　　And ever since then the clapper is still,
　　And the sweeps have fallen from Ha'nacker Mill.

Ha'nacker Hill is in Desolation:
　　Ruin a-top and a field unploughed.
And Spirits that call on a fallen nation
　　Spirits that loved her calling aloud:
　　Spirits abroad in a windy cloud.

Spirits that call and no one answers;
　　Ha'nacker's down and England's done.
Wind and Thistle for pipe and dancers
　　And never a ploughman under the Sun.
　　Never a ploughman. Never a one.

101 *On a General Election*

THE accursèd power which stands on Privilege
(And goes with Women, and Champagne and Bridge)
Broke—and Democracy resumed her reign:
(Which goes with Bridge, and Women and Champagne).

102 *On Mundane Acquaintances*

GOOD morning, Algernon: Good morning, Percy.
Good morning, Mrs. Roebeck. Christ have mercy!

103   *Fatigue*

I'M tired of Love: I'm still more tired of Rhyme.
But Money gives me pleasure all the time.

J. M. SYNGE
1871–1909

104   *A Question*

I ASKED if I got sick and died, would you
With my black funeral go walking too,
If you'd stand close to hear them talk or pray
While I'm let down in that steep bank of clay.

And, No, you said, for if you saw a crew
Of living idiots, pressing round that new
Oak coffin—they alive, I dead beneath
That board,—you'd rave and rend them with your teeth.

105   *Winter*
              With little money in a great city

THERE'S snow in every street
Where I go up and down,
And there's no woman, man, or dog
That knows me in the town.

I know each shop, and all
These Jews, and Russian Poles,
For I go walking night and noon
To spare my sack of coals.

W. H. DAVIES
1871–1940

106 *The Rain*

I HEAR leaves drinking rain;
  I hear rich leaves on top
Giving the poor beneath
  Drop after drop;
'Tis a sweet noise to hear
These green leaves drinking near.

And when the Sun comes out,
  After this rain shall stop,
A wondrous light will fill
  Each dark, round drop;
I hope the Sun shines bright;
'Twill be a lovely sight.

107 *The Dumb World*

I CANNOT see the short, white curls
  Upon the forehead of an Ox,
But what I see them dripping with
  That poor thing's blood, and hear the axe;
When I see calves and lambs, I see
  Them led to death; I see no bird
Or rabbit cross the open field
  But what a sudden shot is heard;
A shout that tells me men aim true,
  For death or wound, doth chill me through.

The shot that kills a hare or bird
  Doth pass through me; I feel the wound
When those poor things find peace in death,
  And when I hear no more that sound.

These cat-like men do hate to see
   Small lives in happy motion; I
Would almost rather hide my face
   From Nature than pass these men by;
And rather see a battle than
A dumb thing near a drunken man.

108   *The Inquest*

I TOOK my oath I would inquire,
   Without affection, hate, or wrath,
Into the death of Ada Wright—
   So help me God! I took that oath.

When I went out to see the corpse,
   The four months' babe that died so young,
I judged it was seven pounds in weight,
   And little more than one foot long.

One eye, that had a yellow lid,
   Was shut—so was the mouth, that smiled;
The left eye open, shining bright—
   It seemed a knowing little child.

For as I looked at that one eye,
   It seemed to laugh, and say with glee:
'What caused my death you'll never know—
   Perhaps my mother murdered me.'

When I went into court again
   To hear the mother's evidence—
It was a love-child, she explained.
   And smiled, for our intelligence.

'Now, Gentlemen of the Jury,' said
   The coroner—'this woman's child
By misadventure met its death.'
   'Aye, aye,' said we. The mother smiled.

And I could see that child's one eye
   Which seemed to laugh, and say with glee:
'What caused my death you'll never know—
   Perhaps my mother murdered me.'

109   *The Villain*

WHILE joy gave clouds the light of stars,
   That beamed where'er they looked;
And calves and lambs had tottering knees,
   Excited, while they sucked;
While every bird enjoyed his song,
Without one thought of harm or wrong—
I turned my head and saw the wind,
   Nor far from where I stood,
Dragging the corn by her golden hair,
   Into a dark and lonely wood.

110   *The Rat*

'THAT woman there is almost dead,
Her feet and hands like heavy lead;
Her cat's gone out for his delight,
He will not come again this night.

'Her husband in a pothouse drinks,
Her daughter at a soldier winks;
Her son is at his sweetest game,
Teasing the cobbler old and lame.

'Now with these teeth that powder stones,
I'll pick at one of her cheek-bones:
When husband, son and daughter come,
They'll soon see who was left at home.'

111   *The White Horse*

WHAT do I stare at—not the colt
   That frisks in yon green field; so strong
That he can leap about and run,
   Yet is too weak to stand up straight
When his mother licks him with her tongue.

No, no, my eyes go far beyond,
   Across that field to yon far hill,
Where one white horse stands there alone;
   And nothing else is white to see,
Outside a house all dark and still.

'Death, are you in that house?' think I—
   'Is that horse there on your account?
Can I expect a shadow soon,
   Seen in that horse's ghostly ribs—
When you come up behind, to mount?'

RALPH HODGSON
1871–1962

112   *The Hammers*

NOISE of hammers once I heard,
Many hammers, busy hammers,
Beating, shaping, night and day,
Shaping, beating dust and clay
To a palace; saw it reared;
Saw the hammers laid away.

And I listened, and I heard
Hammers beating, night and day,
In the palace newly reared,
Beating it to dust and clay:
Other hammers, muffled hammers,
Silent hammers of decay.

113 *Stupidity Street*

I SAW with open eyes
Singing birds sweet
Sold in the shops
For the people to eat,
Sold in the shops of
Stupidity Street.

I saw in vision
The worm in the wheat,
And in the shops nothing
For people to eat;
Nothing for sale in
Stupidity Street.

114 *The Bull*

SEE an old unhappy bull,
Sick in soul and body both,
Slouching in the undergrowth
Of the forest beautiful,
Banished from the herd he led,
Bulls and cows a thousand head.

Cranes and gaudy parrots go
Up and down the burning sky;
Tree-top cats purr drowsily
In the dim-day green below;
And troops of monkeys, nutting, some,
All disputing, go and come;

And things abominable sit
Picking offal buck or swine,
On the mess and over it
Burnished flies and beetles shine,
And spiders big as bladders lie
Under hemlocks ten foot high;

And a dotted serpent curled
Round and round and round a tree,
Yellowing its greenery,
Keeps a watch on all the world,
All the world and this old bull
In the forest beautiful.

Bravely by his fall he came:
One he led, a bull of blood
Newly come to lustihood,
Fought and put his prince to shame,
Snuffed and pawed the prostrate head
Tameless even while it bled.

There they left him, every one,
Left him there without a lick,
Left him for the birds to pick,
Left him there for carrion,
Vilely from their bosom cast
Wisdom, worth and love at last.

When the lion left his lair
And roared his beauty through the hills,
And the vultures pecked their quills
And flew into the middle air,
Then this prince no more to reign
Came to life and lived again.

He snuffed the herd in far retreat,
He saw the blood upon the ground,
And snuffed the burning airs around
Still with beevish odours sweet,
While the blood ran down his head
And his mouth ran slave red.

Pity him, this fallen chief,
All his splendour, all his strength,
All his body's breadth and length
Dwindled down with shame and grief,
Half the bull he was before,
Bones and leather, nothing more.

See him standing dewlap-deep
In the rushes at the lake,
Surly, stupid, half asleep,
Waiting for his heart to break
And the birds to join the flies
Feasting at his bloodshot eyes;

Standing with his head hung down
In a stupor, dreaming things:
Green savannas, jungles brown,
Battlefields and bellowings,
Bulls undone and lions dead
And vultures flapping overhead.

Dreaming things: of days he spent
With his mother gaunt and lean
In the valley warm and green,
Full of baby wonderment,
Blinking out of silly eyes
At a hundred mysteries;

Dreaming over once again
How he wandered with a throng
Of bulls and cows a thousand strong,
Wandered on from plain to plain,
Up the hill and down the dale,
Always at his mother's tail;

How he lagged behind the herd,
Lagged and tottered, weak of limb,
And she turned and ran to him
Blaring at the loathly bird
Stationed always in the skies,
Waiting for the flesh that dies.

Dreaming maybe of a day
When her drained and drying paps
Turned him to the sweets and saps,
Richer fountains by the way,
And she left the bull she bore
And he looked to her no more;

And his little frame grew stout,
And his little legs grew strong,
And the way was not so long;
And his little horns came out,
And he played at butting trees
And boulder-stones and tortoises,

Joined a game of knobby skulls
With the youngsters of his year,
All the other little bulls,
Learning both to bruise and bear,
Learning how to stand a shock
Like a little bull of rock.

Dreaming of a day less dim,
Dreaming of a time less far,
When the faint but certain star
Of destiny burned clear for him,
And a fierce and wild unrest
Broke the quiet of his breast,

And the gristles of his youth
Hardened in his comely pow,
And he came to fighting growth,
Beat his bull and won his cow,
And flew his tail and trampled off
Past the tallest, vain enough,

And curved about in splendour full
And curved again and snuffed the airs
As who should say Come out who dares!
And all beheld a bull, a Bull,
And knew that here was surely one
That backed for no bull, fearing none.

And the leader of the herd
Looked and saw, and beat the ground,
And shook the forest with his sound,
Bellowed at the loathly bird
Stationed always in the skies,
Waiting for the flesh that dies.

Dreaming, this old bull forlorn,
Surely dreaming of the hour
When he came to sultan power,
And they owned him master-horn,
Chiefest bull of all among
Bulls and cows a thousand strong;

And in all the tramping herd
Not a bull that barred his way,
Not a cow that said him nay,
Not a bull or cow that erred
In the furnace of his look
Dared a second, worse rebuke;

Not in all the forest wide,
Jungle, thicket, pasture, fen,
Not another dared him then,
Dared him and again defied;
Not a sovereign buck or boar
Came a second time for more;

Not a serpent that survived
Once the terrors of his hoof
Risked a second time reproof,
Came a second time and lived,
Not a serpent in its skin
Came again for discipline;

Not a leopard bright as flame,
Flashing fingerhooks of steel
That a wooden tree might feel,
Met his fury once and came
For a second reprimand,
Not a leopard in the land;

Not a lion of them all,
Not a lion of the hills,
Hero of a thousand kills,
Dared a second fight and fall,
Dared that ram terrific twice,
Paid a second time the price. . . .

Pity him, this dupe of dream,
Leader of the herd again
Only in his daft old brain,
Once again the bull supreme
And bull enough to bear the part
Only in his tameless heart.

Pity him that he must wake;
Even now the swarm of flies
Blackening his bloodshot eyes
Bursts and blusters round the lake,
Scattered from the feast half-fed,
By great shadows overhead.

And the dreamer turns away
From his visionary herds
And his splendid yesterday,
Turns to meet the loathly birds
Flocking round him from the skies,
Waiting for the flesh that dies.

115   *Silver Wedding*

In the middle of the night
He started up
At a cry from his sleeping Bride—
A bat from some ruin
In a heart he'd never searched,
Nay, hardly seen inside:

'Want me and take me
For the woman that I am
And not for her that died,
The lovely chit nineteen
I one time was,
And am no more'—she cried.

Hymn to Moloch

O THOU who didst furnish
The fowls of the air
With loverly feathers
For leydies to wear,
Receive this Petition
For blessin an aid,
From the principal Ouses
Engaged in the Trade.

The trouble's as follows:
A white-livered Scum,
What if they was choked
'Twould be better for some,
S'been pokin about an
Creatin a fuss
An talkin too loud to be
Ealthy for us.

Thou'lt ardly believe
Own damn friendly they are,
They say there's a time
In the future not far
When birds worth good money'll
Waste by the ton
An the Trade can look
Perishin pleased to look on,

With best lines in Paradies
Equal to what
Is fetchin a pony
A time in the at,
An ospreys an ummins
An other choice goods,
Wastefully oppin
About in the woods.

They're kiddin the papers,
An callin us names,
Not Yorkshire ones neither,
That's one of their games,

They've others as pleasin
An soakin with spite,
An it dont make us appy,
Ow can it do, quite!

We thank thee most earty
For mercies to date,
The Olesales is pickin
Nice profits per crate,
Reports from the Retails
Is pleasin to read;
We certainly thank thee
Most earty indeed.

Vouchsafe, then, to muzzle
These meddlesome swine,
An learn em to andle goods
More in their line,
Be faithful, be foxy
Till peril is past,
An plant thy strong sword
In their livers at last.

SIR MAX BEERBOHM

1872–1956

117   *A Luncheon* [1]

LIFT latch, step in, be welcome, Sir,
Albeit to see you I'm unglad
And your face is fraught with a deathly shyness
Bleaching what pink it may have had.
Come in, come in, Your Royal Highness.

[1] 'On July 20 [1923] the Prince of Wales paid a visit to Dorchester . . . and Hardy
was invited to meet him there, and to drive back to Max Gate where the Prince and
the party accompanying him were to lunch. It was a hot day . . .'
    —*The Later Years of Thomas Hardy 1892–1928*,
    by Florence Emily Hardy.

Beautiful weather?—Sir, that's true,
Though the farmers are casting rueful looks
At tilth's and pasture's dearth of spryness.—
Yes, Sir, I've written several books.—
A little more chicken, Your Royal Highness?

Lift latch, step out, your car is there,
To bear you hence from this antient vale.
We are both of us aged by our strange brief nighness
But each of us lives to tell the tale.
Farewell, farewell, Your Royal Highness.

JOHN COWPER POWYS

1872–1963

118

In a Hotel Writing-Room

WE artists have strange nerves!
That man in front of me,
I had been hating him
Implacably,
Just for the lines and curves
Of his unconscious face,
Lines that brought no disgrace
Upon humanity.
But when that same man spoke,
And with a grunt and wheeze
Asked me how many *c*s
Had the word 'Necessity,'
The cord of my hatred broke.
'For how's a beggar to tell'
He said;—and I loved him for it—
'With a word as long as hell,
If no wise blighter tell us?'
—'You are right, my friend. We may score it
Over and over with c;
But at last it is not we
Who spell "Necessity,"
But Necessity who spells us!'

He smiled. I smiled. And between
Your artist and your drummer
Swept, on a breeze of summer,
A wave of sympathy;
And we even came to wonder
Where—in the name of thunder—
We had met before this scene.

WALTER DE LA MARE

1873–1956

119   *Autumn*

THERE is a wind where the rose was;
Cold rain where sweet grass was;
   And clouds like sheep
   Stream o'er the steep
Grey skies where the lark was.

Nought gold where your hair was;
Nought warm where your hand was;
   But phantom, forlorn,
   Beneath the thorn,
Your ghost where your face was.

Sad winds where your voice was;
Tears, tears where my heart was;
   And ever with me,
   Child, ever with me,
Silence where hope was.

Miss Loo

WHEN thin-strewn memory I look through,
I see most clearly poor Miss Loo;
Her tabby cat, her cage of birds,
Her nose, her hair, her muffled words,
And how she'd open her green eyes,
As if in some immense surprise,
Whenever as we sat at tea
She made some small remark to me.
It's always drowsy summer when
From out the past she comes again;
The westering sunshine in a pool
Floats in her parlour still and cool;
While the slim bird its lean wires shakes,
As into piercing song it breaks;

Till Peter's pale-green eyes ajar
Dream, wake; wake, dream, in one brief bar.
And I am sitting, dull and shy,
And she with gaze of vacancy,
And large hands folded on the tray,
Musing the afternoon away;
Her satin bosom heaving slow
With sighs that softly ebb and flow,
And her plain face in such dismay,
It seems unkind to look her way:
Until all cheerful back will come
Her gentle gleaming spirit home:
And one would think that poor Miss Loo
Asked nothing else, if she had you.

The Scarecrow

ALL winter through I bow my head
    Beneath the driving rain;
The North Wind powders me with snow
    And blows me black again;

At midnight in a maze of stars
　　I flame with glittering rime,
And stand, above the stubble, stiff
　　As mail at morning-prime.
But when that child, called Spring, and all
　　His host of children, come,
Scattering their buds and dew upon
　　These acres of my home,
Some rapture in my rags awakes;
　　I lift void eyes and scan
The skies for crows, those ravening foes,
　　Of my strange master, Man.
I watch him striding lank behind
　　His clashing team, and know
Soon will the wheat swish body high
　　Where once lay sterile snow;
Soon shall I gaze across a sea
　　Of sun-begotten grain,
Which my unflinching watch hath sealed
　　For harvest once again.

122

Nod

SOFTLY along the road of evening,
　　In a twilight dim with rose,
Wrinkled with age, and drenched with dew,
　　Old Nod, the shepherd, goes.

His drowsy flock streams on before him,
　　Their fleeces charged with gold,
To where the sun's last beam leans low
　　On Nod the shepherd's fold.

The hedge is quick and green with brier,
　　From their sand the conies creep;
And all the birds that fly in heaven
　　Flock singing home to sleep.

His lambs outnumber a noon's roses,
    Yet, when night's shadows fall,
His blind old sheep-dog, Slumber-soon,
    Misses not one of all.

His are the quiet steeps of dreamland,
    The waters of no-more-pain,
His ram's bell rings 'neath an arch of stars,
    'Rest, rest, and rest again.'

123   *All That's Past*

VERY old are the woods;
    And the buds that break
Out of the brier's boughs,
    When March winds wake,
So old with their beauty are—
    Oh, no man knows
Through what wild centuries
    Roves back the rose.

Very old are the brooks;
    And the rills that rise
Where snow sleeps cold beneath
    The azure skies
Sing such a history
    Of come and gone,
Their every drop is as wise
    As Solomon.

Very old are we men;
    Our dreams are tales
Told in dim Eden
    By Eve's nightingales;
We wake and whisper awhile,
    But, the day gone by,
Silence and sleep like fields
    Of amaranth lie.

124 *The Stranger*

HALF-HIDDEN in a graveyard,
  In the blackness of a yew,
Where never living creature stirs,
  Nor sunbeam pierces through,

Is a tomb-stone, green and crooked—
  Its faded legend gone—
With one rain-worn cherub's head
  To sing of the unknown.

There, when the dusk is falling,
  Silence broods so deep
It seems that every air that breathes
  Sighs from the fields of sleep.

Day breaks in heedless beauty,
  Kindling each drop of dew,
But unforsaking shadow dwells
  Beneath this lonely yew.

And, all else lost and faded,
  Only this listening head
Keeps with a strange unanswering smile
  Its secret with the dead.

125 *The Ghost*

'WHO knocks?' 'I, who was beautiful,
  Beyond all dreams to restore,
I, from the roots of the dark thorn am hither,
  And knock on the door.'

'Who speaks?' 'I—once was my speech
  Sweet as the bird's on the air,
When echo lurks by the waters to heed;
  'Tis I speak thee fair.'

'Dark is the hour!' 'Ay, and cold.'
  'Lone is my house.' 'Ah, but mine?'
'Sight, touch, lips, eyes yearned in vain.'
  'Long dead these to thine . . .'

Silence. Still faint on the porch
  Brake the flames of the stars.
In gloom groped a hope-wearied hand
  Over keys, bolts, and bars.

A face peered. All the grey night
  In chaos of vacancy shone;
Nought but vast sorrow was there—
  The sweet cheat gone.

126   *The Railway Junction*

FROM here through tunnelled gloom the track
Forks into two; and one of these
Wheels onward into darkening hills,
And one toward distant seas.

How still it is; the signal light
At set of sun shines palely green;
A thrush sings; other sound there's none,
Nor traveller to be seen—

Where late there was a throng. And now,
In peace awhile, I sit alone;
Though soon, at the appointed hour,
I shall myself be gone.

But not their way; the bow-legged groom,
The parson in black, the widow and son,
The sailor with his cage, the gaunt
Gamekeeper with his gun,

That fair one, too, discreetly veiled—
All, who so mutely came, and went,
Will reach those far nocturnal hills,
Or shores, ere night is spent.

I nothing know why thus we met—
Their thoughts, their longings, hopes, their fate:
And what shall I remember, except—
The evening growing late—

That here through tunnelled gloom the track
Forks into two; of these
One into darkening hills leads on,
And one toward distant seas?

G. K. CHESTERTON
1874–1936

127   *The Secret People*

SMILE at us, pay us, pass us; but do not quite forget,
For we are the people of England, that never has spoken yet.
There is many a fat farmer that drinks less cheerfully,
There is many a free French peasant who is richer and sadder than we.
There are no folk in the whole world so helpless or so wise.
There is hunger in our bellies, there is laughter in our eyes;
You laugh at us and love us, both mugs and eyes are wet:
Only you do not know us. For we have not spoken yet.

The fine French kings came over in a flutter of flags and dames.
We liked their smiles and battles, but we never could say their names.
The blood ran red to Bosworth and the high French lords went down;
There was naught but a naked people under a naked crown.
And the eyes of the King's Servants turned terribly every way,
And the gold of the King's Servants rose higher every day.
They burnt the homes of the shaven men, that had been quaint and
    kind,
Till there was no bed in a monk's house, nor food that man could find.
The inns of God where no man paid, that were the wall of the weak,
The King's Servants ate them all. And still we did not speak.

And the face of the King's Servants grew greater than the King:
He tricked them, and they trapped him, and stood round him in a ring.
The new grave lords closed round him, that had eaten the abbey's
    fruits,
And the men of the new religion, with their Bibles in their boots,
We saw their shoulders moving, to menace or discuss,
And some were pure and some were vile; but none took heed of us.
We saw the King as they killed him, and his face was proud and pale;
And a few men talked of freedom, while England talked of ale.

A war that we understood not came over the world and woke
Americans, Frenchmen, Irish; but we knew not the things they spoke.
They talked about rights and nature and peace and the people's reign:
And the squires, our masters, bade us fight; and never scorned us
    again.
Weak if we be for ever, could none condemn us then;
Men called us serfs and drudges; men knew that we were men.
In foam and flame at Trafalgar, on Albuera plains,
We did and died like lions, to keep ourselves in chains,
We lay in living ruins; firing and fearing not
The strange fierce face of the Frenchman who knew for what they
    fought,
And the man who seemed to be more than man we strained against and
    broke;
And we broke our own rights with him. And still we never spoke.

Our path of glory ended; we never heard guns again.
But the squire seemed struck in the saddle; he was foolish, as if in pain
He leaned on a staggering lawyer, he clutched a cringing Jew,
He was stricken; it may be, after all, he was stricken at Waterloo.
Or perhaps the shades of the shaven men, whose spoil is in his house,
Come back in shining shapes at last to spoil his last carouse:
We only know the last sad squires ride slowly towards the sea,
And a new people takes the land: and still it is not we.

They have given us into the hands of the new unhappy lords,
Lords without anger and honour, who dare not carry their swords.
They fight by shuffling papers; they have bright dead alien eyes;
They look at our labour and laughter as a tired man looks at flies.
And the load of their loveless pity is worse than the ancient wrongs,
Their doors are shut in the evening; and they know no songs.

We hear men speaking for us of new laws strong and sweet,
Yet is there no man speaketh as we speak in the street.
It may be we shall rise the last as Frenchmen rose the first,
Our wrath come after Russia's wrath and our wrath be the worst.
It may be we are meant to mark with our riot and our rest
God's scorn for all men governing. It may be beer is best.
But we are the people of England; and we have not spoken yet.
Smile at us, pay us, pass us. But do not quite forget.

128   *The Rolling English Road*

BEFORE the Roman came to Rye or out to Severn strode,
The rolling English drunkard made the rolling English road.
A reeling road, a rolling road, that rambles round the shire,
And after him the parson ran, the sexton and the squire;
A merry road, a mazy road, and such as we did tread
The night we went to Birmingham by way of Beachy Head.

I knew no harm of Bonaparte and plenty of the Squire,
And for to fight the Frenchman I did not much desire;
But I did bash their baggonets because they came arrayed
To straighten out the crooked road an English drunkard made,
Where you and I went down the lane with ale-mugs in our hands,
The night we went to Glastonbury by way of Goodwin Sands.

His sins they were forgiven him; or why do flowers run
Behind him; and the hedges all strengthening in the sun?
The wild thing went from left to right and knew not which was which,
But the wild rose was above him when they found him in the ditch.
God pardon us, nor harden us; we did not see so clear
The night we went to Bannockburn by way of Brighton Pier.

My friends, we will not go again or ape an ancient rage,
Or stretch the folly of our youth to be the shame of age,
But walk with clearer eyes and ears this path that wandereth,
And see undrugged in evening light the decent inn of death;
For there is good news yet to hear and fine things to be seen
Before we go to Paradise by way of Kensal Green.

129   *Gold Leaves*

Lo! I am come to autumn,
    When all the leaves are gold;
Grey hairs and golden leaves cry out
    The year and I are old.

In youth I sought the prince of men,
    Captain in cosmic wars,
Our Titan, even the weeds would show
    Defiant, to the stars.

But now a great thing in the street
    Seems any human nod,
Where shift in strange democracy
    The million masks of God.

In youth I sought the golden flower
    Hidden in wood or wold,
But I am come to autumn,
    When all the leaves are gold.

EDWARD THOMAS
1878–1917

130   *As the Team's Head-Brass*

As the team's head-brass flashed out on the turn
The lovers disappeared into the wood.
I sat among the boughs of the fallen elm
That strewed the angle of the fallow, and
Watched the plough narrowing a yellow square
Of charlock. Every time the horses turned
Instead of treading me down, the ploughman leaned
Upon the handles to say or ask a word,
About the weather, next about the war.
Scraping the share he faced towards the wood,
And screwed along the furrow till the brass flashed
Once more.

The blizzard felled the elm whose crest
I sat in, by a woodpecker's round hole,
The ploughman said. 'When will they take it away?'
'When the war's over.' So the talk began—
One minute and an interval of ten,
A minute more and the same interval.
'Have you been out?' 'No.' 'And don't want to, perhaps?'
'If I could only come back again, I should.
I could spare an arm. I shouldn't want to lose
A leg. If I should lose my head, why, so,
I should want nothing more. . . . Have many gone
From here?' 'Yes.' 'Many lost?' 'Yes, a good few.
Only two teams work on the farm this year.
One of my mates is dead. The second day
In France they killed him. It was back in March,
The very night of the blizzard, too. Now if
He had stayed here we should have moved the tree.'
'And I should not have sat here. Everything
Would have been different. For it would have been
Another world.' 'Ay, and a better, though
If we could see all all might seem good.' Then
The lovers came out of the wood again:
The horses started and for the last time
I watched the clods crumble and topple over
After the ploughshare and the stumbling team.

131 *Thaw*

OVER the land freckled with snow half-thawed
The speculating rooks at their nests cawed
And saw from elm-tops, delicate as flower of grass,
What we below could not see, Winter pass.

132 *In Memoriam (Easter, 1915)*

THE flowers left thick at nightfall in the wood
This Eastertide call into mind the men,
Now far from home, who, with their sweethearts, should
Have gathered them and will do never again.

133   *It Rains*

IT rains, and nothing stirs within the fence
Anywhere through the orchard's untrodden, dense
Forest of parsley. The great diamonds
Of rain on the grassblades there is none to break,
Or the fallen petals further down to shake.

And I am nearly as happy as possible
To search the wilderness in vain though well,
To think of two walking, kissing there,
Drenched, yet forgetting the kisses of the rain:
Sad, too, to think that never, never again,

Unless alone, so happy shall I walk
In the rain. When I turn away, on its fine stalk
Twilight has fined to naught, the parsley flower
Figures, suspended still and ghostly white,
The past hovering as it revisits the light.

134   *The Glory*

THE glory of the beauty of the morning,—
The cuckoo crying over the untouched dew;
The blackbird that has found it, and the dove
That tempts me on to something sweeter than love;
White clouds ranged even and fair as new-mown hay;
The heat, the stir, the sublime vacancy
Of sky and meadow and forest and my own heart:—
The glory invites me, yet it leaves me scorning
All I can ever do, all I can be,
Beside the lovely of motion, shape, and hue,
The happiness I fancy fit to dwell
In beauty's presence. Shall I now this day
Begin to seek as far as heaven, as hell,
Wisdom or strength to match this beauty, start
And tread the pale dust pitted with small dark drops,
In hope to find whatever it is I seek,

Hearkening to short-lived happy-seeming things
That we know naught of, in the hazel copse?
Or must I be content with discontent
As larks and swallows are perhaps with wings?
And shall I ask at the day's end once more
What beauty is, and what I can have meant
By happiness? And shall I let all go,
Glad, weary, or both? Or shall I perhaps know
That I was happy oft and oft before,
Awhile forgetting how I am fast pent,
How dreary-swift, with naught to travel to,
Is Time? I cannot bite the day to the core.

135   *Adlestrop*

Yes, I remember Adlestrop—
The name, because one afternoon
Of heat the express-train drew up there
Unwontedly. It was late June.

The steam hissed. Someone cleared his throat.
No one left and no one came
On the bare platform. What I saw
Was Adlestrop—only the name

And willows, willow-herb, and grass,
And meadowsweet, and haycocks dry,
Not whit less still and lonely fair
Than the high cloudlets in the sky.

And for that minute a blackbird sang
Close by, and round him, mistier,
Farther and farther, all the birds
Of Oxfordshire and Gloucestershire.

136 *Rain*

RAIN, midnight rain, nothing but the wild rain
On this bleak hut, and solitude, and me
Remembering again that I shall die
And neither hear the rain nor give it thanks
For washing me cleaner than I have been
Since I was born into this solitude.
Blessed are the dead that the rain rains upon:
But here I pray that none whom once I loved
Is dying to-night or lying still awake
Solitary, listening to the rain,
Either in pain or thus in sympathy
Helpless among the living and the dead,
Like a cold water among broken reeds,
Myriads of broken reeds all still and stiff,
Like me who have no love which this wild rain
Has not dissolved except the love of death,
If love it be for what is perfect and
Cannot, the tempest tells me, disappoint.

137 *Celandine*

THINKING of her had saddened me at first,
Until I saw the sun on the celandines lie
Redoubled, and she stood up like a flame,
A living thing, not what before I nursed,
The shadow I was growing to love almost,
The phantom, not the creature with bright eye
That I had thought never to see, once lost.

She found the celandines of February
Always before us all. Her nature and name
Were like those flowers, and now immediately
For a short swift eternity back she came,
Beautiful, happy, simply as when she wore
Her brightest bloom among the winter hues
Of all the world; and I was happy too,
Seeing the blossoms and the maiden who
Had seen them with me Februarys before,
Bending to them as in and out she trod
And laughed, with locks sweeping the mossy sod.

But this was a dream: the flowers were not true,
Until I stooped to pluck from the grass there
One of five petals and I smelt the juice
Which made me sigh, remembering she was no more,
Gone like a never perfectly recalled air.

138   *Digging*

To-day I think
Only with scents,—scents dead leaves yield,
And bracken, and wild carrot's seed,
And the square mustard field;

Odours that rise
When the spade wounds the root of tree,
Rose, currant, raspberry, or goutweed,
Rhubarb or celery;

The smoke's smell, too,
Flowing from where a bonfire burns
The dead, the waste, the dangerous,
And all to sweetness turns.

It is enough
To smell, to crumble the dark earth,
While the robin sings over again
Sad songs of Autumn mirth.

OLIVER ST. JOHN GOGARTY
1878–1957

139   *Ringsend*
                    (*After reading Tolstoi*)

I will live in Ringsend
With a red-headed whore,
And the fan-light gone in
Where it lights the hall-door;

And listen each night
For her querulous shout,
As at last she streels in
And the pubs empty out
To soothe that wild breast
With my old-fangled songs,
Till she feels it redressed
From inordinate wrongs,
Imagined, outrageous,
Preposterous wrongs,
Till peace at last comes,
Shall be all I will do,
Where the little lamp blooms
Like a rose in the stew;
And up the back-garden
The sound comes to me
Of the lapsing, unsoilable,
Whispering sea.

140   *Farrell O'Reilly*

You, Farrell O'Reilly, I feared as a boy
With your thin riding legs and your turned-in toes;
I feared the sharp, gimlet-like look in your eye,
Your rumbling brown beard and your pocketed nose.
Old friend of my Father what brings you back now?
You died fifty-nine years or sixty ago.

They say, when a man is about to be drowned,
His youth flashes back and he sees his life clear;
So, maybe, because I am nearing the ground
The days of my youth and my childhood are here.
If so, they are welcome if they compensate
For days that are yearly increasing in weight.

My Father no sooner would talk of Kilbeg
And carefully measure the charge for each cartridge,
Than I saw myself strutting behind with the bag
And heard the men talk as they walked up the partridge.
The coveys were scarce, and the cause of the trouble
Was 'Farrell O'Reilly's too proud to have stubble.'

O thick-sodded fields that have fattened the herds
From the days of the kings in the dawn of our time,
O fields of Moynalty, The Plain of the Birds,
None ever drew plough through your land on the lime!
King Leary of Tara just over the way
Knew more about Meath than the men of to-day.

My young eyes were good and rejoiced at the sight
Of a drake with the sun all a blaze on his green
That flew on a sudden from left to the right:
What banging! But only a feather was seen.
When each man exclaimed to the other, 'Bad luck!'
I could not help thinking 'twas good for the duck.

Remote as the days in an old mezzotint
When Farrell O'Reilly would lean to his gun
Top-hatted; and aim with a vigilant squint,
(If he missed, it was due to the wind or the sun)
My Father stands clear; but I see clearer Farrell
His left eye shut tight and his hand up the barrel.

In spite of their failure, I gaped at the men,
Their failures were feats to me looking for wonder.
How little I doubted Authority then!
Authority added distinction to blunder.
They could not do wrong, though they played ducks and drakes,
For great men can lend a prestige to mistakes.

'Now hand me that bag, for you can't lift a leg.'
I said, 'It's so light I can carry it farther'—
A thousand wide acres surrounded Kilbeg—
And Farrell said nothing, but looked at my Father;
Then carried me home; and I found, for a truth,
There's sometimes great kindness behind the uncouth.

The little pine wood with its floor of dense laurels;
The river slow-moving with bulrushes rimmed;
The well-house, the lis—all the things that were Farrell's,
Though half were forbidden, are shining undimmed:
The harness room filled with bits, saddles and bridles,
A room where the dairy maid gossips and idles.

I feel the lull now that came over the men,
And I see the groom wafting his smoke with his hand,
Intent as his polishing started again;
'The Master!' A hint that they all understand;
The dairy maid holding her blouse at her throat,
As he enters the yard in his cut-away coat.

Like everyone else who was in his employ,
Alert, lest, surprised, I be taken in error,
In spite of foreboding, I snatched at my joy,
For joy is a pleasance surrounded by terror.
Wood, river and well—to maid and to man
Sharp Farrell O'Reilly appeared as god Pan.

Wood, river and well—the wild things of the fields;
The lis with its lonely and wind-twisted thorn,
Enchanted me early; now everything yields
To the breath I drew first from the winds of my morn:
So, Farrell O'Reilly, in token from me,
Accept this wild leaf from your own twisted tree.

WILFRID GIBSON

1878–1962

The Ice

141

Her day out from the workhouse-ward, she stands,
A grey-haired woman decent and precise,
With prim black bonnet and neat paisley shawl,
Among the other children by the stall,
And with grave relish eats a penny ice.

To wizened toothless gums with quaking hands
She holds it, shuddering with delicious cold,
Nor heeds the jeering laughter of young men—
The happiest, in her innocence, of all:
For, while their insolent youth must soon grow old,
She, who's been old, is now a child again.

142   *Breakfast*

WE ate our breakfast lying on our backs
Because the shells were screeching overhead.
I bet a rasher to a loaf of bread
That Hull United would beat Halifax
When Jimmy Stainthorpe played full-back instead
Of Billy Bradford. Ginger raised his head
And cursed, and took the bet, and dropt back dead.
We ate our breakfast lying on our backs
Because the shells were screeching overhead.

143   *The Drove-Road*

'TWAS going to snow—'twas snowing! Curse his luck!
And fifteen mile to travel. Here was he
With nothing but an empty pipe to suck,
And half a flask of rum—but that would be
More welcome later on. He'd had a drink
Before he left, and that would keep him warm
A tidy while; and 'twould be good to think
He'd something to fall back on if the storm
Should come to much. You never knew with snow.
A sup of rain he didn't mind at all,
But snow was different with so far to go—
Full fifteen mile, and not a house of call.
Ay, snow was quite another story, quite—
Snow on the fell-tops with a north-east wind
Behind it, blowing steadily with a bite
That made you feel that you were stark and skinned.

And those poor beasts—and they just off the boat
A day or so, and hardly used to land—
Still dizzy with the sea, their wits afloat.
When they first reached the dock they scarce could stand,
They'd been so joggled. It's gey bad to cross,
After a long day's jolting in the train,
Thon Irish Channel, always pitch and toss—
And, heads or tails, not much for them to gain!

And then the market, and the throng and noise
Of yapping dogs; and they stung mad with fear,
Welted with switches by those senseless boys—
He'd like to dust their jackets! But 'twas queer,
A beast's life, when you came to think of it,
From start to finish—queerer, ay, a lot
Than any man's, and chancier a good bit.
With his ash-sapling at their heels they'd got
To travel before night those fifteen miles
Of hard fell road against the driving snow,
Half-blinded, on and on. He thought at whiles
'Twas just as well for them they couldn't know. . . .
Though, as for that, 'twas little that he knew
Himself what was in store for him. He took
Things as they came: 'twas all a man could do;
And he'd kept going somehow by hook or crook.
And here he was, with fifteen mile of fell,
And snow and . . . God, but it was blowing stiff!
And no tobacco. Blest if he could tell
Where he had lost it—but for half a whiff
He'd swop the very jacket off his back—
Not that he'd miss the cobweb of old shreds
That held the holes together.
                Thon cheap-jack
Who'd sold it him had said it was Lord Ted's,
And London cut: but Teddy had grown fat
Since he'd been made an alderman. . . . His bid?
And did the gentleman not want a hat
To go with it, a topper? If he did,
Here was the very . . .
              Hell, but it was cold,
And driving dark it was—nigh dark as night.
He'd almost think he must be getting old
To feel the wind so. And long out of sight
The beasts had trotted. Well, what odds! The way
Ran straight for ten miles on, and they'd go straight:
They'd never heed a by-road. Many a day
He'd had to trudge on, trusting them to fate,
And always found them safe. They scamper fast,
But in the end a man could walk them down:
They're showy trotters, but they cannot last:
He'd race the fastest beast for half-a-crown

On a day's journey. Beasts were never made
For steady travelling—drive them twenty mile
And they were done; while he was not afraid
To travel twice that distance with a smile.

But not a day like this! He'd never felt
A wind with such an edge. 'Twas like the blade
Of the rasper in the pocket of his belt
He kept for easy shaving. In his trade
You'd oft to make your toilet under a dyke—
And he was always one for a clean chin,
And carried soap.
           He'd never felt the like—
That wind, it cut clean through you to the skin.
He might be mother-naked, walking bare,
For all the use his clothes were, with the snow
Half blinding him and clagging to his hair
And trickling down his spine. He'd like to know
What was the sense of pegging steadily,
Chilled to the marrow, after a daft herd
Of draggled beasts he couldn't even see!

But that was him all over—just a word,
A nod, a wink, the price of half-and-half,
And he'd be setting out for God-knows-where
With no more notion than a yearling calf
Where he would find himself when he got there.
And he'd been travelling hard on sixty year
The same old road, the same old giddy gait;
And he'd be walking, for a pint of beer,
Into his coffin one day, soon or late—
But not with such a tempest in his teeth,
Half-blinded and half-dothered, that he hoped!
He'd met a sight of weather on the heath,
But this beat all.
           'Twas worse than when he'd groped
His way that evening down the Mallerstang—
Thon was a blizzard, thon, and he was done
And almost dropping, when he came a bang
Against a house—slap-bang, and like to stun!

Though that just saved his senses: and right there
He saw a lighted window he'd not seen,
Although he'd nearly staggered through its glare
Into a goodwife's kitchen, where she'd been
Baking hot griddle-cakes upon the peat . . .
And he could taste them now, and feel the glow
Of steady, aching, tingly, drowsy heat
As he sat there and let the caking snow
Melt off his boots, staining the sanded floor.
And that brown jug she took down from the shelf—
And every time he'd finished fetching more
And piping, *Now reach up and help yourself!*
She was a wonder, thon, the gay old wife—
But no such luck this journey. Things like that
Could hardly happen every day of life,
Or no one would be dying but the fat
And oily undertakers, starved to death
For want of custom. . . . Hell! but he would soon
Be giving them a job. . . . It caught your breath,
That throttling wind. And it was not yet noon.
And he'd be travelling through it until dark.
Dark! 'Twas already dark, and might be night
For all that he could see.
                And not a spark
Of comfort for him! Just to strike a light
And press the kindling shag down in the bowl,
Keeping the flame well shielded with his hand,
And puff and puff! He'd give his very soul
For half a pipe. He couldn't understand
How he had come to lose it. He'd the rum—
Ay, that was safe enough, but it would keep
A while: you never knew what chance might come
In such a storm. . . .
              If he could only sleep . . .
If he could only sleep. . . . That rustling sound
Of drifting snow, it made him sleepy-like—
Drowsy and dizzy, dithering round and round. . . .
If he could only curl up under a dyke
And sleep and sleep. . . . It dazzled him, that white,
Drifting and drifting round and round . . .
Just half a moment's snooze. . . . He'd be all right,
It made his head quite dizzy, that dry sound

Of rustling snow: it made his head go round,
That rustling in his ears . . . and drifting, drifting. . . .
If only he could sleep . . . he would sleep sound. . . .
God! he was nearly gone. . . .
                              The storm was lifting;
And he'd run into something soft and warm—
Slap into his own beasts, and never knew.
Huddled they were, bamboozled by the storm—
And little wonder either when it blew
A blasted blizzard. Still, they'd got to go:
They couldn't stand there snoozing until night.

But they were sniffing something in the snow:
'Twas that had stopped them, something big and white—
A bundle—nay, a woman . . . and she slept—
But it was death to sleep.
                              He'd nearly dropped
Asleep himself. 'Twas well that he had kept
That rum, and lucky that the beasts had stopped.
Ay, it was well that he had kept the rum:
He liked his drink, but he had never cared
For soaking by himself and sitting mum:
Even the best rum tasted better shared.

144   *Lament*

WE who are left, how shall we look again
Happily on the sun or feel the rain,
Without remembering how they who went
Ungrudgingly, and spent
Their all for us, loved too the sun and rain?

A bird among the rain-wet lilac sings—
But we, how shall we turn to little things,
And listen to the birds and winds and streams
Made holy by their dreams,
Nor feel the heart-break in the heart of things?

145 *Long Tom*

HE talked of Delhi brothels half the night,
Quaking with fever; and then, dragging tight
The frowsy blankets to his chattering chin,
Cursed for an hour because they were so thin
And nothing would keep out that gnawing cold—
Scarce forty years of age, and yet so old,
Haggard and worn with burning eyes set deep—
Until at last he cursed himself asleep.

Before I'd shut my eyes reveille came;
And as I dressed by the one candle-flame
The mellow golden light fell on his face
Still sleeping, touching it to tender grace,
Rounding the features life had scarred so deep,
Till youth came back to him in quiet sleep:
And then what women saw in him I knew
And why they'd love him all his brief life through.

146 *All Being Well*

ALL being well, I'll come to you,
Sweetheart, before the year is through;
And we shall find so much to do,
So much to tell.

I read your letter through and through,
And dreamt of all we'd say and do,
Till in my heart the thought of you
Rang like a bell.

Now the bell tolls, my love, for you;
For long before the year is through
You've gone where there is naught to do
And naught to tell.

Yet mayn't I find when life is through
The best is still to say and do,
When I at last may come to you,
All being well?

JOHN MASEFIELD
1878–1967

147 FROM *Biography*

OTHER bright days of action have seemed great;
Wild days in a pampero off the Plate;
Good swimming days, at Hog Back or the Coves
Which the young gannet and the corbie loves;
Surf-swimming between rollers, catching breath
Between the advancing grave and breaking death,
Then shooting up into the sunbright smooth
To watch the advancing roller bare her tooth,
And days of labour also, loading, hauling;
Long days at winch or capstan, heaving, pawling;
The days with oxen, dragging stone from blasting,
And dusty days in mills, and hot days masting.
Trucking on dust-dry deckings smooth like ice,
And hunts in mighty wool-racks after mice;
Mornings with buckwheat when the fields did blanch
With White Leghorns come from the chicken ranch.
Days near the spring upon the sunburnt hill,
Plying the maul or gripping tight the drill.
Delights of work most real—delights that change
The headache life of towns to rapture strange
Not known by townsmen, nor imagined; health
That puts new glory upon mental wealth
And makes the poor man rich. But that ends, too,
Health with its thoughts of life; and that bright view
That sunny landscape from life's peak, that glory,
And all a glad man's comments on life's story,
And thoughts of marvellous towns and living men,
And what pens tell and all beyond the pen,
End, and are summed in words so truly dead,
They raise no image of the heart and head,
The life, the man alive, the friend we knew,
The mind ours argued with or listened to,
None; but are dead, and all life's keenness, all,
Is dead as print before the funeral,
Even deader after, when the dates are sought,
And cold minds disagree with what we thought.

This many pictured world of many passions
Wears out the nations as a woman fashions,
And what life is is much to very few,
Men being so strange, so mad, and what men do
So good to watch or share; but when men count
Those hours of life that were a bursting fount,
Sparkling the dusty heart with living springs,
There seems a world, beyond our earthly things,
Gated by golden moments, each bright time
Opening to show the city white like lime,
High-towered and many-peopled. This made sure,
Work that obscures those moments seems impure,
Making our not-returning time of breath
Dull with the ritual and records of death,
That frost of fact by which our wisdom gives
Correctly stated death to all that lives.

Best trust the happy moments. What they gave
Makes man less fearful of the certain grave,
And gives his work compassion and new eyes,
The days that make us happy make us wise.

148   FROM *Reynard the Fox*
                    OR
          The Ghost Heath Run

THE meet was at 'The Cock and Pye
By Charles and Martha Enderby,'
The grey, three-hundred-year-old inn
Long since the haunt of Benjamin
The highwayman, who rode the bay.
The tavern fronts the coaching way,
The mail changed horses there of old.
It has a strip of grassy mould
In front of it, a broad green strip.
A trough, where horses' muzzles dip,
Stands opposite the tavern front,
And there that morning came the hunt,
To fill that quiet width of road
As full of men as Framilode
Is full of sea when tide is in.

The stables were alive with din
From dawn until the time of meeting.
A pad-groom gave a cloth a beating,
Knocking the dust out with a stake.
Two men cleaned stalls with fork and rake,
And one went whistling to the pump,
The handle whined, ker-lump, ker-lump,
The water splashed into the pail,
And, as he went, it left a trail,
Lipped over on the yard's bricked paving.
Two grooms (sent on before) were shaving
There in the yard, at glasses propped
On jutting bricks; they scraped and stropped,
And felt their chins and leaned and peered,
A woodland day was what they feared
(As second horseman), shaving there.
Then, in the stalls where hunters were,
Straw rustled as the horses shifted,
The hayseeds ticked and haystraws drifted
From racks as horses tugged their feed.
Slow gulping sounds of steady greed
Came from each stall, and sometimes stampings,
Whinnies (at well-known steps) and rampings,
To see the horse in the next stall.

Outside, the spangled cock did call
To scattering grain that Martha flung.
And many a time a mop was wrung
By Susan ere the floor was clean.
The harness-room, that busy scene,
Clinked and chinked from ostler's brightening
Rings and bits with dips of whitening,
Rubbing fox-flecks out of stirrups,
Dumbing buckles of their chirrups
By the touch of oily feathers.
Some, with stag's bones rubbed at leathers,
Brushed at saddle-flaps or hove
Saddle-linings to the stove.
Blue smoke from strong tobacco drifted
Out of the yard, the passers snifft it,
Mixed with the strong ammonia flavour
Of horses' stables and the savour

Of saddle-paste and polish spirit
Which put the gleam on flap and tirrit,
The grooms in shirts with rolled-up sleeves,
Belted by girths of coloured weaves,
Groomed the clipped hunters in their stalls.
One said: 'My dad cured saddle-galls,
He called it Dr. Barton's cure—
Hog's lard and borax, laid on pure.'
And others said: 'Ge' back, my son.'
'Stand over, girl; now, girl, ha' done.'
'Now, boy, no snapping; gently. Crikes!
He gives a rare pinch when he likes.'

'Drawn blood? I thought he looked a biter.'
'I give 'em all sweet spit of nitre
For that, myself: that sometimes cures.'
'Now, Beauty, mind them feet of yours.'
They groomed, and sissed with hissing notes
To keep the dust out of their throats.

149 *The Crowd*

THEY had secured their beauty to the dock,
First having decked her to delight the eye.
After long months of water and the sky
These twenty saw the prison doors unlock;

These twenty men were free to quit the ship,
To tread dry land and slumber when they chose,
To count no bells that counted their repose,
To waken free from python Duty's grip.

What they had suffered and had greatly been
Was stamped upon their faces; they were still
Haggard with the indomitable will
That singleness of purpose had made clean.

These twenty threadbare men with frost-bit ears
And canvas bags and little chests of gears.

150   *Partridges*

HERE they lie mottled to the ground unseen,
This covey linked together from the nest.
The nosing pointers put them from their rest,
The wings whirr, the guns flash and all has been.

The lucky crumple to the clod, shot clean,
The wounded drop and hurry and lie close;
The sportsmen praise the pointer and his nose,
Until he scents the hiders and is keen.

Tumbled in bag with rabbits, pigeons, hares,
The crumpled corpses have forgotten all
The covey's joys of strong or gliding flight.

But when the planet lamps the coming night,
The few survivors seek those friends of theirs;
The twilight hears and darkness hears them call.

151   *Sea-Fever*

I MUST go down to the seas again, to the lonely sea and the sky,
And all I ask is a tall ship and a star to steer her by,
And the wheel's kick and the wind's song and the white sails shaking,
And a grey mist on the sea's face and a grey dawn breaking.

I must go down to the seas again, for the call of the running tide
Is a wild call and a clear call that may not be denied;
And all I ask is a windy day with the white clouds flying,
And the flung spray and the blown spume, and the sea-gulls crying.

I must go down to the seas again, to the vagrant gypsy life,
To the gull's way and the whale's way where the wind's like a whetted
    knife;
And all I ask is a merry yarn from a laughing fellow-rover,
And quiet sleep and a sweet dream when the long trick's over.

152 *Twilight*

TWILIGHT it is, and the far woods are dim, and the rooks cry and
    call.
Down in the valley the lamps, and the mist, and a star over all,
There by the rick, where they thresh, is the drone at an end,
Twilight it is, and I travel the road with my friend.

I think of the friends who are dead, who were dear long ago in the past,
Beautiful friends who are dead, though I know that death cannot last;
Friends with the beautiful eyes that the dust has defiled,
Beautiful souls who were gentle when I was a child.

153 *C. L. M.*

IN the dark womb where I began
My mother's life made me a man.
Through all the months of human birth
Her beauty fed my common earth.
I cannot see, nor breathe, nor stir,
But through the death of some of her.

Down in the darkness of the grave
She cannot see the life she gave.
For all her love, she cannot tell
Whether I use it ill or well,
Nor knock at dusty doors to find
Her beauty dusty in the mind.

If the grave's gates could be undone,
She would not know her little son,
I am so grown. If we should meet
She would pass by me in the street,
Unless my soul's face let her see
My sense of what she did for me.

What have I done to keep in mind
My debt to her and womankind?
What woman's happier life repays
Her for those months of wretched days?
For all my mouthless body leeched
Ere Birth's releasing hell was reached?

What have I done, or tried, or said
In thanks to that dear woman dead?
Men triumph over women still,
Men trample women's rights at will,
And man's lust roves the world untamed.

        *   *   *   *

O grave, keep shut lest I be shamed.

154   *An Epilogue*

I HAVE seen flowers come in stony places
And kind things done by men with ugly faces,
And the gold cup won by the worst horse at the races,
So I trust, too.

HAROLD MONRO

1879–1932

155   *Thistledown*

THIS might have been a place for sleep
But, as from that small hollow there
Hosts of bright thistledown begin
Their dazzling journey through the air,
An idle man can only stare.

They grip their withered edge of stalk
In brief excitement for the wind;
They hold a breathless final talk,
And when their filmy cables part
One almost hears a little cry.

Some cling together while they wait
And droop and gaze and hesitate,
But others leap along the sky,
Or circle round and calmly choose
The gust they know they ought to use.

While some in loving pairs will glide,
Or watch the others as they pass,
Or rest on flowers in the grass,
Or circle through the shining day
Like silvery butterflies at play.

Some catch themselves to every mound,
Then lingeringly and slowly move
As if they knew the precious ground
Were opening for their fertile love:
They almost try to dig, they need
So much to plant their thistle-seed.

156 *Midnight Lamentation*

WHEN you and I go down
Breathless and cold,
Our faces both worn back
To earthly mould,
How lonely we shall be!
What shall we do,
You without me,
I without you?

I cannot bear the thought
You, first, may die,
Nor of how you will weep,
Should I.
We are too much alone;
What can we do
To make our bodies one:
You, me; I, you?

We are most nearly born
Of one same kind;
We have the same delight,
The same true mind.
Must we then part, we part;
Is there no way
To keep a beating heart,
And light of day?

I could now rise and run
Through street on street
To where you are breathing—you,
That we might meet,
And that your living voice
Might sound above
Fear, and we two rejoice
Within our love.

How frail the body is,
And we are made
As only in decay
To lean and fade.
I think too much of death;
There is a gloom
When I can't hear your breath
Calm in some room.

O, but how suddenly
Either may droop;
Countenance be so white,
Body stoop.
Then there may be a place
Where fading flowers
Drop on a lifeless face
Through weeping hours.

Is then nothing safe?
Can we not find
Some everlasting life
In our one mind?
I feel it like disgrace
Only to understand
Your spirit through your word,
Or by your hand.

I cannot find a way
Through love and through;
I cannot reach beyond
Body, to you.
When you or I must go
Down evermore,
There'll be no more to say
—But a locked door.

JOSEPH CAMPBELL
1879–1944

157 *The Old Woman*

As a white candle
In a holy place,
So is the beauty
Of an agéd face.

As the spent radiance
Of the winter sun,
So is a woman
With her travail done.

Her brood gone from her,
And her thoughts as still
As the waters
Under a ruined mill.

158 *The Antiquary*

IF you would learn
The why and wherefore of a 'Quern',
A 'kistvaen' or a 'reliquary',
You've but to ask the Antiquary.
He'll tell you that, and lashings more
Of history, and the oral lore
He's taken down from peasants' lips
Who never heard of manuscripts.
As who, for instance, might have thrown
Yon butterlump of basalt stone
That balks the wind of Moran's crop
So slickly from the mountain top.
Or what it is that rings the bell
On certain fasts in Grumly's Well:
A fish, maybe, a sacred trout,
Or virtue dropping from the clout
Some ulcered beggar left behind
To thank his God he is not blind.

Collector, too, and lapidary
As well as Irish antiquary,
His house, the last one in the town
With the brass vane, is coming down
With odds and ends of ancientry
Picked up from Cove to Murloch Bay.—
A hafted pike that killed its man
In 'Ninety-Eight; a copper pan
The Fianna used, and hazel spits
With charred ends from their cooking pits;
A Danish cup; a crucible
Found at the foot of Cullan's hill,
And likely used by him of old
For melting findruiney and gold;
A Jacobean sword; a ball
Shot from a gun on Derry's Wall;
A string of cinerary urns;
A ballad thumbed by Jamey Burns,
The Antrim yeoman, amethysts
From Achill; anchors, treasure chests
Recovered from a Spanish wreck
(The Great Armada!) centuries back;
A murrain charm; a Georgian 'snugg',
And such like age-embrownéd stuff.
Not that the crust on sword or scroll
Has touched the freshness of his soul.
An airy man; his eager mind
Stretching into the dark behind,
And forward; young as fallen dew,
And yet as old as Ireland, too.

ALFRED NOYES

1880–1958

159   *Spring, and the Blind Children*

THEY left the primrose glistening in its dew.
  With empty hands they drifted down the lane,
As though, for them, the Spring held nothing new;
  And not one face was turned to look again.

Like tiny ghosts, along their woodland aisle,
  They stole. They did not leap or dance or run.
Only, at times, without a word or smile,
  Their small blind faces lifted to the sun;

Innocent faces, desolately bright,
  Masks of dark thought that none could ever know;
But O, so small to hide it. In their night
  What dreams of our strange world must come and go;

Groping, as we, too, grope for heavens unseen;
  Guessing—at what those fabulous visions are;
Or wondering, when they learned that leaves were green,
  If colours were like music, heard afar?

Were brooks like bird-song? Was the setting sun
  Like scent of roses, or like evening prayer?
Were stars like chimes in heaven, when day was done;
  Was midnight like their mothers' warm soft hair?

And dawn?—a pitying face against their own,
  A whispered word, an unknown angel's kiss,
That stoops to each, in its own dark, alone;
  But leaves them lonelier for that breath of bliss?

Was it for earth's transgressions that they paid—
  Lambs of that God whose eyes with love grow dim—
Sharing His load on whom all wrongs are laid?
  But O, so small to bear it, even with Him!

God of blind children, through Thy dreadful light
  They pass. We pass. Thy heavens are all so near.
We cannot grasp them in our earth-bound night.
  But O, Thy grief! For Thou canst see and hear.

HERBERT PALMER
1880–1961

160   *Rock Pilgrim*

LET the damned ride their earwigs to Hell, but let me not join them.
For why should I covet the tide, or in meanness purloin them?
They are sick, they have chosen the path of their apple-green folly,
I will turn to my mountains of light, and my mauve melancholy.

Let their hands get the primrose—God wreathe me!—of lowland and
    lagland;
For me the small yellow tormentil of heath-hill and cragland.
Man's days are as grass, his thought but as thistle-seed wind-sown;
I will plod up the pass, and nourish the turf with my shinbone.

I should stay for a day, I should seek in high faith to reclaim them?
But the threadbare beat straw, and the hole in my shirt will inflame
    them.
They are blinder than moles, for they see but the flies in God's honey;
And they eat off their soles; and they kneel to the Moloch of money

They have squeezed my mouth dumb; their clutch for a year yet may
    rankle.
I will tie Robin Death to my side, with his claw on my ankle.
Let them come, stick and drum, and assail me across the grey boulders
I will flutter my toes, and rattle the screes on their shoulders.

Let the damned get to Hell and be quick, while decision is early.
I will tie a red rose to my stick, and plant my feet squarely.
My back shall be blind on their spite, and my rump on their folly;
I will plod up the ridge to the right, past the crimson-green holly.

HERBERT ASQUITH
1881–1947

161 *The Volunteer*

HERE lies a clerk who half his life had spent
Toiling at ledgers in a city grey,
Thinking that so his days would drift away
With no lance broken in life's tournament:
Yet ever 'twixt the books and his bright eyes
The gleaming eagles of the legions came,
And horsemen, charging under phantom skies,
Went thundering past beneath the oriflamme.

And now those waiting dreams are satisfied;
From twilight to the halls of dawn he went;
His lance is broken; but he lies content
With that high hour, in which he lived and died.
And falling thus, he wants no recompense,
Who found his battle in the last resort;
Nor needs he any hearse to bear him hence,
Who goes to join the men of Agincourt.

PADRAIC COLUM
1881–1972

162 *Monkeys*

Two little creatures
With faces the size of
A pair of pennies
Are clasping each other.
'Ah, do not leave me,'
One says to the other,
In the high monkey-
Cage in the beast-shop.

There are no people
To gape at them now,
For people are loth to
Peer in the dimness;
Have they not builded
Streets and playhouses,
Sky-signs and bars,
To lose the loneliness
Shaking the hearts
Of the two little Monkeys?

Yes. But who watches
The penny-small faces
Can hear the voices:
'Ah, do not leave me;
Suck I will give you,
Warmth and clasping,
And if you slip from
This beam I can never
Find you again.'

Dim is the evening,
And chill is the weather;
There, drawn from their coloured
Hemisphere,
The apes lilliputian
With faces the size of
A pair of pennies,
And voices as low as
The flow of my blood.

JOHN DRINKWATER
1882–1937

163 *Birthright*

LORD RAMESES of Egypt sighed
   Because a summer evening passed;
And little Ariadne cried
   That summer fancy fell at last
To dust; and young Verona died
   When beauty's hour was overcast.

Theirs was the bitterness we know
   Because the clouds of hawthorn keep
So short a state, and kisses go
   To tombs unfathomably deep,
While Rameses and Romeo
   And little Ariadne sleep.

164 *Moonlit Apples*

AT the top of the house the apples are laid in rows,
And the skylight lets the moonlight in, and those
Apples are deep-sea apples of green. There goes
   A cloud on the moon in the autumn night.

A mouse in the wainscot scratches, and scratches, and then
There is no sound at the top of the house of men
Or mice; and the cloud is blown, and the moon again
   Dapples the apples with deep-sea light.

They are lying in rows there, under the gloomy beams;
On the sagging floor; they gather the silver streams
Out of the moon, those moonlit apples of dreams,
   And quiet is the steep stair under.

In the corridors under there is nothing but sleep.
And stiller than ever on orchard boughs they keep
Tryst with the moon, and deep is the silence, deep
   On moon-washed apples of wonder.

JAMES JOYCE

1882–1941

165   *The Holy Office*

MYSELF unto myself will give
This name, Katharsis-Purgative.
I, who dishevelled ways forsook
To hold the poets' grammar-book,
Bringing to tavern and to brothel
The mind of witty Aristotle,
Lest bards in the attempt should err
Must here be my interpreter:
Wherefore receive now from my lip
Peripatetic scholarship.
To enter heaven, travel hell,
Be piteous or terrible,
One positively needs the ease
Of plenary indulgences.
For every true-born mysticist
A Dante is, unprejudiced,
Who safe at ingle-nook, by proxy,
Hazards extremes of heterodoxy,
Like him who finds a joy at table,
Pondering the uncomfortable.
Ruling one's life by commonsense
How can one fail to be intense?
But I must not accounted be
One of that mumming company—
With him[1] who hies him to appease
His giddy dames'[2] frivolities
While they console him when he whinges
With gold-embroidered Celtic fringes—
Or him who sober all the day
Mixes a naggin in his play[3]—
Or him whose conduct 'seems to own'
His preference for a man of 'tone'[4]—

---

[1] William Butler Yeats.
[2] Lady Gregory, Miss Horniman, and perhaps Maud Gonne MacBride.
[3] J. M. Synge.
[4] Oliver St. John Gogarty.

Or him who plays the ragged patch
To millionaires in Hazelhatch
But weeping after holy fast
Confesses all his pagan past[1]—
Or him who will his hat unfix
Neither to malt nor crucifix
But show to all that poor-dressed be
His high Castilian courtesy[2]—
Or him who loves his Master dear[3]—
Or him who drinks his pint in fear[4]—
Or him who once when snug abed
Saw Jesus Christ without his head
And tried so hard to win for us
The long-lost works of Eschylus.[5]
But all these men of whom I speak
Make me the sewer of their clique.
That they may dream their dreamy dreams
I carry off their filthy streams
For I can do those things for them
Through which I lost my diadem,
Those things for which Grandmother Church
Left me severely in the lurch.
Thus I relieve their timid arses,
Perform my office of Katharsis.
My scarlet leaves them white as wool.
Through me they purge a bellyful.
To sister mummers one and all
I act as vicar-general,
And for each maiden, shy and nervous,
I do a similar kind service.
For I detect without surprise
That shadowy beauty in her eyes,
The 'dare not' of sweet maidenhood
That answers my corruptive 'would'.
Whenever publicly we meet
She never seems to think of it;
At night when close in bed she lies
And feels my hand between her thighs

[1] Padraic Colum.
[2] W. K. Magee ('John Eglinton').
[3] George Roberts, who referred to 'AE' (George Russell) thus in a poem.
[4] James S. Starkey ('Seumas O'Sullivan').
[5] 'AE' (George Russell).

My little love in light attire
Knows the soft flame that is desire.
But Mammon places under ban
The uses of Leviathan
And that high spirit ever wars
On Mammon's countless servitors,
Nor can they ever be exempt
From this taxation of contempt.
So distantly I turn to view
The shamblings of that motley crew,
Those souls that hate the strength that mine has
Steeled in the school of old Aquinas.
Where they have crouched and crawled and prayed
I stand the self-doomed, unafraid,
Unfellowed, friendless and alone,
Indifferent as the herring-bone,
Firm as the mountain-ridges where
I flash my antlers on the air.
Let them continue as is meet
To adequate the balance-sheet.
Though they may labour to the grave
My spirit shall they never have
Nor make my soul with theirs as one
Till the Mahamanvantara be done:
And though they spurn me from their door
My soul shall spurn them evermore.

166

I HEAR an army charging upon the land,
    And the thunder of horses plunging, foam about their knees:
Arrogant, in black armour, behind them stand,
    Disdaining the reins, with fluttering whips, the charioteers.

They cry unto the night their battle-name:
    I moan in sleep when I hear afar their whirling laughter.
They cleave the gloom of dreams, a blinding flame,
    Clanging, clanging upon the heart as upon an anvil.

They come shaking in triumph their long, green hair:
  They come out of the sea and run shouting by the shore.
My heart, have you no wisdom thus to despair?
  My love, my love, my love, why have you left me alone?

JAMES STEPHENS

1882–1950

167   *Seumas Beg*

A MAN was sitting underneath a tree
Outside the village; and he asked me what
Name was upon this place; and said that he
Was never here before—He told a lot

Of stories to me too. His nose was flat!
I asked him how it happened, and he said
—The first mate of the Holy Ghost did that
With a marling-spike one day; but he was dead,

And jolly good job too; and he'd have gone
A long way to have killed him—Oh, he had
A gold ring in one ear; the other one
—'Was bit off by a crocodile, bedad!'—

That's what he said. He taught me how to chew!
He was a real nice man! He liked me too!

168   *The Cage*

IT tried to get from out the cage;
    Here and there it ran, and tried
    At the edges and the side,
In a busy, timid rage.

Trying yet to find the key
   Into freedom, trying yet,
   In a timid rage, to get
To its old tranquillity.

It did not know, it did not see,
   It did not turn an eye, or care
   That a man was watching there
While it raged so timidly.

It ran without a sound, it tried,
   In a busy, timid rage,
   To escape from out the cage
By the edges and the side.

169   *A Glass of Beer*

THE lanky hank of a she in the inn over there
Nearly killed me for asking the loan of a glass of beer;
May the devil grip the whey-faced slut by the hair,
And beat bad manners out of her skin for a year.

That parboiled ape, with the toughest jaw you will see
On virtue's path, and a voice that would rasp the dead,
Came roaring and raging the minute she looked at me,
And threw me out of the house on the back of my head!

If I asked her master he'd give me a cask a day;
But she, with the beer at hand, not a gill would arrange!
May she marry a ghost and bear him a kitten, and may
The High King of Glory permit her to get the mange.

T. E. HULME
1883–1917

170 *The Embankment*

(The fantasia of a fallen gentleman on a cold, bitter night)

ONCE, in finesse of fiddles found I ecstasy,
In a flash of gold heels on the hard pavement.
Now see I
That warmth's the very stuff of poesy.
Oh, God, make small
The old star-eaten blanket of the sky,
That I may fold it round me and in comfort lie.

171 *Image*

OLD houses were scaffolding once
              and workmen whistling.

JAMES ELROY FLECKER
1884–1915

172 *Oxford Canal*

WHEN you have wearied of the valiant spires of this County Town,
Of its wide white streets and glistening museums, and black monastic
walls,
Of its red motors and lumbering trams, and self-sufficient people,
I will take you walking with me to a place you have not seen—
Half town and half country—the land of the Canal.

It is dearer to me than the antique town: I love it more than the
rounded hills:
Straightest, sublimest of rivers is the long Canal.
I have observed great storms and trembled: I have wept for fear of
the dark.

But nothing makes me so afraid as the clear water of this idle canal
on a summer's noon.

Do you see the great telephone poles down in the water, how every
wire is distinct?

If a body fell into the canal it would rest entangled in those wires
for ever, between earth and air.

For the water is as deep as the stars are high.

One day I was thinking how if a man fell from that lofty pole

He would rush through the water toward me till his image was
scattered by his splash,

When suddenly a train rushed by: the brazen dome of the engine
flashed: the long white carriages roared;

The sun veiled himself for a moment, and the signals loomed in
fog;

A savage woman screamed at me from a barge: little children began
to cry;

The untidy landscape rose to life; a sawmill started;

A cart rattled down to the wharf, and workmen clanged over the
iron footbridge;

A beautiful old man nodded from the first story window of a square
red house,

And a pretty girl came out to hang up clothes in a small delightful
garden.

O strange motion in the suburb of a county town: slow regular
movement of the dance of death!

Men and not phantoms are these that move in light.

Forgotten they live, and forgotten die.

173   *In Hospital*

WOULD I might lie like this, without the pain,
    For seven years—as one with snowy hair,
Who in the high tower dreams his dying reign—

    Lie here and watch the walls—how grey and bare,
The metal bed-post, the uncoloured screen,
    The mat, the jug, the cupboard, and the chair;

And served by an old woman, calm and clean,
    Her misted face familiar, yet unknown,
Who comes in silence, and departs unseen,

And with no other visit, lie alone,
Nor stir, except I had my food to find
    In that dull bowl Diogenes might own.

And down my window I would draw the blind,
    And never look without, but, waiting, hear
A noise of rain, a whistling of the wind,

    And only know that flame-foot Spring is near
By trilling birds, or by the patch of sun
    Crouching behind my curtains. So, in fear,

Noon-dreams should enter, softly, one by one,
    And throng about the floor, and float and play
And flicker on the screen, while minutes run—

    The last majestic minutes of the day—
And with the mystic shadows, Shadow grow.
    Then the grey square of wall should fade away,

And glow again, and open, and disclose
    The shimmering lake in which the planets swim,
And all that lake a dewdrop on a rose.

174   *The Golden Journey to Samarkand*
                    Prologue

WE who with songs beguile your pilgrimage
    And swear that Beauty lives though lilies die,
We Poets of the proud old lineage
    Who sing to find your hearts, we know not why,—

What shall we tell you? Tales, marvellous tales
    Of ships and stars and isles where good men rest,
Where nevermore the rose of sunset pales,
    And winds and shadows fall toward the West:

And there the world's first huge white-bearded kings
    In dim glades sleeping, murmur in their sleep,
And closer round their breasts the ivy clings,
    Cutting its pathway slow and red and deep.

II

And how beguile you? Death has no repose
    Warmer and deeper than that Orient sand
Which hides the beauty and bright faith of those
    Who made the Golden Journey to Samarkand.

And now they wait and whiten peaceably,
    Those conquerors, those poets, those so fair:
They know time comes, not only you and I,
    But the whole world shall whiten, here or there;

When those long caravans that cross the plain
    With dauntless feet and sound of silver bells
Put forth no more for glory or for gain,
    Take no more solace from the palm-girt wells.

When the great markets by the sea shut fast
    All that calm Sunday that goes on and on:
When even lovers find their peace at last,
    And Earth is but a star, that once had shone.

ANNA WICKHAM

1884-1947

175   *The Fired Pot*

IN our town, people live in rows.
The only irregular thing in a street is the steeple;
And where that points to, God only knows,
And not the poor disciplined people!

And I have watched the women growing old,
Passionate about pins, and pence, and soap,
Till the heart within my wedded breast grew cold,
And I lost hope.

But a young soldier came to our town,
He spoke his mind most candidly.
He asked me quickly to lie down,
And that was very good for me.

ANNA WICKHAM

For though I gave him no embrace—
Remembering my duty—
He altered the expression of my face,
And gave me back my beauty.

GILBERT FRANKAU

1884–1952

176 *Gun Teams*

(Loos, September 1915)

THEIR rugs are sodden, their heads are down, their tails are turned to
    the storm:
(Would you know them, you who groomed them in the sleek fat days
    of peace,
When the tiles rang to their pawings in the lighted stalls, and warm,
Now the foul clay cakes on breeching strap and clogs the quick-
    release?)

The blown rain stings; there is never a star; the tracks are rivers of
    slime:
(You must harness-up by guesswork with a failing torch for light,
Instep-deep in unmade standings; for it's active-service time,
And our resting weeks are over, and we move the guns to-night.)

The tyres slither; the traces sag; their blind hoofs stumble and slide;
They are war-worn, they are weary, soaked with sweat and sopped
    with rain:
(You must hold them, you must help them, swing your lead and
    centre wide,
Where the greasy granite *pavé* peters out to squelching drain.)

There is shrapnel bursting a mile in front on the road that the guns
    must take:
(You are thoughtful, you are nervous, you are shifting in your seat,
As you watch the ragged feathers flicker orange, flame and break):
But the teams are pulling steady down the battered village street.

You have shod them cold, and their coats are long, and their bellies
    stiff with the mud;
They have done with gloss and polish, but the fighting heart's un-
    broke . . .
We, who saw them hobbling after us down white roads patched with
    blood,
Patient, wondering why we left them, till we lost them in the smoke;

Who have felt them shiver between our knees, when the shells rain
    black from the skies,
When the bursting terrors find us and the lines stampede as one;
Who have watched the pierced limbs quiver and the pain in stricken
    eyes;
Know the worth of humble servants, foolish-faithful to their gun.

FRANCIS BRETT YOUNG

1884–1954

177   *Seascape*

OVER that morn hung heaviness, until,
Near sunless noon, we heard the ship's bell beating
A melancholy staccato on dead metal;
Saw the bare-footed watch come running aft;
Felt, far below, the sudden telegraph jangle
Its harsh metallic challenge, thrice repeated:
Stand by. Half-speed ahead. Slow. Stop her!
    They stopped.
The plunging pistons sank like a stopt heart:
She held, she swayed, a bulk, a hollow carcass
Of blistered iron that the grey-green, waveless,
Unruffled tropic waters slapped languidly.
Burial at sea! A Portuguese official. . . .
Poor fever-broken devil from Mozambique:
Came on half-tight: the doctor calls it heat-stroke.
Why do they travel steerage? It's the exchange:
So many million reis to the pound.
What did he look like? No one ever saw him:
Took to his bunk, and drank and drank and died.
They're ready! Silence!

                                    We clustered to the rail,
Curious and half-ashamed. The well-deck spread
A comfortable gulf of segregation
Between ourselves and death. *Burial at sea.* . . .
The master holds a black book at arm's length;
His droning voice comes for'ard: *This our brother.* . . .
We therefore commit his body to the deep
To be turned into corruption. . . .
                                    The bo's'n whispers
Hoarsely behind his hand: *Now, all together!*
The hatch-cover is tilted; a mummy of sail-cloth
Well ballasted with iron shoots clear of the poop;
Falls, like a diving gannet. The green sea closes
Its burnished skin; the snaky swell smooths over. . . .
While he, the man of the steerage, goes down, down,
Feet-foremost, sliding swiftly down the dim water:
Swift to escape
Those plunging shapes with pale, empurpled bellies
That swirl and veer about him. He goes down
Unerringly, as though he knew the way
Through green, through gloom, to absolute watery darkness,
Where no weed sways nor curious fin quivers:
To the sad, sunless deeps, where, endlessly,
A downward drift of death spreads its wan mantle
In the wave-moulded valleys that shall enfold him
Till the sea give up its dead.
There shall he lie dispersed amid great riches:
Such gold, such arrogance, so many bold hearts!
All the sunken armadas pressed to powder
By weight of incredible seas! That mingled wrack
No livening sun shall visit till the crust
Of earth be riven, or this rolling planet
Reel on its axis; till the moon-chained tides,
Unloosed, deliver up that white Atlantis,
Whose naked peaks shall bleach above the slaked
Thirst of Sahara, fringed by weedy tangles
Of Atlas's drown'd cedars, frowning Eastward
To where the sands of India lie cold,
And heaped Himalaya's a rib of coral
Slowly uplifted, grain on grain. . . .
                                    We dream
Too long! Another jangle of alarum
Stabs at the engines: *Slow. Half-speed. Full-speed!*

The great bearings rumble; the screw churns, frothing
Opaque water to downward swelling plumes
Milky as woodsmoke. A shoal of flying-fish
Spurts out like animate spray. The warm breeze wakens,
And we pass on, forgetting,
Toward the solemn horizon of bronzed cumulus
That bounds our brooding sea, gathering gloom
That, when night falls, will dissipate in flaws
Of watery lightning, washing the hot sky,
Cleansing all hearts of heat and restlessness,
Until, with day, another blue be born.

WYNDHAM LEWIS

1884–1957

178   *The Song of the Militant Romance*

I

AGAIN let me do a lot of extraordinary talking.
Again let me do a lot!
Let me abound in speeches—let me abound!—publicly polyglot.
Better a blind word to bluster with—better a bad word than none
   lieber Gott!
Watch me push into my witch's vortex all the Englishman's got
To cackle and rattle with—you catch my intention?—to be busily
   balking
The tongue-tied Briton—that is my outlandish plot!

To put a spark in his damp peat—a squib for the Scotchman—
Starch for the Irish—to give a teutonic-cum-Scot
Breadth to all that is slender in Anglo-cum-Oxfordshire-Saxony,
Over-pretty in Eire—to give to this watery galaxy
A Norseman's seasalted stamina, a dram of the Volsung's salt blood.

II

As to the trick of the prosody, the method of conveying the matter,
Frankly I shall provoke the maximum of saxophone clatter.
I shall not take 'limping' iambics, nor borrow from Archilochous
His 'light-horse gallop', nor drive us into a short distich that would
   bog us.

I shall *not* go back to Skeltonics, nor listen to Doctor Guest.
I know with my bold Fourteener I have the measure that suits us best.
I shall drive the matter along as I have driven it from the first,
My peristalsis is well-nigh perfect in burst upon well-timed burst—
I shall drive my coach and four through the strictest of hippical
    treatises,
I do not want to know too closely the number of beats it is.
So shipwreck the nerves to enable the vessel the better to float.
This cockle shell's what it first was built for, and a most seaworthy
    boat.
At roll-call *Byron Dominus* uttered at a fool-school,
Shouted by scottish ushers, caused his lordship to sob like a fool,
Yet Byron was the first to laugh at the over-sensitive Keats
'Snuffed out by an article', those were the words. A couple of rubber
    teats
Should have been supplied beyond any question to these over-touchy
    pets—
For me, you are free to spit your hardest and explode your bloody
    spleen
Regarding my bold compact Fourteener, or my four less than fourteen.

III

So set up a shouting for me! Get a Donnybrook racket on!
Hound down the drosy latin goliaths that clutter the lexicon—
Send a contingent over to intone in our battle-line—
Wrench the trumpet out of the centre of a monkish leonine—
Courtmartial the stripling slackers who dance in the dull Rhyme
    Royal—
Send staggering out all the stammerers who stick round as Chaucer's
    foil—
Dig out the dogs from the doggerel of the hudibrastic couplet—
Hot up the cold-as-mutton songbirds of the plantagenet cabinet!
Go back to the Confessor's palace and disentangle some anglo-saxon,
And borrow a bellow or two from the pictish or from the Manxman.
Set all our mother-tongue reeling, with the eruption of obsolete
    vocables,
Disrupt it with all the grammars, that are ground down to cement it—
    with obstacles
Strew all the cricket pitches, the sleek tennis-lawns of our tongue—
Instal a nasty cold in our larynx—a breathlessness in our lung!

173

IV

But let me have silence always, in the centre of the shouting—
That is essential! Let me have silence so that no pin may drop
And not be heard, and not a whisper escape us for all our spouting,
Nor the needle's scratching upon this gramophone of a circular cosmic
    spot.
Hear me! Mark me! Learn me! Throw the mind's ear open—
Shut up the mind's eye—all will be music! What
Sculpture of sound cannot—what cannot as a fluid token
Words—that nothing else cannot!

V

But when the great blind talking is set up and thoroughly got going—
When you are accustomed to be stunned—
When the thunder of this palaver breaks with a gentle soughing
Of discreet Zephyrs, or of dull surf underground—
Full-roaring, when sinus sinus is outblowing,
Backed up by a bellow of sheer blarney loudest-lunged—
That is the moment to compel from speech
That hybrid beyond language—hybrid only words can reach.

VI

Break out word-storms!—a proper tongue-burst! Split
Our palate down the middle—shatter it!
Give us hare-lip and cross us with a seal
That we may emit the most ear-splitting squeal!
Let words forsake their syntax and ambit—
The dam of all the lexicons gone west!—
Chaos restored, why then by such storms hit
The brain can mint its imagery best.
Whoever heard of perfect sense or perfect rhythm
Matching the magic of extreme verbal schism?

VII

Swept off your feet, be on the look out for the pattern.
It is the chart that matters—the graph is everything!
In such wild weather you cannot look too closely at 'em—
Cleave to the abstract of this blossoming.

I shall, I perhaps should say, make use of a duplicate screen—
And upper and a lower (the pattern lies between)
But most observe the understrapper—the second-string.
The counterpart's the important—keep your eye on the copy—
What's plainest seen is a mere buffer. But if that's too shoppy,
Just say to yourself—'He talks around the compass
To get back at last to the thing that started all the rumpus!'

VIII

Do not expect a work of the classic canon.
Take binoculars to these nests of camouflage—
Spy out what is *half-there*—the page-under-the-page.
Never demand the integral—never completion—
Always what is fragmentary—the promise, the presage—
Eavesdrop upon the soliloquy—stop calling the spade spade—
Neglecting causes always in favour of their effects—
Reading between the lines—surprising things half-made—
Preferring shapes spurned by our intellects.
Plump for the thing, however odd, that's ready to do duty for another,
Sooner than one kowtowing to causation and the living-image of its
    mother.

IX

Do your damnedest! Be yourself! Be an honest-to-goodness sport!
Take all on trust! Shut up the gift-nag's mouth! Batten upon report!
And you'll hear a great deal more, where a sentence breaks in two,
Believe me, than ever the most certificated school-master's darlings do!
When a clause breaks down (that's natural, for it's been probably
    overtaxed)
Or the sense is observed to squint, or in a dashing grammatical tort,
You'll find more of the stuff of poetry than ever in stupid syntax!

I sabotage the sentence! With me is the naked word.
I spike the verb—all parts of speech are pushed over on their backs.
I am the master of all that is half-uttered and imperfectly heard.
Return with me where I am crying out with the gorilla and the bird!

SIR JOHN SQUIRE
1884–1958

Winter Nightfall

THE old yellow stucco
Of the time of the Regent
Is flaking and peeling:
The rows of square windows
In the straight yellow building
   Are empty and still;
And the dusty dark evergreens
Guarding the wicket
Are draped with wet cobwebs,
And above this poor wilderness
Toneless and sombre
   Is the flat of the hill.

They said that a colonel
Who long ago died here
Was the last one to live here:
An old retired colonel,
Some Fraser or Murray,
   I don't know his name;
Death came here and summoned him,
And the shells of him vanished
Beyond all speculation;
And silence resumed here,
Silence and emptiness,
   And nobody came.

Was it wet when he lived here,
Were the skies dun and hurrying,
Was the rain so irresolute?
Did he watch the night coming,
Did he shiver at nightfall,
   Before he was dead?
Did the wind go so creepily,
Chilly and puffing,

With drops of cold rain in it?
Was the hill's lifted shoulder
So lowering and menacing,
   So dark and so dread?

Did he turn through his doorway
And go to his study,
And light many candles?
And fold in the shutters,
And heap up the fireplace
   To fight off the damps?
And muse on his boyhood,
And wonder if India
Ever was real?
And shut out the loneliness
With pig-sticking memoirs
   And collections of stamps?

Perhaps. But he's gone now,
He and his furniture
Dispersed now for ever;
And the last of his trophies,
Antlers and photographs,
   Heaven knows where.
And there's grass in his gateway,
Grass on his footpath,
Grass on his door-step;
The garden's grown over,
The well-chain is broken,
   The windows are bare.

And I leave him behind me,
For the straggling, discoloured
Rags of the daylight,
And hills and stone walls
And a rick long forgotten
   Of blackening hay:
The road pale and sticky,
And cart-ruts and nail-marks,
And wind-ruffled puddles,
And the slop of my footsteps
In this desolate country's
   Cadaverous clay.

The Stockyard
(TO ROBERT FROST)

I

DID you go at all to Chicago?

We came to Chicago over the wide plain,
Travelling all a day on the Illinois plain,
Dappled with distant woodlands and cosy farms.
And the weather as time went on grew constantly colder
And wetter; and we got there at night in a storm.

Did it clear next day?

It was cold and snowed a little,
But we moved about and saw what we went to see.

And what did you go to see?

The University,
A football match, the lake, some Chicago people,
A play at the Opera . . .

You did not go to the Stockyards?

We went to a Stockyard.
We spent a morning there.

I should not have thought it. How could you? What was it like?
Was there cruelty?

I should not say so, nothing so human.
I will tell you. Keep still, if you really want to know.

II

It was cushioned and warm in the car,
And I had a cigar;
But icy outside. A few
Thin snowflakes fell through the air or flew
When a small gust blew.

They spotted the rapid diverging lines
Of buildings, waste-spaces, heaps
Like the litter at tops of mines,
Scabrous cottages, dirty forlorn little shops,
Railroad crossings, canals and telegraph posts. . . .
I watched till monotony tired me,
Then sank away, staring only
At the driver's back and the featureless grey of the sky.

But at last we stopped at a place
Of dingy yards with towering buildings behind,
And backed and turned down a lane between high walls,
Where bumping or halted by doorways
We passed loaded wagons, and horses
Who knew not what service they did there
Plodding in the purlieus of slaughter.
And I thought as I looked about me,
Was it truth when I called it a duty
That a man who ate flesh should come out here,
Being answerable for all that is done here
In this place that I dread to approach?

We came to a yard and the door of a great new building
Square and clean; and up in a lift, and into
A spacious hall and rows of small clerks receding,
At rows of desks, girls and their typewriters,
Inkstands, ledgers, and cords of electric lights;
And then to a neat little office with pictures and carpet
Where a little old man awaited us, smiling and shrewd,
A man with a close white beard and twinkling eyes.
He was witty and kind, he cracked us a few little jokes
About mixing up men with beasts, and the need of guides;
So he rang for guides, and two tidy young men came and fetched us
And we picked up our hats and sticks and walked downstairs:
And I heard at my ear in a quiet sad voice
A sad reproach that I could not answer:
'You have come to see the filthiest thing in the world:
Why have you come to a thing so loathsome,
To ask trite questions and act indifference
As now you are doing before you have started
To stroll through the filthiest place in the world?'

So we stepped out into the cold,
And walked in pairs, wincing at wind and sleet,
Through gates, across gravel, and then to a range of buildings.
The explanations began, my guide talked profusely,
I professed an interest. But my heart was unquiet, afraid,
Trembling with fear at the expectation of strangeness,
Pledged to encounter something I could not guess:
What people? What duties? What infamies done in the light
Yet hid from the world? . . . Who but a fool would come?
Would I go away now if I could? . . . But now was too late,
The threshold was crossed at the lowest plank of a stairway
Rising outside a high wall. Came a whiff of the sty.
We climbed to a gallery running along outside
A windowless wooden loft. They were here for a day,
The hogs who would die to-morrow. They were through that wall.
We must pass, for we did not come to see feeding hogs. . . .
Yet I could not help but linger and peep through a crack:
And there in a filtered light they were scattered about,
Scores of squat steadfast hogs, snouting at roots,
Arrived that day with only a day's respite,
Fattening after a journey, contentedly grunting,
At the rest and the space and the food. . . . No notice would *they* take
Of the new tall sides of the sty, the numerous company,
Yet I looked at them full of fear and awe:
Not pigs did I see but Life in a doom-filled place,
All things and their destiny, not to be understood,
Till my name in a courteous voice broke into my trance:
'We have only an hour and a half: there is much to see.'

The gallery led to a door and we left the sky
And stood among beams by a flat revolving drum.
Pigs slung by the hinder feet went round with that drum
Squealing, and when they had soared and drooped again
A man with a rhythmical knife let blood from their throats,
And they passed down the shed on an endless chain, smoothly,
At regular intervals, pig after pig after pig
Hung downwards, slate-coloured, pouring blood, to vanish
Through a door. The smell came hot and enveloped us round.
I dared not look at the others. I held my breath,
Breathed through my mouth, thought about other things . . .
I had to walk slowly and could not ask to go back.

A sound of perpetual scraping, a warm wet stench . . .
And then, still steaming, moved evenly into a hall
A line of pinkish-white pigs, atrociously naked,
Their unders gashed with a wound from tail to head,
Suspended parallel, a quivering pattern of trunks
And dangling snouts and smooth flapping pointed ears,
A shifting geometrical maze of bodies
That trembled when turning the corners. Men stood at their posts
Jabbing and slicing and plucking. The file moved slowly,
And evenly opposite, over against the chain,
A belt flowed on with tight little heaps that were entrails,
The gaping body above, the entrails below it,
Each pile gliding in line with the belly that owned it,
Till it came in the middle to the front of a blue-smocked figure,
Who worked with his fingers, who dipped and peered and dipped
In time like a clock, a man who would stand all a day,
All a year, all a life, groping and peering in entrails
Watching for something there that would mean disease . . .
I remember: a negro: he'd an armlet 'U.S. Inspector'.

Somewhere the heads went off: when we next stood still
In a narrow high passage, half-hogs came tumbling outward
To the top of an inclined plane of wood, slid down
And stuck at the base a second to be smitten in two.
A dark young man with an axe was standing there,
Lean-waisted, strong-armed; one fancied a mask like a headsman's.
He waited, axe downwards, his eyes looking at us and through us,
His mouth was firm, chin square, he'd a slight dark moustache:
Slavonic perhaps. There was pride and contempt in his eyes,
And nothing else lived in his face to show what he thought.
A carcass rushed down; his hands went steadily upwards,
Then down flew the axe and severed it clean between bones,
To tumble down funnels. . . . I answered ashamed his gaze
As he stood, imperious, erect, his eyes looking forward,
Axe at rest, straight down from his forearm, a waiting headsman,
A figure from allegory, a symbol of Doom.

And beyond were cool chambers where browning hogs of the past
Hung quiet in lines that dwindled away in the distance
In twilight and fume, being cured. The blood was behind us,
The corridors now were steely and bare, and at last

We came to light and the human; in a varnished room
Hams slid in and were placed in paper wrappers,
Packed and sealed by pretty aproned girls,
Dainty and clean like nursery-rhyme dairymaids;
And a clock marked noon as we watched, and they all broke off,
And two of them put their arms round each other's waists,
And went tripping upstairs to their meal, whispering and laughing;
All under the one vast roof with the knives and the steam.

They were hurrying outside in the grey cold yards,
Men and women with anxious faces,
Crossing the yard, hurrying for dinner. . . .
But there was no rest in that place from continuous killing,
The work with the sheep and the cattle went clanking on,
And we threaded the bleak-faced crowd to go on with our day. . . .
A sawdusty room, very clean, surrounded with meat,
Where dealers would come, but none as yet were there;
Cool stores of pieces all still in a blue half-light;
And then a glimpse of the sheep-sheds: an open door
And a flock huddling in, led by a trotting goat
Trained to betray those simpletons; woolly backs
Jammed in the pen, and further, a struggling sheep
Hauled through, and another, then dangling bodies and chains . . .
We passed through a place where a row of throat-cut calves
Hung downwards, their muzzles and tongues dripping blood to the
    floor:
One of them started to kick like a marionette:
We glanced and went on to the largest shed of all.

So at last we stood
In an old black gallery whose wood was dewy with death,
Old death soaked in. Across, there were bullocks entering
From the light to the dimness, patient. Were they conscious of death?
Did they wonder what this was to which they were brought in a herd
Of strange companions, these fields with no pools, no trees,
No grass on the ground, no gentle light from above,
No leisure to kneel and sleep? They were strangely silent;
But once from them came most quiet and pitiful
A brief little lowing, a little plaintive moo,
Like a question that got no answer. There was not another,
No sound but the shuffling of bodies as we sauntered around
And halted above them and gazed right down on their backs.

They stood there stolid like prisoners under a guard,
And were pushed one by one to their end. For beyond a partition
We moved, and could see, directly below us, two men
Half screened by the shadows, and one had a hammer he swung.
The bullock came in and waited, staring ahead,
The hammer leapt down on his head with a loud smack,
And the beast collapsed and crumpled along the ground
To be hooked and slung and raised and swung for the slitting.

But some I saw that, dazed, fell to their knees
And needed a second blow, and one
That came to its knees and looked with uplifted head,
Bewildered, appealing, as against a dread mistake,
And the loud crack drove it down, and it lay like the rest,
And went off like the rest in the gloom and another one came,
And another, another, and passed to the high dark hall,
Where great carcasses slowly moved, or were held by men
With plunging arms, who slashed and stripped and clove.
They were dabbled with blood, the place was all painted with blood,
Splashings and drippings and clots; blood trickled to the gutters
Specked with white fragments of flesh. In the open space
Of the middle men padded about in the dark red slime
Of a flat floor paved with blood. . . .

Dazzled and sick I passed into the light,
Down steps, along scaffolding, moving with the others,
Crossing the firm's museum where they preserve
Relics of the founder's humble beginnings,
A rude machine and photographs of a shop.
I talked and smiled with effort, wishing for solitude
In an air heavy with the neighbourhood of death;
At moments marching mechanically, empty and vague,
Till the thought came back again, dizzying, frightening,
That within those pale insubstantial walls of brick
The wheels of death were grinding, death at each stroke,
Life pouring down a shoot to the dark Pit,
A manufacture of death. And when we were parting,
Shaking hands in the bright white carpeted office
Thanking our host, while floated through the partition
The muted multitudinous tapping of typewriters,
Everything swam before me, I felt like falling,
I saw again that antechamber of slaughter,
And heard the timid lowing of that poor beast. . . .

A varied day, many people, chat about books,
Journeys, sight-seeing, shops. In pauses outdoors,
In streets and courts, at the edge of the ruffled grey lake,
My nostrils were suddenly filled with a scent from the suburbs,
A sickening, pungent, invisible reek blowing in
Over miles of roofs. I set my teeth to my retching,
And told myself, 'It is only wood-smoke from the curing,
It gets in your clothes in those vaults with the files of hams,
Or even if not, if it blows, it is only wood-smoke.'
But a whisper came. 'No, not smoke; it's the scent of death,
The odour of death that hangs always over Chicago.
Chicago lives always in the breath from the caverns of Death,
And her people walk always, knowing it, trying to forget it;
Buying and selling and playing, fringed by that horror,
They smell it and do not speak.'
                               But at night in the Opera
We sat in a box surrounded by pensive faces,
Soft hair, glinting jewels, silks, white elbows on velvet,
Curving around in an arc. There were rows below
Of bare-armed women and quiet white-fronted men,
And far above us, mounting in tiers to the roof,
A slope, thick-speckled with faces. The lights went down,
The people glimmered in shadow all silent, watching
The enchanted gold of the stage, cut square in the darkness.
They saw a pageant of white-cowled monks who chanted,
Feigned worship and grief, a woman dressed as a boy;
They were fired and lifted, comforted, saddened, delighted,
By chains of pearly song, deep organ-like choruses. . . .
Across that circle of thousands
At the summit of civilisation
In a pause of the wandering music
Like the boding voice of disaster
I heard a desolate lowing.
They were happy in song and colour,
Flushed and tender and yearning:
But wanning the air a cloud came over,
A poisonous breath that choked my nostrils.

We talked. The lights went up, then down for a ballet.
In the lovely fairyland world of the stage,
A shepherdess sweetly beribboned
Drooped sighing by a faltering fountain
That sprayed and sobbed in the twilight,

Circled by dark-green bushes
And the pedestalled heads of fauns;
And a ring of shepherds came leaping,
Brown-limbed, in a noiseless motion,
Joining hands and dividing and joining again
To delicate minglings of music. . . . .
O harp and horn and Arcadian pipe!
Again from the marshes of blood beyond
It stole to me, chilling my spirit,
The inveterate miasma of death,
A presence drifting as only I knew
Over all that gaiety, sensibility,
Refinement, innocent playing with toys.
And I thought no longer of only Chicago
But of all our haunted race and its world.
The auditorium was rent like a veil
And I saw in a chasm of infinite darkness
Killing, devouring, and charnel smoking,
Writhing, flames and a rain of blood,
The faceless phantoms of Baal and Moloch . . .
Till it closed and again I resumed my life.

D. H. LAWRENCE

1885–1930

181   *The Collier's Wife*

SOMEBODY's knockin' at th' door
     Mother, come down an' see!
—I's think it's nobbut a beggar;
     Say I'm busy.

It's not a beggar, mother; hark
     How 'ard 'e knocks!
—Eh, tha'rt a mard-arsed kid,
     'E'll gie thee socks!

Shout an' ax what 'e wants,
     I canna come down.
—'E says, is it Arthur Holliday's?
     —Say Yes, tha clown.

'E says: Tell your mother as 'er mester's
  Got hurt i' th' pit——
What? Oh my Sirs, 'e never says that.
  That's not it!

Come out o' th' way an' let me see!
  Eh, there's no peace!
An' stop thy scraightin', childt,
  Do shut thy face!

'Your mester's 'ad a accident
  An' they ta'ein' 'im i' th' ambulance
Ter Nottingham.'—Eh dear o' me,
  If 'e's not a man for mischance!

Wheer's 'e hurt this time, lad?
  —I dunna know,
They on'y towd me it wor bad—
  It would be so!

Out o' my way, childt! dear o' me, wheer
  'Ave I put 'is clean stockin's an' shirt?
Goodness knows if they'll be able
  To take off 'is pit-dirt!

An' what a moan 'e'll make! there niver
  Was such a man for fuss
If anything ailed 'im; at any rate
  I shan't 'ave 'im to nuss.

I do 'ope as it's not very bad!
  Eh, what a shame it seems
As some should ha'e hardly a smite o' trouble
  An' others 'as reams!

It's a shame as 'e should be knocked about
  Like this, I'm sure it is!
'E's 'ad twenty accidents, if 'e's 'ad one;
  Owt bad, an' it's his!

There's one thing, we s'll 'ave a peaceful 'ouse f'r a bit,
  Thank heaven for a peaceful house!
An' there's compensation, sin' it's accident,
  An' club-money—I won't growse.

An' a fork an' a spoon 'e'll want—an' what else?
I s'll never catch that train!
What a traipse it is, if a man gets hurt!
I sh'd think 'e'll get right again.

182   *The Bride*

MY love looks like a girl tonight,
          But she is old.
The plaits that lie along her pillow
          Are not gold,
But threaded with filigree silver,
          And uncanny cold.

She looks like a young maiden, since her brow
          Is smooth and fair;
Her cheeks are very smooth, her eyes are closed,
          She sleeps a rare,
Still, winsome sleep, so still, and so composed.

Nay, but she sleeps like a bride, and dreams her dreams
          Of perfect things.
She lies at last, the darling, in the shape of her dream,
          And her dead mouth sings
By its shape, like thrushes in clear evenings.

183   *The Song of a Man who has Come Through*

NOT I, not I, but the wind that blows through me!
A fine wind is blowing the new direction of Time.
If only I let it bear me, carry me, if only it carry me!
If only I am sensitive, subtle, oh, delicate, a winged gift!
If only, most lovely of all, I yield myself and am borrowed
By the fine, fine wind that takes its course through the chaos of the
    world
Like a fine, an exquisite chisel, a wedge-blade inserted;
If only I am keen and hard like the sheer tip of a wedge
Driven by invisible blows,
The rock will split, we shall come at the wonder, we shall find the
    Hesperides.

Oh, for the wonder that bubbles into my soul,
I would be a good fountain, a good well-head,
Would blur no whisper, spoil no expression.

What is the knocking?
What is the knocking at the door in the night?
It is somebody wants to do us harm.

No, no, it is the three strange angels.
Admit them, admit them.

184   *Kangaroo*

IN the northern hemisphere
Life seems to leap at the air, or skim under the wind
Like stags on rocky ground, or pawing horses, or springly scut-tailed
    rabbits.

Or else rush horizontal to charge at the sky's horizon,
Like bulls or bisons or wild pigs.

Or slip like water slippery towards its ends,
As foxes, stoats, and wolves, and prairie dogs.

Only mice, and moles, and rats, and badgers, and beavers, and perhaps
    bears
Seem belly-plumbed to the earth's mid-navel.
Or frogs that when they leap come flop, and flop to the centre of the
    earth.

But the yellow antipodal Kangaroo, when she sits up,
Who can unseat her, like a liquid drop that is heavy, and just touches
    earth.

The downward drip
The down-urge.
So much denser than cold-blooded frogs.

Delicate mother Kangaroo
Sitting up there rabbit-wise, but huge, plumb-weighted,
And lifting her beautiful slender face, oh! so much more gently and
    finely lined than a rabbit's, or than a hare's,
Lifting her face to nibble at a round white peppermint drop which she
    loves, sensitive mother Kangaroo.

Her sensitive, long, pure-bred face.
Her full antipodal eyes, so dark,
So big and quiet and remote, having watched so many empty dawns in
    silent Australia.

Her little loose hands, and drooping Victorian shoulders.
And then her great weight below the waist, her vast pale belly
With a thin young yellow little paw hanging out, and straggle of a long
    thin ear, like ribbon,
Like a funny trimming to the middle of her belly, thin little dangle of
    an immature paw, and one thin ear.

Her belly, her big haunches
And, in addition, the great muscular python-stretch of her tail.

There, she shan't have any more peppermint drops.
So she wistfully, sensitively sniffs the air, and then turns, goes off in
    slow sad leaps

On the long flat skis of her legs,
Steered and propelled by that steel-strong snake of a tail.

Stops again, half turns, inquisitive to look back.
While something stirs quickly in her belly, and a lean little face comes
    out, as from a window,
Peaked and a bit dismayed,
Only to disappear again quickly away from the sight of the world, to
    snuggle down in the warmth,
Leaving the trail of a different paw hanging out.

Still she watches with eternal, cocked wistfulness!
How full her eyes are, like the full, fathomless, shining eyes of an
    Australian black-boy
Who has been lost so many centuries on the margins of existence!

She watches with insatiable wistfulness.
Untold centuries of watching for something to come,
For a new signal from life, in that silent lost land of the South.

Where nothing bites but insects and snakes and the sun, small life.
Where no bull roared, no cow ever lowed, no stag cried, no leopard
  screeched, no lion coughed, no dog barked,
But all was silent save for parrots occasionally, in the haunted blue
  bush.

Wistfully watching, with wonderful liquid eyes.
And all her weight, all her blood, dripping sack-wise down towards the
  earth's centre,
And the live little-one taking in its paw at the door of her belly.

Leap then, and come down on the line that draws to the earth's deep,
  heavy centre.

185   *Mountain Lion*

CLIMBING through the January snow, into the Lobo Canyon
Dark grow the spruce-trees, blue is the balsam, water sounds still
  unfrozen, and the trail is still evident.

Men!
Two men!
Men! The only animal in the world to fear!

They hesitate
We hesitate.
They have a gun.
We have no gun.

Then we all advance, to meet.

Two Mexicans, strangers, emerging out of the dark and snow and in-
  wardness of the Lobo valley.
What are they doing here on this vanishing trail?

What is he carrying?
Something yellow.
A deer?

Qué tiene, amigo?
León—

He smiles, foolishly, as if he were caught doing wrong.
And we smile, foolishly, as if we didn't know.
He is quite gentle and dark-faced.

It is a mountain lion,
A long, long slim cat, yellow like a lioness.
Dead.

He trapped her this morning, he says, smiling foolishly.
Lift up her face,
Her round, bright face, bright as frost.
Her round, fine-fashioned head, with two dead ears;
And stripes in the brilliant frost of her face, sharp, fine dark rays,
Dark, keen, fine rays in the brilliant frost of her face.
Beautiful dead eyes.

Hermoso es!

They go out towards the open;
We go on into the gloom of Lobo.
And above the trees I found her lair,
A hole in the blood-orange brilliant rocks that stick up, a little cave.
And bones, and twigs, and a perilous ascent.

So, she will never leap up that way again, with the yellow flash of a
mountain lion's long shoot!
And her bright striped frost-face will never watch any more, out of the
shadow of the cave in the blood-orange rock,
Above the trees of the Lobo dark valley-mouth!

Instead, I look out.
And out to the dim of the desert, like a dream, never real;
To the snow of the Sangre de Cristo mountains, the ice of the mountains
of Picoris,
And near across at the opposite steep of snow, green trees motionless
standing in snow, like a Christmas toy.

And I think in this empty world there was room for me and a mountain
  lion.
And I think in the world beyond, how easily we might spare a million
  or two of humans
And never miss them.
Yet what a gap in the world, the missing white frost-face of that slim
  yellow mountain lion!

186   *We Are Transmitters—*

As we live, we are transmitters of life.
And when we fail to transmit life, life fails to flow through us.

That is part of the mystery of sex, it is a flow onwards.
Sexless people transmit nothing.

And if, as we work, we can transmit life into our work,
life, still more life, rushes into us to compensate, to be ready
and we ripple with life through the days.

Even if it is a woman making an apple dumpling, or a man a stool,
if life goes into the pudding, good is the pudding
good is the stool,
content is the woman, with fresh life rippling in to her,
content is the man.

Give, and it shall be given unto you
is still the truth about life.
But giving life is not so easy.
It doesn't mean handing it out to some mean fool, or letting the living
  dead eat you up.
It means kindling the life-quality where it was not,
even if it's only in the whiteness of a washed pocket-handkerchief.

187 *Self-Pity*

I NEVER saw a wild thing
sorry for itself.
A small bird will drop frozen dead from a bough
without ever having felt sorry for itself.

188 *The Gazelle Calf*

THE gazelle calf, O my children,
goes behind its mother across the desert,
goes behind its mother on blithe bare foot
requiring no shoes, O my children!

189 *Little Fish*

THE tiny fish enjoy themselves
in the sea.
Quick little splinters of life,
their little lives are fun to them
in the sea.

190 *The Mosquito Knows—*

THE mosquito knows full well, small as he is
he's a beast of prey.
But after all
he only takes his bellyful,
he doesn't put my blood in the bank.

191 *Stand Up!—*

STAND up, but not for Jesus!
It's a little late for that.
Stand up for justice and a jolly life.
I'll hold your hat.

Stand up, stand up for justice,
ye swindled little blokes!
Stand up and do some punching,
give 'em a few hard pokes.

Stand up for jolly justice
you haven't got much to lose:
a job you don't like and a scanty chance
for a dreary little booze.

Stand up for something different,
and have a little fun
fighting for something worth fighting for
before you've done.

Stand up for a new arrangement
for a chance of life all round,
for freedom, and the fun of living
bust in, and hold the ground!

192 *Shadows*

AND if tonight my soul may find her peace
in sleep, and sink in good oblivion,
and in the morning wake like a new-opened flower
then I have been dipped again in God, and new-created.

And if, as weeks go round, in the dark of the moon
my spirit darkens and goes out, and soft strange gloom
pervades my movements and my thoughts and words
then I shall know that I am walking still
with God, we are close together now the moon's in shadow.

And if, as autumn deepens and darkens
I feel the pain of falling leaves, and stems that break in storms
and trouble and dissolution and distress
and then the softness of deep shadows folding, folding
around my soul and spirit, around my lips
so sweet, like a swoon, or more like the drowse of a low, sad song
singing darker than the nightingale, on, on to the solstice
and the silence of short days, the silence of the year, the shadow,

then I shall know that my life is moving still
with the dark earth, and drenched
with the deep oblivion of earth's lapse and renewal.

And if, in the changing phases of man's life
I fall in sickness and in misery
my wrists seem broken and my heart seems dead
and strength is gone, and my life
is only the leavings of a life:

and still, among it all, snatches of lovely oblivion, and snatches of
    renewal
odd, wintry flowers upon the withered stem, yet new, strange flowers
such as my life has not brought forth before, new blossoms of me—

then I must know that still
I am in the hands [of] the unknown God,
he is breaking me down to his own oblivion
to send me forth on a new morning, a new man.

GERALD GOULD

1885–1936

193   FROM *Monogamy*

You were young—but that was scarcely to your credit:
    Pretty—as one expects the young to be:
    And you were very much in love with me,
And half I lured it on, and half I fled it,
    Till honour turned its foolish face on mine
    Taking for allies music and good wine—
And told me what I ought to say: I said it.

Folk, overawed by so much happiness,
    Decided on a quiet wedding.—Well,
    That doesn't leave the poet much to tell;
The bride was married in a travelling-dress;
    The mothers, weeping, sold remarks by retail;
    Good taste had been observed in every detail;
The quiet wedding was a great success.

And then—the night! the happy sacred night
    With the soft flame of bridal lamps aglow!
    Your white face in its terror moved me so,
I nearly learned life's lesson—but not quite:
    I touched the skirts of Purity-in-Passion;
    Almost, to use the satyr-words of fashion,
Did I forbear to press the husband's right.

One moment, then, we clung together thus,
    Your face down-turned and trembling to my breast,
    My heart desiring only what was best—
The stuff of moments is too perilous;
    But God, perhaps, when we lie racked in Hell,
    Will think—when for one moment we loved well,
How close we were to Him!—and weep for us.

Behold the strife of virtues and of sins,
    Of soul and body!—Let the trumpets sound
    From the four corners of the battle-ground!
The loud and fortunate blaze of war begins!
    —But different is the case with neither pride
    Nor faith nor hope nor love on the soul's side,
Nor good digestion.—So the body wins.

And now we have a boy—like me, they say;
    Also, I think, a little bit like you
    —The pledge of what is wrong between us two;
And night by night, and day by sordid day,
    I must fulfil the blasphemy, and live
    To get the filthy gift not fit to give,
That he may thank me when his hair is grey.

And always through the sunshine, like a tune
  Played softly from a green-and-golden bower,
  The women walk in gentleness of power,
Ready to share, but not with me, their boon:
  Everywhere pass, with lips for me unmoved,
  The lovely ladies that I might have loved,
That never now will love me, late or soon.

O happy girls, discreet in joviality!
  Decoy of fingers and appeal of eyes,
  Summoning the soul to be sincere and wise,
And love not in the flesh, but in totality!
  O loves forbidden, I'll go home and start
  My pipe and light my fire and break my heart,
And read a book on sexual morality.

194

THIS is the horror that, night after night,
  Sits grinning on my pillow—that I meant
  To mix the peace of being innocent
With the warm thrill of seeking out delight:
This is the final blasphemy, the blight
  On all pure purpose and divine intent—
  To dress the selfish thought, the indolent,
In the priest's sable or the angel's white.

For God's sake, if you sin, take pleasure in it,
  And do it for the pleasure. Do not say:
'Behold the spirit's liberty!—a minute
  Will see the earthly vesture break away
And God shine through.' Say: 'Here's a sin—I'll sin it;
  And there's the price of sinning—and I'll pay.'

F. S. FLINT
1885–1960

195

Eau-Forte

ON black bare trees a stale cream moon
Hangs dead, and sours the unborn buds.

Two gaunt old hacks, knees bent, heads low,
Tug, tired and spent, an old horse tram.

Damp smoke, rank mist fill the dark square;
And round the bend six bullocks come.

A hobbling, dirt-grimed drover guides
Their clattering feet—
        their clattering feet!
          to the slaughterhouse.

ANDREW YOUNG
1885–1971

196

Last Snow

ALTHOUGH the snow still lingers
Heaped on the ivy's blunt webbed fingers
And painting tree-trunks on one side,
Here in this sunlit ride
The fresh unchristened things appear,
Leaf, spathe and stem,
With crumbs of earth clinging to them
To show the way they came
But no flower yet to tell their name,
And one green spear
Stabbing a dead leaf from below
Kills winter at a blow.

197 *Wiltshire Downs*

THE cuckoo's double note
Loosened like bubbles from a drowning throat
Floats through the air
In mockery of pipit, lark and stare.

The stable-boys thud by
Their horses slinging divots at the sky
And with bright hooves
Printing the sodden turf with lucky grooves.

As still as a windhover
A shepherd in his flapping coat leans over
His tall sheep-crook
And shearlings, tegs and yoes cons like a book.

And one tree-crowned long barrow
Stretched like a sow that has brought forth her farrow
Hides a king's bones
Lying like broken sticks among the stones.

198 *Culbin Sands*

HERE lay a fair fat land;
  But now its townships, kirks, graveyards
Beneath bald hills of sand
  Lie buried deep as Babylonian shards.

But gales may blow again;
  And like a sand-glass turned about
The hills in a dry rain
  Will flow away and the old land look out;

And where now hedgehog delves
  And conies hollow their long caves
Houses will build themselves
  And tombstones rewrite names on dead men's graves.

199 *The Shepherd's Hut*

THE smear of blue peat smoke
That staggered on the wind and broke,
The only sign of life,
Where was the shepherd's wife,
Who left those flapping clothes to dry,
Taking no thought for her family?
For, as they bellied out
And limbs took shape and waved about,
I thought, She little knows
That ghosts are trying on her children's clothes.

HUMBERT WOLFE

1886–1940

200 *Wardour Street*

THERE'S a small café off the Avenue
    Where Alphonse, that old sinner, used to fix
    A five-course dinner up at one and six,
And trust to luck and youth to pull him through.
I can't remember much about the wine
    Except that it was ninepence for the quart
    Called claret and was nothing of the sort,
Cheap like the rest and like the rest divine.
But Alphonse, I suppose, is long since sped
    And Madame's knitting needles rusted through
    And even Marguerite, like us she flew
To wait on, waited on by death instead.
Well Alphonse, well Madame, well Marguerite!
They've no more use for us in Wardour Street.

201

YOU cannot hope
    to bribe or twist,
thank God! the
    British journalist.

But, seeing what
    the man will do
unbribed, there's
    no occasion to.

FRANCES CORNFORD
1886–1960

202

The Watch

I WAKENED on my hot, hard bed,
Upon the pillow lay my head;
Beneath the pillow I could hear
My little watch was ticking clear.
I thought the throbbing of it went
Like my continual discontent;
I thought it said in every tick:
I am so sick, so sick, so sick;
O Death, come quick, come quick, come quick,
Come quick, come quick, come quick, come quick.

203

Childhood

I USED to think that grown-up people chose
To have stiff backs and wrinkles round their nose,
And veins like small fat snakes on either hand,
On purpose to be grand.
Till through the banisters I watched one day
My great-aunt Etty's friend who was going away,

And how her onyx beads had come unstrung.
I saw her grope to find them as they rolled;
And then I knew that she was helplessly old,
As I was helplessly young.

204   *The Coast : Norfolk*

As on the highway's quiet edge
He mows the grass beside the hedge,
The old man has for company
The distant, grey, salt-smelling sea,
A poppied field, a cow and calf,
The finches on the telegraph.

Across his faded back a hone,
He slowly, slowly scythes alone
In silence of the wind-soft air,
With ladies' bedstraw everywhere,
With whitened corn, and tarry poles,
And far-off gulls like risen souls.

205   *All Souls' Night*

My love came back to me
Under the November tree
Shelterless and dim.
He put his hand upon my shoulder,
He did not think me strange or older,
Nor I, him.

SIEGFRIED SASSOON
1886–1967

206   *Attack*

AT dawn the ridge emerges massed and dun
In the wild purple of the glow'ring sun,
Smouldering through spouts of drifting smoke that shroud
The menacing scarred slope; and, one by one,
Tanks creep and topple forward to the wire.
The barrage roars and lifts. Then, clumsily bowed
With bombs and guns and shovels and battle-gear,
Men jostle and climb to meet the bristling fire.
Lines of grey, muttering faces, masked with fear,
They leave their trenches, going over the top,
While time ticks blank and busy on their wrists,
And hope, with furtive eyes and grappling fists,
Flounders in mud. O Jesus, make it stop!

207   *The General*

'GOOD-MORNING; good-morning!' the General said
When we met him last week on our way to the line.
Now the soldiers he smiled at are most of 'em dead,
And we're cursing his staff for incompetent swine.
'He's a cheery old card,' grunted Harry to Jack
As they slogged up to Arras with rifle and pack.

   .   .   .   .

But he did for them both by his plan of attack.

208   *Falling Asleep*

VOICES moving about in the quiet house:
Thud of feet and a muffled shutting of doors:
Everyone yawning. Only the clocks are alert.

Out in the night there's autumn-smelling gloom
Crowded with whispering trees; across the park
A hollow cry of hounds like lonely bells:
And I know that the clouds are moving across the moon;
The low, red, rising moon. Now herons call
And wrangle by their pool; and hooting owls
Sail from the wood above pale stooks of oats.

Waiting for sleep, I drift from thoughts like these;
And where to-day was dream-like, build my dreams.
Music . . . there was a bright white room below,
And someone singing a song about a soldier,
One hour, two hours ago: and soon the song
Will be '*last night*'; but now the beauty swings
Across my brain, ghost of remembered chords
Which still can make such radiance in my dream
That I can watch the marching of my soldiers,
And count their faces; faces, sunlit faces.

Falling asleep . . . the herons, and the hounds. . . .
September in the darkness; and the world
I've known; all fading past me into peace.

209 *Everyone Sang*

EVERYONE suddenly burst out singing;
And I was filled with such delight
As prisoned birds must find in freedom,
Winging wildly across the white
Orchards and dark-green fields; on—on—and out
    of sight.

Everyone's voice was suddenly lifted;
And beauty came like the setting sun:
My heart was shaken with tears; and horror
Drifted away . . . O, but Everyone
Was a bird; and the song was wordless; the singing
    will never be done.

210 *Sporting Acquaintances*

I WATCHED old squatting Chimpanzee: he traced
His painful patterns in the dirt: I saw
Red-haired Ourang-Utang, whimsical-faced,
Chewing a sportsman's meditative straw.
I'd known them years ago, and half-forgotten
They'd come to grief. (But how, I'd never heard,
Poor beggars!) Still, it seemed so rude and rotten
To stand and gape at them with never a word.

I ventured 'Ages since we met,' and tried
My candid smile of friendship. No success.
One scratched his hairy thigh, while t'other sighed
And glanced away. I saw they liked me less
Than when, on Epsom Downs, in cloudless weather,
We backed The Tetrarch and got drunk together.

211

'*WHEN I'm alone*'—the words tripped off his tongue
As though to be alone were nothing strange.
'*When I was young,*' he said; '*when I was young. . . .*'

I thought of age, and loneliness, and change.
I thought how strange we grow when we're alone,
And how unlike the selves that meet, and talk,
And blow the candles out, and say good-night.
Alone . . . The word is life endured and known.
It is the stillness where our spirits walk
And all but inmost faith is overthrown.

212 *Two Old Ladies*

HERE'S an old lady, almost ninety-one.
Fragile in dark blue velvet, from her chair
She talks to me about Lord Palmerston,
With whom her father 'often took the air'.

I watch her tiny black-lace-mittened hands—
When tea-time's ended—slowly crumble a rusk
For feeding peacocks with. Reflective stands
My memory-mirror in the autumn dusk.

Memory records the scene; and straightway plays
One of its dream-like unexpected tricks;
Transports me forty years to summer days
On time's first page, when I was only six . . .
Miss Clara, deaf and old, alert and queer,
With scraps of bread heaped on a dark blue dish,
Conducts me—I can catch her voice quite clear—
Out to the lily-pond to feed the fish.

RUPERT BROOKE

1887–1915

213 *Success*

I THINK if you had loved me when I wanted;
  If I'd looked up one day, and seen your eyes,
And found my wild sick blasphemous prayer granted,
  And your brown face, that's full of pity and wise,
Flushed suddenly; the white godhead in new fear
  Intolerably so struggling, and so shamed;
Most holy and far, if you'd come all too near,
  If earth had seen Earth's lordliest wild limbs tamed,
Shaken, and trapped, and shivering, for *my* touch—
  Myself should I have slain? or that foul you?
But this the strange gods, who had given so much,
  To have seen and known you, this they might not do.
One last shame's spared me, one black word's unspoken;
And I'm alone; and you have not awoken.

Dust

WHEN the white flame in us is gone,
  And we that lost the world's delight
Stiffen in darkness, left alone
  To crumble in our separate night;

When your swift hair is quiet in death,
  And through the lips corruption thrust
Has stilled the labour of my breath—
  When we are dust, when we are dust!—

Not dead, not undesirous yet,
  Still sentient, still unsatisfied,
We'll ride the air, and shine, and flit,
  Around the places where we died,

And dance as dust before the sun,
  And light of foot, and unconfined,
Hurry from road to road, and run
  About the errands of the wind.

And every mote, on earth or air,
  Will speed and gleam, down later days,
And like a secret pilgrim fare
  By eager and invisible ways,

Nor ever rest, nor ever lie,
  Till, beyond thinking, out of view,
One mote of all the dust that's I
  Shall meet one atom that was you.

Then in some garden hushed from wind,
  Warm in a sunset's afterglow,
The lovers in the flowers will find
  A sweet and strange unquiet grow

Upon the peace; and, past desiring,
  So high a beauty in the air,
And such a light, and such a quiring,
  And such a radiant ecstasy there,

They'll know not if it's fire, or dew,
    Or out of earth, or in the height,
Singing, or flame, or scent, or hue,
    Or two that pass, in light, to light,

Out of the garden higher, higher. . . .
    But in that instant they shall learn
The shattering ecstasy of our fire,
    And the weak passionless hearts will burn

And faint in that amazing glow,
    Until the darkness close above;
And they will know—poor fools, they'll know!—
    One moment, what it is to love.

215   *The Hill*

BREATHLESS, we flung us on the windy hill,
    Laughed in the sun, and kissed the lovely grass.
    You said, 'Through glory and ecstasy we pass;
Wind, sun, and earth remain, the birds sing still,
When we are old, are old. . . .' 'And when we die
    All's over that is ours; and life burns on
Through other lovers, other lips,' said I,
    'Heart of my heart, our heaven is now, is won!'

'We are Earth's best, that learnt her lesson here.
    Life is our cry. We have kept the faith!' we said;
    'We shall go down with unreluctant tread
Rose-crowned into the darkness!' . . . Proud we were,
And laughed, that had such brave true things to say.
—And then you suddenly cried, and turned away.

216   *The Old Vicarage, Grantchester*
          (*Café des Westens, Berlin, May 1912*)

JUST now the lilac is in bloom,
All before my little room;
And in my flower-beds, I think,
Smile the carnation and the pink;
And down the borders, well I know,
The poppy and the pansy blow . . .
Oh! there the chestnuts, summer through,
Beside the river make for you
A tunnel of green gloom, and sleep
Deeply above; and green and deep
The stream mysterious glides beneath,
Green as a dream and deep as death.
—Oh, damn! I know it! and I know
How the May fields all golden show,
And when the day is young and sweet,
Gild gloriously the bare feet
That run to bathe . . .
                Du lieber Gott!

Here am I, sweating, sick, and hot,
And there the shadowed waters fresh
Lean up to embrace the naked flesh.
Temperamentvoll German Jews
Drink beer around;—and *there* the dews
Are soft beneath a morn of gold.
Here tulips bloom as they are told;
Unkempt about those hedges blows
An English unofficial rose;
And there the unregulated sun
Slopes down to rest when day is done,
And wakes a vague unpunctual star,
A slippered Hesper; and there are
Meads towards Haslingfield and Coton
Where *das Betreten*'s not *verboten.*

εἴθε γενοίμην . . . would I were
In Grantchester, in Grantchester!—
Some, it may be, can get in touch
With Nature there, or Earth, or such.
And clever modern men have seen
A Faun a-peeping through the green,
And felt the Classics were not dead,
To glimpse a Naiad's reedy head,
Or hear the Goat-foot piping low: . . .
But these are things I do not know.
I only know that you may lie
Day-long and watch the Cambridge sky,
And, flower-lulled in sleepy grass,
Hear the cool lapse of hours pass,
Until the centuries blend and blur
In Grantchester, in Grantchester. . . .
Still in the dawnlit waters cool
His ghostly Lordship swims his pool,
And tries the strokes, essays the tricks,
Long learnt on Hellespont, or Styx.
Dan Chaucer hears his river still
Chatter beneath a phantom mill.
Tennyson notes, with studious eye,
How Cambridge waters hurry by . . .
And in that garden, black and white,
Creep whispers through the grass all night;
And spectral dance, before the dawn,
A hundred Vicars down the lawn;
Curates, long dust, will come and go
On lissom, clerical, printless toe;
And oft between the boughs is seen
The sly shade of a Rural Dean . . .
Till, at a shiver in the skies,
Vanishing with Satanic cries,
The prim ecclesiastic rout
Leaves but a startled sleeper-out,
Grey heavens, the first bird's drowsy calls,
The falling house that never falls.

God! I will pack, and take a train,
And get me to England once again!
For England's the one land, I know,
Where men with Splendid Hearts may go;

And Cambridgeshire, of all England,
The shire for Men who Understand;
And of *that* district I prefer
The lovely hamlet Grantchester.
For Cambridge people rarely smile,
Being urban, squat, and packed with guile;
And Royston men in the far South
Are black and fierce and strange of mouth;
At Over they fling oaths at one,
And worse than oaths at Trumpington,
And Ditton girls are mean and dirty,
And there's none in Harston under thirty,
And folks in Shelford and those parts
Have twisted lips and twisted hearts,
And Barton men make Cockney rhymes,
And Coton's full of nameless crimes,
And things are done you'd not believe
At Madingley, on Christmas Eve.
Strong men have run for miles and miles,
When one from Cherry Hinton smiles;
Strong men have blanched, and shot their wives,
Rather than send them to St. Ives;
Strong men have cried like babes, bydam,
To hear what happened at Babraham.
But Grantchester! ah, Grantchester!
There's peace and holy quiet there,
Great clouds along pacific skies,
And men and women with straight eyes,
Lithe children lovelier than a dream,
A bosky wood, a slumbrous stream,
And little kindly winds that creep
Round twilight corners, half asleep.
In Grantchester their skins are white;
They bathe by day, they bathe by night;
The women there do all they ought;
The men observe the Rules of Thought.
They love the Good; they worship Truth;
They laugh uproariously in youth;
(And when they get to feeling old,
They up and shoot themselves, I'm told) . . .

Ah God! to see the branches stir
Across the moon at Grantchester!
To smell the thrilling-sweet and rotten
Unforgettable, unforgotten
River-smell, and hear the breeze
Sobbing in the little trees.
Say, do the elm-clumps greatly stand
Still guardians of that holy land?
The chestnuts shade, in reverend dream,
The yet unacademic stream?
Is dawn a secret shy and cold
Anadyomene, silver-gold?
And sunset still a golden sea
From Haslingfield to Madingley?
And after, ere the night is born,
Do hares come out about the corn?
Oh, is the water sweet and cool,
Gentle and brown, above the pool?
And laughs the immortal river still
Under the mill, under the mill?
Say, is there Beauty yet to find?
And Certainty? and Quiet kind?
Deep meadows yet, for to forget
The lies, and truths, and pain? . . . oh! yet
Stands the Church clock at ten to three?
And is there honey still for tea?

217   *Clouds*

DOWN the blue night the unending columns press
   In noiseless tumult, break and wave and flow,
   Now tread the far South, or lift rounds of snow
Up to the white moon's hidden loveliness.
Some pause in their grave wandering comradeless,
   And turn with profound gesture vague and slow,
   As who would pray good for the world, but know
Their benediction empty as they bless.

They say that the Dead die not, but remain
  Near to the rich heirs of their grief and mirth.
    I think they ride the calm mid-heaven, as these,
In wise majestic melancholy train,
    And watch the moon, and the still-raging seas,
  And men, coming and going on the earth.

218   *The Soldier*

IF I should die, think only this of me:
  That there's some corner of a foreign field
That is for ever England. There shall be
  In that rich earth a richer dust concealed;
A dust whom England bore, shaped, made aware,
  Gave, once, her flowers to love, her ways to roam,
A body of England's, breathing English air,
  Washed by the rivers, blest by suns of home.

And think, this heart, all evil shed away,
  A pulse in the eternal mind, no less
    Gives somewhere back the thoughts by England given;
Her sights and sounds; dreams happy as her day;
  And laughter, learnt of friends; and gentleness,
    In hearts at peace, under an English heaven.

EDWIN MUIR

1887–1959

219   *Suburban Dream*

WALKING the suburbs in the afternoon
In summer when the idle doors stand open
  And the air flows through the rooms
  Fanning the curtain hems,

You wander through a cool elysium
Of women, schoolgirls, children, garden talks,
  With a schoolboy here and there
  Conning his history book.

The men are all away in offices,
Committee-rooms, laboratories, banks,
  Or pushing cotton goods
  In Wick or Ilfracombe.

The massed unanimous absence liberates
The light keys of the piano and sets free
  Chopin and everlasting youth,
  Now, with the masters gone.

And all things turn to images of peace,
The boy curled over his book, the young girl poised
  On the path as if beguiled
  By the silence of a wood.

It is a child's dream of a grown-up world.
But soon the brazen evening clocks will bring
  The tramp of feet and brisk
  Fanfare of motor horns
  And the masters come.

220   *Love's Remorse*

I FEEL remorse for all that time has done
To you, my love, as if myself, not time,
Had set on you the never-resting sun
And the little deadly days, to work this crime.

For not to guard what by such grace was given,
But leave it for the idle hours to take,
Let autumn bury away our summer heaven:
To such a charge what answer can I make

But the old saw still by the heart retold,
'Love is exempt from time.' And that is true.
But we, the loved and the lover, we grow old;
Only the truth, the truth is always new:

'Eternity alone our wrong can right,
That makes all young again in time's despite.'

221 *Scotland's Winter*

Now the ice lays its smooth claws on the sill,
The sun looks from the hill
Helmed in his winter casket,
And sweeps his arctic sword across the sky.
The water at the mill
Sounds more hoarse and dull.
The miller's daughter walking by
With frozen fingers soldered to her basket
Seems to be knocking
Upon a hundred leagues of floor
With her light heels, and mocking
Percy and Douglas dead,
And Bruce on his burial bed,
Where he lies white as may
With wars and leprosy,
And all the kings before
This land was kingless,
And all the singers before
This land was songless,
This land that with its dead and living waits the Judgment Day.
But they, the powerless dead,
Listening can hear no more
Than a hard tapping on the sounding floor
A little overhead
Of common heels that do not know
Whence they come or where they go
And are content
With their poor frozen life and shallow banishment.

222 *The Horses*

Barely a twelvemonth after
The seven days war that put the world to sleep,
Late in the evening the strange horses came.
By then we had made our covenant with silence,
But in the first few days it was so still
We listened to our breathing and were afraid.

On the second day
The radios failed; we turned the knobs; no answer.
On the third day a warship passed us, heading north,
Dead bodies piled on the deck. On the sixth day
A plane plunged over us into the sea. Thereafter
Nothing. The radios dumb;
And still they stand in corners of our kitchens,
And stand, perhaps, turned on, in a million rooms
All over the world. But now if they should speak,
If on a sudden they should speak again,
If on the stroke of noon a voice should speak,
We would not listen, we would not let it bring
That old bad world that swallowed its children quick
At one great gulp. We would not have it again.
Sometimes we think of the nations lying asleep,
Curled blindly in impenetrable sorrow,
And then the thought confounds us with its strangeness.
The tractors lie about our fields; at evening
They look like dank sea-monsters couched and waiting.
We leave them where they are and let them rust:
'They'll moulder away and be like other loam'.
We make our oxen drag our rusty ploughs,
Long laid aside. We have gone back
Far past our fathers' land.
                              And then, that evening
Late in the summer the strange horses came.
We heard a distant tapping on the road,
A deepening drumming; it stopped, went on again
And at the corner changed to hollow thunder.
We saw the heads
Like a wild wave charging and were afraid.
We had sold our horses in our fathers' time
To buy new tractors. Now they were strange to us
As fabulous steeds set on an ancient shield
Or illustrations in a book of knights.
We did not dare go near them. Yet they waited,
Stubborn and shy, as if they had been sent
By an old command to find our whereabouts
And that long-lost archaic companionship.
In the first moment we had never a thought
That they were creatures to be owned and used.
Among them were some half-a-dozen colts
Dropped in some wilderness of the broken world,

Yet new as if they had come from their own Eden.
Since then they have pulled our ploughs and borne our loads,
But that free servitude still can pierce our hearts.
Our life is changed; their coming our beginning.

EDITH SITWELL

1887–1964

223   *Sir Beelzebub*

WHEN
Sir
Beelzebub called for his syllabub in the hotel in Hell
      Where Proserpine first fell,
Blue as the gendarmerie were the waves of the sea,
      (Rocking and shocking the barmaid).

Nobody comes to give him his rum but the
Rim of the sky hippopotamus-glum
Enhances the chances to bless with a benison
Alfred Lord Tennyson crossing the bar laid
With cold vegetation from pale deputations
Of temperance workers (all signed In Memoriam)
Hoping with glory to trip up the Laureate's feet,
      (Moving in classical metres) . . .

Like Balaclava, the lava came down from the
Roof, and the sea's blue wooden gendarmerie
Took them in charge while Beelzebub roared for his rum.
      . . . None of them come!

224   FROM *The Sleeping Beauty*

IN the great gardens, after bright spring rain,
We find sweet innocence come once again,
White periwinkles, little pensionnaires
With muslin gowns and shy and candid airs,

That under saint-blue skies, with gold stars sown,
Hide their sweet innocence by spring winds blown,
From zephyr libertines that like Richelieu
And d'Orsay their gold-spangled kisses blew;

And lilies of the valley whose buds blond and tight
Seem curls of little school-children that light
The priests' procession, when on some saint's day
Along the country paths they make their way;

Forget-me-nots, whose eyes of childish blue,
Gold-starred like heaven, speak of love still true;
And all the flowers that we call 'dear heart,'
Who say their prayers like children, then depart

Into the dark. Amid the dew's bright beams
The summer airs, like Weber waltzes, fall
Round the first rose who, flushed with her youth, seems
Like a young Princess dressed for her first ball:

Who knows what beauty ripens from dark mould
After the sad wind and the winter's cold?—
But a small wind sighed, colder than the rose
Blooming in desolation, 'No one knows.'

225   *Heart and Mind*

SAID the Lion to the Lioness—'When you are amber dust,—
No more a raging fire like the heat of the Sun
(No liking but all lust)—
Remember still the flowering of the amber blood and bone,
The rippling of bright muscles like a sea,
Remember the rose-prickles of bright paws
Though we shall mate no more
Till the fire of that sun the heart and the moon-cold bone are one.'

Said the Skeleton lying upon the sands of Time—
'The great gold planet that is the mourning heat of the Sun
Is greater than all gold, more powerful
Than the tawny body of a Lion that fire consumes
Like all that grows or leaps . . . so is the heart

More powerful than all dust. Once I was Hercules
Or Samson, strong as the pillars of the seas:
But the flames of the heart consumed me, and the mind
Is but a foolish wind.'

Said the Sun to the Moon—'When you are but a lonely white crone,
And I, a dead King in my golden armour somewhere in a dark wood,
Remember only this of our hopeless love
That never till Time is done
Will the fire of the heart and the fire of the mind be one.'

226   *The Shadow of Cain*

TO C. M. BOWRA

UNDER great yellow flags and banners of the ancient Cold
Began the huge migrations
From some primeval disaster in the heart of Man.

There were great oscillations
Of temperature. . . . You knew there had once been warmth;

But the Cold is the highest mathematical Idea . . . the Cold is Zero—
The Nothing from which arose
All Being and all variation. . . . It is the sound too high for our hearing,
    the Point that flows

Till it becomes the line of Time . . . an endless positing
Of Nothing, or the Ideal that tries to burgeon
Into Reality through multiplying. Then Time froze

To immobility and changed to Space.
Black flags among the ice, blue rays
And the purple perfumes of the polar Sun
Freezing the bone to sapphire and to zircon—
These were our days.

And now in memory of great oscillations
Of temperature in that epoch of the Cold,
We found a continent of turquoise, vast as Asia
In the yellowing airs of the Cold: the tooth of a mammoth;
And there, in a gulf, a dark pine-sword

To show there had once been warmth and the gulf stream in our veins
Where only the Chaos of the Antarctic Pole
Or the peace of its atonic coldness reigns.

And sometimes we found the trace
Of a bird's claw in the immensity of the Cold:
The trace of the first letters we could not read:
Some message of Man's need,

And of the slow subsidence of a Race;
And of great heats in which the Pampean mud was formed,
In which the Megatherium Mylodon
Lies buried under Mastodon-trumpetings of leprous Suns.

The Earth had cloven in two in that primal disaster.
But when the glacial period began
There was still some method of communication
Between Man and his brother Man—
Although their speech
Was alien, each from each
As the Bird's from the Tiger's, born from the needs of our opposing
    famines.

Each said 'This is the Race of the Dead . . . their blood is cold. . . .
For the heat of those more recent on the Earth
Is higher . . . the blood-beat of the Bird more high
Than that of the ancient race of the primeval Tiger':
The Earth had lived without the Bird

In that Spring when there were no flowers like thunders in the air.
And now the Earth lies flat beneath the shade of an iron wing.
And of what does the Pterodactyl sing—
Of what red buds in what tremendous Spring?'

The thunders of the Spring began. . . . We came again
After that long migration
To the city built before the Flood by our brother Cain.

And when we reached an open door
The Fate said 'My feet ache.'
The Wanderers said 'Our hearts ache.'

There was great lightning
In flashes coming to us over the floor:
The Whiteness of the Bread—
The Whiteness of the Dead—
The Whiteness of the Claw—
All this coming to us in flashes through the open door.

There were great emerald thunders in the air
In the violent Spring, the thunders of the sap and the blood in the
    heart
—The Spiritual Light, the physical Revelation.

In the streets of the City of Cain there were great Rainbows
Of emeralds: the young people, crossing and meeting.

And everywhere
The great voice of the Sun in sap and bud
Fed from the heart of Being, the panic Power,
The sacred Fury, shouts of Eternity
To the blind eyes, the heat in the wingèd seed, the fire in the blood.

And through the works of Death,
The dust's aridity, is heard the sound
Of mounting saps like monstrous bull-voices of unseen fearful mimes:
And the great rolling world-wide thunders of that drumming under-
    ground

Proclaim our Christ, and roar 'Let there be harvest!
Let there be no more Poor—
For the Son of God is sowed in every furrow!'

We did not heed the Cloud in the Heavens shaped like the hand
Of Man. . . . But there came a roar as if the Sun and Earth had come
    together—
The Sun descending and the Earth ascending
To take its place above . . . the Primal Matter
Was broken, the womb from which all life began.
Then to the murdered Sun a totem pole of dust arose in memory of
    Man.

The cataclysm of the Sun down-pouring
Seemed the roar
Of those vermilion Suns the drops of the blood
That bellowing like Mastodons at war
Rush down the length of the world—away—away—

The violence of torrents, cataracts, maelstroms, rains
That went before the Flood—
These covered the earth from the freshets of our brothers' veins;

And with them, the forked lightnings of the gold
From the split mountains,
Blasting their rivals, the young foolish wheat-ears
Amid those terrible rains.

The gulf that was torn across the world seemed as if the beds of all the
    Oceans
Were emptied. . . . Naked, and gaping at what once had been the Sun,
Like the mouth of the Universal Famine
It stretched its jaws from one end of the Earth to the other.

And in that hollow lay the body of our brother
Lazarus, upheaved from the world's tomb.
He lay in that great Death like the gold in the husk
Of the world . . . and round him, like spent lightnings, lay the Ore—
The balm for the world's sore.

And the gold lay in its husk of rough earth like the core
In the furred almond, the chestnut in its prickly
Bark, the walnut in a husk green and bitter.

And to that hollow sea
The civilisation of the Maimed, and, too, Life's lepers, came
As once to Christ near the Sea of Galilee.

They brought the Aeons of Blindness and the Night
Of the World, crying to him, 'Lazarus, give us sight!
O you whose sores are of gold, who are the new Light
Of the World!'
                They brought to the Tomb
The Condemned of Man, who wear as stigmata from the womb
The depression of the skull as in the lesser
Beasts of Prey, the marks of Ape and Dog,
The canine and lemurine muscle . . . the pitiable, the terrible,
The loveless, whose deformities arose
Before their birth, or from a betrayal by the gold wheatear.
'Lazarus, for all love we knew the great Sun's kiss

On the loveless cheek. He came to the dog-fang and the lion-claw
That Famine gave the empty mouth, the workless hands.
He came to the inner leaf of the forsaken heart—
He spoke of our Christ, and of a golden love. . . .
But our Sun is gone . . . will your gold bring warmth to the loveless
    lips, and harvest to barren lands?'

Then Dives was brought. . . . He lay like a leprous Sun
That is covered with the sores of the world . . . the leprosy
Of gold encrusts the world that was his heart.

Like a great ear of wheat that is swoln with grain,
Then ruined by white rain,
He lay. . . . His hollow face, dust white, was cowled with a hood of
    gold:
But you saw there was no beat or pulse of blood—
You would not know him now from Lazarus!

He did not look at us.
He said 'What was spilt still surges like the Flood.
But Gold shall be the Blood
Of the world. . . . Brute gold condensed to the primal essence
Has the texture, smell, warmth, colour of Blood. We must take

A quintessence of the disease for remedy. Once hold
The primal matter of all gold—
From which it grows
(That Rose of the World) as the sharp clear tree from the seed of the
    great rose,

Then give of this, condensed to the transparency
Of the beryl, the weight of twenty barley grains:
And the leper's face will be full as the rose's face
After great rains.

It will shape again the Shadow of Man. Or at least will take
From all roots of life the symptoms of the leper—
And make the body sharp as the honeycomb,
The roots of life that are left like the red roots of the rose-branches.'

But near him a gold sound—
The voice of an unborn wheat-ear accusing Dives—
Said 'Soon I shall be more rare, more precious than gold.'

There are no thunders, there are no fires, no suns, no earthquakes
Left in our blood. . . . But yet like the rolling thunders of all the fires
   in the world, we cry
To Dives: 'You are the shadow of Cain. Your shade is the primal
   Hunger.'
'I lie under what condemnation?'
'The same as Adam, the same as Cain, the same as Sodom, the same as
   Judas.

'And the fires of your Hell shall not be quenched by the rain
From those torn and parti-coloured garments of Christ, those rags
That once were Men. Each wound, each stripe,
Cries out more loudly than the voice of Cain—
Saying "Am I my brother's keeper?" ' Think! When the last clamour
   of the Bought and Sold
The agony of Gold
Is hushed. . . . When the last Judas-kiss
Has died upon the cheek of the Starved Man Christ, those ashes that
   were men
Will rise again
To be our Fires upon the Judgment Day!
And yet—who dreamed that Christ has died in vain?
He walks again on the Seas of Blood, He comes in the terrible Rain.

SUSAN MILES
(URSULA ROBERTS)

1887–

227   *Microcosmos*

THE brown-faced nurse has murmured something unintelligible
And is clucking distressedly.
She is apparently perturbed because I have not eaten my dinner.
Deprecatingly she takes from the chair by my bed
The heavy plate of liver and rice which I have not touched.
She turns the rice with a slow-moving fork
And gently proffers a brown chunk of liver cased in congealing gravy.
I raise myself in the bed and hold up my mouth.
But the stitch in my wound is pricking me,

And the smell of the liver makes me sick.
Through the wall beside me
Penetrates the sound of sobbing from the Sergeant's wife,
Whose baby is dead.
'Memsahib cry,' the brown-faced nurse is murmuring.
'Memsahib cry, cry, cry—all the day,
All the night.
Memsahib never smile; only cry.
Memsahib not happy. No.'
As she moves away
Her kind eyes are filled with tenderness
And with deep and impotent pity
For the sobbing woman.

Carrying on her fore-arm a minute bundle,
The Sister enters.
She has brought for my inspection a brown baby,
Aged twenty minutes.
She tells me that his child mother
Has died.
The baby clenches frail and infinitesimal fists,
And makes vague movements with pale curled feet.
His unseeing eyes stare through the Sister's pity-wrenched face.
She speaks rapidly and a little brusquely,
Fearing lest her voice should sound blurred by emotion.
Now she has thrown me a quick jest
And is gone.

From across the compound creeps a child,
Naked and inevitable.
She squats on the verandah near my bed,
And surveys me with patient eyes.
I fold my hands upon the bed-clothes
And watch her,
Patient too.
Her utterances, which are many,
Are wholly unintelligible to me.
Around her neck yellow marigolds
Dangle in rich beauty.
She holds them out, proudly:
And babbles, proudly.
Now she has ceased to hold out
The marigolds.
She is pointing,

Apparently with equal pride,
To the sores on her little body,
And she is babbling, exultantly it seems,
Of them.

And while I listen to her unintelligible babble,
As she displays now her marigolds,
Now her sores,
Her little voice becomes for me the voice
Of the unintelligible universe,
Beautiful and appalling.

JULIAN GRENFELL

1888–1915

228 *Into Battle*

THE naked earth is warm with Spring,
   And with green grass and bursting trees
Leans to the sun's gaze glorying,
   And quivers in the sunny breeze;

And life is colour and warmth and light,
   And a striving evermore for these;
And he is dead who will not fight;
   And who dies fighting has increase.

The fighting man shall from the sun
   Take warmth, and life from the glowing earth;
Speed with the light-foot winds to run,
   And with the trees to newer birth;
And find, when fighting shall be done,
   Great rest, and fullness after dearth.

All the bright company of Heaven
   Hold him in their high comradeship,
The Dog-Star, and the Sisters Seven,
   Orion's Belt and sworded hip.

The woodland trees that stand together,
   They stand to him each one a friend;
They gently speak in the windy weather;
   They guide to valley and ridge's end.

The kestrel hovering by day,
   And the little owls that call by night,
Bid him be swift and keen as they,
   As keen of ear, as swift of sight.

The blackbird sings to him, 'Brother, brother,
   If this be the last song you shall sing,
Sing well, for you may not sing another;
   Brother, sing.'

In dreary, doubtful waiting hours,
   Before the brazen frenzy starts,
The horses show him nobler powers;
   O patient eyes, courageous hearts!

And when the burning moment breaks,
   And all things else are out of mind,
And only joy of battle takes
   Him by the throat, and makes him blind,

Through joy and blindness he shall know,
   Not caring much to know, that still
Nor lead nor steel shall reach him, so
   That it be not the Destined Will.

The thundering line of battle stands,
   And in the air Death moans and sings;
But Day shall clasp him with strong hands,
   And Night shall fold him in soft wings.

F. W. HARVEY
1888–1957

229 *November*

HE has hanged himself—the Sun.
   He dangles
A scarecrow in thin air.

He is dead for love—the Sun,
   He who in forest tangles
Wooed all things fair

That great lover—the Sun,
   Now spangles
The wood with blood-stains.

He has hanged himself—the Sun.
   How thin he dangles
In these gray rains!

T. S. ELIOT
1888–1965

230 *The Love Song of J. Alfred Prufrock*

S'io credessi che mia risposta fosse
a persona che mai tornasse al mondo,
questa fiamma staria senza più scosse.
Ma per ciò che giammai di questo fondo
non tornò vivo alcun, s'i'odo il vero,
senza tema d'infamia ti rispondo.

LET us go then, you and I,
When the evening is spread out against the sky
Like a patient etherised upon a table;
Let us go, through certain half-deserted streets,
The muttering retreats

Of restless nights in one-night cheap hotels
And sawdust restaurants with oyster-shells:
Streets that follow like a tedious argument
Of insidious intent
To lead you to an overwhelming question . . .
Oh, do not ask, 'What is it?'
Let us go and make our visit.

In the room the women come and go
Talking of Michelangelo.

The yellow fog that rubs its back upon the window-panes,
The yellow smoke that rubs its muzzle on the window-panes,
Licked its tongue into the corners of the evening,
Lingered upon the pools that stand in drains,
Let fall upon its back the soot that falls from chimneys,
Slipped by the terrace, made a sudden leap,
And seeing that it was a soft October night,
Curled once about the house, and fell asleep.

And indeed there will be time
For the yellow smoke that slides along the street
Rubbing its back upon the window-panes;
There will be time, there will be time
To prepare a face to meet the faces that you meet;
There will be time to murder and create,
And time for all the works and days of hands
That lift and drop a question on your plate;
Time for you and time for me,
And time yet for a hundred indecisions,
And for a hundred visions and revisions,
Before the taking of a toast and tea.

In the room the women come and go
Talking of Michelangelo.

And indeed there will be time
To wonder, 'Do I care?' and, 'Do I dare?'
Time to turn back and descend the stair,
With a bald spot in the middle of my hair—
(They will say: 'How his hair is growing thin!')
My morning coat, my collar mounting firmly to the chin,
My necktie rich and modest, but asserted by a simple pin—

(They will say: 'But how his arms and legs are thin!')
Do I dare
Disturb the universe?
In a minute there is time
For decisions and revisions which a minute will reverse.

For I have known them all already, known them all—
Have known the evenings, mornings, afternoons,
I have measured out my life with coffee spoons;
I know the voices dying with a dying fall
Beneath the music from a farther room.
  So how should I presume?

And I have known the eyes already, known them all—
The eyes that fix you in a formulated phrase,
And when I am formulated, sprawling on a pin,
When I am pinned and wriggling on the wall,
Then how should I begin
To spit out all the butt-ends of my days and ways?
  And how should I presume?

And I have known the arms already, known them all—
Arms that are braceleted and white and bare
(But in the lamplight, downed with light brown hair!)
Is it perfume from a dress
That makes me so digress?
Arms that lie along a table, or wrap about a shawl.
  And should I then presume?
  And how should I begin?

        .   .   .   .

Shall I say, I have gone at dusk through narrow streets
And watched the smoke that rises from the pipes
Of lonely men in shirt-sleeves, leaning out of windows? . . .

I should have been a pair of ragged claws
Scuttling across the floors of silent seas.

        .   .   .   .

And the afternoon, the evening, sleeps so peacefully!
Smoothed by long fingers,
Asleep . . . tired . . . or it malingers,
Stretched on the floor, here beside you and me.
Should I, after tea and cakes and ices,
Have the strength to force the moment to its crisis?

But though I have wept and fasted, wept and prayed,
Though I have seen my head (grown slightly bald) brought in upon a
     platter,
I am no prophet—and here's no great matter;
I have seen the moment of my greatness flicker,
And I have seen the eternal Footman hold my coat, and snicker,
And in short, I was afraid.

   And would it have been worth it, after all,
After the cups, the marmalade, the tea,
Among the porcelain, among some talk of you and me,
Would it have been worth while,
To have bitten off the matter with a smile,
To have squeezed the universe into a ball
To roll it towards some overwhelming question,
To say: 'I am Lazarus, come from the dead,
Come back to tell you all, I shall tell you all'—
If one, settling a pillow by her head,
     Should say: 'That is not what I meant at all.
     That is not it, at all.'

   And would it have been worth it, after all,
Would it have been worth while,
After the sunsets and the dooryards and the sprinkled streets,
After the novels, after the teacups, after the skirts that trail along the
     floor—
And this, and so much more?—
It is impossible to say just what I mean!
But as if a magic lantern threw the nerves in patterns on a screen:
Would it have been worth while
If one, settling a pillow or throwing off a shawl,
And turning toward the window, should say:
     'That is not it at all,
     That is not what I meant, at all.'

                .   .   .   .   .

   No! I am not Prince Hamlet, nor was meant to be;
Am an attendant lord, one that will do
To swell a progress, start a scene or two,
Advise the prince; no doubt, an easy tool,
Deferential, glad to be of use,
Politic, cautious, and meticulous;

Full of high sentence, but a bit obtuse;
At times, indeed, almost ridiculous—
Almost, at times, the Fool.

I grow old . . . I grow old . . .
I shall wear the bottoms of my trousers rolled.

Shall I part my hair behind? Do I dare to eat a peach?
I shall wear white flannel trousers, and walk upon the beach.
I have heard the mermaids singing, each to each.

I do not think that they will sing to me.

I have seen them riding seaward on the waves
Combing the white hair of the waves blown back
When the wind blows the water white and black.

We have lingered in the chambers of the sea
By sea-girls wreathed with seaweed red and brown
Till human voices wake us, and we drown.

231 *La Figlia Che Piange*

O quam te memorem virgo . . .

STAND on the highest pavement of the stair—
Lean on a garden urn—
Weave, weave the sunlight in your hair—
Clasp your flowers to you with a pained surprise—
Fling them to the ground and turn
With a fugitive resentment in your eyes:
But weave, weave the sunlight in your hair.

So I would have had him leave,
So I would have had her stand and grieve,
So he would have left
As the soul leaves the body torn and bruised,
As the mind deserts the body it has used.
I should find
Some way incomparably light and deft,
Some way we both should understand,
Simple and faithless as a smile and shake of the hand.

She turned away, but with the autumn weather
Compelled my imagination many days,
Many days and many hours:
Her hair over her arms and her arms full of flowers.
And I wonder how they should have been together!
I should have lost a gesture and a pose.
Sometimes these cogitations still amaze
The troubled midnight and the noon's repose.

232   *Sweeney Erect*

> *And the trees about me,*
> *Let them be dry and leafless; let the rocks*
> *Groan with continual surges; and behind me*
> *Make all a desolation. Look, look, wenches!*

PAINT me a cavernous waste shore
    Cast in the unstilled Cyclades,
Paint me the bold anfractuous rocks
    Faced by the snarled and yelping seas.

Display me Aeolus above
    Reviewing the insurgent gales
Which tangle Ariadne's hair
    And swell with haste the perjured sails.

Morning stirs the feet and hands
    (Nausicaa and Polypheme).
Gesture of orang-outang
    Rises from the sheets in steam.

This withered root of knots of hair
    Slitted below and gashed with eyes,
This oval O cropped out with teeth:
    The sickle motion from the thighs

Jackknifes upward at the knees
    Then straightens out from heel to hip
Pushing the framework of the bed
    And clawing at the pillow slip.

Sweeney addressed full length to shave
  Broadbottomed, pink from nape to base,
Knows the female temperament
  And wipes the suds around his face.

(The lengthened shadow of a man
  Is history, said Emerson
Who had not seen the silhouette
  Of Sweeney straddled in the sun.)

Tests the razor on his leg
  Waiting until the shriek subsides.
The epileptic on the bed
  Curves backward, clutching at her sides.

The ladies of the corridor
  Find themselves involved, disgraced,
Call witness to their principles
  And deprecate the lack of taste

Observing that hysteria
  Might easily be misunderstood;
Mrs. Turner intimates
  It does the house no sort of good.

But Doris, towelled from the bath,
  Enters padding on broad feet,
Bringing sal volatile
  And a glass of brandy neat.

233   *The Waste Land*

'Nam Sibyllam quidem Cumis ego ipse oculis meis vidi in ampulla pendere, et cum illi pueri dicerent: Σίβυλλα τί θέλεις; respondebat illa: ἀποθανεῖν θέλω.'

For Ezra Pound
il miglior fabbro.

I. *The Burial of the Dead*

APRIL is the cruellest month, breeding
Lilacs out of the dead land, mixing
Memory and desire, stirring

Dull roots with spring rain.
Winter kept us warm, covering
Earth in forgetful snow, feeding
A little life with dried tubers.
Summer surprised us, coming over the Starnbergersee
With a shower of rain; we stopped in the colonnade,
And went on in sunlight, into the Hofgarten,
And drank coffee, and talked for an hour.
Bin gar keine Russin, stamm' aus Litauen, echt deutsch.
And when we were children, staying at the arch-duke's,
My cousin's, he took me out on a sled,
And I was frightened. He said, Marie,
Marie, hold on tight. And down we went.
In the mountains, there you feel free.
I read, much of the night, and go south in the winter.

What are the roots that clutch, what branches grow
Out of this stony rubbish? Son of man,
You cannot say, or guess, for you know only
A heap of broken images, where the sun beats,
And the dead tree gives no shelter, the cricket no relief,
And the dry stone no sound of water. Only
There is shadow under this red rock,
(Come in under the shadow of this red rock),
And I will show you something different from either
Your shadow at morning striding behind you
Or your shadow at evening rising to meet you;
I will show you fear in a handful of dust.
                    Frisch weht der Wind
                    Der Heimat zu
                    Mein Irisch Kind
                    Wo weilest du?
'You gave me hyacinths first a year ago;
'They called me the hyacinth girl.'
—Yet when we came back, late, from the hyacinth
        garden,
Your arms full, and your hair wet, I could not
    Speak, and my eyes failed, I was neither
Living nor dead, and I knew nothing,
Looking into the heart of light, the silence.
Oed' und leer das Meer.

Madame Sosostris, famous clairvoyante,
Had a bad cold, nevertheless
Is known to be the wisest woman in Europe,
With a wicked pack of cards. Here, said she,
Is your card, the drowned Phœnician Sailor,
(Those are pearls that were his eyes. Look!)
Here is Belladonna, the Lady of the Rocks,
The lady of situations.
Here is the man with three staves, and here the Wheel,
And here is the one-eyed merchant, and his card,
Which is blank, is something he carries on his back,
Which I am forbidden to see. I do not find
The Hanged Man. Fear death by water.
I see crowds of people, walking round in a ring.
Thank you. If you see dear Mrs. Equitone,
Tell her I bring the horoscope myself:
One must be so careful these days.

    Unreal City,
Under the brown fog of a winter dawn,
A crowd flowed over London Bridge, so many,
I had not thought death had undone so many.
Sighs, short and infrequent, were exhaled,
And each man fixed his eyes before his feet.
Flowed up the hill and down King William Street,
To where Saint Mary Woolnoth kept the hours
With a dead sound on the final stroke of nine.
There I saw one I knew, and stopped him, crying: 'Stetson!
'You who were with me in the ships at Mylae!
'That corpse you planted last year in your garden,
'Has it begun to sprout? Will it bloom this year?
'Or has the sudden frost disturbed its bed?
'O keep the Dog far hence, that's friend to men,
'Or with his nails he'll dig it up again!
'You! hypocrite lecteur!—mon semblable,—mon frère!'

II. *A Game of Chess*

    The Chair she sat in, like a burnished throne,
Glowed on the marble, where the glass
Held up by standards wrought with fruited vines
From which a golden Cupidon peeped out
(Another hid his eyes behind his wing)
Doubled the flames of sevenbranched candelabra

Reflecting light upon the table as
The glitter of her jewels rose to meet it,
From satin cases poured in rich profusion.
In vials of ivory and coloured glass
Unstoppered, lurked her strange synthetic perfumes,
Unguent, powdered, or liquid—troubled, confused
And drowned the sense in odours; stirred by the air
That freshened from the window, these ascended
In fattening the prolonged candle-flames,
Flung their smoke into the laquearia,
Stirring the pattern on the coffered ceiling.
Huge sea-wood fed with copper
Burned green and orange, framed by the coloured stone,
In which sad light a carvèd dolphin swam.
Above the antique mantel was displayed
As though a window gave upon the sylvan scene
The change of Philomel, by the barbarous king
So rudely forced; yet there the nightingale
Filled all the desert with inviolable voice
And still she cried, and still the world pursues,
'Jug Jug' to dirty ears.
And other withered stumps of time
Were told upon the walls; staring forms
Leaned out, leaning, hushing the room enclosed.
Footsteps shuffled on the stair.
Under the firelight, under the brush, her hair
Spread out in fiery points
Glowed into words, then would be savagely still.

'My nerves are bad to-night. Yes, bad. Stay with me.
'Speak to me. Why do you never speak. Speak.
'What are you thinking of? What thinking? What?
'I never know what you are thinking. Think.'

I think we are in rats' alley
Where the dead men lost their bones.

'What is that noise?'
                The wind under the door.
'What is that noise now? What is the wind doing?'
                Nothing again nothing.
                            'Do
'You know nothing? Do you see nothing? Do you remember
'Nothing?'

I remember
Those are pearls that were his eyes.
'Are you alive, or not? Is there nothing in your head?'

But

O O O O that Shakespeherian Rag—
It's so elegant
So intelligent
'What shall I do now? What shall I do?'
'I shall rush out as I am, and walk the street
'With my hair down, so. What shall we do tomorrow?
'What shall we ever do?'

The hot water at ten.
And if it rains, a closed car at four.
And we shall play a game of chess,
Pressing lidless eyes and waiting for a knock upon the door.

When Lil's husband got demobbed, I said—
I didn't mince my words, I said to her myself,
HURRY UP PLEASE ITS TIME
Now Albert's coming back, make yourself a bit smart.
He'll want to know what you done with that money he gave you
To get herself some teeth. He did, I was there.
You have them all out, Lil, and get a nice set,
He said, I swear, I can't bear to look at you.
And no more can't I, I said, and think of poor Albert,
He's been in the army four years, he wants a good time,
And if you don't give it him, there's others will, I said.
Oh is there, she said. Something o' that, I said.
Then I'll know who to thank, she said, and give me a straight look.
HURRY UP PLEASE ITS TIME
If you don't like it you can get on with it, I said.
Others can pick and choose if you can't.
But if Albert makes off, it won't be for lack of telling.
You ought to be ashamed, I said, to look so antique.
(And her only thirty-one.)
I can't help it, she said, pulling a long face,
It's them pills I took, to bring it off, she said.
(She's had five already, and nearly died of young George.)
The chemist said it would be all right, but I've never been the same.
You *are* a proper fool, I said.
Well, if Albert won't leave you alone, there it is, I said,
What you get married for if you don't want children?
HURRY UP PLEASE ITS TIME

Well, that Sunday Albert was home, they had a hot gammon,
And they asked me in to dinner, to get the beauty of it hot—
HURRY UP PLEASE ITS TIME
HURRY UP PLEASE ITS TIME
Goonight Bill. Goonight Lou. Goonight May. Goonight.
Ta ta. Goonight. Goonight.
Good night, ladies, good night, sweet ladies, good night, good night.

III. *The Fire Sermon*

   The river's tent is broken; the last fingers of leaf
Clutch and sink into the wet bank. The wind
Crosses the brown land, unheard. The nymphs are departed.
Sweet Thames, run softly, till I end my song.
The river bears no empty bottles, sandwich papers,
Silk handkerchiefs, cardboard boxes, cigarette ends
Or other testimony of summer nights. The nymphs are departed.
And their friends, the loitering heirs of City directors;
Departed, have left no addresses.
By the waters of Leman I sat down and wept . . .
Sweet Thames, run softly till I end my song,
Sweet Thames, run softly, for I speak not loud or long,
But at my back in a cold blast I hear
The rattle of the bones, and chuckle spread from ear to ear.

A rat crept softly through the vegetation
Dragging its slimy belly on the bank
While I was fishing in the dull canal
On a winter evening round behind the gashouse
Musing upon the king my brother's wreck
And on the king my father's death before him.
White bodies naked on the low damp ground
And bones cast in a little low dry garret,
Rattled by the rat's foot only, year to year.
But at my back from time to time I hear
The sound of horns and motors, which shall bring
Sweeney to Mrs. Porter in the spring.
O the moon shone bright on Mrs. Porter
And on her daughter
They wash their feet in soda water
Et O ces voix d'enfants, chantant dans la coupole!

Twit twit twit
Jug jug jug jug jug jug

So rudely forc'd.
Tereu

   Unreal City
Under the brown fog of a winter noon
Mr. Eugenides, the Smyrna merchant
Unshaven, with a pocket full of currants
C.i.f. London: documents at sight,
Asked me in demotic French
To luncheon at the Cannon Street Hotel
Followed by a weekend at the Metropole.

   At the violet hour, when the eyes and back
Turn upward from the desk, when the human engine waits
Like a taxi throbbing waiting,
I Tiresias, though blind, throbbing between two lives,
Old man with wrinkled female breasts, can see
At the violet hour, the evening hour that strives
Homeward, and brings the sailor home from sea,
The typist home at teatime, clears her breakfast, lights
Her stove, and lays out food in tins.
Out of the window perilously spread
Her drying combinations touched by the sun's last rays,
On the divan are piled (at night her bed)
Stockings, slippers, camisoles, and stays.
I Tiresias, old man with wrinkled dugs
Perceived the scene, and foretold the rest—
I too awaited the expected guest.
He, the young man carbuncular, arrives,
A small house agent's clerk, with one bold stare,
One of the low on whom assurance sits
As a silk hat on a Bradford millionaire.
The time is now propitious, as he guesses,
The meal is ended, she is bored and tired,
Endeavours to engage her in caresses
Which still are unreproved, if undesired.
Flushed and decided, he assaults at once;
Exploring hands encounter no defence;
His vanity requires no response,
And makes a welcome of indifference.

(And I Tiresias have foresuffered all
Enacted on this same divan or bed;
I who have sat by Thebes below the wall
And walked among the lowest of the dead.)
Bestows one final patronising kiss,
And gropes his way, finding the stairs unlit . . .

   She turns and looks a moment in the glass,
Hardly aware of her departed lover;
Her brain allows one half-formed thought to pass:
'Well now that's done: and I'm glad it's over.'
When lovely woman stoops to folly and
Paces about her room again, alone,
She smoothes her hair with automatic hand,
And puts a record on the gramophone.

   'This music crept by me upon the waters'
And along the Strand, up Queen Victoria Street.
O City city, I can sometimes hear
Beside a public bar in Lower Thames Street,
The pleasant whining of a mandoline
And a clatter and a chatter from within
Where fishmen lounge at noon: where the walls
Of Magnus Martyr hold
Inexplicable splendour of Ionian white and gold.

The river sweats
Oil and tar
The barges drift
With the turning tide
Red sails
Wide
To leeward, swing on the heavy spar.
The barges wash
Drifting logs
Down Greenwich reach
Past the Isle of Dogs.
        Weialala leia
        Wallala leialala

Elizabeth and Leicester
Beating oars
The stern was formed
A gilded shell
Red and gold
The brisk swell
Rippled both shores
Southwest wind
Carried down stream
The peal of bells
White towers
       Weialala leia
       Wallala leialala

'Trams and dusty trees.
Highbury bore me. Richmond and Kew
Undid me. By Richmond I raised my knees
Supine on the floor of a narrow canoe.'

'My feet are at Moorgate, and my heart
Under my feet. After the event
He wept. He promised "a new start."
I made no comment. What should I resent?'

'On Margate Sands.
I can connect
Nothing with nothing.
The broken fingernails of dirty hands.
My people humble people who expect
Nothing.'
       la la

To Carthage then I came

Burning burning burning burning
O Lord Thou pluckest me out
O Lord Thou pluckest

burning

IV. *Death by Water*

Phlebas the Phœnician, a fortnight dead,
Forgot the cry of gulls, and the deep sea swell
And the profit and loss.
                              A current under sea
Picked his bones in whispers. As he rose and fell
He passed the stages of his age and youth
Entering the whirlpool.
                              Gentile or Jew
O you who turn the wheel and look to windward,
Consider Phlebas, who was once handsome and tall as you.

V. *What the Thunder said*

After the torchlight red on sweaty faces
After the frosty silence in the gardens
After the agony in stony places
The shouting and the crying
Prison and palace and reverberation
Of thunder of spring over distant mountains
He who was living is now dead
We who were living are now dying
With a little patience

Here is no water but only rock
Rock and no water and the sandy road
The road winding above among the mountains
Which are mountains of rock without water
If there were water we should stop and drink
Amongst the rock one cannot stop or think
Sweat is dry and feet are in the sand
If there were only water amongst the rock
Dead mountain mouth of carious teeth that cannot spit
Here one can neither stand nor lie nor sit
There is not even silence in the mountains
But dry sterile thunder without rain
There is not even solitude in the mountains
But red sullen faces sneer and snarl
From doors of mudcracked houses
                              If there were water

And no rock
If there were rock
And also water
And water
A spring
A pool among the rock
If there were the sound of water only
Not the cicada
And dry grass singing
But sound of water over a rock
Where the hermit-thrush sings in the pine trees
Drip drop drip drop drop drop drop
But there is no water

Who is the third who walks always beside you?
When I count, there are only you and I together
But when I look ahead up the white road
There is always another one walking beside you
Gliding wrapt in a brown mantle, hooded
I do not know whether a man or a woman
—But who is that on the other side of you?

What is that sound high in the air
Murmur of maternal lamentation
Who are those hooded hordes swarming
Over endless plains, stumbling in cracked earth
Ringed by the flat horizon only

What is the city over the mountains
Cracks and reforms and bursts in the violet air
Falling towers
Jerusalem Athens Alexandria
Vienna London
Unreal

A woman drew her long black hair out tight
And fiddled whisper music on those strings
And bats with baby faces in the violet light
Whistled, and beat their wings
And crawled head downward down a blackened wall
And upside down in air were towers
Tolling reminiscent bells, that kept the hours
And voices singing out of empty cisterns and exhausted wells.

In this decayed hole among the mountains
In the faint moonlight, the grass is singing
Over the tumbled graves, about the chapel
There is the empty chapel, only the wind's home.
It has no windows, and the door swings,
Dry bones can harm no one.
Only a cock stood on the rooftree
Co co rico co co rico
In a flash of lightning. Then a damp gust
Bringing rain

Ganga was sunken, and the limp leaves
Waited for rain, while the black clouds
Gathered far distant, over Himavant.
The jungle crouched, humped in silence.
Then spoke the thunder
DA
Datta : what have we given?
My friend, blood shaking my heart
The awful daring of a moment's surrender
Which an age of prudence can never retract
By this, and this only, we have existed
Which is not to be found in our obituaries
Or in memories draped by the beneficent spider
Or under seals broken by the lean solicitor
In our empty rooms
DA
Dayadhvam : I have heard the key
Turn in the door once and turn once only
We think of the key, each in his prison
Thinking of the key, each confirms a prison
Only at nightfall, aethereal rumours
Revive for a moment a broken Coriolanus
DA
Damyata : The boat responded
Gaily, to the hand expert with sail and oar
The sea was calm, your heart would have responded
Gaily, when invited, beating obedient
To controlling hands
                  I sat upon the shore
Fishing, with the arid plain behind me
Shall I at least set my lands in order?

London Bridge is falling down falling down falling down
Poi s'ascose nel foco che gli affina
Quando fiam uti chelidon—O swallow swallow
Le Prince d'Aquitaine à la tour abolie
These fragments I have shored against my ruins
Why then Ile fit you. Hieronymo's mad againe.
Datta. Dayadhvam. Damyata.
            Shantih shantih shantih

234   *Journey of the Magi*

    'A COLD coming we had of it,
Just the worst time of the year
For a journey, and such a long journey:
The ways deep and the weather sharp,
The very dead of winter.'
And the camels galled, sore-footed, refractory,
Lying down in the melting snow.
There were times we regretted
The summer palaces on slopes, the terraces,
And the silken girls bringing sherbet.
Then the camel men cursing and grumbling
And running away, and wanting their liquor and women,
And the night-fires going out, and the lack of shelters,
And the cities hostile and the towns unfriendly
And the villages dirty and charging high prices:
A hard time we had of it.
At the end we preferred to travel all night,
Sleeping in snatches,
With the voices singing in our ears, saying
That this was all folly.

    Then at dawn we came down to a temperate valley,
Wet, below the snow line, smelling of vegetation,
With a running stream and a water-mill beating the darkness,
And three trees on the low sky.
And an old white horse galloped away in the meadow.
Then we came to a tavern with vine-leaves over the lintel,
Six hands at an open door dicing for pieces of silver,
And feet kicking the empty wine-skins.

But there was no information, so we continued
And arrived at evening, not a moment too soon
Finding the place; it was (you may say) satisfactory.

   All this was a long time ago, I remember,
And I would do it again, but set down
This set down
This: were we led all that way for
Birth or Death? There was a Birth, certainly,
We had evidence and no doubt. I had seen birth and death,
But had thought they were different; this Birth was
Hard and bitter agony for us, like Death, our death.
We returned to our places, these Kingdoms,
But no longer at ease here, in the old dispensation,
With an alien people clutching their gods.
I should be glad of another death.

235   CHORUSES FROM *Murder in the Cathedral*

I

WE do not wish anything to happen.
Seven years we have lived quietly,
Succeeded in avoiding notice,
Living and partly living.
There have been oppression and luxury,
There have been poverty and licence,
There has been minor injustice.
Yet we have gone on living,
Living and partly living.
Sometimes the corn has failed us,
Sometimes the harvest is good,
One year is a year of rain,
Another a year of dryness,
One year the apples are abundant,
Another year the plums are lacking.
Yet we have gone on living,
Living and partly living.
We have kept the feasts, heard the masses,
We have brewed beer and cider,
Gathered wood against the winter,

Talked at the corner of the fire,
Talked at the corners of streets,
Talked not always in whispers,
Living and partly living.
We have seen births, deaths and marriages,
We have had various scandals,
We have been afflicted with taxes,
We have had laughter and gossip,
Several girls have disappeared
Unaccountably, and some not able to.
We have all had our private terrors,
Our particular shadows, our secret fears.
But now a great fear is upon us, a fear not of one but of many,
A fear like birth and death, when we see birth and death alone
In a void apart. We
Are afraid in a fear which we cannot know, which we cannot face, which
    none understands,
And our hearts are torn from us, our brains unskinned like the layers of
    an onion, our selves are lost lost
In a final fear which none understands.

236   II

We have not been happy, my Lord, we have not been too happy.
We are not ignorant women, we know what we must expect and not
    expect.
We know of oppression and torture,
We know of extortion and violence,
Destitution, disease,
The old without fire in winter,
The child without milk in summer,
Our labour taken away from us,
Our sins made heavier upon us.
We have seen the young man mutilated,
The torn girl trembling by the mill-stream.
And meanwhile we have gone on living,
Living and partly living,
Picking together the pieces,
Gathering faggots at nightfall,
Building a partial shelter,
For sleeping, and eating and drinking and laughter.

God gave us always some reason, some hope; but now a new terror has
    soiled us, which none can avert, none can avoid, flowing under our
    feet and over the sky;
Under doors and down chimneys, flowing in at the ear and the mouth
    and the eye.
God is leaving us, God is leaving us, more pang, more pain than birth
    or death.
Sweet and cloying through the dark air
Falls the stifling scent of despair;
The forms take shape in the dark air:
Puss-purr of leopard, footfall of padding bear,
Palm-pat of nodding ape, square hyaena waiting
For laughter, laughter, laughter. The Lords of Hell are here.
They curl round you, lie at your feet, swing and wing through the
    dark air.

237   *Gus: The Theatre Cat*

GUS is the Cat at the Theatre Door.
His name, as I ought to have told you before,
Is really Asparagus. That's such a fuss
To pronounce, that we usually call him just Gus.
His coat's very shabby, he's thin as a rake,
And he suffers from palsy that makes his paw shake.
Yet he was, in his youth, quite the smartest of Cats—
But no longer a terror to mice and to rats.

For he isn't the Cat that he was in his prime;
Though his name was quite famous, he says, in its time.
And whenever he joins his friends at their club
(Which takes place at the back of the neighbouring pub)
He loves to regale them, if someone else pays,
With anecdotes drawn from his palmiest days.
For he once was a Star of the highest degree—
He has acted with Irving, he's acted with Tree.
And he likes to relate his success on the Halls,
Where the Gallery once gave him seven cat-calls.
But his grandest creation, as he loves to tell,
Was Firefrorefiddle, the Fiend of the Fell.

'I have played', so he says, 'every possible part,
And I used to know seventy speeches by heart.
I'd extemporize back-chat, I knew how to gag,
And I knew how to let the cat out of the bag.
I knew how to act with my back and my tail;
With an hour of rehearsal, I never could fail.
I'd a voice that would soften the hardest of hearts,
Whether I took the lead, or in character parts.
I have sat by the bedside of poor Little Nell;
When the Curfew was rung, then I swung on the bell.
In the Pantomime season I never fell flat,
And I once understudied Dick Whittington's Cat.
But my grandest creation, as history will tell,
Was Firefrorefiddle, the Fiend of the Fell.'

Then, if someone will give him a toothful of gin,
He will tell how he once played a part in *East Lynne*.
At a Shakespeare performance he once walked on pat,
When some actor suggested the need for a cat.
He once played a Tiger—could do it again—
Which an Indian Colonel pursued down a drain.
And he thinks that he still can, much better than most,
Produce blood-curdling noises to bring on the Ghost.
And he once crossed the stage on a telegraph wire,
To rescue a child when a house was on fire.
And he says: 'Now, these kittens, they do not get trained
As we did in the days when Victoria reigned.
They never get drilled in a regular troupe,
And they think they are smart, just to jump through a hoop.'

And he'll say, as he scratches himself with his claws,
'Well, the Theatre's certainly not what it was.
These modern productions are all very well,
But there's nothing to equal, from what I hear tell,
    That moment of mystery
    When I made history
As Firefrorefiddle, the Fiend of the Fell.'

238

Little Gidding

I

MIDWINTER spring is its own season
Sempiternal though sodden towards sundown,
Suspended in time, between pole and tropic.
When the short day is brightest, with frost and fire,
The brief sun flames the ice, on pond and ditches,
In windless cold that is the heart's heat,
Reflecting in a watery mirror
A glare that is blindness in the early afternoon.
And glow more intense than blaze of branch, or brazier,
Stirs the dumb spirit: no wind, but pentecostal fire
In the dark time of the year. Between melting and freezing
The soul's sap quivers. There is no earth smell
Or smell of living thing. This is the spring time
But not in time's covenant. Now the hedgerow
Is blanched for an hour with transitory blossom
Of snow, a bloom more sudden
Than that of summer, neither budding nor fading,
Not in the scheme of generation.
Where is the summer, the unimaginable
Zero summer?

If you came this way,
Taking the route you would be likely to take
From the place you would be likely to come from,
If you came this way in may time, you would find the hedges
White again, in May, with voluptuary sweetness.
It would be the same at the end of the journey,
If you came at night like a broken king,

If you came by day not knowing what you came for,
It would be the same, when you leave the rough road
And turn behind the pig-sty to the dull façade
And the tombstone. And what you thought you came for
Is only a shell, a husk of meaning
From which the purpose breaks only when it is fulfilled
If at all. Either you had no purpose
Or the purpose is beyond the end you figured
And is altered in fulfilment. There are other places

Which also are the world's end, some at the sea jaws,
Or over a dark lake, in a desert or a city—
But this is the nearest, in place and time,
Now and in England.

                    If you came this way,
Taking any route, starting from anywhere,
At any time or at any season,
It would always be the same: you would have to put off
Sense and notion. You are not here to verify,
Instruct yourself, or inform curiosity
Or carry report. You are here to kneel
Where prayer has been valid. And prayer is more
Than an order of words, the conscious occupation
Of the praying mind, or the sound of the voice praying.
And what the dead had no speech for, when living,
They can tell you, being dead: the communication
Of the dead is tongued with fire beyond the language of the living.
Here, the intersection of the timeless moment
Is England and nowhere. Never and always.

II

Ash on an old man's sleeve
Is all the ash the burnt roses leave.
Dust in the air suspended
Marks the place where the story ended.
Dust inbreathed was a house—
The wall, the wainscot and the mouse.
The death of hope and despair,
    This is the death of air.

There are flood and drouth
Over the eyes and in the mouth,
Dead water and dead sand
Contending for the upper hand.
The parched eviscerate soil
    Gapes at the vanity of toil,
Laughs without mirth.
This is the death of earth.

Water and fire succeed
The town, the pasture and the weed.
Water and fire deride
The sacrifice that we denied.
Water and fire shall rot
The marred foundations we forgot,
Of sanctuary and choir.
　　This is the death of water and fire.

In the uncertain hour before the morning
　　Near the ending of interminable night
　　At the recurrent end of the unending
After the dark dove with the flickering tongue
　　Had passed below the horizon of his homing
　　While the dead leaves still rattled on like tin
Over the asphalt where no other sound was
　　Between three districts whence the smoke arose
　　I met one walking, loitering and hurried
As if blown towards me like the metal leaves
　　Before the urban dawn wind unresisting.
　　And as I fixed upon the down-turned face
That pointed scrutiny with which we challenge
　　The first-met stranger in the waning dusk
　　I caught the sudden look of some dead master
Whom I had known, forgotten, half recalled
　　Both one and many; in the brown baked features
The eyes of a familiar compound ghost
　　Both intimate and unidentifiable.
　　So I assumed a double part, and cried
　　And heard another's voice cry: 'What! are *you* here?'
Although we were not. I was still the same,
　　Knowing myself yet being someone other—
　　And he a face still forming; yet the words sufficed
To compel the recognition they preceded.
　　And so, compliant to the common wind,
　　Too strange to each other for misunderstanding,
In concord at this intersection time
　　Of meeting nowhere, no before and after,
　　We trod the pavement in a dead patrol.
I said: 'The wonder that I feel is easy,
　　Yet ease is cause of wonder. Therefore speak:
　　I may not comprehend, may not remember.'
And he: 'I am not eager to rehearse

My thoughts and theory which you have forgotten.
These things have served their purpose: let them be.
So with your own, and pray they be forgiven
By others, as I pray you to forgive
Both bad and good. Last season's fruit is eaten
And the fullfed beast shall kick the empty pail.
For last year's words belong to last year's language
And next year's words await another voice.
But, as the passage now presents no hindrance
To the spirit unappeased and peregrine
Between two worlds become much like each other,
So I find words I never thought to speak
In streets I never thought I should revisit
When I left my body on a distant shore.
Since our concern was speech, and speech impelled us
To purify the dialect of the tribe
And urge the mind to aftersight and foresight,
Let me disclose the gifts reserved for age
To set a crown upon your lifetime's effort.
First, the cold friction of expiring sense
Without enchantment, offering no promise
But bitter tastelessness of shadow fruit
As body and soul begin to fall asunder.
Second, the conscious impotence of rage
At human folly, and the laceration
Of laughter at what ceases to amuse.
And last, the rending pain of re-enactment
Of all that you have done, and been; the shame
Of motives late revealed, and the awareness
Of things ill done and done to others' harm
Which once you took for exercise of virtue.
Then fools' approval stings, and honour stains.

From wrong to wrong the exasperated spirit
Proceeds, unless restored by that refining fire
Where you must move in measure, like a dancer.'
The day was breaking. In the disfigured street
He left me, with a kind of valediction,
And faded on the blowing of the horn.

III

There are three conditions which often look alike
Yet differ completely, flourish in the same hedgerow:
Attachment to self and to things and to persons, detachment
From self and from things and from persons; and, growing between
    them, indifference
Which resembles the others as death resembles life,
Being between two lives—unflowering, between
The live and the dead nettle. This is the use of memory:
For liberation—not less of love but expanding
Of love beyond desire, and so liberation
From the future as well as the past. Thus, love of a country
Begins as attachment to our own field of action
And comes to find that action of little importance
Though never indifferent. History may be servitude,
History may be freedom. See, now they vanish,
The faces and places, with the self which, as it could, loved them,
To become renewed, transfigured, in another pattern.
Sin is Behovely, but
All shall be well, and
All manner of thing shall be well.
If I think, again, of this place,
And of people, not wholly commendable,
Of no immediate kin or kindness,
But some of peculiar genius,
All touched by a common genius,
United in the strife which divided them;
If I think of a king at nightfall,
Of three men, and more, on the scaffold
And a few who died forgotten
In other places, here and abroad,
And of one who died blind and quiet,
Why should we celebrate
These dead men more than the dying?

It is not to ring the bell backward
Nor is it an incantation
To summon the spectre of a Rose.
We cannot revive old factions
We cannot restore old policies
Or follow an antique drum.
These men, and those who opposed them

And those whom they opposed
Accept the constitution of silence
And are folded in a single party.
Whatever we inherit from the fortunate
We have taken from the defeated
What they had to leave us—a symbol:
A symbol perfected in death.
And all shall be well and
All manner of thing shall be well
By the purification of the motive
In the ground of our beseeching.

IV

The dove descending breaks the air
With flame of incandescent terror
Of which the tongues declare
The one discharge from sin and error.
The only hope, or else despair
   Lies in the choice of pyre or pyre—
   To be redeemed from fire by fire.

Who then devised the torment? Love.
Love is the unfamiliar Name
Behind the hands that wove
The intolerable shirt of flame
Which human power cannot remove.
   We only live, only suspire
   Consumed by either fire or fire.

V

What we call the beginning is often the end
And to make an end is to make a beginning.
The end is where we start from. And every phrase
And sentence that is right (where every word is at home,
Taking its place to support the others,
The word neither diffident nor ostentatious,
An easy commerce of the old and the new,
The common word exact without vulgarity,
The formal word precise but not pedantic,
The complete consort dancing together)
Every phrase and every sentence is an end and a beginning,

Every poem an epitaph. And any action
Is a step to the block, to the fire, down the sea's throat
Or to an illegible stone: and that is where we start.
We die with the dying:
See, they depart, and we go with them.
We are born with the dead:
See, they return, and bring us with them.
The moment of the rose and the moment of the yew-tree
Are of equal duration. A people without history
Is not redeemed from time, for history is a pattern
Of timeless moments. So, while the light fails
On a winter's afternoon, in a secluded chapel
History is now and England.

With the drawing of this Love and the voice of this Calling

We shall not cease from exploration
And the end of all our exploring
Will be to arrive where we started
And know the place for the first time.
Through the unknown, remembered gate
When the last of earth left to discover
Is that which was the beginning;
At the source of the longest river
The voice of the hidden waterfall
And the children in the apple-tree
Not known, because not looked for
But heard, half-heard, in the stillness
Between two waves of the sea.
Quick now, here, now, always—
A condition of complete simplicity
(Costing not less than everything)
And all shall be well and
All manner of thing shall be well
When the tongues of flame are in-folded
Into the crowned knot of fire
And the fire and the rose are one.

MURIEL STUART

239 *In the Orchard*

'I THOUGHT you loved me.' 'No, it was only fun.'
'When we stood there, closer than all?' 'Well, the harvest moon
Was shining and queer in your hair, and it turned my head.'
'That made you?' 'Yes.' 'Just the room and the light it made
Under the tree?' 'Well, your mouth, too.' 'Yes, my mouth?'
'And the quiet there that sang like the drum in the booth.
You shouldn't have danced like that.' 'Like what?' 'So close,
With your head turned up, and the flower in your hair, a rose
That smelt all warm.' 'I loved you. I thought you knew
I wouldn't have danced like that with any but you.'
'I didn't know. I thought you knew it was fun.'
'I thought it was love you meant.' 'Well, it's done.' 'Yes, it's done.
I've seen boys stone a blackbird, and watched them drown
A kitten . . . it clawed at the reeds, and they pushed it down
Into the pool while it screamed. Is that fun, too?'
'Well, boys are like that . . . Your brothers . . .' 'Yes, I know.
But you, so lovely and strong! Not you! Not you!'
'They don't understand it's cruel. It's only a game.'
'And are girls fun, too?' 'No, still in a way it's the same.
It's queer and lovely to have a girl . . .' 'Go on.'
'It makes you mad for a bit to feel she's your own,
And you laugh and kiss her, and maybe you give her a ring,
But it's only in fun.' 'But I gave you everything.'
'Well, you shouldn't have done it. You know what a fellow thinks
When a girl does that.' 'Yes, he talks of her over his drinks
And calls her a—' 'Stop that now. I thought you knew.'
'But it wasn't with anyone else. It was only you.'
'How did I know? I thought you wanted it too.
I thought you were like the rest. Well, what's to be done?'
'To be done?' 'Is it all right?' 'Yes.' 'Sure?' 'Yes, but why?'
'I don't know. I thought you were going to cry.
You said you had something to tell me.' 'Yes, I know.
It wasn't anything really . . . I think I'll go.'
'Yes, it's late. There's thunder about, a drop of rain
Fell on my hand in the dark. I'll see you again
At the dance next week. You're sure that everything's right?'
'Yes.' 'Well, I'll be going.' 'Kiss me . . .' 'Good night.' . . . 'Good
      night.'

DOROTHY WELLESLEY
1889–1956

240

Horses
'*Newmarket or St. Leger*'

WHO, in the garden-pony carrying skeps
Of grass or fallen leaves, his knees gone slack,
Round belly, hollow back,
Sees the Mongolian Tarpan of the Steppes?
Or, in the Shire with plaits and feathered feet,
The war-horse like the wind the Tartar knew?
Or, in the Suffolk Punch, spells out anew
The wild grey asses fleet
With stripe from head to tail, and moderate ears?
In cross sea-donkeys, sheltering as storm gathers,
The mountain zebras maned upon the withers,
With round enormous ears?

And who in thoroughbreds in stable garb
Of blazoned rug, ranged orderly, will mark
The wistful eyelashes so long and dark,
And call to mind the old blood of the Barb?
And that slim island on whose bare campaigns
Galloped with flying manes
For a king's pleasure, churning surf and scud,
A white Arabian stud?

That stallion, teazer to Hobgoblin, free
And foaled upon a plain of Barbary:
Godolphin Barb, who dragged a cart for hire
In Paris, but became a famous sire,
Covering all lovely mares, and she who threw
Rataplan to the Baron, loveliest shrew;
King Charles's royal mares; the Dodsworth Dam;
And the descendants: Yellow Turk, King Tom;
And Lath out of Roxana, famous foal;
Careless; Eclipse, unbeaten in the race,
With white blaze on his face;
Prunella who was dam to Parasol.

Blood Arab, pony, pedigree, no name,
All horses are the same:
The Shetland stallion stunted by the damp,
Yet filled with self-importance, stout and small;
The Cleveland slow and tall;
New Forests that may ramp
Their lives out, being branded, breeding free
When bluebells turn the Forest to a sea,
When mares with foal at foot flee down the glades,
Sheltering in bramble coverts
From mobs of corn-fed lovers;
Or, at the acorn harvest, in stockades,
A round-up being afoot, will stand at bay,
Or, making for the heather clearings, splay
Widespread towards the bogs by gorse and whin,
Roped as they flounder in
By foresters.

But hunters as day fails
Will take the short-cut home across the fields;
With slackened rein will stoop through darkening wealds;
With creaking leathers skirt the swedes and kales.
Patient, adventuring still,
A horse's ears bob on the distant hill;
He starts to hear
A pheasant chuck or whirr, having the fear
In him of ages filled with war and raid,
Night gallop, ambuscade;
Remembering adventures of his kin
With giant winged worms that coiled round mountain bases,
And Nordic tales of young gods riding races
Up courses of the rainbow; here, within
The depth of Hampshire hedges, does he dream
How Athens woke, to hear above her roofs
The welkin flash and thunder to the hoofs
Of Dawn's tremendous team?

G. D. H. COLE
1889–1959

FROM *Civil Riot*

AND you'll say a nation totters
When it can't control its mobs.
But how'd you feel
If some rotters
Made a dash
For your cash?
Wouldn't you hit back and hurt 'em,
Manhandle and unshirt 'em,
If you could?
By God, you would,
Like these others,
Men and brothers,
Whose mobs are all they've got,
You'd give it to 'em hot.
So don't talk so damned superior
All because the other chap,
Whom in gaol you'd like to clap,
Ranks to-day as your inferior.

For it's hard to say who's right,
And who's wrong,
When men begin to fight,
Hot and strong,
Because they think they're being swindled,
And savage passions kindled
In the mind
Make them blind.
Yet you mustn't think I blame
The police.
They've got their job to do,
The same as me and you,
To keep the peace.
And perhaps they only did
What they simply had to do,
When someone lifted off the lid
Of the stew.

And, whatever view you take
Of the moral side of scabbing—
Which, to me, is merely grabbing
What's another's, and not yours—
I'm not making any claims
That our strikers showed good morals
When they hit to pay off scores.
For the essence of most quarrels
Is that ethics get forgot;
So I'm not
Passing judgment, only saying
What I saw
When some men I know and like,
After seven months on strike,
Got the wrong side of the law,
Tried to stop the scabs from smashing
All their chances of a win,
Did their bit of vulgar bashing,
Tried their best to do them in,
Seeing red,
And instead
Got beaten up and battered
Plenty and to spare.
Oh, I don't suppose it mattered;
But I happened to be there.

ARTHUR WALEY

1889–1966

242   *Censorship*

I HAVE been a censor for fifteen months,
The building where I work has four times been bombed.
Glass, boards and paper, each in turn,
Have been blasted from the windows—where windows are left at all.
It is not easy to wash, keep warm and eat;
At times we lack gas, water or light.
The rules for censors are difficult to keep;
In six months there were over a thousand 'stops'.

The Air Raid Bible alters from day to day;
Official orders are not clearly expressed.
One may mention Harrods, but not Derry and Toms;
One may write of mist but may not write of rain.
Japanese scribbled on thin paper
In faint scrawl tires the eyes to read.
In a small room with ten telephones
And a tape-machine concentration is hard.
Yet the Blue Pencil is a mere toy to wield,
There are worse knots than the tangles of Red Tape.
It is not difficult to censor foreign news,
What is hard today is to censor one's own thoughts—
To sit by and see the blind man
On the sightless horse, riding into the bottomless abyss.

ISAAC ROSENBERG

1890–1918

243   *August 1914*

WHAT in our lives is burnt
In the fire of this?
The heart's dear granary?
The much we shall miss?

Three lives hath one life—
Iron, honey, gold.
The gold, the honey gone—
Left is the hard and cold.

Iron are our lives
Molten right through our youth.
A burnt space through ripe fields
A fair mouth's broken tooth.

244 *Louse Hunting*

NUDES—stark and glistening,
Yelling in lurid glee. Grinning faces
And raging limbs
Whirl over the floor one fire.
For a shirt verminously busy
Yon soldier tore from his throat, with oaths
Godhead might shrink at, but not the lice.
And soon the shirt was aflare
Over the candle he'd lit while we lay.

Then we all sprang up and stript
To hunt the verminous brood.
Soon like a demons' pantomime
The place was raging.
See the silhouettes agape,
See the gibbering shadows
Mixed with the battled arms on the wall.
See gargantuan hooked fingers
Pluck in supreme flesh
To smutch supreme littleness.
See the merry limbs in hot Highland fling
Because some wizard vermin
Charmed from the quiet this revel
When our ears were half lulled
By the dark music
Blown from Sleep's trumpet.

IVOR GURNEY

1890–1937

245 *Strange Hells*

THERE are strange Hells within the minds War made
Not so often, not so humiliatingly afraid
As one would have expected—the racket and fear guns made.

One Hell the Gloucester soldiers they quite put out;
Their first bombardment, when in combined black shout
Of fury, guns aligned, they ducked low their heads
And sang with diaphragms fixed beyond all dreads,
That tin and stretched-wire tinkle, that blither of tune;
'Après la guerre fini' till Hell all had come down,
Twelve-inch, six-inch, and eighteen pounders hammering Hell's
    thunders.

Where are they now on State-doles, or showing shop patterns
Or walking town to town sore in borrowed tatterns
Or begged. Some civic routine one never learns.
The heart burns—but has to keep out of face how heart burns.

SIR ALAN HERBERT

1890–1971

246   *'Less Nonsense'*

LET'S have less nonsense from the friends of Joe;
We laud, we love him, but the nonsense—NO.
In 1940, when we bore the brunt,
WE could have done, boys, with a Second Front.
A continent went down a cataract,
But Russia did not think it right to act.
Not ready? No. And who shall call her wrong?
Far better not to strike till you are strong.
Better, perhaps (though this was not our fate),
To make new treaties with the man you hate.
Alas! These shy manœuvres had to end
When Hitler leaped upon his largest friend
(And if he'd not, I wonder, by the way,
If Russia would be in the war to-day?).
But who rushed out to aid the giant then—
A giant rich in corn, and oil, and men,
Long, long prepared, and having, so they say,
The most enlightened leaders of the day?

THIS tiny island, antiquated, tired,
Effete, capitalist, and uninspired!
THIS tiny island, wounded in the war
Through taking tyrants on two years before!
This tiny isle of muddles and mistakes—
Having a front on every wave that breaks.
We might have said, 'Our shipping's on the stretch—
You shall have all the tanks that you can fetch.'
But that is not the way we fight this war:
We give them tanks, *and* take them to the door.
And now we will not hear from anyone
That it's for us to show we hate the Hun.
It does not profit much to sing this tune,
But those who 'prod' cannot be quite immune;
And those who itch to conquer and to kill
Should waste less breath on tubs on Tower Hill.
Honour the Kremlin, boys, but now and then
Admit some signs of grace at Number Ten.

STELLA BENSON

1892–1933

247   *'Now I Have Nothing'*

NOW I have nothing. Even the joy of loss—
Even the dreams I had I now am losing.
Only this thing I know; that you are using
My heart as a stone to bear your foot across. . . .
I am glad—I am glad—the stone is of your choosing. . . .

248   *Frost*

AH, nobody knows
The thing I would learn
But the star of the frost
That is still in the night for a while
And is burned in the morning and lost.

So would I be frozen,
So would I be burned
Into silence
And lost;
So would I return—
Not I—not I—
But a wind from the wild,
Besieging the blossoming
Towers of the roses.

EDWARD SHANKS
1892–1953

249 *Going in to Dinner*

BEAT the knife on the plate and the fork on the can,
For we're going in to dinner, so make all the noise you can.
Up and down the officer wanders, looking blue,
Sing a song to cheer him up, he wants his dinner too.

March into the dining-hall, make the tables rattle
Like a dozen dam' machine guns in the bloody battle,
Use your forks for drum-sticks, use your plates for drums,
Make a most infernal clatter, here the dinner comes!

V. SACKVILLE-WEST
1892–1962

250 *Young Stock*

NOR shall you for your fields neglect your stock;
Spring is the season when the young things thrive,
Having the kindly months before them. Lambs,
Already sturdy, straggle from the flock;
Frisk tails; tug grass-tufts; stare at children; prance;
Then panic-stricken scuttle for their dams.
Calves learn to drink from buckets; foals
Trot laxly in the meadow, with soft glance
Inquisitive; barn, sty and shed
Teem with young innocence newly come alive.

Round collie puppies, on the sunny step,
Buffet each other with their duffer paws
And pounce at flies, and nose the plaited skep,
And with tucked tail slink yelping from the hive.
Likewise the little secret beasts
That open eyes on a world of death and dread,
Thirst, hunger, and mishap,
The covert denizens of holts and shaws,
The little creatures of the ditch and hedge,
Mice nested in a tussock, shrews, and voles,
Inhabitants of the wood,
The red-legged dabchick, paddling in the sedge,
Followed by chubby brood;
The vixen, prick-eared for the first alarm
Beside her tumbling cubs at foot of tree,—
All in the spring begin their precarious round,
Not cherished as the striplings on the farm,
Sheltered, and cosseted, and kept from harm,
But fang and claw against them, snare and trap,
For life is perilous to the small wild things,
Danger's their lot, and fears abound;
Great cats destroy unheedful wings,
And nowhere's safety on the hunted ground;
And who's to blame them, though they be
Sly, as a man would think him shame?
Man in security walks straight and free,
And shall not measure blame,
For they, that each on other preys,
Weasel on rabbit, owl on shrew,
Their cowardly and murderous ways
In poor defence of life pursue,
Not for a wanton killing, not for lust,
As stags will fight among the trampled brake
With antlers running red; with gore and thrust,
With hoofs that stamp, and royal heads that shake
Blood from their eyes,—in vain,
Since still their splendid anger keeps them blind,
And lowers their entangled brows again,
For brief possession of a faithless hind;—
Not thus, but furtive through the rustling leaves
Life preys on little life; the frightened throat
Squeals once beneath the yellow bite of stoat,

Destroyers all, necessity of kind;
Talon rips fur, and fang meets sharper fang,
And even sleeping limbs must be alert.
But fortunate, if death with sudden pang
Leaps, and is ended; if no lingering hurt,
Dragging a broken wing or mangled paw,
Brings the slow anguish that no night reprieves,
In the dark refuge of a lonely shaw.

So do they venture on their chance of life
When months seem friendliest; so shall men
Repair their herds in spring by natural law
In byre and farrowing pen.
Thus shall you do, with calves that you would rear,
—Heifer, not driven to the slaughterer's knife,
And bull-calf, early cut from bull to steer,—
Two to one udder run, till they may feed
Alone; then turn the little foster-siblings out;
Or wean from birth, and teach to drink from pail,
With fair allowance of their mother's milk,
(But watch, for as the calf grows hale,
He's rough, and knocks the empty pail about).
By either method shall you safely breed
Moist muzzles, thrifty coats of silk,
Well-uddered heifers, bullocks strong and stout.

251   *Craftsmen*

ALL craftsmen share a knowledge. They have held
Reality down fluttering to a bench;
Cut wood to their own purposes; compelled
The growth of pattern with the patient shuttle;
Drained acres to a trench.
Control is theirs. They have ignored the subtle
Release of spirit from the jail of shape.
They have been concerned with prison, not escape;
Pinioned the fact, and let the rest go free,
And out of need made inadvertent art.
All things designed to play a faithful part
Build up their plain particular poetry.
Tools have their own integrity;

The sneath of scythe curves rightly to the hand,
The hammer knows its balance, knife its edge,
All tools inevitably planned,
Stout friends, with pledge
Of service; with their crotchets too
That masters understand,
And proper character, and separate heart,
But always to their chosen temper true.
—So language, smithied at the common fire,
Grew to its use; as sneath and shank and haft
Of well-grained wood, nice instruments of craft,
Curve to the simple mould the hands require,
Born of the needs of man.
The poet like the artisan
Works lonely with his tools; picks up each one,
Blunt mallet knowing, and the quick thin blade,
And plane that travels when the hewing's done;
Rejects, and chooses; scores a fresh faint line;
Sharpens, intent upon his chiselling;
Bends lower to examine his design,
If it be truly made,
And brings perfection to so slight a thing
But in the shadows of his working-place,
Dust-moted, dim,
Among the chips and lumber of his trade,
Lifts never his bowed head, a breathing-space
To look upon the world beyond the sill,
The world framed small, in distance, for to him
The world and all its weight are in his will.
Yet in the ecstasy of his rapt mood
There's no retreat his spirit cannot fill,
No distant leagues, no present, and no past,
No essence that his need may not distil,
All pressed into his service, but he knows
Only the immediate care, if that be good;
The little focus that his words enclose;
As the poor joiner, working at his wood,
Knew not the tree from which the planks were taken,
Knew not the glade from which the trunk was brought,
Knew not the soil in which the roots were fast,
Nor by what centuries of gales the boughs were shaken,
But holds them all beneath his hands at last.

J. B. S. HALDANE
1892–1964

252   *Cancer's a Funny Thing*[1]

I WISH I had the voice of Homer
To sing of rectal carcinoma,
Which kills a lot more chaps, in fact,
Than were bumped off when Troy was sacked.

I noticed I was passing blood
(Only a few drops, not a flood)
So pausing on my homeward way
From Tallahassee to Bombay
I asked a doctor, now my friend,
To peer into my hinder end,
To prove or to disprove the rumour
That I had a malignant tumour.
They pumped in Ba SO_4
Till I could really stand no more,
And, when sufficient had been pressed in,
They photographed my large intestine.
In order to decide the issue
They next scraped out some bits of tissue.
(Before they did so, some good pal
Had knocked me out with pentothal,
Whose action is extremely quick,
And does not leave me feeling sick.)
The microscope returned the answer
That I had certainly got cancer.
So I was wheeled to the theatre
Where holes were made to make me better.
One set is in my perineum
Where I can feel, but can't yet see 'em.
Another made me like a kipper
Or female prey of Jack the Ripper.

---

[1] A rare example of the truly public poem: 'The main functions of my rhyme', wrote Professor Haldane, who died in 1964 at the age of 73, were 'to induce cancer patients to be operated on early and to be cheerful about it.'

J. B. S. HALDANE

Through this incision, I don't doubt,
The neoplasm was taken out,
Along with colon, and lymph nodes
Where cancer cells might find abodes.
A third much smaller hole is meant
To function as a ventral vent:
So now I am like two-faced Janus
The only[1] god who sees his anus.
I'll swear, without the risk of perjury,
It was a snappy bit of surgery.
My rectum is a serious loss to me,
But I've a very neat colostomy,
And hope, as soon as I am able,
To make it keep a fixed time-table.

So do not wait for aches and pains
To have a surgeon mend your drains;
If he says 'cancer' you're a dunce
Unless you have it out at once,
For if you wait it's sure to swell,
And may have progeny as well.
My final word, before I'm done,
Is 'Cancer can be rather fun.'
Thanks to the nurses and Nye Bevan
The NHS is quite like heaven
Provided one confronts the tumour
With a sufficient sense of humour.
I know that cancer often kills,
But so do cars and sleeping pills;
And it can hurt one till one sweats,
So can bad teeth and unpaid debts.
A spot of laughter, I am sure,
Often accelerates one's cure;
So let us patients do our bit
To help the surgeons make us fit.

[1] In India there are several more
With extra faces, up to four,
But both in Brahma and in Shiva
I own myself an unbeliever.

SIR OSBERT SITWELL
1892–1969

253   *Mrs. Busk*

ON dull mornings
        When the sun was bolstered,
            Buried in feathers,
It yet shone whitely in the fish-market,
        Playing on the scaly surfaces of quays,
Among the glistening curves and planes of iridescent mounds.
Here, as on a stone raft between the seas,
            The fish-wives,
            Armed with knives,
Called to each other over damp, slimy stalls
            With thick briny laughter.
Here Mrs. Busk, a mountain in oilskin
        With a creased tarpaulin face,
            Bought her wares,
        Squeezing, testing, prodding with appraising thumb and finger.

Later, in a voice like a loving cat,
She cried '*Fish*' over every street.
Her howl, without pity, seemed to govern the town,
Making all men equal.
Inhuman, it floated in at fashionable windows
And at those that gaped like caves,
Over the rain-grey slates and the red-ribbed roofs,
Oracular, like that of a prophetess foretelling doom universal;
        '*Fresh Whiting, Fine Whiting!*
            Fresh Codfish, Fine Codfish!'

HUGH MACDIARMID
(CHRISTOPHER MURRAY GRIEVE)
1892–

254   *Cattle Show*

I SHALL go among red faces and virile voices,
See stylish sheep, with fine heads and well-wooled,
And great bulls mellow to the touch,
Brood mares of marvellous approach, and geldings
With sharp and flinty bones and silken hair.

And through th'enclosure draped in red and gold
I shall pass on to spheres more vivid yet
Where countesses' coque feathers gleam and glow
And, swathed in silks, the painted ladies are
Whose laughter plays like summer lightning there.

255   FROM *Lament for the Great Music*

YET there is no great problem in the world to-day
Except disease and death men cannot end
If no man tries to dominate another.
The struggle for material existence is over. It has been won.
The need for repressions and disciplines has passed.
The struggle for truth and that indescribable necessity,
Beauty, begins now, hampered by none of the lower needs.
No one now needs live less or be less than his utmost.
And in the slow and devious development that has brought men to
     this stage
Scottish genius has played a foremost role. Yet I turn to you,
For unselfish intellect rises like a perfume
Above the faults and follies of the world of will.
But for the excellence of the typical swift life no nation
Deserves to be remembered more than the sands of the sea.

I am only that Job in feathers, a heron myself,
Gaunt and unsubstantial—yet immune to the vicissitudes
Other birds accept as a matter of course; impervious to the effects
Of even the wildest weather, no mean consideration in a country like
　　this;
And my appetite is not restricted to any particular fare.
Hence I am encountered in places far removed from one another
And widely different in an intimately topographical sense
—Spearing a rat at the mouth of a culvert at midnight
And bolting an eel on the seashore in the halflight of dawn—
Communal dweller yet lone hunter, lumbering yet swift and sustained
　　flier,
The usual steely expression of my eyes does not flatter me;
Few birds perhaps have so successfully solved
The problem of existence as my grey lanky self
That in light or darkness, wet or shine, subsists
By a combination of alertness, patience, and passivity.
A kind of Caolite mac Ronain[1] too; but it takes
　　All my wits in Scotland to-day.

This is the darkness where you have been; and have left
I think forever. It is the darkness from which nothing is cast out,
No loss, no wanton pain, no disease, no insanity,
None of the unripe intelligence of so-called dead nature,
Abortive attempts of nature to reflect itself.
All the unintelligible burden that alone leads to the height
Where it seems that extremes meet and I could reach you
i bh-fogus do dhul ar neamh-nidh,[2] with a *leim eanamhail*.[3]
In this depth that I dare not leave
I who am no dilettante of chaos and find
No bitter gratification in the contemplation of ultimate Incoherence
Know that the world is at any given moment anything it may be called
And even more difficult to group round any central character,
Yet it is out of this aimless dispersion, all these zig-zagging efforts,
All this disorderly growth, that the ideal of an epoch ends
By disentangling itself. Myriads of human activities
Are scattered in all directions by the indifferent forces

---

　[1] 'The grey spare swift runner, he who saved Fionn once by that wonderful feat of gathering couples of all the wild beasts and birds of Ireland (a ram and a crimson sheep from Inis, two water-birds from the Erne, two cormorants from the Cliath, two foxes from Slieve Gullion, and the rest).'
　[2] 'On the confines of vanishing.'
　[3] 'Bird-like leap.'

Of self-interest, passion, crime, madness—but out of their number
Some few of these activities are endowed with a little constancy
By the pure in heart, for reasons which seem to respond
To the most elementary designs of the spirit.
Civilisation, culture, all the good in the world
Depends ultimately on the existence of a few men of good will.
The perspective will converge upon them yet.
I dare not leave this dark and distracted scene.
I believe in the necessary and unavoidable responsibility of man
And in the ineluctable certainty of the resurrection
And know that the mind of man creates no ideas
Though it is ideas alone that create.
Mind is the organ through which the Universe reaches
Such consciousness of itself as is possible now, and I must not brood
On the intermittence of genius, the way consciousness varies
Or declines, as in Scotland here, till it seems
Heaven itself may be only the best that is feasible
For most people, but a sad declension from music like yours.
Yes, I am prepared to see the Heavens open
And find the celestial music poor by comparison.
Yet my duty is here. It is now the duty of the Scottish genius
Which has provided the economic freedom for it
To lead in the abandonment of creeds and moral compromises
Of every sort and to commence to express the unity of life
By confounding the curse of short-circuited thought
Circumscribing consciousness, for that is the thought
Of compromise, the medium of the time-server.
This must be done to lead men to cosmic consciousness
And as it cannot be quick, except on occasion
And *that* the creative instant, the moment of divine realisation,
When the self is lit up by its own inner light
Caused in the self by its intensity of thought
Possibly over a long period, it must be thought of as a craft
In which the consummation of the idea, not in analysis but in synthesis,
Must be the subject of the object—life.
Wherefore I cannot take the bird-like leap to you
Though well I know that: 'He that can endure
To follow with allegiance a fallen lord
Does conquer him that did his master conquer.'

I dare not leap to you now. But after all since I cannot believe
You will ever be really for everyone or even for many
And are likely to pursue in the hereafter

A separate destiny from theirs—or simply because
I long to hear the great pipers play their great music themselves.
And they all dead (save one) centuries before I was born,
And have one glimpse of my beloved Scotland yet
As the land I have dreamt of where the supreme values
Which the people recognise are states of mind
Their ruling passion the attainment of higher consciousness,
And their actual rulers those in whom they find,
Or think they do, the requisite knowledge for such attainments
And where one is not required to believe anything
But even warned of the dangers of doing so
Except with infinite qualifications and care,
My duty done, I will try to follow you on the last day of the world,
And pray I may see you all standing shoulder to shoulder
With Patrick Mor MacCrimmon and Duncan Ban MacCrimmon in
    the centre
In the hollow[1] at Boreraig or in front of Dunvegan Castle
Or on the lip of the broken graves in Kilmuir Kirkyard[2]
While, the living stricken ghastly in the eternal light
And the rest of the dead all risen blue-faced from their graves
(Though, the pipes to your hand, you will be once more
Perfectly at ease, and as you were in your prime)
All ever born crowd the islands and the West Coast of Scotland
Which has standing room for them all, and the air curdled with angels,
And everywhere that feeling seldom felt on the earth before
Save in the hearts of parents or in youth untouched by tragedy
That in its very search for personal experience often found
A like impersonality and self-forgetfulness,
And you playing: 'Farewell to Scotland, and the rest of the Earth,'
The only fit music there can be for that day
—And I will leap then and hide behind one of you,
Us Caismeachd phiob-mora bras shroiceadh am puirt.[3]

Look! Is that only the setting sun again?
Or a piper coming from far away?

[1] i.e. the pipers' hollow where the students at the college of the MacCrimmons (1500–1800) practised. Ten generations of MacCrimmons were the hereditary pipers of MacLeod of MacLeod, whose seat is at Dunvegan Castle in the Isle of Skye. Boreraig was where the MacCrimmons lived.

[2] Near Dunvegan.

[3] 'While the notes of the great pipes shrilly sound out their cries' (from Alasdair MacMhaighstir Alasdair).

256 *The Two Parents*

I LOVE my little son, and yet when he was ill
I could not confine myself to his bedside.
I was impatient of his squalid little needs,
His laboured breathing and the fretful way he cried
And longed for my wide range of interests again,
Whereas his mother sank without another care
To that dread level of nothing but life itself
And stayed day and night, till he was better, there.

Women may pretend, yet they always dismiss
Everything but mere being just like this.

257 *The Storm-Cock's Song*

MY song today is the storm-cock's song.
When the cold winds blow and the driving snow
Hides the tree-tops, only his song rings out
In the lulls in the storm. So let mine go!

On the topmost twig of a leafless ash
He sits bolt upright against the sky
Surveying the white fields and the leafless woods
And distant red in the East with his buoyant eye.

Surely he has little enough cause to sing
When even the hedgerow berries are already pulped by the frost
Or eaten by other birds—yet alone and aloft
To another hungry day his greeting is tossed.

Blessed are those who have songs to sing
When others are silent; poor song though it be,
Just a message to the silence that someone is still
Alive and glad, though on a naked tree.

What if it is only a few churning notes
Flung out in a loud and artless way?
His 'Will I do it? Do it I will!' is worth a lot
When the rest have nothing at all to say.

258 *Old Wife in High Spirits*
In an Edinburgh Pub

AN auld wumman cam' in, a mere rickle o' banes, in a faded black dress
And a bonnet wi' beads o' jet rattlin' on it;
A puir-lookin' cratur, you'd think she could haurdly ha'e had less
Life left in her and still lived, but dagonit!

He gied her a stiff whisky—she was nervous as a troot
And could haurdly haud the tumbler, puir cratur;
Syne he gied her anither, joked wi' her, and anither, and syne
Wild as the whisky up cam' her nature.

The rod that struck water frae the rock in the desert
Was naething to the life that sprang oot o' her;
The dowie auld soul was twinklin' and fizzin' wi' fire;
You never saw ocht sae souple and kir.

Like a sackful o' monkeys she was, and her lauchin'
Loupit up whiles to incredible heights;
Wi' ane owre the eight her temper changed and her tongue
Flew juist as the forkt lichtnin' skites.

The heich skeich auld cat was fair in her element;
Wanton as a whirlwind, and shairly better that way
Than a' crippen thegither wi' laneliness and cauld
Like a foretaste o' the graveyaird clay.

Some folk nae doot'll condemn gie'in' a guid spree
To the puir dune body and raither she endit her days
Like some auld tashed copy o' the Bible yin sees
On a street book-barrow's tipenny trays.

A' I ken is weel-fed and weel-put-on though they be
Ninety per cent o' respectable folk never hae
As muckle life in their creeshy carcases frae beginnin' to end
As kythed in that wild auld carline that day!

WILFRED OWEN

1893–1918

259 *Insensibility*

I

HAPPY are men who yet before they are killed
Can let their veins run cold.
Whom no compassion fleers
Or makes their feet
Sore on the alleys cobbled with their brothers.
The front line withers,
But they are troops who fade, not flowers
For poets' tearful fooling:
Men, gaps for filling:
Losses, who might have fought
Longer; but no one bothers.

II

And some cease feeling
Even themselves or for themselves.
Dullness best solves
The tease and doubt of shelling,
And Chance's strange arithmetic
Comes simpler than the reckoning of their shilling.
They keep no check on armies' decimation.

III

Happy are these who lose imagination:
They have enough to carry with ammunition.
Their spirit drags no pack,
Their old wounds, save with cold, can not more ache.
Having seen all things red,
Their eyes are rid
Of the hurt of the colour of blood for ever.
And terror's first constriction over,
Their hearts remain small-drawn.
Their senses in some scorching cautery of battle
Now long since ironed,
Can laugh among the dying, unconcerned.

IV

Happy the soldier home, with not a notion
How somewhere, every dawn, some men attack,
And many sighs are drained.
Happy the lad whose mind was never trained:
His days are worth forgetting more than not.
He sings along the march
Which we march taciturn, because of dusk,
The long, forlorn, relentless trend
From larger day to huger night.

V

We wise, who with a thought besmirch
Blood over all our soul,
How should we see our task
But through his blunt and lashless eyes?
Alive, he is not vital overmuch;
Dying, not mortal overmuch;
Nor sad, nor proud,
Nor curious at all.
He cannot tell
Old men's placidity from his.

VI

But cursed are dullards whom no cannon stuns,
That they should be as stones;
Wretched are they, and mean
With paucity that never was simplicity.
By choice they made themselves immune
To pity and whatever mourns in man
Before the last sea and the hapless stars;
Whatever mourns when many leave these shores;
Whatever shares
The eternal reciprocity of tears.

260   *Anthem for Doomed Youth*

WHAT passing-bells for these who die as cattle?
   Only the monstrous anger of the guns.
   Only the stuttering rifles' rapid rattle
Can patter out their hasty orisons.
No mockeries now for them; no prayers nor bells,
   Nor any voice of mourning save the choirs,—
The shrill, demented choirs of wailing shells;
   And bugles calling for them from sad shires.

What candles may be held to speed them all?
   Not in the hands of boys, but in their eyes
Shall shine the holy glimmers of good-byes.
   The pallor of girls' brows shall be their pall;
Their flowers the tenderness of patient minds,
And each slow dusk a drawing-down of blinds.

261   *Disabled*

HE sat in a wheeled chair, waiting for dark,
And shivered in his ghastly suit of grey,
Legless, sewn short at elbow. Through the park
Voices of boys rang saddening like a hymn,
Voices of play and pleasure after day,
Till gathering sleep had mothered them from him.

   .   .   .   .   .   .

About this time Town used to swing so gay
When glow-lamps budded in the light blue trees,
And girls glanced lovelier as the air grew dim,—
In the old times, before he threw away his knees.
Now he will never feel again how slim
Girls' waists are, or how warm their subtle hands;
All of them touch him like some queer disease.

   .   .   .   .   .   .

There was an artist silly for his face,
For it was younger than his youth, last year.
Now, he is old; his back will never brace;
He's lost his colour very far from here,
Poured it down shell-holes till the veins ran dry,
And half his lifetime lapsed in the hot race,
And leap of purple spurted from his thigh.

.   .   .   .

One time he liked a blood-smear down his leg,
After the matches, carried shoulder-high.
It was after football, when he'd drunk a peg,
He thought he'd better join.—He wonders why.
Someone had said he'd look a god in kilts,
That's why; and may be, too, to please his Meg;
Aye, that was it, to please the giddy jilts
He asked to join. He didn't have to beg;
Smiling they wrote his lie; aged nineteen years.
Germans he scarcely thought of; all their guilt,
And Austria's, did not move him. And no fears
Of Fear came yet. He thought of jewelled hilts
For daggers in plaid socks; of smart salutes;
And care of arms; and leave; and pay arrears;
Esprit de corps; and hints for young recruits.
And soon, he was drafted out with drums and cheers.

.   .   .   .   .   .

Some cheered him home, but not as crowds cheer Goal.
Only a solemn man who brought him fruits
Thanked him; and then inquired about his soul.

.   .   .   .   .   .

Now, he will spend a few sick years in Institutes,
And do what things the rules consider wise,
And take whatever pity they may dole.
To-night he noticed how the women's eyes
Passed from him to the strong men that were whole.
How cold and late it is! Why don't they come
And put him into bed? Why don't they come?

262 *The Show*

We have fallen in the dreams the ever-living
Breathe on the tarnished mirror of the world,
And then smooth out with ivory hands and sigh.
W. B. Yeats

MY soul looked down from a vague height, with Death,
As unremembering how I rose or why,
And saw a sad land, weak with sweats of dearth,
Gray, cratered like the moon with hollow woe,
And pitted with great pocks and scabs of plagues.

Across its beard, that horror of harsh wire,
There moved thin caterpillars, slowly uncoiled.
It seemed they pushed themselves to be as plugs
Of ditches, where they writhed and shrivelled, killed.

By them had slimy paths been trailed and scraped
Round myriad warts that might be little hills.

From gloom's last dregs these long-strung creatures crept,
And vanished out of dawn down hidden holes.

(And smell came up from those foul openings
As out of mouths, or deep wounds deepening.)

On dithering feet upgathered, more and more,
Brown strings, towards strings of gray, with bristling spines,
All migrants from green fields, intent on mire.

Those that were gray, of more abundant spawns,
Ramped on the rest and ate them and were eaten.

I saw their bitten backs curve, loop, and straighten,
I watched those agonies curl, lift, and flatten.
Whereat, in terror what that sight might mean,
I reeled and shivered earthward like a feather.

And Death fell with me, like a deepening moan.
And He, picking a manner of worm, which half had hid
Its bruises in the earth, but crawled no further,
Showed me its feet, the feet of many men,
And the fresh-severed head of it, my head.

284

263   *The Send-off*

DOWN the close, darkening lanes they sang their way
To the siding-shed,
And lined the train with faces grimly gay.

Their breasts were stuck all white with wreath and spray
As men's are, dead.

Dull porters watched them, and a casual tramp
Stood staring hard,
Sorry to miss them from the upland camp.
Then, unmoved, signals nodded, and a lamp
Winked to the guard.

So secretly, like wrongs hushed-up, they went.
They were not ours:
We never heard to which front these were sent.

Nor there if they yet mock what women meant
Who gave them flowers.

Shall they return to beatings of great bells
In wild train-loads?
A few, a few, too few for drums and yells,
May creep back, silent, to still village wells
Up half-known roads.

264   *The Chances*

I MIND as 'ow the night afore that show
Us five got talkin',—we was in the know.
'Over the top to-morrer; boys, we're for it.
First wave we are, first ruddy wave; that's tore it!'
'Ah well,' says Jimmy,—an' 'e's seen some scrappin'—
'There ain't no more nor five things as can 'appen:
Ye get knocked out; else wounded—bad or cushy;
Scuppered; or nowt except yer feelin' mushy.'

One of us got the knock-out, blown to chops.
T'other was 'urt, like, losin' both 'is props.
An' one, to use the word of 'ypocrites,
'Ad the misfortoon to be took be Fritz.
Now me, I wasn't scratched, praise God Amighty,
(Though next time please I'll thank 'im for a blighty).
But poor young Jim, 'e's livin' an' 'e's not;
'E reckoned 'e'd five chances, an' 'e 'ad;
'E's wounded, killed, and pris'ner, all the lot,
The bloody lot all rolled in one. Jim's mad.

265   *A Terre*

(Being the Philosophy of Many Soldiers)

SIT on the bed. I'm blind, and three parts shell.
Be careful; can't shake hands now; never shall.
Both arms have mutinied against me,—brutes.
My fingers fidget like ten idle brats.

I tried to peg out soldierly,—no use!
One dies of war like any old disease.
This bandage feels like pennies on my eyes.
I have my medals?—Discs to make eyes close.
My glorious ribbons?—Ripped from my own back
In scarlet shreds. (That's for your poetry book.)

A short life and a merry one, my buck!
We used to say we'd hate to live dead-old,—
Yet now . . . I'd willingly be puffy, bald,
And patriotic. Buffers catch from boys
At least the jokes hurled at them. I suppose
Little I'd ever teach a son, but hitting,
Shooting, war, hunting, all the arts of hurting.
Well, that's what I learnt,—that, and making money.

Your fifty years ahead seem none too many?
Tell me how long I've got? God! For one year
To help myself to nothing more than air!
One Spring! Is one too good to spare, too long?
Spring wind would work its own way to my lung,
And grow me legs as quick as lilac-shoots.

My servant's lamed, but listen how he shouts!
When I'm lugged out, he'll still be good for that.
Here in this mummy-case, you know, I've thought
How well I might have swept his floors for ever.
I'd ask no nights off when the bustle's over,
Enjoying so the dirt. Who's prejudiced
Against a grimed hand when his own's quite dust,
Less live than specks that in the sun-shafts turn,
Less warm than dust that mixes with arms' tan?
I'd love to be a sweep, now, black as Town,
Yes, or a muckman. Must I be his load?

O Life, Life, let me breathe,—a dug-out rat!
Not worse than ours the existences rats lead—
Nosing along at night down some safe rut,
They find a shell-proof home before they rot.
Dead men may envy living mites in cheese,
Or good germs even. Microbes have their joys,
And subdivide, and never come to death.
Certainly flowers have the easiest time on earth.
'I shall be one with nature, herb, and stone',
Shelley would tell me. Shelley would be stunned:
The dullest Tommy hugs that fancy now.
'Pushing up daisies' is their creed, you know.
To grain, then, go my fat, to buds my sap,
For all the usefulness there is in soap.
D'you think the Boche will ever stew man-soup?
Some day, no doubt, if . . .

                              Friend, be very sure
I shall be better off with plants that share
More peaceably the meadow and the shower.
Soft rains will touch me,—as they could touch once,
And nothing but the sun shall make me ware.
Your guns may crash around me. I'll not hear;
Or, if I wince, I shall not know I wince.
Don't take my soul's poor comfort for your jest.
Soldiers may grow a soul when turned to fronds,
But here the thing's best left at home with friends.

My soul's a little grief, grappling your chest,
To climb your throat on sobs; easily chased
On other sighs and wiped by fresher winds.

Carry my crying spirit till it's weaned
To do without what blood remained these wounds.

SIR HERBERT READ

1893–1968

266   *1945*

THEY came running over the perilous sands
    Children with their golden eyes
Crying: *Look! We have found samphire*
    Holding out their bone-ridden hands.

It might have been the spittle of wrens
    Or the silver nest of a squirrel
For I was invested with the darkness
    Of an ancient quarrel whose omens
Lay scatter'd on the silted beach.
    The children came running toward me

But I saw only the waves behind them
    Cold, salt and disastrous
Lift their black banners and break
    Endlessly, without resurrection.

RICHARD CHURCH

1893–1972

267   *The Alchemist*

THE sheet of writing paper
Slowly became a leaf of gold,
Changing under my hand.

I looked up,
And close about the window
Saw soft mallets of fog
Thudding upon the sun;
Saw him cool from fire to bronze,
To aluminium,
To water,
And vanish.

268 *Be Frugal*

BE frugal in the gift of love,
Lest you should kindle in return
Love like your own, that may survive
Long after yours has ceased to burn.

For in life's later years you may
Meet with the ghost of what you woke
And shattered at a second stroke.
God help you on that fatal day.

LILIAN BOWES LYON

1895–1949

269 *The White Hare*

AT the field's edge,
In the snow-furred sedge,
Couches the white hare;
Her stronghold is there.

Brown as the seeding grass
In summer she was,
With a creamed belly soft as ermine;
Beautiful she was among vermin.
Silky young she had,
For her spring was glad;

LILIAN BOWES LYON

On the fell above
She ran races with love.
Softly she went
In and out of the tent
Of the tasselled corn;
Till the huntsman's horn
Raised the bogey death
And she was gone, like breath.

Thanks to her senses five
This charmer is alive:
Who cheated the loud pack,
Biting steel, poacher's sack;
Among the steep rocks
Outwitted the fanged fox.

And now winter has come;
Winds have made dumb
Water's crystal chime;
In a cloak of rime
Stands the stiff bracken;
Until the cold slacken
Beauty and terror kiss;
There is no armistice.
Low must the hare lie,
With great heart and round eye.

Wind-scoured and sky-burned
The fell was her feet spurned
In the flowery season
Of her swift unreason;
Gone is her March rover;
Now noon is soon over;
Now the dark falls
Heavily from sheer walls
Of snow-cumbering cloud,
And Earth shines in her shroud.
All things now fade
That were in love's image made.

She too must decrease
Unto a thorny peace,
Who put her faith
In this flesh, in this wraith.
A hoar habit borrows
Our light lady of sorrows,
Nor is her lot strange;
Time rings a snow-change.

COLIN ELLIS

1895–1969

270   *The Old Ladies*

THEY walked in straitened ways,
   They had not great possessions;
They lived before the days
   When ladies learned professions.

And one was rather mad
   And all were rather trying,
So little life they had,
   So long they spent a-dying.

In spotless white lace caps,
   Just sitting, sitting, sitting,
Their hands upon their laps
   Or occupied with knitting.

And now they all are gone,
   Miss Alice and Miss Ella,
Miss Jane (at ninety-one)
   And poor Miss Arabella.

The house they loved so well
   And always kept so nicely,
Some auctioneer will sell
   'At six o'clock precisely.'

It seemed as though their lives
    Were wasted more than others':
They would have made good wives,
    They might have made good mothers.

Yet this was their reward:
    Through ninety years of leisure
Small precious things to guard,
    None else had time to treasure.

Their crystal was their pride,
    Their porcelain a token,
Kept safe until they died
    And handed on unbroken.

271   *An Epitaph*
            (*Twopence coloured, penny plain*)

HE worshipped at the altar of Romance
(*Tried to seduce a woman half his age*)
And dared to stake his fortune on a chance
(*Gambled away his children's heritage*).

He valued only what the world held cheap
(*Refused to work, from laziness and pride*):
Dreams were his refuge and he welcomed sleep
(*He failed in business, took to drink and died*).

ROBERT GRAVES
1895–

272   *Star-Talk*

'ARE you awake, Gemelli,
    This frosty night?'
'We'll be awake till reveillé,
Which is Sunrise,' say the Gemelli,
'It's no good trying to go to sleep:
If there's wine to be got we'll drink it deep,
    But sleep is gone for to-night,
    But sleep is gone for to-night.'

'Are you cold too, poor Pleiads,
 This frosty night?'
'Yes, and so are the Hyads:
See us cuddle and hug,' say the Pleiads,
'All six in a ring: it keeps us warm:
We huddle together like birds in a storm:
 It's bitter weather to-night,
 It's bitter weather to-night.'

'What do you hunt, Orion,
 This starry night?'
'The Ram, the Bull and the Lion,
And the Great Bear,' says Orion,
'With my starry quiver and beautiful belt
I am trying to find a good thick pelt
 To warm my shoulders to-night,
 To warm my shoulders to-night.'

'Did you hear that, Great She-bear,
 This frosty night?'
'Yes, he's talking of stripping *me* bare
Of my own big fur,' says the She-bear,
I'm afraid of the man and his terrible arrow:
The thought of it chills my bones to the marrow,
 And the frost so cruel to-night!
 And the frost so cruel to-night!'

'How is your trade, Aquarius,
 This frosty night?'
'Complaints is many and various
And my feet are cold,' says Aquarius,
'There's Venus objects to Dolphin-scales,
And Mars to Crab-spawn found in my pails,
 And the pump has frozen to-night,
 And the pump has frozen to-night.'

A Frosty Night

'ALICE, dear, what ails you,
   Dazed and lost and shaken?
Has the chill night numbed you?
   Is it fright you have taken?'

'Mother, I am very well,
   I was never better.
Mother, do not hold me so,
   Let me write my letter.'

'Sweet, my dear, what ails you?'
   'No, but I am well.
The night was cold and frosty—
   There's no more to tell.'

'Ay, the night was frosty,
   Coldly gaped the moon,
Yet the birds seemed twittering
   Through green boughs of June.

'Soft and thick the snow lay,
   Stars danced in the sky—
Not all the lambs of May-day
   Skip so bold and high.

'Your feet were dancing, Alice,
   Seemed to dance on air,
You looked a ghost or angel
   In the star-light there.

'Your eyes were frosted star-light;
   Your heart, fire and snow.
Who was it said, "I love you"?'
   'Mother, let me go!'

274 *The Cool Web*

CHILDREN are dumb to say how hot the day is,
How hot the scent is of the summer rose,
How dreadful the black wastes of evening sky,
How dreadful the tall soldiers drumming by.

But we have speech, to chill the angry day,
And speech, to dull the rose's cruel scent.
We spell away the overhanging night,
We spell away the soldiers and the fright.

There's a cool web of language winds us in,
Retreat from too much joy or too much fear:
We grow sea-green at last and coldly die
In brininess and volubility.

But if we let our tongues lose self-possession,
Throwing off language and its watery clasp
Before our death, instead of when death comes,
Facing the wide glare of the children's day,
Facing the rose, the dark sky and the drums,
We shall go mad no doubt and die that way.

275 *It Was All Very Tidy*

WHEN I reached his place,
The grass was smooth,
The wind was delicate,
The wit well timed,
The limbs well formed,
The pictures straight on the wall:
It was all very tidy.

He was cancelling out
The last row of figures,
He had his beard tied up in ribbons,
There was no dust on his shoe,
Everyone nodded:
It was all very tidy.

Music was not playing,
There were no sudden noises,
The sun shone blandly,
The clock ticked:
It was all very tidy.

'Apart from and above all this,'
I reassured myself,
'There is now myself.'
It was all very tidy.

Death did not address me,
He had nearly done:
It was all very tidy.
They asked, did I not think
It was all very tidy?

I could not bring myself
To laugh, or untie
His beard's neat ribbons,
Or jog his elbow,
Or whistle, or sing,
Or make disturbance.
I consented, frozenly,
He was unexceptionable:
It was all very tidy.

276 *Welsh Incident*

'BUT that was nothing to what things came out
From the sea-caves of Criccieth yonder.'
'What were they? Mermaids? dragons? ghosts?'
'Nothing at all of any things like that.'
'What were they, then?'
                              'All sorts of queer things,
Things never seen or heard or written about,
Very strange, un-Welsh, utterly peculiar
Things. Oh, solid enough they seemed to touch,
Had anyone dared it. Marvellous creation,

All various shapes and sizes, and no sizes,
All new, each perfectly unlike his neighbour,
Though all came moving slowly out together.'
'Describe just one of them.'
                         'I am unable.'
'What were their colours?'
                    'Mostly nameless colours,
Colours you'd like to see; but one was puce
Or perhaps more like crimson, but not purplish.
Some had no colour.'
                'Tell me, had they legs?'
'Not a leg nor foot among them that I saw.'
'But did these things come out in any order?
What o'clock was it? What was the day of the week?
Who else was present? How was the weather?'
'I was coming to that. It was half-past three
On Easter Tuesday last. The sun was shining.
The Harlech Silver Band played *Marchog Jesu*
On thirty-seven shimmering instruments,
Collecting for Caernarvon's (Fever) Hospital Fund.
The populations of Pwllheli, Criccieth,
Portmadoc, Borth, Tremadoc, Penrhyndeudraeth,
Were all assembled. Criccieth's mayor addressed them
First in good Welsh and then in fluent English,
Twisting his fingers in his chain of office,
Welcoming the things. They came out on the sand,
Not keeping time to the band, moving seaward
Silently at a snail's pace. But at last
The most odd, indescribable thing of all,
Which hardly one man there could see for wonder,
Did something recognizably a something.'
'Well, what?'
            'It made a noise.'
                          'A frightening noise?'
'No, no.'
          'A musical noise? A noise of scuffling?'
'No, but a very loud, respectable noise—
Like groaning to oneself on Sunday morning
In Chapel, close before the second psalm.'
'What did the mayor do?'
                    'I was coming to that.'

277 *She Tells Her Love While Half Asleep*

SHE tells her love while half asleep,
   In the dark hours,
     With half-words whispered low:
As Earth stirs in her winter sleep
   And puts out grass and flowers
     Despite the snow,
     Despite the falling snow.

278 *Counting the Beats*

YOU, love, and I,
(He whispers) you and I,
And if no more than only you and I
What care you or I?

Counting the beats,
Counting the slow heart beats,
The bleeding to death of time in slow heart beats,
Wakeful they lie.

Cloudless day,
Night, and a cloudless day,
Yet the huge storm will burst upon their heads one day
From a bitter sky.

Where shall we be,
(She whispers) where shall we be,
When death strikes home, O where then shall we be
Who were you and I?

Not there but here,
(He whispers) only here,
As we are, here, together, now and here,
Always you and I.

Counting the beats,
Counting the slow heart beats,
The bleeding to death of time in slow heart beats,
Wakeful they lie.

279

The Straw

PEACE, the wild valley streaked with torrents,
A hoopoe perched on the warm rock. Then why
This tremor of the straw between my fingers?

What should I fear? Have I not testimony
In her own hand, signed with her own name
That my love fell as lightning on her heart?

These questions, bird, are not rhetorical.
Watch how the straw twitches and leaps
As though the earth quaked at a distance.

Requited love; but better unrequited
If this chance instrument gives warning
Of cataclysmic anguish far away.

Were she at ease, warmed by the thought of me,
Would not my hand stay steady as this rock?
Have I undone her by my vehemence?

280

A Slice of Wedding Cake

WHY have such scores of lovely, gifted girls
   Married impossible men?
Simple self-sacrifice may be ruled out,
   And missionary endeavour, nine times out of ten.

Repeat 'impossible men': not merely rustic,
   Foul-tempered or depraved
(Dramatic foils chosen to show the world
   How well women behave, and always have behaved).

Impossible men: idle, illiterate,
   Self-pitying, dirty, sly,
For whose appearance even in City parks
   Excuses must be made to casual passers-by.

Has God's supply of tolerable husbands
    Fallen, in fact, so low?
Or do I always over-value woman
    At the expense of man?
                  Do I?
                        It might be so.

281   *Hedges Freaked With Snow*

No argument, no anger, no remorse,
    No dividing of blame.
There was poison in the cup—why should we ask
    From whose hand it came?

No grief for our dead love, no howling gales
    That through darkness blow,
But the smile of sorrow, a wan winter landscape,
    Hedges freaked with snow.

282   *Change*

'THIS year she has changed greatly'—meaning you—
My sanguine friends agree,
And hope thereby to reassure me.

No, child, you never change; neither do I.
Indeed all our lives long
We are still fated to do wrong,

Too fast caught by care of humankind,
Easily vexed and grieved,
Foolishly flattered and deceived;

And yet each knows that the changeless other
Must love and pardon still,
Be the new error what it will:

Assured by that same glint of deathlessness
Which neither can surprise
In any other pair of eyes.

MAY WEDDERBURN CANNAN

Rouen
26 April–25 May 1915

EARLY morning over Rouen, hopeful, high, courageous morning,
And the laughter of adventure and the steepness of the stair,
And the dawn across the river, and the wind across the bridges,
And the empty littered station and the tired people there.

Can you recall those mornings and the hurry of awakening,
And the long-forgotten wonder if we should miss the way,
And the unfamiliar faces, and the coming of provisions,
And the freshness and the glory of the labour of the day?

Hot noontide over Rouen, and the sun upon the city,
Sun and dust unceasing, and the glare of cloudless skies,
And the voices of the Indians and the endless stream of soldiers,
And the clicking of the tatties, and the buzzing of the flies.

Can you recall those noontides and the reek of steam and coffee,
Heavy-laden noontides with the evening's peace to win,
And the little piles of Woodbines, and the sticky soda bottles,
And the crushes in the 'Parlour', and the letters coming in?

Quiet night-time over Rouen, and the station full of soldiers,
All the youth and pride of England from the ends of all the earth;
And the rifles piled together, and the creaking of the sword-belts,
And the faces bent above them, and the gay, heart-breaking mirth.

Can I forget the passage from the cool white-bedded Aid Post
Past the long sun-blistered coaches of the khaki Red Cross train
To the truck train full of wounded, and the weariness and laughter,
And 'Good-bye, and thank you, Sister', and the empty yards again?

Can you recall the parcels that we made them for the railroad,
Crammed and bulging parcels held together by their string,
And the voices of the sergeants who called the Drafts together,
And the agony and splendour when they stood to save the King?

Can you forget their passing, the cheering and the waving,
The little group of people at the doorway of the shed,
The sudden awful silence when the last train swung to darkness,
And the lonely desolation, and the mocking stars o'erhead?

Can you recall the midnights, and the footsteps of night watchers,
Men who came from darkness and went back to dark again,
And the shadows on the rail-lines and the all-inglorious labour,
And the promise of the daylight firing blue the window-pane?

Can you recall the passing through the kitchen door to morning,
Morning very still and solemn breaking slowly on the town,
And the early coastways engines that had met the ships at daybreak,
And the Drafts just out from England, and the day shift coming down?

Can you forget returning slowly, stumbling on the cobbles,
And the white-decked Red Cross barges dropping seawards for the
   tide,
And the search for English papers, and the blessed cool of water,
And the peace of half-closed shutters that shut out the world outside?

Can I forget the evenings and the sunsets on the island,
And the tall black ships at anchor far below our balcony,
And the distant call of bugles, and the white wine in the glasses,
And the long line of the street lamps, stretching Eastwards to the sea?

. . . When the world slips slow to darkness, when the office fire burns
   lower,
My heart goes out to Rouen, Rouen all the world away;
When other men remember I remember our Adventure
And the trains that go from Rouen at the ending of the day.

F. R. HIGGINS

1896–1941

284   *The Old Jockey*

His last days linger in that low attic
That barely lets out the night,
With its gabled window on Knackers' Alley,
Just hoodwinking the light.

He comes and goes by that gabled window
And then on the window-pane
He leans, as thin as a bottled shadow—
A look and he's gone again:

Eyeing, maybe, some fine fish-women
In the best shawls of the Coombe
Or, maybe, the knife-grinder plying his treadle,
A run of sparks from his thumb!

But, O you should see him gazing, gazing,
When solemnly out on the road
The horse-drays pass overladen with grasses,
Each driver lost in his load;

Gazing until they return; and suddenly,
As galloping by they race,
From his pale eyes, like glass breaking,
Light leaps on his face.

L. A. G. STRONG

1896–1958

285   *Evening Before Rain*

WALKING at last by the tame little edge of the sea
I have found a quieter haven and rest for my thought
Than any I called to my comfort, the time I crept
Watchfully through those fields there in dread of the bull.

The bull broke loose and tore up my neighbour's garden.
Four men went out with a rope, but they have not caught him.
He is roaming the fields, yet I am already rested
Looking across the quiet water to the Isle of Skye.

The sea is pale as a sheet, the dark Island
Mottled with tiny fields, touch-close, clear;
A silence has fallen over the rocks and sea-birds
Who will soon be listening to the tingle and whisper of the rain.

My fear has gone, I can scarcely remember it.
There is a magic in this hour that calms behaviour.
I am going back in the stillness, and if he is abroad
The gray bull will browse, his back to me, when I go by.

286   *Coroner's Jury*

HE was the doctor up to Combe,
Quiet-spoke, dark, weared a moustache,
And one night his wife's mother died
After her meal, and he was tried
    For poisoning her.

Evidence come up dark's a bag,
But onions is like arsenic:
'Twas eating they, his lawyer said,
And rabbit, 'fore she went to bed,
    That took her off.

Jury withdrew. 'He saved my child,'
Says 'Lias Lee. 'Think to his wife,'
Says one. 'I tell 'ee, a nit's life
That there old 'ooman lead 'em both—
    Tedious old toad.'

'Give en six months,' says easy Joe.
'You can't do that, sirs,' foreman said,
' 'Tis neck or nothing, yes or no.'
'All right then, sir,' says Joe. ' 'Tis no,
    Not guilty, sir.'

'You, Jabez Halls?' 'I brings it in
Rabbit and onions; that's my thought.
If that didn' kill her, sirs, it ought,
To her age.' So us brought it in
    Rabbit and onions.

Doctor went free, but missis died
Soon afterward, she broke her heart.
Still Doctor bide on twenty year
Walking the moors, keeping apart
    And quiet, like.

287   *The Appointment*

YES, he said, darling, yes, of course you tried
To come, but you were kept. That's what I thought—
But something in his heart struggled and cried
Mortally, like a bird the cat has caught.

EDMUND BLUNDEN
1896–

288   *Almswomen*

AT Quincey's moat the squandering village ends,
And there in the almshouse dwell the dearest friends
Of all the village, two old dames that cling
As close as any trueloves in the spring.
Long, long ago they passed three-score-and-ten,
And in this doll's-house lived together then;
All things they have in common being so poor,
And their one fear, Death's shadow at the door.
Each sundown makes them mournful, each sunrise
Brings back the brightness in their failing eyes.

How happy go the rich fair-weather days
When on the roadside folk stare in amaze
At such a honeycomb of fruit and flowers
As mellows round their threshold; what long hours
They gloat upon their steepling hollyhocks,
Bee's balsam, feathery southernwood and stocks,
Fiery dragon's-mouths, great mallow leaves
For salves, and lemon-plants in bushy sheaves,
Shagged Esau's-hands with five green finger-tips.
Such old sweet names are ever on their lips.

As pleased as little children where these grow
In cobbled pattens and worn gowns they go,
Proud of their wisdom when on gooseberry shoots
They stuck egg shells to fright from coming fruits

The brisk-billed rascals; scanning still to see
Their neighbour owls saunter from tree to tree,
Or in the hushing half-light mouse the lane
Long-winged and lordly.
                But when those hours wane
Indoors they ponder, scared by the harsh storm
Whose pelting saracens on the window swarm,
And listen for the mail to clatter past
And church clock's deep bay withering on the blast;
They feed the fire that flings its freakish light
On pictured kings and queens grotesquely bright,
Platters and pitchers, faded calendars
And graceful hourglass trim with lavenders.

Many a time they kiss and cry and pray
That both be summoned in the selfsame day,
And wiseman linnet tinkling in his cage
End too with them the friendship of old age,
And all together leave their treasured room
Some bell-like evening when the May's in bloom.

289   *Forefathers*

HERE they went with smock and crook,
   Toiled in the sun, lolled in the shade,
Here they mudded out the brook
   And here their hatchet cleared the grade:
Harvest-supper woke their wit,
Huntsman's moon their wooings lit.

From this church they led their brides,
   From this church themselves were led
Shoulder-high; on these waysides
   Sat to take their beer and bread.
Names are gone—what men they were
These their cottages declare.

Names are vanished, save the few
   In the old brown Bible scrawled;
These were men of pith and thew,
   Whom the city never called;
Scarce could read or hold a quill,
Built the barn, the forge, the mill.

On the green they watched their sons
   Playing till too dark to see,
As their fathers watched them once,
   As my father once watched me;
While the bat and beetle flew
On the warm air webbed with dew.

Unrecorded, unrenowned,
   Men from whom my ways begin,
Here I know you by your ground
   But I know you not within—
There is silence, there survives
Not a moment of your lives.

Like the bee that now is blown
   Honey-heavy on my hand,
From his toppling tansy-throne
   In the green tempestuous land—
I'm in clover now, nor know
Who made honey long ago.

290   *Winter: East Anglia*

In a frosty sunset
   So fiery red with cold
The footballers' onset
   Rings out glad and bold;
Then boys from daily tether
   With famous dogs at heel
In starlight meet together
   And to farther hedges steal;
Where the rats are pattering
   In and out the stacks,
Owls with hatred chattering
   Swoop at the terriers' backs
And, frost forgot, the chase grows hot
   Till a rat's a foolish prize,
But the cornered weasel stands his ground,
Shrieks at the dogs and boys set round,
Shrieks as he knows they stand all round,
   And hard as winter dies.

291   *Lonely Love*

I LOVE to see those loving and beloved
Whom Nature seems to have spited; unattractive,
Unnoticeable people, whose dry track
No honey-drop of praise, or understanding,
Or bare acknowledgment that they existed,
Perhaps yet moistened. Still, they make their world.

She with her arm in his—O Fate, be kind,
Though late, be kind; let her have never cause
To live outside her dream, nor unadore
This underlying in body, mind and type,
Nor part from him what makes her dwarfish form
Take grace and fortune, envy's antitone.

I saw where through the plain a river and road
Ran quietly, and asked no more event
Than sun and rain and wind, and night and day,
Two walking—from what cruel show escaped?
Deformity, defect of mind their portion.
But I forget the rest of that free day of mine,
And in what flowerful coils, what airy music
It led me there and on; those two I see
Who, loving, walking slowly, saw not me,
But shared with me the strangest happiness.

AUSTIN CLARKE

1896–

292   *The Planter's Daughter*

WHEN night stirred at sea
And the fire brought a crowd in,
They say that her beauty
Was music in mouth
And few in the candlelight
Thought her too proud,
For the house of the planter
Is known by the trees.

Men that had seen her
Drank deep and were silent,
The women were speaking
Wherever she went—
As a bell that is rung
Or a wonder told shyly,
And O she was the Sunday
In every week.

293   *The Fair at Windgap*

THERE was airy music and sport at the fair
And showers were tenting on the bare field,
Laughter had knotted a crowd where the horses
And mares were backing, when carts from the wheelwright
Were shafted: bargains on sale everywhere and the barmen
Glassing neat whiskey or pulling black porter
On draught—and O the red brandy, the oatmeal
And the whiteness of flour in the weighing scale!

Calico petticoats, cashmere and blouses,
Blankets of buttermilk, flannel on stalls there,
Caps of bright tweed and corduroy trousers
And green or yellow ribbon with a stripe;
The tanner was hiding, the saddler plied the bradawl;
Barrows had chinaware, knives and blue razors,
Black twisted tobacco to pare in the claypipe
And the ha'penny harp that is played on a finger.

Soft as rain slipping through rushes, the cattle
Came: dealers were brawling at seven-pound-ten,
On heifers in calf a bargain was clapped
When ewes, that are nearer the grass, had taken
Two guineas; the blacksmith was filing the horn in his lap
For the fillies called up more hands than their height,
Black goats were cheap; for a sow in the stock
O'Flaherty got but the half of her farrow.

Balladmen, beggarmen, trick o' the loop men
And cardmen, hiding Queen Maeve up their sleeve,
Were picking red pennies and soon a prizefighter
Enticed the young fellows and left them all grieving:
While the marriageable girls were walking up and down
And the folk were saying that the Frenchmen
Had taken the herring from the brown tide
And sailed at daybreak, they were saying.

Twenty-five tinkers that came from Glentartan,
Not counting the jennets and barefooted women,
Had a white crop of metal upon every cart;
The neighbours were buying, but a red-headed man
Of them, swearing no stranger could bottom a kettle,
Leaped over the droves going down to the ocean,
Glibbed with the sunlight: blows were around him
And so the commotion arose at the fair.

'SAGITTARIUS'
(OLGA KATZIN)
1896–

294

Nerves
[2 Sept. 1939]

I THINK I'll get a paper,
I think I'd better wait.
I'll hear the news at six o'clock,
That's much more up to date.

It's just like last September,
Absurd how time stands still;
They're bound to make a statement.
I don't suppose they will.

I think I'd better stroll around.
Perhaps it's best to stay.
I think I'll have a whisky neat,
I can't this time of day.

I think I'll have another smoke.
I don't know what to do.
I promised to ring someone up,
I can't remember who.

They say it's been averted.
They say we're on the brink.
I'll wait for the 'New Statesman',
I wonder what they think.

They're shouting. It's a Special.
It's not. It's just street cries.
I think the heat is frightful.
God damn these bloody flies.

I see the nation's keeping cool,
The public calm is fine.
This crisis can't shake England's nerves.
It's playing hell with mine.

RUTH PITTER

1897–

295   *The Eternal Image*

HER angel looked upon God's face
As eagles gaze upon the sun,
Fair in the everlasting place.

And saw that everything is one
And moveless, in the eternal light:
Never completed, not begun.

She on the earth, with steadfast sight,
Stood like an image of the Muse
Amid the falling veils of night:

Her feet were silvered in the dews,
Dew fell upon her darkling tree,
And washed the plain with whitish hues.

Standing so still, what does she see?
She sees the changeless creature shine
Apparelled in eternity:

She knows the constancy divine;
The whole of life sees harvested,
And frozen into crystalline

And final form, the quick, the dead,
All that has ever seemed to change,
Possess at once the pale and red:

All that from birth to death may range
Newborn and dead she sees, nor says
The vision to be sad or strange.

How may this serve her mortal ways?
Truly it cannot buy her bread
Nor ease the labour of her days:

But calm her waking, quiet her bed,
For she has seen the perfect round
That binds the infant to the dead,

And one by one draws underground
All men; and still, and one by one,
Into the air the living bound,

Never completed, not begun.
With burning hair, with moveless grace,
As eagles gaze against the sun

Her angel looks upon God's face.

296   *Time's Fool*

TIME's fool, but not heaven's: yet hope not for any return.
The rabbit-eaten dry branch and the halfpenny candle
Are lost with the other treasure: the sooty kettle
Thrown away, become redbreast's home in the hedge, where the nettle
Shoots up, and bad bindweed wreathes rust-fretted handle.
Under that broken thing no more shall the dry branch burn.

Poor comfort all comfort: once what the mouse had spared
Was enough, was delight, there where the heart was at home;
The hard cankered apple holed by the wasp and the bird,
The damp bed, with the beetle's tap in the headboard heard,
The dim bit of mirror, three inches of comb:
Dear enough, when with youth and with fancy shared.

I knew that the roots were creeping under the floor,
That the toad was safe in his hole, the poor cat by the fire,
The starling snug in the roof, each slept in his place:
The lily in splendour, the vine in her grace,
The fox in the forest, all had their desire,
As then I had mine, in the place that was happy and poor.

297   *But for Lust*

BUT for lust we could be friends,
    On each other's necks could weep:
In each other's arms could sleep
    In the calm the cradle lends:

Lends awhile, and takes away.
    But for hunger, but for fear,
Calm could be our day and year
    From the yellow to the grey:

From the gold to the grey hair,
    But for passion we could rest,
But for passion we could feast
    On compassion everywhere.

Even in this night I know
    By the awful living dead,
By this craving tear I shed,
    Somewhere, somewhere it is so.

298   *Hen Under Bay-Tree*

A SQUALID, empty-headed Hen,
Resolved to rear a private brood,
Has stolen from the social pen
To this, the noblest solitude.

She feels this tree is magical.
She knows that spice, beneath her breast
That sweet dry death; for after all
Her cradle was the holy East.

Alert she sits, and all alone;
She breathes a time-defying air:
Above her, songbirds many a one
Shake the dark spire, and carol there.

Unworthy and unwitting, yet
She keeps love's vigil glorious;
Immovably her faith is set,
The plant of honour is her house.

C. S. LEWIS
1898–1963

299   *On a Vulgar Error*

No. It's an impudent falsehood. Men did not
Invariably think the newer way
Prosaic, mad, inelegant, or what not.

Was the first pointed arch esteemed a blot
Upon the church? Did anybody say
How modern and how ugly? They did not.

Plate-armour, or windows glazed, or verse fire-hot
With rhymes from France, or spices from Cathay,
Were these at first a horror? They were not.

If, then, our present arts, laws, houses, food
All set us hankering after yesterday,
Need this be only an archaising mood?

Why, any man whose purse has been let blood
By sharpers, when he finds all drained away
Must compare how he stands with how he stood.

If a quack doctor's breezy ineptitude
Has cost me a leg, must I forget straightway
All that I can't do now, all that I could?

So, when our guides unanimously decry
The backward glance, I think we can guess why.

ROBERT RENDALL
1898–1967

300   *Angle of Vision*

But, John, have you seen the world, said he,
Trains and tramcars and sixty-seaters,
Cities in lands across the sea—
Giotto's tower and the dome of St. Peter's?

No, but I've seen the arc of the earth,
From the Birsay shore, like the edge of a planet,
And the lifeboat plunge through the Pentland Firth
To a cosmic tide with the men that man it.

EDGELL RICKWORD
1898–

301   *Winter Warfare*

COLONEL Cold strode up the Line
  (tabs of rime and spurs of ice);
stiffened all who met his glare:
  horses, men, and lice.

Visited a forward post,
  left them burning, ear to foot;
fingers stuck to biting steel,
  toes to frozen boot.

Stalked on into No Man's Land,
  turned the wire to fleecy wool,
iron stakes to sugar sticks
  snapping at a pull.

Those who watched with hoary eyes
  saw two figures gleaming there;
Hauptman Kalte, Colonel Cold,
  gaunt in the grey air.

Stiffly, tinkling spurs they moved,
  glassy eyed, with glinting heel
stabbing those who lingered there
  torn by screaming steel.

302   *The Encounter*

TWITTINGPAN seized my arm, though I'd have gone
willingly. To be seen with him alone,
the choicest spirit of the present age,
flattered my vanity into quite a rage.
His was the presence always in dispute
by every cocktail hostess of repute;

And I'd long enjoyed seeing his drooping form
breast each successive, new-aesthetic storm.
He had championed Epstein, Gertrude, and *Parade*,
and even now was nothing of a die-hard;
(I had last heard him on some Red-film show-day
expounding *tonal montage* in the foyer);
being two days nimbler than the smartest clique
he gave the cachet to the safest chic.
    We turned from Regent Street to Conduit Street.
He thought my overcoat was far from neat,
offered his tailor's name and then forgot.
His mind was in a turmoil and overshot
immediate objects in transcendent aims.
Juggling voluptuously with Christian names
he listed for me each new partnership
contracted since I'd given Town the slip
for ten days in the wilds near Sevenoaks;
and Lord! I thought, no wonder Douglas[1] croaks
imminent fire and brimstone; though no Prudhomme,
I could never quite regret the fate of Sodom.
    This intellectual athlete next began
praising the freedom of the modern man
from dogma, morals, and the plagues of nature—
a scientific, half-angelic creature,
immune from all—my hero almost winces—
Tokyo is down,[2] but dancing's on at Prince's.
He summed up briefly all religion means
and then explained the universe by Jeans.
Burly Jack Haldane next supplied his text
(and as the Sacred Writ is always vext
into queer meanings for sectarian ends),
Twittingpan preached the marriage of true friends
when blessed parthenogenesis arrives
and he-uranians can turn honest wives.
    'Consider Bond Street,' as we reached it, cried
falsetto Twittingpan our period's pride,
'Does it not realise in microcosm
the whole ideal Time nurses in its bosom?

[1] James, not Norman. A vice-hound and high-brow baiter employed by the *Sunday Express*.
[2] This refers to the 1923 catastrophe. Also to Voltaire.

Luxury, cleanliness and objets d'art,
the modern Trinity for us all who are
freed from the burden of the sense of sin.
Lord Russell says . . .' I feared he would begin
an exposition of the free man's worship,
that neo-anabaptist, compelled to dip
not now from mystic but hygienic motives.
'But look, in Shanks's[1] shop the Past still lives;
those gross utensils symbolically bind us
to the brute part we soon shall leave behind us,
for Haldane promises in the world-to-come
excretion's inoffensive minimum.'[2]
He gestured freely and drew inquiring stares
from elegant shoppers wrapped like dainty bears,
whilst I blushed like a country cousin come
to the Time-metropolis from an archaic home.
He saw my red cheeks, and with a kindly air
proclaimed sophistication everywhere.
'You must meet Iris, she who lives serene
in the intense confession of the obscene
and drags her tea-time sex-affair all fresh
to the dinner-table, like a cat with flesh.
Her new book is, I hear, just too, *too* topical,
though Janet's peeved not to be in it at all.
But Basil's poems are far more utter than
you can imagine, as you don't know the man.'
With that he handed me a deckled sheet
where these lines staggered on uncertain feet:

> you the one onely
> not more but one than
> two is superfluous two is
> i reminds you of me
> me reminds i of you
> i is another
> identity unidentifiable
> then say is love not
> the word
> all love is perhaps no love
> or is perhaps luck
> or no luck is no love rather.

---

[1] Sanitary engineers.   [2] See *Daedalus*.

'Chaste, isn't it? and yes, I must explain
that I inspired it, at risk of seeming vain;
otherwise you might miss its fine notations
which do convey so subtly my relations
with the dear fellow. You two must really meet;
he would impress you even in the street.'
I fixed my look at 'silent admiration'
and paced along all tense with expectation,
though bashful at my Siamese-like linking
with the lank oracle of modern thinking.
   'Lewis and Middleton Murry are, I'm sure,
the only moderns likely to endure
of the older crowd; for Eliot's later works
are merely sanctimonious quips and quirks;
and Huxley is portentously obsessed
with the problems that make City clerks depressed.
Don't you think Wyndham Lewis too divine?
That brute male strength he shows in every line!
I swear if he'd flogged me in his last book but one,
as some kind person informed me he has done,
I'd have forgiven him for the love of art.
And you, too, ought to take his works to heart
as I have done, for torn by inner strife,
I've made him mentor of my mental life.
You cannot imagine what a change that worked.
I who was all emotion, and always shirked
the cold chaste isolation of male mind,
now thrust in front all I had kept behind.
I'd lived in Time and Motion and Sensation,
then smashed my watch and burnt the Bloomsbury *Nation* ...
But here comes Clarence,—Clarence with Basil!' So
like a hot poker then he let my arm go;
and, stifling jealousy, hailed them with 'How nice!'
They flaunted gay shirts and a grand old vice.
Poor Twittingpan had no novelty to produce;
I was not shabby enough to be of use
as a quaint genius, nor smart enough for friend.
Poor wretch! To put his agony at an end
I touched my hat, *good-day*, *sir*-ed, like a tout,
and left my Twittingpan to lie it out.

SIR NOEL COWARD
1899–

303 *The Boy Actor*

I CAN remember. I can remember.
The months of November and December
  Were filled for me with peculiar joys
So different from those of other boys
  For other boys would be counting the days
Until end of term and holiday times
  But I was acting in Christmas plays
While they were taken to pantomimes.
  I didn't envy their Eton suits,
Their children's dances and Christmas trees.
  My life had wonderful substitutes
For such conventional treats as these.
  I didn't envy their country larks,
Their organized games in panelled halls:
  While they made snow-men in stately parks
I was counting the curtain calls.

I remember the auditions, the nerve-racking auditions:
Darkened auditorium and empty, dusty stage,
Little girls in ballet dresses practising 'positions',
Gentlemen with pince-nez asking you your age.
Hopefulness and nervousness struggling within you,
Dreading that familiar phrase, 'Thank you dear, no more.'
Straining every muscle, every tendon, every sinew
To do your dance much better than you'd ever done before.
Think of your performance. Never mind the others,
Never mind the pianist, talent must prevail.
Never mind the baleful eyes of other children's mothers
Glaring from the corners and willing you to fail.

SIR NOEL COWARD

I can remember. I can remember.
The months of November and December
  Were more significant to me
Than other months could ever be
  For they were the months of high romance
When destiny waited on tip-toe,
  When every boy actor stood a chance
Of getting into a Christmas show,
  Not for me the dubious heaven
Of being some prefect's protégé!
  Not for me the Second Eleven.
For me, two performances a day.

    Ah those first rehearsals! Only very few lines:
    Rushing home to mother, learning them by heart,
    'Enter Left through window'—Dots to mark the cue lines:
    'Exit with the others'—Still it *was* a part.
    Opening performance; legs a bit unsteady,
    Dedicated tension, shivers down my spine,
    Powder, grease and eye-black, sticks of make-up ready
    Leichner number three and number five and number nine.
    World of strange enchantment, magic for a small boy
    Dreaming of the future, reaching for the crown,
    Rigid in the dressing-room, listening for the call-boy
    'Overture Beginners—Everybody Down!'

I can remember. I can remember.
The months of November and December,
  Although climatically cold and damp,
Meant more to me than Aladdin's lamp.
I see myself, having got a job,
Walking on wings along the Strand,
Uncertain whether to laugh or sob
And clutching tightly my mother's hand,
  I never cared who scored the goal
Or which side won the silver cup,
  I never learned to bat or bowl
But I heard the curtain going up.

BASIL BUNTING

1900–

304   *On the Fly-Leaf of Pound's Cantos*

THERE are the Alps. What is there to say about them?
They don't make sense. Fatal glaciers, crags cranks climb,
jumbled boulder and weed, pasture and boulder, scree,
et l'on entend, maybe, *le refrain joyeux et leger.*
Who knows what the ice will have scraped on the rock it is smoothing?

There they are, you will have to go a long way round
if you want to avoid them.
It takes some getting used to. There are the Alps,
fools! Sit down and wait for them to crumble!

305   *Chomei at Toyama*

*(Kamo-no-Chomei, born at Kamo 1154, died at Toyama on
Mount Hino, 24 June 1216)*

THE swirl sleeping in the waterfall!
The scum on motionless pools appearing
           disappearing!

Eaves formal on the zenith,
lofty city Kyoto,
wealthy, without antiquities!

Housebreakers clamber about,
builders raising floor upon floor
at the corner sites, replacing
gardens by bungalows.

In the town where I was known
the young men stare at me.
A few faces I know remain.

Whence comes man at his birth? or where
does death lead him? Whom do you mourn?
Whose steps wake your delight?
Dewy hibiscus dries: though dew
outlast the petals.

I have been noting events forty years.

On the twentyseventh May eleven hundred
and seventyseven, eight p.m., fire broke out
at the corner of Tomi and Higuchi streets.
In a night
palace, ministries, university, parliament
were destroyed. As the wind veered
flames spread out in the shape of an open fan.
Tongues torn by the gusts stretched and leapt.
In the sky clouds of cinders lit red with the blaze.

Some choked, some burned, some barely escaped.
Sixteen great officials lost houses and
very many poor. A third of the city burned;
several thousands died; and of beasts,
oxen and horses and such, limitless numbers.

Men are fools to invest in real estate.

Three years less three days later a wind
starting near the outer boulevard
broke a path a quarter mile across
to Sixth Avenue.

Not a house stood. Some were felled whole,
some in splinters; some had left
great beams upright in the ground
and round about
lay rooves scattered where the wind flung them.
Flocks of furniture in the air,
everything flat fluttered like dead leaves.
A dust like fog or smoke,
you could hear nothing for the roar,
         'bufera infernal!'
Lamed some, wounded some.
This cyclone turned southwest.

Massacre without cause.

Portent?

The same year thunderbolted change of capital,
fixed here, Kyoto, for ages.
Nothing compelled the change nor was it an easy matter
but the grumbling was disproportionate.
We moved, those with jobs
or wanting jobs or hangers on of the rest,
in haste haste fretting to be the first.
Rooftrees overhanging empty rooms;
dismounted: floating down the river;
The soil returned to heath.

I visited the new site: narrow and too uneven,
cliffs and marshes, deafening shores, perpetual strong winds;
the palace a logcabin dumped amongst the hills
(yet not altogether inelegant).
There was no flat place for houses, many vacant lots,
the former capital wrecked, the new a camp,
and thoughts like clouds changing, frayed by a breath:
peasants bewailing lost land, newcomers aghast at prices.
No one in uniform: the crowds
resembled demobilized conscripts.

There were murmurs. Time defined them.
In the winter the decree was rescinded,
we returned to Kyoto;
but the houses were gone and none
could afford to rebuild them.

I have heard of a time when kings beneath bark rooves
watched the chimneys.
When smoke was scarce, taxes were remitted.

To appreciate present conditions
collate them with those of antiquity.

Drought, floods, and a dearth. Two fruitless autumns.
Empty markets, swarms of beggars. Jewels
sold for a handful of rice. Dead stank
on the curb, lay so thick on
Riverside Drive a car couldn't pass.
The pest bred.
That winter my fuel was the walls of my own house.

Fathers fed their children and died,
babies died sucking the dead.
The priest Hoshi went about marking their foreheads
A, Amida, their requiem;
he counted them in the East End in the last two months,
fortythree thousand A's.

Crack, rush, ye mountains, bury your rills!
Spread your green glass, ocean, over the meadows!
Scream, avalanche, boulders amok, strangle the dale!
O ships in the sea's power, O horses
On shifting roads, in the earth's power, without hoofhold!
This is the earthquake, this was
the great earthquake of Genryaku!

The chapel fell, the abbey, the minister and the small shrines
fell, their dust rose and a thunder of houses falling.
O to be birds and fly or dragons and ride on a cloud!
The earthquake, the great earthquake of Genryaku!

A child building a mud house against a high wall:
I saw him crushed suddenly, his eyes hung
from their orbits like two tassels.
His father howled shamelessly—an officer.
I was not abashed at his crying.

Such shocks continued three weeks; then lessening,
but still a score daily as big as an average earthquake;
then fewer, alternate days, a tertian ague of tremors.
There is no record of any greater.
It caused a religious revival.
Months . . .
Years . . .

  .   .   .   .
Nobody mentions it now.

This is the unstable world and
we in it unstable and our houses.

The poor man living amongst the rich
gives no rowdy parties, doesn't sing.
Dare he keep his child at home, keep a dog?
He dare not pity himself above a whimper.

But he visits, he flatters, he is put in his place,
he remembers the patch on his trousers.
His wife and sons despise him for being poor.
He has no peace.

If he lives in an alley of rotting frame houses
he dreads a fire.
If he commutes he loses his time
and leaves his house daily to be plundered by gunmen.

The bureaucrats are avaricious.
He who has no relatives in the Inland Revenue,
poor devil!

Whoever helps him enslaves him
and follows him crying out: '*Gratitude!*'
If he wants success he is wretched.
If he doesn't he passes for mad.

Where shall I settle, what trade choose
that the mind may practise, the body rest?

My grandmother left me a house
but I was always away
for my health and because I was alone there.
When I was thirty I couldn't stand it any longer,
I built a house to suit myself:
one bamboo room, you would have thought it was a cartshed,
poor shelter from snow or wind.
It stood on the flood plain. And that quarter
is also flooded with gangsters.

One generation
I saddened myself with idealistic philosophies,
but before I was fifty
I perceived that there was no time to lose,
left home and conversation.
Among the cloudy mountains of Ohara
spring and autumn, spring and autumn, spring and autumn,
emptier than ever.

The dew evaporates from my sixty years,
I have built my last house, or hovel,
a hunter's bivouac, an old
silkworm's cocoon:
ten feet by ten, seven high: and I,
reckoning it a lodging not a dwelling,
omitted the usual foundation ceremony.

I have filled the frames with clay,
set hinges at the corners;
easy to take it down and carry it away
when I get bored with this place.
Two barrowloads of junk
and the cost of a man to shove the barrow,
no trouble at all.

Since I have trodden Hino mountain
noon has beaten through the awning
over my bamboo balcony, evening
shone on Amida.
I have shelved my books above the window,
lute and mandolin near at hand,
piled bracken and a little straw for bedding,
a smooth desk where the light falls, stove for bramblewood.
I have gathered stones, fitted
stones for a cistern, laid bamboo
pipes. No woodstock,
wood enough in the thicket.

Toyama, sung in the creepers!
Toyama, deep in the dense gully, open
westward whence the dead ride out of Eden
squatting on blue clouds of wistaria.
(Its scent drifts west to Amida.)

Summer? Cuckoo's *Follow, follow*—to
harvest Purgatory hill!
Fall? The nightgrasshopper will
shrill *Fickle life*!
Snow will thicken on the doorstep,
melt like a drift of sins.
No friend to break silence,
no one will be shocked if I neglect the rite.
There's a Lent of commandments kept
where there's no way to break them.

A ripple of white water after a boat,
shining water after the boats Mansami saw
rowing at daybreak
at Okinoya.
'*Between the maple leaf and the caneflower*'
murmurs the afternoon—Po Lo-tien
saying goodbye on the verge of Jinyo river.
(I am playing scales on my mandolin.)

Be limber, my fingers, I am going to play 'Autumn Wind'
to the pines, I am going to play 'Hastening Brook'
to the water. I am no player
but there's nobody listening,
I do it for my own amusement.

Sixteen and sixty, I and the gamekeeper's boy,
one zest and equal, chewing tsubana buds,
One zest and equal, persimmon, pricklypear,
ears of sweetcorn pilfered from Valley Farm.

The view from the summit: sky bent over Kyoto,
picnic villages, Fushimi and Toba:
a very economical way of enjoying yourself.
Thought runs along the crest, climbs Sumiyama;
beyond Kasatori it visits the great church,
goes on pilgrimage to Ishiyama (no need to foot it!)
or the graves of poets, of Semimaru who said:
>   '*Somehow or other*
>   *we scuttle through a lifetime.*
>   *Somehow or other*
>   *neither palace nor straw-hut*
>   *is quite satisfactory.*'

Not emptyhanded, with cherryblossom, with red maple
as the season gives it to decorate my Buddha
or offer a sprig at a time to chancecomers, home!

A fine moonlit night,
I sit at the window with a headful of old verses.

'Whenever a monkey howls there are tears on my cuff.'

*'Those are fireflies that seem
the fishermen's lights
off Maki island.'*

A shower at dawn
sings
like the hillbreeze in the leaves.

*'At the pheasant's chirr I recall
my father and mother uncertainly.'*

I rake my ashes.

         *'Chattering fire,
soon kindled, soon burned out,
fit wife for an old man!'*

Neither closed in one landscape
nor in one season
the mind moving in illimitable
recollection.

I came here for a month
five years ago.
There's moss on the roof.

And I hear Soanso's dead
back in Kyoto.
I have as much room as I need.

I know myself and mankind.
   .   .   .   .
I don't want to be bothered.

BASIL BUNTING

(You will make me editor
of the Imperial Anthology?

I don't want to be bothered.)

You build for your wife, children,
cousins and cousins' cousins.
You want a house to entertain in.

A man like me can have neither servants nor friends
in the present state of society.
If I did not build for myself
for whom should I build?

Friends fancy a rich man's riches,
friends suck up to a man in high office.
If you keep straight you will have no friends
but catgut and blossom in season.

Servants weigh out their devotion
in proportion to their perquisites.
What do they care for peace and quiet?
There are more pickings in town.

I sweep my own floor
—less fuss.
I walk; I get tired
but do not have to worry about a horse.

My hands and feet will not loiter
when I am not looking.
I will not overwork them.
Besides, it's good for the health.

My jacket's wistaria flax,
my blanket hemp,
berries and young greens
my food.

(Let it be quite understood,
all this is merely personal.
I am not preaching the simple life
to those who enjoy being rich.)

BASIL BUNTING

I am shifting rivermist, not to be trusted.
I do not ask anything extraordinary of myself.
I like a nap after dinner
and to see the seasons come round in good order.

Hankering, vexation and apathy,
that's the run of the world.
Hankering, vexation and apathy,
keeping a carriage won't cure it.

Keeping a man in livery
won't cure it. Keeping a private fortress
won't cure it. These things satisfy no craving.
Hankering, vexation and apathy . . .

I am out of place in the capital,
people take me for a beggar,
as you would be out of place in this sort of life,
you are so—I regret it—so welded to your vulgarity.

The moonshadow merges with darkness
on the cliffpath,
a tricky turn near ahead.

Oh! There's nothing to complain about.
Buddha says: 'None of the world is good'.
I am fond of my hut . . .

I have renounced the world;
have a saintly
appearance.

I do not enjoy being poor,
I've a passionate nature.
My tongue
clacked a few prayers.

306   *What the Chairman Told Tom*

POETRY? It's a hobby.
I run model trains.
Mr Shaw there breeds pigeons.

It's not work. You don't sweat.
Nobody pays for it.
You *could* advertise soap.

Art, that's opera; or repertory—
The Desert Song.
Nancy was in the chorus.

But to ask for twelve pounds a week—
married, aren't you?—
you've got a nerve.

How could I look a bus conductor
in the face
if I paid you twelve pounds?

Who says it's poetry, anyhow?
My ten year old
can do it *and* rhyme.

I get three thousand and expenses,
a car, vouchers,
but I'm an accountant.

They do what I tell them,
my company.
What do *you* do?

Nasty little words, nasty long words,
it's unhealthy.
I want to wash when I meet a poet.

They're Reds, addicts,
all delinquents.
What you write is rot.

Mr Hines says so, and he's a schoolteacher,
he ought to know.
Go and find *work*.

MICHAEL ROBERTS
1902–1948

307   *Hymn to the Sun*

'VOY wawm' said the dustman
one bright August morning—
But that was in Longbenton,
under the trees.

He was Northumbrian, he'd never known
horizons shimmering in the sun,
men with swart noontide faces sleeping, thick with flies,
by roadside cherry trees.

He was Northumbrian, how should he know
mirage among blue hills,
thin streams that tinkle silence in the still
pulsating drone of summer—

How should he know
how cool the darkness in the white-washed inns
after the white road dancing, and the stones,
and quick dry lizards, round Millevaches?

'*Fait chaud*,' as each old woman said,
going over the hill, in Périgord,
prim in tight bonnets, worn black dresses, and content
with the lilt of sunlight in their bones.

308   *H.M.S. Hero*

PALE grey, her guns hooded, decks clear of all impediment,
Easily, between the swart tugs, she glides in the pale October sunshine:
It is Saturday afternoon, and the men are at football,
The wharves and the cobbled streets are silent by the slow river.

Smoothly, rounding the long bend, she glides to her place in history,
Past the grimed windows cracked and broken,
Past Swan Hunter's, Hawthorn Leslie's, Armstrong's,
Down to the North Sea, and trials, and her first commission.

Here is grace; and a job well done; built only for one end.
Women watch from the narrow doorways and give no sign,
Children stop playing by the wall and stare in silence
At gulls wheeling above the Tyne, or the ship passing.

ROY CAMPBELL

1902–1957

309   *Heartbreak Camp*

RED as the guardroom lamp
The moon inspects the trees:
High over Heartbreak Camp,
Orion stands at ease:

With buttons lit, for Sentry,
He challenges who's there
Acceding all the entry
Whose passport is Despair.

All joys are privates there
Who seldom go on leave
And only sorrows wear
Three chevrons on their sleeve:

But boredom wears three pips,
A fiend of monstrous size,
With curses on his lips
And circles round his eyes.

All round, for league on league
And labouring up the hills,
The clouds are on fatigue,
Collecting damps and chills.

ROY CAMPBELL

Sir Dysentery Malaria,
A famous brigadier,
Commands the whole sub-area,
And stalking in his rear,

A more ferocious colonel
Lord Tremens (of the Drunks)
To whose commands infernal
We tremble in our bunks.

Here till the pale aurora
Dismiss the stars from drill,
I dream of my señora
Behind the guardroom grille.

In the outcry of crickets
And the silence of guitars,
I watch the lonely pickets
And the slow patrol of stars.

Our vineyard and the terrace
By the Tagus, they recall,
With the Rose of the Sierras,
Whom I love the best of all!

My heart was once her campfire
And burned for her alone,
Fed with the thyme and samphire
That azure days had grown.

My thoughts for their safari
Have scarcely taken wings
Through spaces wide and starry
To hear her stroke the strings.

But ere one word be spoken
A fiend my elbow jogs,
The reverie is broken
By the tomtom of the wogs:

And, all illusions killing,
Upon the stillness jars
A far hyaena drilling
His company of stars.

310   *Autumn*

I LOVE to see, when leaves depart,
The clear anatomy arrive,
Winter, the paragon of art,
That kills all forms of life and feeling
Save what is pure and will survive.

Already now the clanging chains
Of geese are harnessed to the moon:
Stripped are the great sun-clouding planes:
And the dark pines, their own revealing,
Let in the needles of the noon.

Strained by the gale the olives whiten
Like hoary wrestlers bent with toil
And, with the vines, their branches lighten
To brim our vats where summer lingers
In the red froth and sun-gold oil.

Soon on our hearth's reviving pyre
Their rotted stems will crumble up:
And like a ruby, panting fire,
The grape will redden on your fingers
Through the lit crystal of the cup.

311   FROM *The Golden Shower*

HERE, where relumed by changing seasons, burn
The phoenix trees of Africa in turn,
Each from the other's ashes taking fire
As swiftly to revive as to expire,
Mimosa, jacaranda, kaffirboom,
And tulip-tree, igniting bloom from bloom,
While through their zodiac of flowery signs
The flame-furred sun like some huge moth is whirled
Circling forever, as he fades or shines,
Around the open blossom of the world—

All things as if to Venus' touch ignite
And the grey soil is tinder to her tread
Whence married flowers explode into the light—
And burn with fiery pollen as they wed.
She burns through bark and wood as flame through glass
The dust is fuel to her warm desire
On which, with scintillating plumes, the grass
Runs waving like a disembodied fire:
But we of all her splendours are most splendid
In whom the rest are held and comprehended,
And our clear sprites, whom rays and showers begem,
Burn through each other as the world through them.

Though we seem merely mortal, what we are,
Is clearly mirrored on a deathless flood.
We change and fade: our dust is strewn afar—
Only the ancient river of our blood,
Rising far-off in unimagined spaces,
Red with the silt and ruin of the past
And churning with the strife of savage races,
Like deep Zambezi goes on rolling past,
Swiftens through us its energies unending,
And reaches out, beneath the shades we cast,
To what vast ocean of the night descending
Or in what sunny lake at last to sleep,
We do not know—save that it turns to foam,
Just here, for us; its currents curl and comb
And all its castalies in thunder leap,
Silvering, forth into a white resilience
Of ecstacy, whose momentary brilliance
Must compensate eternities of sleep.
Knowing these things, are not we lovers, then,
Though mortal in our nature, more than men?
Since by our senses, as by rivers, veined,
The hills of primal memory are drained,
And the dim summits of their frosty spars,
Whose tops are nibbled by the grazing stars,
Thawed by the rising noon of our desire,
And fusing into consciousness and fire,
Down through the sounding canyons of the soul
Their rich alluvium of starlight roll.

We bear to future times the secret news
That first was whispered to the new-made earth:
We are like worlds with nations in our thews,
Shaped for delight, and primed for endless birth.
We never kiss but vaster shapes possess
Our bodies: towering up into the skies,
We wear the night and thunder for our dress,
While, vaster than imagination, rise
Two giant forms, like cobras flexed to sting,
Bending their spines in one tremendous ring
With all the starlight burning through their eyes,
Fire in their loins, and on their lips the hiss
Of breath indrawn above some steep abyss.
When, like the sun, our heavenly desire
Has turned this flesh into a cloud of fire
Through which our nerves their strenuous lightnings fork,
Eternity has blossomed in an hour
And as we gaze upon that wondrous flower
We think the world a beetle on its stalk.

312   *On Some South African Novelists*

YOU praise the firm restraint with which they write—
I'm with you there, of course:
They use the snaffle and the curb all right,
But where's the bloody horse?

313   *On the Same*

FAR from the vulgar haunts of men
Each sits in her 'successful room',
Housekeeping with her fountain pen
And writing novels with her broom.

314   FROM *The Georgiad*

NEXT him Jack Squire through his own tear-drops sploshes
In his great, flat, trochaical goloshes,
And far behind him leaves a spoor of mud
To sprout a thousand lilies of Malud—
Now as he would exalt to deathless Fame
His vanished Lycidas, 'Willie' by name,
And to the dead man's pet his grief expresses,
Outslobbering the bulldog he caresses,
Like some strange Orpheus for Eurydice
Inciting Cerberus to sympathy,
The patient monster as he listens drops
A sympathetic trickle from his chops,
And both together mix the mutual moan,
Squire for the dead, and Fido for a bone.
Partners in grief, in watery tourney vie
The rheumy jowl and the poetic eye,
While with its tail for baton, keeping time,
The poet wags his mangy stump of rhyme.
Nor at his football match is Squire more gay—
Heart-rending verse describes funereal play;
While swarming adjectives in idle ranks,
As dumb spectators, load the groaning planks,
See the fat nouns, like porky forwards, sprawl
Into a scrum that never heels the ball—
A mass of moving bottoms like a sea,
All fatter than his head, if that could be;
While still attentive at their clumsy calves
The adverbs pine away, dejected halves,
The verbs hang useless by, like unfed threes
With trousers idly flapping in the breeze,
And while they strike their arm-pits for some heat
Or idly stamp their splayed trochaic feet,
The two full-backs of alternating rhyme
Walk sadly up and down to kill the time.

A. S. J. TESSIMOND
1902–1962

315   *Jamaican Bus Ride*

THE live fowl squatting on the grapefruit and bananas
in the basket of the copper-coloured lady
is gloomy but resigned.
The four very large baskets on the floor
are in everybody's way,
as the conductor points out
loudly, often, but in vain.

Two quadroon dandies are disputing
who is standing on whose feet.

When we stop,
a boy vanishes through the door marked ENTRANCE;
but those entering through the door marked EXIT
are greatly hindered by the fact that when we started
there were twenty standing,
and another ten have somehow inserted themselves
into invisible crannies
between dark sweating body and body.

With an odour of petrol
both excessive and alarming
we hurtle hell-for-leather
between crimson bougainvillea blossom
and scarlet poinsettia
and miraculously do not run over
three goats, seven hens and a donkey
as we pray
that the driver has not fortified himself
at Daisy's Drinking Saloon
with more than four rums:
or by the gods of Jamaica
this day is our last!

STEVIE SMITH

1902–1971

316   *Not Waving but Drowning*

NOBODY heard him, the dead man,
But still he lay moaning:
I was much further out than you thought
And not waving but drowning.

Poor chap, he always loved larking
And now he's dead
It must have been too cold for him his heart gave way,
They said.

Oh, no no no, it was too cold always
(Still the dead one lay moaning)
I was much too far out all my life
And not waving but drowning.

317   *Away, Melancholy*

AWAY, melancholy,
Away with it, let it go.

Are not the trees green,
The earth as green?
Does not the wind blow,
Fire leap and the rivers flow?
Away melancholy.

The ant is busy
He carrieth his meat,
All things hurry
To be eaten or eat.
Away, melancholy.

Man, too, hurries,
Eats, couples, buries,
He is an animal also
With a hey ho melancholy,
Away with it, let it go.

Man of all creatures
Is superlative
(Away melancholy)
He of all creatures alone
Raiseth a stone
(Away melancholy)
Into the stone, the god,
Pours what he knows of good
Calling good, God.
Away melancholy, let it go.

Speak not to me of tears,
Tyranny, pox, wars,
Saying, Can God,
Stone of man's thought, be good?

Say rather it is enough
That the stuffed
Stone of man's good, growing,
By man's called God.
Away, melancholy, let it go.

Man aspires
To good,
To love
Sighs;

Beaten, corrupted, dying
In his own blood lying
Yet heaves up an eye above
Cries, Love, love.
It is his virtue needs explaining,
Not his failing.

Away, melancholy,
Away with it, let it go.

318 *The Singing Cat*

IT was a little captive cat
  Upon a crowded train
His mistress takes him from his box
  To ease his fretful pain.

She holds him tight upon her knee
  The graceful animal
And all the people look at him
  He is so beautiful.

But oh he pricks and oh he prods
  And turns upon her knee
Then lifteth up his innocent voice
  In plaintive melody.

He lifteth up his innocent voice
  He lifteth up, he singeth
And to each human countenance
  A smile of grace he bringeth.

He lifteth up his innocent paw
  Upon her breast he clingeth
And everybody cries, Behold
  The cat, the cat that singeth.

He lifteth up his innocent voice
  He lifteth up, he singeth
And all the people warm themselves
  In the love his beauty bringeth.

319 *Edmonton, thy cemetery . . .*

EDMONTON, thy cemetery
  In which I love to tread
Has roused in me a dreary thought
  For all the countless dead,
  Ah me, the countless dead.

Yet I believe that one is one
And shall for ever be,
And while I hold to this belief
I walk, oh cemetery,
Thy footpaths happily.

And I believe that two and two
Are but an earthly sum
Whose totalling has no part at all
In heavenly kingdom-come,
I love the dead, I cry, I love
Each happy happy one.

Till Doubt returns with dreary face
And fills my heart with dread
For all the tens and tens and tens
That must make up a hundred,
And I begin to sing with him
As if Belief had never been
Ah me, the countless dead, ah me
The countless countless dead.

320   *Tenuous and Precarious*

TENUOUS and Precarious
Were my guardians,
Precarious and Tenuous,
Two Romans.

My father was Hazardous,
Hazardous,
Dear old man,
Three Romans.

There was my brother Spurious,
Spurious Posthumous,
Spurious was Spurious,
Was four Romans.

344

My husband was Perfidious,
He was Perfidious,
Five Romans.

Surreptitious, our son,
Was Surreptitious,
He was six Romans.

Our cat Tedious
Still lives,
Count not Tedious
Yet.

My name is Finis,
Finis, Finis,
I am Finis,
Six, five, four, three, two,
One Roman,
Finis.

321   *Valuable*

(After reading two paragraphs in a newspaper)

ALL these illegitimate babies . . .
Oh girls, girls,
Silly little cheap things,
Why do you not put some value on yourselves,
Learn to say, No?
Did nobody teach you?
Nobody teaches anybody to say No nowadays,
People should teach people to say No.

O poor panther,
Oh your poor black animal,
At large for a few moments in a school for young children in Paris,
Now in your cage again,
How your great eyes bulge with bewilderment,
There is something there that accuses us,
In your angry and innocent eyes,
Something that says:
I am too valuable to be kept in a cage.

Oh these illegitimate babies!
Oh girls, girls,
Silly little valuable things,
You should have said, No, I am valuable,
And again, It is because I am valuable
I say, No.

Nobody teaches anybody they are valuable nowadays.

Girls, you are valuable,
And you, Panther, you are valuable,
But the girls say: I shall be alone
If I say 'I am valuable' and other people do not say it of me,
I shall be alone, there is no comfort there.
No, it is not comforting but it is valuable,
And if everybody says it in the end
It will be comforting. And for the panther too,
If everybody says he is valuable
It will be comforting for him.

F. PRATT GREEN

1903–

322   *The Old Couple*

THE old couple in the brand-new bungalow,
Drugged with the milk of municipal kindness,
Fumble their way to bed. Oldness at odds
With newness, they nag each other to show
Nothing is altered, despite the strangeness
Of being divorced in sleep by twin-beds,
Side by side like the Departed, above them
The grass-green of candlewick bedspreads.

In a dead neighbourhood, where it is rare
For hooligans to shout or dogs to bark,
A footfall in the quiet air is crisper
Than home-made bread; and the budgerigar
Bats an eyelid, as sensitive to disturbance
As a distant needle is to an earthquake
In the Great Deep, then balances in sleep.
It is silence keeps the old couple awake.

Too old for loving now, but not for love,
The old couple lie, several feet apart,
Their chesty breathing like a muted duet
On wind instruments, trying to think of
Things to hang on to, such as the tinkle
That a budgerigar makes when it shifts
Its feather weight from one leg to another,
The way, on windy nights, linoleum lifts.

WILLIAM PLOMER

1903–

323   *In the Snake Park*

A WHITE-HOT midday in the Snake Park.
Lethargy lay here and there in coils,
And here and there a neat obsidian head
Lay dreaming on a plaited pillow of its own
Loops like a pretzel or a true-love-knot.

A giant Python seemed a heap of tyres;
Two Nielsen's Vipers looked for a way out,
Sick of their cage and one another's curves;
And the long Ringsnake brought from Lembuland
Poured slowly through an opening like smoke.

Leaning intently forward a young girl
Discerned in stagnant water on a rock
A dark brown shoestring or discarded whiplash,
Then read the label to find out the name,
Then stared again: it moved. She screamed.

Old Piet Vander leant with us that day
On the low wall around the rocky space
Where amid broken quartz that cast no shade
Snakes twitched or slithered, or appeared to sleep,
Or lay invisible in the singing glare.

The sun throbbed like a fever as he spoke:
'Look carefully at this shrub with glossy leaves.'
Leaves bright as brass. 'That leaf on top
Just there, do you see that it has eyes?
That's a Green Mamba, and it's watching *you*.

'A man I once knew did survive the bite,
Saved by a doctor running with a knife,
Serum and all. He was never the same again.
Vomiting blackness, agonizing, passing blood,
Part paralysed, near gone, he felt

'(He told me later) he would burst apart;
But the worst agony was in his mind—
Unbearable nightmare, worse than total grief
Or final loss of hope, impossibly magnified
To a blind passion of panic and extreme distress.'

'Why should that little head have power
To inject all horror for no reason at all?'
'Ask me another—and beware of snakes.'
The sun was like a burning-glass. Face down
The girl who screamed had fallen in a faint.

324   *The Playboy of the Demi-World : 1938*

ALOFT in Heavenly Mansions, Doubleyou One—
Just Mayfair flats, but certainly sublime—
You'll find the abode of D'Arcy Honeybunn,
A rose-red sissy half as old as time.

Peace cannot age him, and no war could kill
The genial tenant of those cosy rooms,
He's lived there always and he lives there still,
Perennial pansy, hardiest of blooms.

There you'll encounter aunts of either sex,
Their jokes equivocal or over-ripe,
Ambiguous couples wearing slacks and specs
And the stout Lesbian knocking out her pipe.

The rooms are crammed with flowers and objets d'art,
A Ganymede still hands the drinks—and plenty!
D'Arcy still keeps a rakish-looking car
And still behaves the way he did at twenty.

A ruby pin is fastened in his tie,
The scent he uses is *Adieu Sagesse*,
His shoes are suède, and as the years go by
His tailor's bill's not getting any less.

He cannot whistle, always rises late,
Is good at indoor sports and parlour tricks,
Mauve is his favourite colour, and his gait
Suggests a peahen walking on hot bricks.

He prances forward with his hands outspread
And folds all comers in a gay embrace,
A wavy toupee on his hairless head,
A fixed smile on his often-lifted face.

'My dear!' he lisps, to whom all men are dear,
'How perfectly enchanting of you!'; turns
Towards his guests and twitters, 'Look who's here!
Do come and help us fiddle while Rome burns!'

'The kindest man alive,' so people say,
'Perpetual youth!' But have you seen his eyes?
The eyes of some old saurian in decay,
That asks no questions and is told no lies.

Under the fribble lurks a worn-out sage
Heavy with disillusion, and alone;
So never say to D'Arcy, 'Be your age!'—
He'd shrivel up at once or turn to stone.

325 *Seven Rainy Months*

March

Flip, clack! The windscreen wipers clear
A fan of focus as I take the track
To one I love, uncertain if I hear
Them or my heart repeat *Flip, clack!*

April

Like a letter-writing schoolgirl's
Over-eager punctuation
Slantwise on the window April
Dashes marks of exclamation.

May

Dulcet the half-expected shock, to hear
The cuckoo practising its name again,
Then still self-centred but not quite so near
Mocking its echo in the soft May rain.

June

Pattering showers on leaves undoing
Knots of guilt and anxiety freshen
The listening soul, as if the raindrops'
Muttering were a delayed confession.

July

Tidal the hush of rain all day,
Faint as the sea that haunts a shell:
Sunset x-rays a stout late bee
Nuzzling inside a foxglove bell.

August

Little more than a mist, and soon it stops:
Morning will bring that ever-pleasing sight—
Nasturtium leaves that balance trembling drops
Of quicksilver collected in the night.

September

Seed-pearl drizzle at midnight sifting softly
Out of a wide white luminous windless sky
The light of a maximum moon diffused through gauzes
Blind as the gaze of a white blind eye.

A. L. ROWSE
1903–

326   *The White Cat of Trenarren*
(for Beryl Cloke)

HE was a mighty hunter in his youth
At Polmear all day on the mound, on the pounce
For anything moving, rabbit or bird or mouse—
My cat and I grow old together.

After a day's hunting he'd come into the house
Delicate ears stuck all with fleas.
At Trenarren I've heard him sigh with pleasure
After a summer's day in the long-grown leas—
My cat and I grow old together.

When I was a child I played all day,
With only a little cat for companion,
At solitary games of my own invention
Under the table or up in the green bay—
My cat and I grow old together.

When I was a boy I wandered the roads
Up to the downs by gaunt Carn Grey,
Wrapt in a dream at end of day,
All round me the moor, below me the bay—
My cat and I grow old together.

Now we are too often apart, yet
Turning out of Central Park into the Plaza,
Or walking Michigan Avenue against the lake-wind,
I see a little white shade in the shrubbery
Of far-off Trenarren, never far from my mind—
My cat and I grow old together.

When I come home from too much travelling,
Cautiously he comes out of his lair to my call,
Receives me at first with a shy reproach
At long absence to him incomprehensible—
My cat and I grow old together.

Incapable of much or long resentment,
He scratches at my door to be let out
In early morning in the ash moonlight,
Or red dawn breaking through Mother Bond's spinney—
    My cat and I grow old together.

No more frisking as of old,
Or chasing his shadow over the lawn,
But a dignified old person, tickling
His nose against twig or flower in the border,
Until evening falls and bed-time's in order,
Unable to keep eyes open any longer
He waits for me to carry him upstairs
To nestle all night snug at foot of bed—
    My cat and I grow old together.

Careful of his licked and polished appearance,
Ears like shell-whorls pink and transparent,
White plume waving proudly over the paths,
Against a background of sea and blue hydrangeas—
    My cat and I grow old together.

C. DAY-LEWIS

1904–1972

327

Do not expect again a phœnix hour,
The triple-towered sky, the dove complaining,
Sudden the rain of gold and heart's first ease
Tranced under trees by the eldritch light of sundown.

By a blazed trail our joy will be returning:
One burning hour throws light a thousand ways,
And hot blood stays into familiar gestures.
The best years wait, the body's plenitude.

Consider then, my lover, this is the end
Of the lark's ascending, the hawk's unearthly hover:
Spring season is over soon and first heatwave;
Grave-browed with cloud ponders the huge horizon.

Draw up the dew. Swell with pacific violence.
Take shape in silence. Grow as the clouds grew.
Beautiful brood the cornlands, and you are heavy;
Leafy the boughs—they also hide big fruit.

328   *Where are the War Poets?*

THEY who in folly or mere greed
Enslaved religion, markets, laws,
Borrow our language now and bid
Us to speak up in freedom's cause.

It is the logic of our times,
No subject for immortal verse—
That we who lived by honest dreams
Defend the bad against the worse.

329   FROM *Flight to Italy*

THE winged bull trundles to the wired perimeter.
Cumbrously turns. Shivers, brakes clamped,
Bellowing four times, each engine tested
With routine ritual. Advances to the runway.
Halts again as if gathering heart
Or warily snuffing for picador cross-winds.
Then, then, a roar open-throated
Affronts the arena. Then fast, faster
Drawn by the magnet of his *idée fixe*,
Head down, tail up, he's charging the horizon.
          And the grass of the airfield grows smooth as a fur.
The runway's elastic and we the projectile;
Installations control-tower mechanics parked aeroplanes—
Units all woven to a ribbon unreeling,
Concrete melts and condenses to an abstract
Blur, and our blood thickens to think of
Rending, burning, as suburban terraces
Make for us, wave after wave.

                                        The moment
Of Truth is here. We can only trust,
Being as wholly committed to other hands
As a babe at birth, Europa to the bull god.
And as when one dies in his sleep, there's no divining
The instant of take-off, so we who were earth-bound
Are air-borne, it seems, in the same breath.
The neutered terraces subside beneath us.

330   *The Album*

I SEE you, a child
In a garden sheltered for buds and playtime,
Listening as if beguiled
By a fancy beyond your years and the flowering maytime.
The print is faded: soon there will be
No trace of that pose enthralling,
Nor visible echo of my voice distantly calling
'Wait! Wait for me!'

Then I turn the page
To a girl who stands like a questioning iris
By the waterside, at an age
That asks every mirror to tell what the heart's desire is.
The answer she finds in that oracle stream
Only time could affirm or disprove,
Yet I wish I was there to venture a warning, 'Love
Is not what you dream.'

Next you appear
As if garlands of wild felicity crowned you—
Courted, caressed, you wear
Like immortelles the lovers and friends around you.
'They will not last you, rain or shine,
They are but straws and shadows,'
I cry: 'Give not to those charming desperadoes
What was made to be mine.'

One picture is missing—
The last. It would show me a tree stripped bare
By intemperate gales, her amazing
Noonday of blossom spoilt which promised so fair.
Yet, scanning those scenes at your heyday taken,
I tremble, as one who must view
In the crystal a doom he could never deflect—yes, I too
Am fruitlessly shaken.

I close the book;
But the past slides out of its leaves to haunt me
And it seems, wherever I look,
Phantoms of irreclaimable happiness taunt me.
Then I see her, petalled in new-blown hours,
Beside me—'All you love most there
Has blossomed again,' she murmurs, 'all that you missed there
Has grown to be yours.'

331   *Sheepdog Trials in Hyde Park*

for ROBERT FROST

A SHEPHERD stands at one end of the arena.
Five sheep are unpenned at the other. His dog runs out
In a curve to behind them, fetches them straight to the shepherd,
Then drives the flock round a triangular course
Through a couple of gates and back to his master; two
Must be sorted there from the flock, then all five penned.
Gathering, driving away, shedding and penning
Are the plain words for the miraculous game.

An abstract game. What can the sheepdog make of such
Simplified terrain?—no hills, dales, bogs, walls, tracks,
Only a quarter-mile plain of grass, dumb crowds
Like crowds on hoardings around it, and behind them
Traffic or mounds of lovers and children playing.
Well, the dog is no landscape-fancier; his whole concern
Is with his master's whistle, and of course
With the flock—sheep are sheep anywhere for him.

The sheep are the chanciest element. Why, for instance,
Go through this gate when there's on either side of it
No wall or hedge but huge and viable space?
Why not eat the grass instead of being pushed around it?
Like blobs of quicksilver on a tilting board
The flock erratically runs, dithers, breaks up,
Is reassembled: their ruling idea is the dog;
And behind the dog, though they know it not yet, is a shepherd.

The shepherd knows that time is of the essence
But haste calamitous. Between dog and sheep
There is always an ideal distance, a perfect angle;
But these are constantly varying, so the man
Should anticipate each move through the dog, his medium.
The shepherd is the brain behind the dog's brain,
But his control of dog, like dog's of sheep,
Is never absolute—that's the beauty of it.

For beautiful it is. The guided missiles,
The black-and-white angels follow each quirk and jink of
The evasive sheep, play grandmother's steps behind them,
Freeze to the ground, or leap to head off a straggler
Almost before it knows that it wants to stray,
As if radar-controlled. But they are not machines—
You can feel them feeling mastery, doubt, chagrin:
Machines don't frolic when their job is done.

What's needfully done in the solitude of sheep-runs—
Those tough, real tasks—becomes this stylized game,
A demonstration of intuitive wit
Kept natural by the saving grace of error.
To lift, to fetch, to drive, to shed, to pen
Are acts I recognize, with all they mean
Of shepherding the unruly, for a kind of
Controlled woolgathering is my work too.

332   *My Mother's Sister*

I SEE her against the pearl sky of Dublin
Before the turn of the century, a young woman
With all those brothers and sisters, green eyes, hair
She could sit on; for high life, a meandering sermon

(Church of Ireland) each Sunday, window-shopping
In Dawson Street, picnics at Killiney and Howth . . .
To know so little about the growing of one
Who was angel and maid-of-all-work to my growth!

—Who, her sister dying, took on the four-year
Child, and the chance that now she would never make
A child of her own; who, mothering me, flowered in
The clover-soft authority of the meek.

Who, exiled, gossiping home chat from abroad
In roundhand letters to a drift of relations—
Squires', Goldsmiths, Overends, Williams'—sang the songs
Of Zion in a strange land. Hers the patience

Of one who made no claims, but simply loved
Because that was her nature, and loving so
Asked no more than to be repaid in kind.
If she was not a saint, I do not know

What saints are . . . Buying penny toys at Christmas
(The most a small purse could afford) to send her
Nephews and nieces, she'd never have thought the shop
Could shine for me one day in Bethlehem splendour.

Exiled again after ten years, my father
Remarrying, she faced the bitter test
Of charity—to abdicate in love's name
From love's contentful duties. A distressed

Gentle woman housekeeping for strangers;
Later, companion to a droll recluse
Clergyman brother in rough-pastured Wexford,
She lived for all she was worth—to be of use.

She bottled plums, she visited parishioners.
A plain habit of innocence, a faith
Mildly forbearing, made her one of those
Who, we were promised, shall inherit the earth.

. . . Now, sunk in one small room of a Rathmines
Old people's home, helpless, beyond speech
Or movement, yearly deeper she declines
To imbecility—my last link with childhood.

The battery's almost done: yet if I press
The button hard—some private joke in boyhood
I teased her with—there comes upon her face
A glowing of the old, enchanted smile.

So, still alive, she rots. A heart of granite
Would melt at this unmeaning sequel. Lord,
How can this be justified, how can it
Be justified?

CHRISTOPHER ISHERWOOD

1904–

333 *On His Queerness*

WHEN I was young and wanted to see the sights,
They told me: 'Cast an eye over the Roman Camp
If you care to,
But plan to spend most of your day at the Aquarium—
Because, after all, the Aquarium—
Well, I mean to say, the Aquarium—
Till you've seen the Aquarium you ain't seen nothing.'

So I cast an eye over
The Roman Camp—
And that old Roman Camp,
That old, old Roman Camp
Got me
Interested.

So that now, near closing-time,
I find that I still know nothing—
And am not even sorry that I know nothing—
About fish.

NORMAN CAMERON

1905–1953

334 *In the Queen's Room*

IN smoky outhouses of the court of love
I chattered, a recalcitrant underling
Living on scraps. 'Below stairs or above,
All's one,' I said. 'We valets have our fling.'

Now I am come, by a chance beyond reach,
Into your room, my body smoky and soiled
And on my tongue the taint of chattering speech,
Tell me, Queen, am I irredeemably spoiled?

335 *The Compassionate Fool*

MY enemy had bidden me as guest.
His table all set out with wine and cake,
His ordered chairs, he to beguile me dressed
So neatly, moved my pity for his sake.

I knew it was an ambush, but could not
Leave him to eat his cake up by himself
And put his unused glasses on the shelf.
I made pretence of falling in his plot,

And trembled when in his anxiety
He bared it too absurdly to my view.
And even as he stabbed me through and through
I pitied him for his small strategy.

336 *The Disused Temple*

WHEN once the scourging prophet, with his cry
Of 'money-changers' and 'my Father's house,'
Had set his mark upon it, men were shy
To enter, and the fane fell in disuse.

NORMAN CAMERON

Since it was unfrequented and left out
Of living, what was there to do except
Make fast the door, destroy the key? (No doubt
One of our number did it while we slept.)

It stays as a disquieting encumbrance.
We moved the market-place out of its shade;
But still it overhangs our whole remembrance,
Making us both inquisitive and afraid.

Shrewd acousticians hammer on the door
And study from the echoes what is there;
Meaningless yet familiar, these appear
Much what we would expect—but we're not sure.

Disquiet makes us sleepy; shoddiness
Has come upon our crafts. No question that
We'll shortly have to yield to our distress,
Abandon the whole township, and migrate.

337   *Green, Green is El Aghir*

SPRAWLED on the crates and sacks in the rear of the truck,
I was gummy-mouthed from the sun and the dust of the track,
And the two Arab soldiers I'd taken on as hitch-hikers
At a torrid petrol-dump, had been there on their hunkers
Since early morning. I said, in a kind of French
'On m'a dit, qu'il y a une belle source d'eau fraîche,
Plus loin, à El Aghir' . . .

                    It was eighty more kilometres
Until round a corner we heard a splashing of waters,
And there, in a green, dark street, was a fountain with two faces
Discharging both ways, from full-throated faucets
Into basins, thence into troughs and thence into brooks.
Our negro corporal driver slammed his brakes,
And we yelped and leapt from the truck and went at the double
To fill our bidons and bottles and drink and dabble.
Then, swollen with water, we went to an inn for wine.
The Arabs came, too, though their faith might have stood between.
'After all,' they said, 'it's a boisson,' without contrition.

360

NORMAN CAMERON

Green, green is El Aghir. It has a railway-station,
And the wealth of its soil has borne many another fruit,
A mairie, a school and an elegant Salle de Fêtes.
Such blessings, as I remarked, in effect, to the waiter,
Are added unto them that have plenty of water.

IDRIS DAVIES

1905–1953

338 *The Lay Preacher Ponders*

'Isn't the violet a dear little flower? And the daisy, too.
What nice little thoughts arise from a daisy!
If I were a poet now—but no, not a poet,
For a poet is a wild and blasphemous man;
He talks about wine and women too much for me
And he makes mad songs about old pagans, look you.
Poets are dangerous men to have in chapel,
And it is bad enough in chapel as it is
With all the quarrelling over the organ and the deacons;
The deacons are not too nice to saintly young men like me.
(Look at Jenkin John Jones, the old damn scoundrel!)
They know I can pray for hours and hours,
They know what a righteous young man I am,
They know how my Bible is always in my pocket
And Abraham and Jonah like brothers to me,
But they prefer the proper preacher with his collar turned round;
They say he is more cultured than I am,
And what is culture but palaver and swank?
I turn up my nose at culture.
I stand up for faith, and very simple faith,
And knowledge I hate because it is poison.
Think of this devilish thing they call science,
It is Satan's new trick to poison men's minds.
When I shall be local councillor and a famous man—
I look forward to the day when I shall be mayor—
I will put my foot down on clever palaver,
And show what a righteous young man I am.
And they ought to know I am that already,
For I give all my spare cash to the chapel
And all my spare time to God.'

339   *High Summer on the Mountains*

HIGH summer on the mountains
And on the clover leas,
And on the local sidings,
And on the rhubarb leaves.

Brass bands in all the valleys
Blaring defiant tunes,
Crowds, acclaiming carnival,
Prize pigs and wooden spoons

Dust on shabby hedgerows
Behind the colliery wall,
Dust on rail and girder
And tram and prop and all.

High summer on the slag heaps
And on polluted streams,
And old men in the morning
Telling the town their dreams.

GEOFFREY GRIGSON

1905–

340   *By the Road*

SNEAKED about here
The abandoned ghost of an old affair.
'By these trees, by this gate,'
It remarked,
'Much as now you were parked.
She said
She never had heard
That tub-thumping classical bird.
You said—it was June—
If we wait
We shall hear her
Quite soon,

GEOFFREY GRIGSON

And hereabouts in the dark
From that most disobliging throat—
You remember?—
There came not a note.

God, in those nights
What a state you were in,
It wasn't so long ago,
You were more thin,
There was more brown in your hair,
And today——'
'Go away,' I said, 'Go away.'

VERNON WATKINS

1906–1967

Two Decisions

341

    I MUST go back to Winter,
The dark, confiding tree,
The sunflower's eaten centre
That waved so tenderly;
Go back, break fellowship
With bud and leaf,
Break the loud branch and strip
The stillborn grief.
I must restore the thorn,
The naked sentinel,
Call lash of hail, wind-scorn
To laughter's lintel;
End argument in a way
Sudden and swift,
Leave stillness, go away
Beyond this leaf-drift,
Leave the ten-windowed house
And merely remark,
The ivy grew too close:
That house was dark.

Then I look out:
Rut, road and hill I see.
Tracks turn about.
Winter must come to me.
I shall not go.
I shall wait here
Until the snow
Bury the old year,
Until the swallows are gone
And the lintels wet
Tell that the rain that has blown
Is blowing yet.
Let me be nowhere
A melodramatic guest
Since here as anywhere
The light is best.
Though distant things entreat
The afraid, the fanciful,
The near is faithful:
Do not deny it.

342 *Foal*

DARKNESS is not dark, nor sunlight the light of the sun
But a double journey of insistent silver hooves.
Light wakes in the foal's blind eyes as lightning illuminates corn
With a rustle of fine-eared grass, where a starling shivers.

And whoever watches a foal sees two images,
Delicate, circling, born, the spirit with blind eyes leaping
And the left spirit, vanished, yet here, the vessel of ages
Clay-cold, blue, laid low by her great wide belly the hill.

See him break that circle, stooping to drink, to suck
His mother, vaulted with a beautiful hero's back
Arched under the singing mane,
Shaped to her shining, pricked into awareness
By the swinging dug, amazed by the movement of suns;
His blue fellow has run again down into grass,
And he slips from that mother to the boundless horizons of air,
Looking for that other, the foal no longer there.

But perhaps
In the darkness under the tufted thyme and downtrodden winds,
In the darkness under the violet's roots, in the darkness of the pitcher's
music,
In the uttermost darkness of a vase
There is still the print of fingers, the shadow of waters.
And under the dry, curled parchment of the soil there is always a little
foal
Asleep.

So the whole morning he runs here, fulfilling the track
Of so many suns; vanishing the mole's way, moving
Into mole's mysteries under the zodiac,
Racing, stopping in the circle. Startled he stands
Dazzled, where darkness is green, where the sunlight is black,
While his mother, grazing, is moving away
From the lagging star of those stars, the unrisen wonder
In the path of the dead, fallen from the sun in her hooves,
And eluding the dead hands, begging him to play.

343   *Peace in the Welsh Hills*

CALM is the landscape when the storm has passed,
Brighter the fields, and fresh with fallen rain.
Where gales beat out new colour from the hills
Rivers fly faster, and upon their banks
Birds preen their wings, and irises revive.
Not so the cities burnt alive with fire
Of man's destruction: when their smoke is spent,
No phœnix rises from the ruined walls.

I ponder now the grief of many rooms.
Was it a dream, that age, when fingers found
A satisfaction sleeping in dumb stone,
When walls were built responding to the touch
In whose high gables, in the lengthening days,
Martins would nest? Though crops, though lives, would fail,
Though friends dispersed, unchanged the walls would stay,
And still those wings return to build in Spring.

Here, where the earth is green, where heaven is true
Opening the windows, touched with earliest dawn,
In the first frost of cool September days,
Chrysanthemum weather, presaging great birth,
Who in his heart could murmur or complain:
'The light we look for is not in this land'?
That light is present, and that distant time
Is always here, continually redeemed.

There is a city we must build with joy
Exactly where the fallen city sleeps.
There is one road through village, town and field,
On whose robust foundation Chaucer dreamed
A ride could wed the opposites in man.
There proud walls may endure, and low walls feed
The imagination if they have a vine
Or shadowy barn made rich with gathered corn.

Great mansions fear from their surrounding trees
The invasion of a wintry desolation
Filling their rooms with leaves. And cottages
Bring the sky down as flickering candles do,
Leaning on their own shadows. I have seen
Vases and polished brass reflect black windows
And draw the ceiling down to their vibrations,
Thick, deep, and white-washed, like a bank of snow.

To live entwined in pastoral loveliness
May rest the eyes, throw pictures on the mind,
But most we need a metaphor of stone
Such as those painters had whose mountain-cities
Cast long, low shadows on the Umbrian hills.
There, in some courtyard on the cobbled stone,
A fountain plays, and through a cherub's mouth
Ages are linked by water in the sunlight.

All of good faith that fountain may recall,
Woman, musician, boy, or else a scholar
Reading a Latin book. They seem distinct,
And yet are one, because tranquillity
Affirms the Judgment. So, in these Welsh hills,
I marvel, waking from a dream of stone,
That such a peace surrounds me, while the city
For which all long has never yet been built.

344

For a Wine Festival

Now the late fruits are in.
Now moves the leaf-starred year
Down, in the sun's decline.
Stoop. Have no fear.
Glance at the burdened tree:
Dark is the grape's wild skin.
Dance, limbs, be free.
Bring the bright clusters here
And crush them into wine.

Acorns from yellow boughs
Drop to the listening ground.
Spirits who never tire,
Dance, dance your round.
Old roots, old thoughts and dry,
Catch, as your footprints rouse
Flames where they fly,
Knowing the year has found
Its own more secret fire.

Nothing supreme shall pass.
Earth to an ember gone
Wears but the death it feigns
And still burns on.
One note more true than time
And shattered falls his glass.
Steal, steal from rhyme:
Take from the glass that shone
The vintage that remains.

SIR JOHN BETJEMAN
1906–

345 *The Arrest of Oscar Wilde at the Cadogan Hotel*

HE sipped at a weak hock and seltzer
As he gazed at the London skies
Through the Nottingham lace of the curtains
Or was it his bees-winged eyes?

To the right and before him Pont Street
Did tower in her new built red,
As hard as the morning gaslight
That shone on his unmade bed,

'I want some more hock in my seltzer,
And Robbie, please give me your hand—
Is this the end or beginning?
How can I understand?

'So you've brought me the latest *Yellow Book*:
And Buchan has got in it now:
Approval of what is approved of
Is as false as a well-kept vow.

'More hock, Robbie—where is the seltzer?
Dear boy, pull again at the bell!
They are all little better than *cretins*,
Though this *is* the Cadogan Hotel.

'One astrakhan coat is at Willis's—
Another one's at the Savoy:
Do fetch my morocco portmanteau,
And bring them on later, dear boy.'

A thump, and a murmur of voices—
('Oh why must they make such a din?')
As the door of the bedroom swung open
And TWO PLAIN CLOTHES POLICEMEN came in:

'Mr. Woilde, we 'ave come for tew take yew
    Where felons and criminals dwell:
We must ask yew tew leave with us quoietly
    For this *is* the Cadogan Hotel.'

He rose, and he put down *The Yellow Book.*
    He staggered—and, terrible-eyed,
He brushed past the palms on the staircase
    And was helped to a hansom outside.

346   *A Subaltern's Love-song*

Miss J. Hunter Dunn, Miss J. Hunter Dunn,
Furnish'd and burnish'd by Aldershot sun,
What strenuous singles we played after tea,
We in the tournament—you against me!

Love-thirty, love-forty, oh! weakness of joy,
The speed of a swallow, the grace of a boy,
With carefullest carelessness, gaily you won,
I am weak from your loveliness, Joan Hunter Dunn.

Miss Joan Hunter Dunn, Miss Joan Hunter Dunn,
How mad I am, sad I am, glad that you won.
The warm-handled racket is back in its press,
But my shock-headed victor, she loves me no less.

Her father's euonymus shines as we walk,
And swing past the summer-house, buried in talk,
And cool the verandah that welcomes us in
To the six-o'clock news and a lime-juice and gin.

The scent of the conifers, sound of the bath,
The view from my bedroom of moss-dappled path,
As I struggle with double-end evening tie,
For we dance at the Golf Club, my victor and I.

On the floor of her bedroom lie blazer and shorts
And the cream-coloured walls are be-trophied with sports,
And westering, questioning settles the sun
On your low-leaded window, Miss Joan Hunter Dunn.

The Hillman is waiting, the light's in the hall,
The pictures of Egypt are bright on the wall,
My sweet, I am standing beside the oak stair
And there on the landing's the light on your hair.

By roads 'not adopted', by woodlanded ways,
She drove to the club in the late summer haze,
Into nine-o'clock Camberley, heavy with bells
And mushroomy, pine-woody, evergreen smells.

Miss Joan Hunter Dunn, Miss Joan Hunter Dunn,
I can hear from the car-park the dance has begun.
Oh! full Surrey twilight! importunate band!
Oh! strongly adorable tennis-girl's hand!

Around us are Rovers and Austins afar,
Above us, the intimate roof of the car,
And here on my right is the girl of my choice,
With the tilt of her nose and the chime of her voice,

And the scent of her wrap, and the words never said,
And the ominous, ominous dancing ahead.
We sat in the car park till twenty to one
And now I'm engaged to Miss Joan Hunter Dunn.

347   *Ireland with Emily*

BELLS are booming down the bohreens,
    White the mist along the grass.
Now the Julias, Maeves and Maureens
    Move between the fields to Mass.
Twisted trees of small green apple
Guard the decent whitewashed chapel,
Gilded gates and doorway grained
Pointed windows richly stained
    With many-coloured Munich glass.

See the black-shawled congregations
  On the broidered vestment gazes
Murmur past the painted stations
  As Thy Sacred Heart displays
Lush Kildare of scented meadows,
Roscommon, thin in ash-tree shadows,
And Westmeath the lake-reflected,
Spreading Leix the hill-protected,
  Kneeling all in silver haze?

In yews and woodbine, walls and guelder,
  Nettle-deep the faithful rest,
Winding leagues of flowering elder,
  Sycamore with ivy dressed,
Ruins in demesnes deserted,
Bog-surrounded bramble-skirted—
Townlands rich or townlands mean as
These, oh, counties of them screen us
  In the Kingdom of the West.

Stony seaboard, far and foreign,
  Stony hills poured over space,
Stony outcrop of the Burren,
  Stones in every fertile place,
Little fields with boulders dotted,
Grey-stone shoulders saffron-spotted,
Stone-walled cabins thatched with reeds,
Where a Stone Age people breeds
  The last of Europe's stone age race.

Has it held, the warm June weather?
  Draining shallow sea-pools dry,
When we bicycled together
  Down the bohreens fuchsia-high.
Till there rose, abrupt and lonely,
A ruined abbey, chancel only,
Lichen-crusted, time-befriended,
Soared the arches, splayed and splendid,
  Romanesque against the sky.

There in pinnacled protection,
　　One extinguished family waits
A Church of Ireland resurrection
　　By the broken, rusty gates.
Sheepswool, straw and droppings cover,
Graves of spinster, rake and lover,
Whose fantastic mausoleum
Sings its own seablown Te Deum,
　　In and out the slipping slates.

348　　　　　FROM *Beside the Seaside*

GREEN Shutters, shut your shutters! Windyridge,
Let winds unnoticed whistle round your hill!
High Dormers, draw your curtains! Slam the door,
And pack the family in the Morris eight.
Lock up the garage. Put her in reverse,
Back out with care, now, forward, off—away!
The richer people living farther out
O'ertake us in their Rovers. We, in turn,
Pass poorer families hurrying on foot
Towards the station. Very soon the town
Will echo to the groan of empty trams
And sweetshops advertise Ice Cream in vain.
Solihull, Headingley and Golders Green,
Preston and Swindon, Manchester and Leeds,
Braintree and Bocking, hear the sea! the sea!
The smack of breakers upon windy rocks,
Spray blowing backwards from their curling walls
Of green translucent water. England leaves
Her centre for her tide-line. Father's toes,
Though now encased in coloured socks and shoes
And pressing the accelerator hard,
Ache for the feel of sand and little shrimps
To tickle in between them. Mother vows
To be more patient with the family;
Just for its sake she will be young again.
And, at that moment, Jennifer is sick
(Over-excitement must have brought it on,
The hurried breakfast and the early start)
And Michael's rather pale, and as for Anne . . .

'Please stop a moment, Hubert, anywhere.'
    So evening sunlight shows us Sandy Cove
The same as last year and the year before.
Still on the brick front of the Baptist Church
SIX-THIRTY. PREACHER:—*Mr. Pentecost—*
All visitors are welcomed. Still the quartz
Glitters along the tops of garden walls.
Those macrocarpa still survive the gales
They must have had last winter. Still the shops
Remain unaltered on the Esplanade—
The Circulating Library, the Stores,
Jill's Pantry, Cynthia's Ditty Box (Antiques),
Trecarrow (Maps and Souvenirs and Guides).
Still on the terrace of the big hotel
Pale pink hydrangeas turn a rusty brown
Where sea winds catch them, and yet do not die.
The bumpy lane between the tamarisks,
The escallonia hedge, and still it's there—
Our lodging-house, ten minutes from the shore.
Still unprepared to make a picnic lunch
Except by notice on the previous day.
Still nowhere for the children when it's wet
Except that smelly, overcrowded lounge.
And still no garage for the motor-car.
Still on the bedroom wall, the list of rules:
Don't waste the water. It is pumped by hand.
Don't throw old blades into the W.C.
Don't keep the bathroom long and don't be late
For meals and don't hang swim-suits out on sills
(A line has been provided at the back).
Don't empty children's sand-shoes in the hall.
Don't this, Don't that. Ah, still the same, the same
As it was last year and the year before—
But rather more expensive, now, of course.

349 *Christmas*

THE bells of waiting Advent ring,
  The Tortoise stove is lit again
And lamp-oil light across the night
  Has caught the streaks of winter rain
In many a stained-glass window sheen
From Crimson Lake to Hooker's Green.

The holly in the windy hedge
  And round the Manor House the yew
Will soon be stripped to deck the ledge,
  The altar, font and arch and pew,
So that the villagers can say
'The church looks nice' on Christmas Day.

Provincial public houses blaze
  And Corporation tramcars clang,
On lighted tenements I gaze
  Where paper decorations hang,
And bunting in the red Town Hall
Says 'Merry Christmas to you all.'

And London shops on Christmas Eve
  Are strung with silver bells and flowers
As hurrying clerks the City leave
  To pigeon-haunted classic towers,
And marbled clouds go scudding by
The many-steepled London sky.

And girls in slacks remember Dad,
  And oafish louts remember Mum,
And sleepless children's hearts are glad,
  And Christmas-morning bells say 'Come!'
Even to shining ones who dwell
Safe in the Dorchester Hotel.

And is it true? And is it true,
  This most tremendous tale of all,
Seen in a stained-glass window's hue,
  A Baby in an ox's stall?
The Maker of the stars and sea
Become a Child on earth for me?

And is it true? For if it is,
  No loving fingers tying strings
Around those tissued fripperies,
  The sweet and silly Christmas things,
Bath salts and inexpensive scent
And hideous tie so kindly meant,

No love that in a family dwells,
  No carolling in frosty air,
Nor all the steeple-shaking bells
  Can with this single Truth compare—
That God was Man in Palestine
And lives to-day in Bread and Wine.

350   *The Metropolitan Railway*
              Baker Street Station Buffet

EARLY Electric! With what radiant hope
  Men formed this many-branched electrolier,
Twisted the flex around the iron rope
  And let the dazzling vacuum globes hang clear,
And then with hearts the rich contrivance fill'd
Of copper, beaten by the Bromsgrove Guild.

Early Electric! Sit you down and see,
  'Mid this fine woodwork and a smell of dinner,
A stained-glass windmill and a pot of tea,
  And sepia views of leafy lanes in PINNER,—
Then visualise, far down the shining lines,
Your parents' homestead set in murmuring pines.

Smoothly from HARROW, passing PRESTON ROAD,
  They saw the last green fields and misty sky,
At NEASDEN watched a workmen's train unload,
  And, with the morning villas sliding by,
They felt so sure on their electric trip
That Youth and Progress were in partnership.

And all that day in murky London Wall
  The thought of RUISLIP kept him warm inside;
At FARRINGDON that lunch hour at a stall
  He bought a dozen plants of London Pride;
While she, in arc-lit Oxford Street adrift,
Soared through the sales by safe hydraulic lift.

Early Electric! Maybe even here
  They met that evening at six-fifteen
Beneath the hearts of this electrolier
  And caught the first non-stop to WILLESDEN GREEN,
Then out and on, through rural RAYNER'S LANE
To autumn-scented Middlesex again.

Cancer has killed him. Heart is killing her.
  The trees are down. An Odeon flashes fire
Where stood their villa by the murmuring fir
  When 'they would for their children's good conspire.'
Of all their loves and hopes on hurrying feet
Thou art the worn memorial, Baker Street.

351   *Middlesex*

  GAILY into Ruislip Gardens
    Runs the red electric train,
  With a thousand Ta's and Pardon's
    Daintily alights Elaine;
  Hurries down the concrete station
  With a frown of concentration,
  Out into the outskirt's edges
  Where a few surviving hedges
Keep alive our lost Elysium—rural Middlesex again.

  Well cut Windsmoor flapping lightly,
    Jacqmar scarf of mauve and green
  Hiding hair which, Friday nightly,
    Delicately drowns in Drene;
  Fair Elaine the bobby-soxer,
  Fresh-complexioned with Innoxa,
  Gains the garden—father's hobby—
  Hangs her Windsmoor in the lobby,
Settles down to sandwich supper and the television screen.

Gentle Brent, I used to know you
   Wandering Wembley-wards at will,
Now what change your waters show you
   In the meadowlands you fill!
Recollect the elm-trees misty
And the footpaths climbing twisty
Under cedar-shaded palings,
Low laburnum-leaned-on railings,
Out of Northolt on and upward to the heights of Harrow hill.

Parish of enormous hayfields
   Perivale stood all alone,
And from Greenford scent of mayfields
   Most enticingly was blown
Over market gardens tidy,
Taverns for the *bona fide*,
Cockney anglers, cockney shooters,
Murray Poshes, Lupin Pooters
Long in Kensal Green and Highgate silent under soot and stone.

352   *How to Get On in Society*
      Originally set as a competition in 'Time and Tide' [1]

PHONE for the fish-knives, Norman
   As Cook is a little unnerved;
You kiddies have crumpled the serviettes
   And I must have things daintily served.

Are the requisites all in the toilet?
   The frills round the cutlets can wait
Till the girl has replenished the cruets
   And switched on the logs in the grate.

It's ever so close in the lounge dear,
   But the vestibule's comfy for tea
And Howard is out riding on horseback
   So do come and take some with me.

---

[1] In the issue for 29 December 1951: 'These verses contain 34 of what some people might call Social Errors. Competitors are asked to compose one more stanza in the same metre.' The results were printed in the issue for 19 January 1952.

Now here is a fork for your pastries
  And do use the couch for your feet;
I know what I wanted to ask you—
  Is trifle sufficient for sweet?

Milk and then just as it comes dear?
  I'm afraid the preserve's full of stones;
Beg pardon, I'm soiling the doileys
  With afternoon tea-cakes and scones.

353   *Diary of a Church Mouse*

(*Lines, written to order on a set subject, to be spoken on the wireless.*)

HERE among long-discarded cassocks,
Damp stools, and half-split open hassocks,
Here where the Vicar never looks
I nibble through old service books.
Lean and alone I spend my days
Behind this Church of England baize.
I share my dark forgotten room
With two oil-lamps and half a broom.
The cleaner never bothers me,
So here I eat my frugal tea.
My bread is sawdust mixed with straw;
My jam is polish for the floor.
    Christmas and Easter may be feasts
For congregations and for priests,
And so may Whitsun. All the same,
They do not fill my meagre frame.
For me the only feast at all
Is Autumn's Harvest Festival,
When I can satisfy my want
With ears of corn around the font.
I climb the eagle's brazen head
To burrow through a loaf of bread.
I scramble up the pulpit stair
And gnaw the marrows hanging there.
    It is enjoyable to taste
These items ere they go to waste,
But how annoying when one finds
That other mice with pagan minds

SIR JOHN BETJEMAN

Come into church my food to share
Who have no proper business there.
Two field mice who have no desire
To be baptized, invade the choir.
A large and most unfriendly rat
Comes in to see what we are at.
He says he thinks there is no God
And yet he comes . . . it's rather odd.
This year he stole a sheaf of wheat
(It screened our special preacher's seat),
And prosperous mice from fields away
Come in to hear the organ play,
And under cover of its notes
Ate through the altar's sheaf of oats.
A Low Church mouse, who thinks that I
Am too papistical, and High,
Yet somehow doesn't think it wrong
To munch through Harvest Evensong,
While I, who starve the whole year through,
Must share my food with rodents who
Except at this time of the year
Not once inside the church appear.
  Within the human world I know
Such goings-on could not be so,
For human beings only do
What their religion tells them to.
They read the Bible every day
And always, night and morning, pray,
And just like me, the good church mouse,
Worship each week in God's own house.
  But all the same it's strange to me
How very full the church can be
With people I don't see at all
Except at Harvest Festival.

354 *Felixstowe, or The Last of Her Order*

WITH one consuming roar along the shingle
   The long wave claws and rakes the pebbles down
To where its backwash and the next wave mingle,
   A mounting arch of water weedy-brown
Against the tide the off-shore breezes blow.
Oh wind and water, this is Felixstowe.

In winter when the sea winds chill and shriller
   Than those of summer, all their cold unload
Full on the gimcrack attic of the villa
   Where I am lodging off the Orwell Road,
I put my final shilling in the meter
And only make my loneliness completer.

In eighteen ninety-four when we were founded,
   Counting our Reverend Mother we were six,
How full of hope we were and prayer-surrounded
   'The Little Sisters of the Hanging Pyx'.
We built our orphanage. We ran our school.
Now only I am left to keep the rule.

Here in the gardens of the Spa Pavilion
   Warm in the whisper of a summer sea,
The cushioned scabious, a deep vermilion,
   With white pins stuck in it, looks up at me
A sun-lit kingdom touched by butterflies
And so my memory of winter dies.

Across the grass the poplar shades grow longer
   And louder clang the waves along the coast.
The band packs up. The evening breeze is stronger
   And all the world goes home to tea and toast.
I hurry past a cakeshop's tempting scones
Bound for the red brick twilight of St. John's.

'Thou knowest my down sitting and mine uprising'
   Here where the white light burns with steady glow
Safe from the vain world's silly sympathising,
   Safe with the Love that I was born to know,
Safe from the surging of the lonely sea
My heart finds rest, my heart finds rest in Thee.

355   *Lord Cozens Hardy*

OH Lord Cozens Hardy
    Your mausoleum is cold,
The dry brown grass is brittle
    And frozen hard the mould
And where those Grecian columns rise
    So white among the dark
Of yew trees and of hollies in
    That corner of the park
By Norfolk oaks surrounded
    Whose branches seem to talk,
I know, Lord Cozens Hardy,
    I would not like to walk.

And even in the summer,
    On a bright East-Anglian day
When round your Doric portico
    Your children's children play
There's a something in the stillness
    And our waiting eyes are drawn
From the butler and the footman
    Bringing tea out on the lawn,
From the little silver spirit lamp
    That burns so blue and still,
To the half-seen mausoleum
    In the oak trees on the hill.

But when, Lord Cozens Hardy,
    November stars are bright,
And the King's Head Inn at Letheringsett
    Is shutting for the night,
The villagers have told me
    That they do not like to pass
Near your curious mausoleum
    Moon-shadowed on the grass
For fear of seeing walking
    In the season of All Souls
That first Lord Cozens Hardy,
    The Master of the Rolls.

356 FROM *Summoned by Bells*

MY dear deaf father, how I loved him then
Before the years of our estrangement came!
The long calm walks on twilit evenings
Through Highgate New Town to the cinema:
The expeditions by North London trains
To dim forgotten stations, wooden shacks
On oil-lit flimsy platforms among fields
As yet unbuilt-on, deep in Middlesex . . .
We'd stand in dark antique shops while he talked,
Holding his deaf-appliance to his ear,
Lifting the ugly mouthpiece with a smile
Towards the flattered shopman. Most of all
I think my father loved me when we went
In early-morning pipe-smoke on the tram
Down to the Angel, visiting the Works.
'Fourth generation—yes, this is the boy.'
  The smell of sawdust still brings back to me
The rambling workshops high on Pentonville,
Built over gardens to White Lion Street,
Clicking with patents of the family firm
Founded in 1820. When you rang
The front-door bell a watchful packer pulled
A polished lever twenty yards away,
And this released the catch into a world
Of shining showrooms full of secret drawers
And Maharajah's dressing-cases.
                                        Hushed
Be thy green hilltop, handsome Highbury!
Stilled be the traffic roar of Upper Street!
Flash shop-fronts, masts and neon signs, drop off
The now-encumbered houses! O return,
Straw-smelling mornings, to old Islington!
A hint of them still hung about the Works
From the past days of our prosperity—
A hint of them in medals, photographs
And stockrooms heavy with the Tantalus
On which the family fortune had been made.
The Alexandra Palace patent lock,
The Betjemann device for hansom cabs,
Patents exhibited in '51,

Improvements on them shown in '62,
The Betjemann trolley used in coffee-rooms,
The inlaid brass, the figured rosewood box,
The yellow satinwood, the silverware—
What wealth the money from them once had brought
To fill the hot-house half-way up the stairs
With red begonias; what servants' halls;
What terrace houses and what carriage-drives!
   Bang through the packing-room! Then up a step:
'Be careful, Master John,' old William called.
Over the silversmiths' uneven floor
I thought myself a fast electric train,
First stop the silver-plating shop (no time
To watch the locksmiths' and engravers' work):
For there in silence Buckland used to drop
Dull bits of metal into frothing tanks
And bring them out all gold or silver bright—
He'd turn a penny into half-a-crown.
Though he but seldom spoke, yet he and I
Worked there as one. He let me seem to work.
The cabinet-makers' shop, all belts and wheels
And whining saws, would thrill me with the scream
Of tortured wood, starting a blackened plank
Under the cruel plane and coming out
Sweet-scented, pink and smooth and richly grained;
While in a far-off shed, caressingly,
French-polishers, all whistling different tunes,
With reeking swabs would rub the coloured woods,
Bringing the figured surfaces to light;
Dark whirling walnut, deep and deeper brown,
And rare mahogany's pressed butterflies.
Beside the timber yard, a favourite hut
Encased the thumping heartbeat of the Works,
An old gas-engine smelling strong of oil.
Its mighty wheel revolved a leather belt
Which, turning lesser wheels and lesser belts,
Spread like a drawing by Heath Robinson
Through all the rambling length of wooden sheds.
   When lunch-time brought me hopes of ginger-beer
I'd meet my father's smile as there he stood
Among his clerks, with pens behind their ears,
In the stern silence of the counting-house;

And he, perhaps not ready to go out,
Would leave me to explore some upper rooms—
One full of ticking clocks, one full of books;
And once I found a dusty drawing-room,
Completely furnished, where long years ago
My great-grandfather lived above his work
Before he moved to sylvan Highbury.
But in the downstair showrooms I could find
No link between the finished articles
And all the clatter of the factory.
The Works in Birmingham, I knew, made glass;
The stoneworks in Torquay made other things . . .
But what did *we* do? This I did not know,
Nor ever wished to—to my father's grief.
    O Mappin, Webb, Asprey and Finnigan!
You polished persons on the retail side—
Old Mag Tags, Paulines and Old Westminsters—
Why did I never take to you? Why now
When, staying in a quiet country house,
I see an onyx ashtray of the firm,
Or in my bedroom, find the figured wood
Of my smooth-sliding dressing-table drawers
Has got a look about it of the Works,
Does my mind flinch so?
                              Partly it is guilt:
'Following in Father's footsteps' was the theme
Of all my early childhood. With what pride
He introduced me to old gentlemen,
Pin-striped commercial travellers of the firm
And tall proprietors of Bond Street shops.
With joy he showed me old George Betjeman's book.
(He was a one-'n' man before the craze
For all things German tacked another 'n'):
'December eighteen seven. Twelve and six—
For helping brother William with his desk.'
Uninteresting then it seemed to me,
Uninteresting still. Slow walks we took
On sunny afternoons to great-great-aunts
In tall Italianate houses: Aberdeen Park,
Hillmarton Road and upper Pooter-land,
Short gravel drives to steepish flights of steps
And stained-glass windows in a purple hall,

A drawing-room with stands of potted plants,
Lace curtains screening other plants beyond.
'Fourth generation—yes, this is the boy.'
    Partly my guilt is letting down the men—
William our coachman who, turned chauffeur, still
Longed for his mare and feared the motor-car
Which he would hiss at, polishing its sides;
Bradshaw and Pettit of the lathe and plane;
Fieldhouse and Lovely, and the old and bent
With wire-framed spectacles and aproned knees;
The young apprentices old custom called,
Indentures done, to passing-out parade
Down a long alley formed among the men
Beating on bits of metal. How they all
Trusted that I would fill my father's place!
'The Guv'nor's looking for you, Master John . . .'
'Well now, my boy, I want your solemn word
To carry on the firm when I am gone:
Fourth generation, John—they'll look to you.
They're artist-craftsmen to their fingertips . . .
Go on creating beauty!'
                        What is beauty?
Here, where I write, the green Atlantic bursts
In cannonades of white along Pentire.
There's beauty here. There's beauty in the slate
And granite smoothed by centuries of sea,
And washed to life as rain and spray bring out
Contrasting strata higher up the cliff,
But none to me in polished wood and stone
Tortured by Father's craftsmen into shapes
To shine in Asprey's showrooms under glass,
A Maharajah's eyeful.
                        For myself,
I knew as soon as I could read and write
That I must be a poet. Even today,
When all the way from Cambridge comes a wind
To blow the lamps out every time they're lit,
I know that I must light mine up again.

WILLIAM EMPSON
1906–

357 *Camping Out*

AND now she cleans her teeth into the lake:
Gives it (God's grace) for her own bounty's sake
What morning's pale and the crisp mist debars:
Its glass of the divine (that Will could break)
Restores, beyond Nature: or lets Heaven take
(Itself being dimmed, her pattern, who half awake
Milks between rocks a straddled sky of stars.

Soap tension the star pattern magnifies.
Smoothly Madonna through-assumes the skies
Whose vaults are opened to achieve the Lord.
No, it is we soaring explore galaxies,
Our bullet boat light's speed by thousands flies.
Who moves so among stars their frame unties;
See where they blur, and die, and are outsoared.

358 *Aubade*

HOURS before dawn we were woken by the quake.
My house was on a cliff. The thing could take
Bookloads off shelves, break bottles in a row.
Then the long pause and then the bigger shake.
It seemed the best thing to be up and go.

And far too large for my feet to step by.
I hoped that various buildings were brought low.
The heart of standing is you cannot fly.

It seemed quite safe till she got up and dressed.
The guarded tourist makes the guide the test.
Then I said The Garden? Laughing she said No.
Taxi for her and for me healthy rest.
It seemed the best thing to be up and go.

The language problem but you have to try.
Some solid ground for lying could she show?
The heart of standing is you cannot fly.

None of these deaths were her point at all.
The thing was that being woken he would bawl
And finding her not in earshot he would know.
I tried saying Half an Hour to pay this call.
It seemed the best thing to be up and go.

I slept, and blank as that I would yet lie.
Till you have seen what a threat holds below
The heart of standing is you cannot fly.

359   *Success*

I HAVE mislaid the torment and the fear.
You should be praised for taking them away.
Those that doubt drugs, let them doubt which was here.

Well are they doubted for they turn out dear.
I feed on flatness and am last to leave.
Verse likes despair. Blame it upon the beer
I have mislaid the torment and the fear.

All losses haunt us. It was a reprieve
Made Dostoevsky talk out queer and clear.

Those stay most haunting that most soon deceive

And turn out no loss of the various Zoo
The public spirits or the private play.
Praised once for having taken these away
What is it else then such a thing can do?

Lose is Find with great marsh lights like you.
Those that doubt drugs, let them doubt which was here
When this leaves the green afterlight of day.
Nor they nor I know what we shall believe.
You should be praised for taking them away.

360 *The Teasers*

NOT but they die, the teasers and the dreams,
Not but they die,
           and tell the careful flood
To give them what they clamour for and why.

You could not fancy where they rip to blood,
You could not fancy
           nor that mud
I have heard speak that will not cake or dry.

Our claims to act appear so small to these,
Our claims to act
           colder lunacies
That cheat the love, the moment, the small fact.

Make no escape because they flash and die,
Make no escape
           build up your love,
Leave what you die for and be safe to die.

361 *Let it go*

IT is this deep blankness is the real thing strange.
   The more things happen to you the more you can't
      Tell or remember even what they were.

The contradictions cover such a range.
   The talk would talk and go so far aslant.
      You don't want madhouse and the whole thing there.

PATRICK KAVANAGH
1906–1967

FROM *The Great Hunger*

I

CLAY is the word and clay is the flesh
Where the potato-gatherers like mechanised scarecrows move
Along the side-fall of the hill—Maguire and his men.
If we watch them an hour is there anything we can prove
Of life as it is broken-backed over the Book
Of Death? Here crows gabble over worms and frogs
And the gulls like old newspapers are blown clear of the hedges,
    luckily.
Is there some light of imagination in these wet clods?
Or why do we stand here shivering?
                              Which of these men
Loved the light and the queen
Too long virgin? Yesterday was summer. Who was it promised
    marriage to himself
Before apples were hung from the ceilings for Hallowe'en?
We will wait and watch the tragedy to the last curtain,
Till the last soul passively like a bag of wet clay
Rolls down the side of the hill, diverted by the angles
Where a plough missed or a spade stands, straitening the way.

A dog lying on a torn jacket under a heeled-up cart,
A horse nosing along the posied headland, trailing
A rusty plough. Three heads hanging between wide-apart
Legs. October playing a symphony on a slack wire paling.
Maguire watches the drills flattened out
And the flints that lit a candle for him on a June altar
Flameless. The drills slipped by and the days slipped by
And he trembled his head away and ran free from the world's halter,
And thought himself wiser than any man in the townland
When he laughed over pints of porter

Of how he came free from every net spread
In the gaps of experience. He shook a knowing head
And pretended to his soul
That children are tedious in hurrying fields of April
Where men are spanging across wide furrows.
Lost in the passion that never needs a wife—
The pricks that pricked were the pointed pins of harrows.
Children scream so loud that the crows could bring
The seed of an acre away with crow-rude jeers.
Patrick Maguire, he called his dog and he flung a stone in the air
And hallooed the birds away that were the birds of the years.

Turn over the weedy clods and tease out the tangled skeins
What is he looking for there?
He thinks it is a potato, but we know better
Than his mud-gloved fingers probe in this insensitive hair.

'Move forward the basket and balance it steady
In this hollow. Pull down the shafts of that cart, Joe,
And straddle the horse,' Maguire calls.
'The wind's over Brannagan's, now that means rain.
Graip up some withered stalks and see that no potato falls
Over the tail-board going down the ruckety pass—
And *that's* a job we'll have to do in December,
Gravel it and build a kerb on the bog-side. Is that Cassidy's ass
Out in my clover? Curse o' God—
Where is that dog?
Never where he's wanted.' Maguire grunts and spits
Through a clay-wattled moustache and stares about him from the
    height.
His dream changes again like the cloud-swung wind
And he is not so sure now if his mother was right
When she praised the man who made a field his bride.

Watch him, watch him, that man on a hill whose spirit
Is a wet sack flapping about the knees of time.

He lives that his little fields may stay fertile when his own body
Is spread in the bottom of a ditch under two coulters crossed in Christ's
    Name.

He was suspicious in his youth as a rat near strange bread,
When girls laughed; when they screamed he knew that meant
The cry of fillies in season. He could not walk
The easy road to his destiny. He dreamt
The innocence of young brambles to hooked treachery.
O the grip, O the grip of irregular fields! No man escapes.
It could not be that back of the hills love was free
And ditches straight.
No monster hand lifted up children and put down apes
As here.
        'O God if I had been wiser!'
That was his sigh like the brown breeze in the thistles.
He looks towards his house and haggard. 'O God if I had been wiser!'
But now a crumpled leaf from the whitethorn bushes
Darts like a frightened robin, and the fence
Shows the green of after-grass through a little window,
And he knows that his own heart is calling his mother a liar.
God's truth is life—even the grotesque shapes of its foulest fire.

The horse lifts its head and cranes
Through the whins and stones
To lip late passion in the crawling clover.
In the gap there's a bush weighted with boulders like morality,
The fools of life bleed if they climb over.

The wind leans from Brady's, and the coltsfoot leaves are holed with
    rust,
Rain fills the cart-tracks and the sole-plate grooves;
A yellow sun reflects in Donaghmoyne
The poignant light in puddles shaped by hooves.

Come with me, Imagination, into this iron house
And we will watch from the doorway the years run back,
And we will know what a peasant's left hand wrote on the page.
Be easy, October. No cackle hen, horse neigh, tree sough, duck
    quack. . . .

CHRISTOPHER CAUDWELL
(CHRISTOPHER ST. JOHN SPRIGG)

1907–1937

363   *The Progress of Poetry*

I SAW a Gardener with a watering can
Sprinkling dejectedly the heads of men
Buried up to their necks in the wet clay.

I saw a Bishop born in sober black
With a bewildered look on his small face
Being rocked in a cradle by a grey-haired woman.

I saw a man, with an air of painful duty
Binding his privates up with bunches of ribbon.
The woman who helped him was decently veiled in white.

I said to the Gardener: 'When I was a younger poet
At least my reference to death had some sonority.
I sang the danger and the deeps of love.

'Is the world poxy with a fresh disease?
Or is this a maggot I feel here, gnawing my breast
And wrinkling my five senses like a walnut's kernel?'

The Gardener answered: 'I am more vexed by the lichen
Upon my walls. I scraped it off with a spade.
As I did so I heard a very human scream.

'In evening's sacred cool, among my bushes
A Figure was wont to walk. I deemed it angel.
But look at the footprint. There's hair between the toes!'

364 *Classic Encounter*

ARRIVED upon the downs of asphodel
I walked towards the military quarter
To find the sunburnt ghosts of allied soldiers
Killed on the Chersonese.

I met a band of palefaced weary men
Got up in odd equipment. 'Hi,' I said
'Are you Gallipoli?'

And one, the leader, with a voice of gold,
Answered: 'No. Ours, Sir, was an older bungle.
We are Athenian hoplites who sat down
Before young Syracuse.

'Need I recount our too-much-memoired end?
The hesitancy of our General Staff,
The battle in the Harbour, where Hope fled
But we could not?

'Not our disgrace in that,' the leader added,
'But we are those proficient in the arts
Freed in return for the repeated verses
Of our Euripides.

'Those honeyed words did not soothe Cerberus'
(The leader grinned), 'For sulky Charon hire
Deficient, and by Rhadamanthos ruled
No mitigation.

'And yet with men, born victims of their ears
The chorus of the weeping Troades
Prevailed to gain the freedom of our limbs
And waft us back to Athens.

'Through every corridor of this old barracks
We wander without friends; not fallen or
Survivors in a military sense:
Hence our disgrace.'

He turned; and as the rank mists took them in
They chanted of the God to Whom men pray,
Whether He be Compulsion, or All-Fathering,
Or Fate and blind.

393

LOUIS MACNEICE

1907–1963

365   *Wolves*

I DO not want to be reflective any more
Envying and despising unreflective things
Finding pathos in dogs and undeveloped handwriting
And young girls doing their hair and all the castles of sand
Flushed, by the children's bedtime, level with the shore.

The tide comes in and goes out again, I do not want
To be always stressing either its flux or its permanence,
I do not want to be a tragic or philosophic chorus
But to keep my eye only on the nearer future
And after that let the sea flow over us.

Come then all of you, come closer, form a circle,
Join hands and make believe that joined
Hands will keep away the wolves of water
Who howl along our coast. And be it assumed
That no one hears them among the talk and laughter.

366   *Snow*

THE room was suddenly rich and the great bay-window was
Spawning snow and pink roses against it
Soundlessly collateral and incompatible:
World is suddener than we fancy it.

World is crazier and more of it than we think,
Incorrigibly plural. I peel and portion
A tangerine and spit the pips and feel
The drunkenness of things being various.

And the fire flames with a bubbling sound for world
Is more spiteful and gay than one supposes—
On the tongue on the eyes on the ears in the palms of one's hands—
There is more than glass between the snow and the huge roses.

367   *The Sunlight on the Garden*

THE sunlight on the garden
Hardens and grows cold,
We cannot cage the minute
Within its nets of gold,
When all is told
We cannot beg for pardon.

Our freedom as free lances
Advances towards its end;
The earth compels, upon it
Sonnets and birds descend;
And soon, my friend,
We shall have no time for dances.

The sky was good for flying
Defying the church bells
And every evil iron
Siren and what it tells:
The earth compels,
We are dying, Egypt, dying

And not expecting pardon,
Hardened in heart anew,
But glad to have sat under
Thunder and rain with you,
And grateful too
For sunlight on the garden.

368   *Bagpipe Music*

IT'S no go the merrygoround, it's no go the rickshaw,
All we want is a limousine and a ticket for the peepshow.
Their knickers are made of crêpe-de-chine, their shoes are made of
    python,
Their halls are lined with tiger rugs and their walls with heads of
    bison.

John MacDonald found a corpse, put it under the sofa,
Waited till it came to life and hit it with a poker,
Sold its eyes for souvenirs, sold its blood for whisky,
Kept its bones for dumb-bells to use when he was fifty.

It's no go the Yogi-Man, it's no go Blavatsky,
All we want is a bank balance and a bit of skirt in a taxi.

Annie MacDougall went to milk, caught her foot in the heather,
Woke to hear a dance record playing of Old Vienna.
It's no go your maidenheads, it's no go your culture,
All we want is a Dunlop tyre and the devil mend the puncture.

The Laird o' Phelps spent Hogmanay declaring he was sober,
Counted his feet to prove the fact and found he had one foot over.
Mrs. Carmichael had her fifth, looked at the job with repulsion,
Said to the midwife 'Take it away; I'm through with over-production'.

It's no go the gossip column, it's no go the ceilidh,
All we want is a mother's help and a sugar-stick for the baby.

Willie Murray cut his thumb, couldn't count the damage,
Took the hide of an Ayrshire cow and used it for a bandage.
His brother caught three hundred cran when the seas were lavish,
Threw the bleeders back in the sea and went upon the parish.

It's no go the Herring Board, it's no go the Bible,
All we want is a packet of fags when our hands are idle.

It's no go the picture palace, it's no go the stadium,
It's no go the country cot with a pot of pink geraniums,
It's no go the Government grants, it's no go the elections,
Sit on your arse for fifty years and hang your hat on a pension.

It's no go my honey love, it's no go my poppet;
Work your hands from day to day, the winds will blow the profit.
The glass is falling hour by hour, the glass will fall for ever,
But if you break the bloody glass you won't hold up the weather.

LOUIS MACNEICE

FROM *Autumn Journal*

VII

CONFERENCES, adjournments, ultimatums,
  Flights in the air, castles in the air,
The autopsy of treaties, dynamite under the bridges,
  The end of *laissez faire*.
After the warm days the rain comes pimpling
  The paving stones with white
And with the rain the national conscience, creeping,
  Seeping through the night.
And in the sodden park on Sunday protest
  Meetings assemble not, as so often, now
Merely to advertise some patent panacea
  But simply to avow
The need to hold the ditch; a bare avowal
  That may perhaps imply
Death at the doors in a week but perhaps in the long run
  Exposure of the lie.
Think of a number, double it, treble it, square it,
  And sponge it out
And repeat *ad lib.* and mark the slate with crosses;
  There is no time to doubt
If the puzzle really has an answer. Hitler yells on the wireless,
  The night is damp and still
And I hear dull blows on wood outside my window;
  They are cutting down the trees on Primrose Hill.
The wood is white like the roast flesh of chicken,
  Each tree falling like a closing fan;
No more looking at the view from seats beneath the branches,
  Everything is going to plan;
They want the crest of this hill for anti-aircraft,
  The guns will take the view
And searchlights probe the heavens for bacilli
  With narrow wands of blue.
And the rain came on as I watched the territorials
  Sawing and chopping and pulling on ropes like a team
In a village tug-of-war; and I found my dog had vanished
  And thought 'This is the end of the old régime,'

But found the police had got her at St. John's Wood station
    And fetched her in the rain and went for a cup
Of coffee to an all-night shelter and heard a taxi-driver
    Say 'It turns me up
When I see these soldiers in lorries'—rumble of tumbrils
    Drums in the trees
Breaking the eardrums of the ravished dryads—
    It turns me up; a coffee, please.
And as I go out I see a windscreen-wiper
    In an empty car
Wiping away like mad and I feel astounded
    That things have gone so far.
And I come back here to my flat and wonder whether
    From now on I need take
The trouble to go out choosing stuff for curtains
    As I don't know anyone to make
Curtains quickly. Rather one should quickly
    Stop the cracks for gas or dig a trench
And take one's paltry measures against the coming
    Of the unknown Uebermensch.
But one—meaning I—is bored, am bored, the issue
    Involving principle but bound in fact
To squander principle in panic and self-deception—
    Accessories after the act,
So that all we foresee is rivers in spate sprouting
    With drowning hands
And men like dead frogs floating till the rivers
    Lose themselves in the sands.
And we who have been brought up to think of 'Gallant Belgium'
    As so much blague
Are now preparing again to essay good through evil
    For the sake of Prague;
And must, we suppose, become uncritical, vindictive,
    And must, in order to beat
The enemy, model ourselves upon the enemy,
    A howling radio for our paraclete.
The night continues wet, the axe keeps falling,
    The hill grows bald and bleak
No longer one of the sights of London but maybe
    We shall have fireworks here by this day week.

370 *Dublin*

GREY brick upon brick,
Declamatory bronze
On sombre pedestals—
O'Connell, Grattan, Moore—
And the brewery tugs and the swans
On the balustraded stream
And the bare bones of a fanlight
Over a hungry door
And the air soft on the cheek
And porter running from the taps
With a head of yellow cream
And Nelson on his pillar
Watching his world collapse.

This was never my town,
I was not born nor bred
Nor schooled here and she will not
Have me alive or dead
But yet she holds my mind
With her seedy elegance,
With her gentle veils of rain
And all her ghosts that walk
And all that hide behind
Her Georgian façades—
The catcalls and the pain,
The glamour of her squalor,
The bravado of her talk.

The lights jig in the river
With a concertina movement
And the sun comes up in the morning
Like barley-sugar on the water.
And the mist on the Wicklow hills
Is close, as close
As the peasantry were to the landlord,
As the Irish to the Anglo-Irish,
As the killer is close one moment
To the man he kills,
Or as the moment itself
Is close to the next moment.

She is not an Irish town
And she is not English,
Historic with guns and vermin
And the cold renown
Of a fragment of Church latin,
Of an oratorical phrase.
But oh the days are soft,
Soft enough to forget
The lesson better learnt,
The bullet on the wet
Streets, the crooked deal,
The steel behind the laugh,
The Four Courts burnt.

Fort of the Dane,
Garrison of the Saxon,
Augustan capital
Of a Gaelic nation,
Appropriating all
The alien brought,
You give me time for thought
And by a juggler's trick
You poise the toppling hour—
O greyness run to flower,
Grey stone, grey water,
And brick upon grey brick.

371   *The Taxis*

IN the first taxi he was alone tra-la,
No extras on the clock. He tipped ninepence
But the cabby, while he thanked him, looked askance
As though to suggest someone had bummed a ride.

In the second taxi he was alone tra-la
But the clock showed sixpence extra; he tipped according
And the cabby from out his muffler said: 'Make sure
You have left nothing behind tra-la between you'.

In the third taxi he was alone tra-la
But the tip-up seats were down and there was an extra
Charge of one-and-sixpence and an odd
Scent that reminded him of a trip to Cannes.

As for the fourth taxi, he was alone
Tra-la when he hailed it but the cabby looked
Through him and said: 'I can't tra-la well take
So many people, not to speak of the dog.'

372   *Tree Party*

YOUR health, Master Willow. Contrive me a bat
To strike a red ball; apart from that
In the last resort I must hang my harp on you.

Your health, Master Oak. You emblem of strength,
Why must your doings be done at such length?
Beware lest the ironclad ages catch up with you.

Your health, Master Blackthorn. Be live and be quick,
Provide the black priest with a big black stick
That his ignorant flock may go straight for the fear of you.

Your health, Master Palm. If you brew us some toddy
To deliver to us out of by means of the body,
We will burn all our bridges and rickshaws in praise of you.

Your health, Master Pine. Though sailing be past
Let you fly your own colours upon your own mast
And rig us a crow's nest to keep a look out from you.

Your health, Master Elm. Of giants arboreal
Poets have found you the most immemorial
And yet the big winds may discover the fault in you.

Your health, Master Hazel. On Halloween
Your nuts are to gather but not to be seen
Are the twittering ghosts that perforce are alive in you.

Your health, Master Holly. Of all the trees
That decorate parlour walls you please
Yet who would have thought you had so much blood in you?

Your health, Master Apple. Your topmost bough
Entices us to come climbing now
For all that old rumour there might be a snake in you.

Your health, Master Redwood. The record is yours
For the girth that astounds, the sap that endures,
But where are the creatures that once came to nest in you?

Your health, Master Banyan, but do not get drunk
Or you may not distinguish your limbs from your trunk
And the sense of Above and Below will be lost on you.

Your health, Master Bo-Tree. If Buddha should come
Yet again, yet again make your branches keep mum
That his words yet again may drop honey by leave of you.

Your health, Master Yew. My bones are few
And I fully admit my rent is due,
But do not be vexed, I will postdate a cheque for you.

W. H. AUDEN

1907–

373   *Missing*

FROM scars where kestrels hover,
The leader looking over
Into the happy valley,
Orchard and curving river,
May turn away to see
The slow fastidious line
That disciplines the fell,
Hear curlew's creaking call
From angles unforeseen,

The drumming of a snipe
Surprise where driven sleet
Had scalded to the bone
And streams are acrid yet
To an unaccustomed lip;
The tall unwounded leader
Of doomed companions, all
Whose voices in the rock
Are now perpetual,
Fighters for no one's sake,
Who died beyond the border.

Heroes are buried who
Did not believe in death,
And bravery is now,
Not in the dying breath
But resisting the temptations
To skyline operations.
Yet glory is not new;
The summer visitors
Still come from far and wide,
Choosing their spots to view
The prize competitors,
Each thinking that he will
Find heroes in the wood,
Far from the capital,
Where lights and wine are set
For supper by the lake,
But leaders must migrate:
'Leave for Cape Wrath to-night,'
And the host after waiting
Must quench the lamps and pass
Alive into the house.

No Change of Place

Who will endure
Heat of day and winter danger,
Journey from one place to another,
Nor be content to lie
Till evening upon headland over bay,
Between the land and sea
Or smoking wait till hour of food,
Leaning on chained-up gate
At edge of wood?

Metals run,
Burnished or rusty in the sun,
From town to town,
And signals all along are down;
Yet nothing passes
But envelopes between these places,
Snatched at the gate and panting read indoors,
And first spring flowers arriving smashed,
Disaster stammered over wires,
And pity flashed.

For should professional traveller come,
Asked at the fireside, he is dumb,
Declining with a secret smile,
And all the while
Conjectures on our maps grow stranger
And threaten danger.

There is no change of place:
No one will ever know
For what conversion brilliant capital is waiting,
What ugly feast may village band be celebrating;
For no one goes
Further than railhead or the ends of piers,
Will neither go nor send his son
Further through foothills than the rotting stack
Where gaitered gamekeeper with dog and gun
Will shout 'Turn back'.

375 *This Lunar Beauty*

THIS lunar beauty
Has no history,
Is complete and early;
If beauty later
Bear any feature,
It had a lover
And is another.

This like a dream
Keeps other time,
And daytime is
The loss of this;
For time is inches
And the heart's changes,
Where ghost has haunted
Lost and wanted.

But this was never
A ghost's endeavour
Nor, finished this,
Was ghost at ease;
And till it pass
Love shall not near
The sweetness here,
Nor sorrow take
His endless look.

376

THAT night when joy began
Our narrowest veins to flush,
We waited for the flash
Of morning's levelled gun.

But morning let us pass,
And day by day relief
Outgrows his nervous laugh,
Grown credulous of peace,

As mile by mile is seen
No trespasser's reproach,
And love's best glasses reach
No fields but are his own.

377   *The Exiles*

WHAT siren zooming is sounding our coming
Up frozen fjord forging from freedom,
       What shepherd's call
       When stranded on hill,
       With broken axle
       On track to exile?

With labelled luggage we alight at last,
Joining joking at the junction on the moor,
       With practised smile
       And harmless tale
       Advance to meet
       Each new recruit.

Expert from uplands, always in oilskins,
Recliner from library, laying down law,
       Owner from shire,
       All meet on this shore,
       Facing each prick
       With ginger pluck.

Our rooms are ready, the register signed,
There is time to take a turn before dark,
       See the blistering paint
       On the scorching front,
       Or icicle sombre
       On pierhead timber.

To climb the cliff path to the coastguard's point
Past the derelict dock deserted by rats,
       Look from concrete sill
       Of fort for sale
       To the bathers' rocks,
       The lovers' ricks.

Our boots will be brushed, our bolsters pummelled,
Cupboards are cleared for keeping our clothes:
    Here we shall live
    And somehow love
    Though we only master
    The sad posture.

Picnics are promised and planned for July
To the wood with the waterfall, walks to find,
    Traces of birds,
    A mole, a rivet,
    In factory yards
    Marked strictly private.

There will be skating and curling at Christmas—indoors
Charades and ragging; then riders pass
    Some afternoons
    In snowy lanes,
    Shut in by wires,
    Surplus from wars.

In Spring we shall spade the soil on the border
For blooming of bulbs; we shall bow in Autumn,
    When trees make passes,
    As high gale pushes,
    And bewildered leaves
    Fall on our lives.

Watching through windows the wastes of evening,
The flare of foundries at fall of the year,
    The slight despair
    At what we are,
    The marginal grief
    Is source of life.

In groups forgetting the gun in the drawer
Need pray for no pardon, are proud till recalled
    By music on water
    To lack of stature,
    Saying Alas
    To less and less.

Till holding our hats in our hands for talking,
Or striding down streets for something to see,
  Gas-light in shops,
  The fate of ships,
  And the tide-wind
  Touch the old wound.

Till our nerves are numb and their now is a time
Too late for love or for lying either,
  Grown used at last
  To having lost,
  Accepting dearth,
  The shadow of death.

CHORUSES FROM

378 *The Dog Beneath the Skin*

I

THE Summer holds: upon its glittering lake
Lie Europe and the islands; many rivers
Wrinkling its surface like a ploughman's palm.
Under the bellies of the grazing horses
On the far side of posts and bridges
The vigorous shadows dwindle; nothing wavers.
Calm at this moment the Dutch sea so shallow
That sunk St. Pauls would ever show its golden cross
And still the deep water that divides us still from Norway.
We would show you at first an English village: You shall choose its
 location
Wherever your heart directs you most longingly to look; you are loving
 towards it:
Whether north to Scots Gap and Bellingham where the black rams
 defy the panting engine:
Or west to the Welsh Marches; to the lilting speech and the magicians'
 faces:
Wherever you were a child or had your first affair
There it stands amidst your darling scenery:
A parish bounded by the wreckers' cliff; or meadows where browse the
 Southern and the maplike Frisian
As at Trent Junction where the Soar comes gliding out of green
 Leicestershire to swell the ampler current.

Hiker with sunburn blisters on your office pallor,
Cross-country champion with corks in your hands,
When you have eaten your sandwich, your salt and your apple,
When you have begged your glass of milk from the ill-kept farm,
What is it you see?

I see barns falling, fences broken,
Pasture not ploughland, weeds not wheat.
The great houses remain but only half are inhabited,
Dusty the gunrooms and the stable clocks stationary.
Some have been turned into prep-schools where the diet is in the hands
    of an experienced matron,
Others into club-houses for the golf-bore and the top-hole.
Those who sang in the inns at evening have departed; they saw their
    hope in another country,
Their children have entered the service of the suburban areas; they
    have become typists, mannequins and factory operatives; they
    desired a different rhythm of life.
But their places are taken by another population, with views about
    nature,
Brought in charabanc and saloon along arterial roads;
Tourists to whom the Tudor cafés
Offer Bovril and buns upon Breton ware
With leather work as a sideline: Filling stations
Supplying petrol from rustic pumps.
Those who fancy themselves as foxes or desire a special setting for
    spooning
Erect their villas at the right places,
Airtight, lighted, elaborately warmed;
And nervous people who will never marry
Live upon dividends in the old-world cottages
With an animal for friend or a volume of memoirs.

Man is changed by his living; but not fast enough.
His concern to-day is for that which yesterday did not occur.
In the hour of the Blue Bird and the Bristol Bomber, his thoughts are
    appropriate to the years of the Penny Farthing:
He tosses at night who at noonday found no truth.

Stand aside now: The play is beginning
In the village of which we have spoken; called Pressan Ambo:
Here too corruption spreads its peculiar and emphatic odours
And Life lurks, evil, out of its epoch.

379

II

YOU are the town and We are the clock.
We are the guardians of the gate in the rock,
  The Two.
On your left and on your right,
In the day and in the night,
  We are watching you.

Wiser not to ask just what has occurred
To them who disobeyed our word;
  To those
We were the whirlpool, we were the reef,
We were the formal nightmare, grief
  And the unlucky rose.

Climb up the crane, learn the sailor's words
When the ships from the islands laden with birds
  Come in;
Tell your stories of fishing and other men's wives,
The expansive dreams of constricted lives,
  In the lighted inn.

But do not imagine We do not know,
Or that what you hide with such care won't show
  At a glance:
Nothing is done, nothing is said,
But don't make the mistake of believing us dead;
  I shouldn't dance.

We're afraid in that case you'll have a fall;
We've been watching you over the garden wall
  For hours:
The sky is darkening like a stain;
Something is going to fall like rain,
  And it won't be flowers.

When the green field comes off like a lid,
Revealing what was much better hid—
    Unpleasant:
And look, behind you without a sound
The woods have come up and are standing round
    In deadly crescent.

The bolt is sliding in its groove;
Outside the window is the black remov-
    er's van:
And now with sudden swift emergence
Come the hooded women, the hump-backed surgeons,
    And the Scissor Man.

This might happen any day;
So be careful what you say
    And do:
Be clean, be tidy, oil the lock,
Weed the garden, wind the clock;
    Remember the Two.

380   *Night Mail*
            (*Commentary for a G.P.O. Film*)

                        I

    THIS is the Night Mail crossing the Border,
    Bringing the cheque and the postal order,

    Letters for the rich, letters for the poor,
    The shop at the corner, the girl next door.

    Pulling up Beattock, a steady climb:
    The gradient's against her, but she's on time.

    Past cotton-grass and moorland boulder,
    Shovelling white steam over her shoulder,

    Snorting noisily, she passes
    Silent miles of wind-bent grasses.

Birds turn their heads as she approaches,
Stare from bushes at her blank-faced coaches.

Sheep-dogs cannot turn her course;
They slumber on with paws across.

In the farm she passes no one wakes,
But a jug in a bedroom gently shakes.

II

Dawn freshens. Her climb is done.
Down towards Glasgow she descends,
Towards the steam tugs yelping down a glade of cranes,
Towards the fields of apparatus, the furnaces
Set on the dark plain like gigantic chessmen.
All Scotland waits for her:
In dark glens, beside pale-green lochs,
Men long for news.

III

Letters of thanks, letters from banks,
Letters of joy from girl and boy,
Receipted bills and invitations
To inspect new stock or to visit relations,
And applications for situations,
And timid lovers' declarations,
And gossip, gossip from all the nations,
News circumstantial, news financial,
Letters with holiday snaps to enlarge in,
Letters with faces scrawled on the margin,
Letters from uncles, cousins and aunts,
Letters to Scotland from the South of France,
Letters of condolence to Highlands and Lowlands,
Written on paper of every hue,
The pink, the violet, the white and the blue,
The chatty, the catty, the boring, the adoring,
The cold and official and the heart's outpouring,
Clever, stupid, short and long,
The typed and the printed and the spelt all wrong.

IV

Thousands are still asleep,
Dreaming of terrifying monsters
Or a friendly tea beside the band in Cranston's or Crawford's:
Asleep in working Glasgow, asleep in well-set Edinburgh,
Asleep in granite Aberdeen,
They continue their dreams,
But shall wake soon and hope for letters,
And none will hear the postman's knock
Without a quickening of the heart.
For who can bear to feel himself forgotten?

381   *Lullaby*

LAY your sleeping head, my love,
Human on my faithless arm;
Time and fevers burn away
Individual beauty from
Thoughtful children, and the grave
Proves the child ephemeral:
But in my arms till break of day
Let the living creature lie,
Mortal, guilty, but to me
The entirely beautiful.

Soul and body have no bounds:
To lovers as they lie upon
Her tolerant enchanted slope
In their ordinary swoon,
Grave the vision Venus sends
Of supernatural sympathy,
Universal love and hope;
While an abstract insight wakes
Among the glaciers and the rocks
The hermit's carnal ecstasy.

Certainty, fidelity
On the stroke of midnight pass
Like vibrations of a bell
And fashionable madmen raise
Their pedantic boring cry:
Every farthing of the cost,
All the dreaded cards foretell,
Shall be paid, but from this night
Not a whisper, not a thought,
Not a kiss nor look be lost.

Beauty, midnight, vision dies:
Let the winds of dawn that blow
Softly round your dreaming head
Such a day of welcome show
Eye and knocking heart may bless,
Find our mortal world enough;
Noons of dryness find you fed
By the involuntary powers,
Nights of insult let you pass
Watched by every human love.

382 *Miss Gee*

LET me tell you a little story
    About Miss Edith Gee;
She lived in Clevedon Terrace
    At Number 83.

She'd a slight squint in her left eye,
    Her lips they were thin and small,
She had narrow sloping shoulders
    And she had no bust at all.

She'd a velvet hat with trimmings,
    And a dark grey serge costume,
She lived in Clevedon Terrace
    In a small bed-sitting room.

414

She'd a purple mac for wet days,
    A green umbrella too to take,
She'd a bicycle with shopping basket
    And a harsh back-pedal brake.

The Church of Saint Aloysius
    Was not so very far;
She did a lot of knitting,
    Knitting for that Church Bazaar.

Miss Gee looked up at the starlight
    And said, 'Does anyone care
That I live in Clevedon Terrace
    On one hundred pounds a year?'

She dreamed a dream one evening
    That she was the Queen of France
And the Vicar of Saint Aloysius
    Asked Her Majesty to dance.

But a storm blew down the palace,
    She was biking through a field of corn,
And a bull with the face of the Vicar
    Was charging with lowered horn.

She could feel his hot breath behind her,
    He was going to overtake;
And the bicycle went slower and slower
    Because of that back-pedal brake.

Summer made the trees a picture,
    Winter made them a wreck;
She bicycled to the evening service
    With her clothes buttoned up to her neck.

She passed by the loving couples,
    She turned her head away;
She passed by the loving couples
    And they didn't ask her to stay.

Miss Gee sat down in the side-aisle,
    She heard the organ play;
And the choir it sang so sweetly
    At the ending of the day,

Miss Gee knelt down in the side-aisle,
   She knelt down on her knees;
'Lead me not into temptation
   But make me a good girl, please.'

The days and nights went by her
   Like waves round a Cornish wreck;
She bicycled down to the doctor
   With her clothes buttoned up to her neck.

She bicycled down to the doctor,
   And rang the surgery bell;
'O, doctor, I've a pain inside me,
   And I don't feel very well.'

Doctor Thomas looked her over,
   And then he looked some more;
Walked over to his wash-basin,
   Said, 'Why didn't you come before?'

Doctor Thomas sat over his dinner,
   Though his wife was waiting to ring,
Rolling his bread into pellets;
   Said, 'Cancer's a funny thing.

'Nobody knows what the cause is,
   Though some pretend they do;
It's like some hidden assassin
   Waiting to strike at you.

'Childless women get it,
   And men when they retire;
It's as if there had to be some outlet
   For their foiled creative fire.'

His wife she rang for the servant,
   Said, 'Don't be so morbid, dear';
He said: 'I saw Miss Gee this evening
   And she's a goner, I fear.'

They took Miss Gee to the hospital,
   She lay there a total wreck,
Lay in the ward for women
   With the bedclothes right up to her neck.

They laid her on the table,
    The students began to laugh;
And Mr. Rose the surgeon
    He cut Miss Gee in half.

Mr. Rose he turned to his students,
    Said, 'Gentlemen, if you please,
We seldom see a sarcoma
    As far advanced as this.'

They took her off the table,
    They wheeled away Miss Gee
Down to another department
    Where they study Anatomy.

They hung her from the ceiling,
    Yes, they hung up Miss Gee;
And a couple of Oxford Groupers
    Carefully dissected her knee.

383   *Brussels in Winter*

WANDERING through cold streets tangled like old string,
Coming on fountains rigid in the frost,
Its formula escapes you; it has lost
The certainty that constitutes a thing.

Only the old, the hungry and the humbled
Keep at this temperature a sense of place,
And in their misery are all assembled;
The winter holds them like an Opera-House.

Ridges of rich apartments loom to-night
Where isolated windows glow like farms,
A phrase goes packed with meaning like a van,

A look contains the history of man,
And fifty francs will earn a stranger right
To take the shuddering city in his arms.

384 *In Memory of W. B. Yeats*
(d. Jan. 1939)

I

HE disappeared in the dead of winter:
The brooks were frozen, the airports almost deserted,
And snow disfigured the public statues;
The mercury sank in the mouth of the dying day.
What instruments we have agree
The day of his death was a dark cold day.

Far from his illness
The wolves ran on through the evergreen forests,
The peasant river was untempted by the fashionable quays;
By mourning tongues
The death of the poet was kept from his poems.

But for him it was his last afternoon as himself,
An afternoon of nurses and rumours;
The provinces of his body revolted,
The squares of his mind were empty,
Silence invaded the suburbs,
The current of his feeling failed; he became his admirers.

Now he is scattered among a hundred cities
And wholly given over to unfamiliar affections,
To find his happiness in another kind of wood
And be punished under a foreign code of conscience.
The words of a dead man
Are modified in the guts of the living.

But in the importance and noise of to-morrow
When the brokers are roaring like beasts on the floor of the Bourse,
And the poor have the sufferings to which they are fairly accustomed,
And each in the cell of himself is almost convinced of his freedom,
A few thousand will think of this day
As one thinks of a day when one did something slightly unusual.
What instruments we have agree
The day of his death was a dark cold day.

II

You were silly like us; your gift survived it all:
The parish of rich women, physical decay,
Yourself. Mad Ireland hurt you into poetry.
Now Ireland has her madness and her weather still,
For poetry makes nothing happen: it survives
In the valley of its making where executives
Would never want to tamper, flows on south
From ranches of isolation and the busy griefs,
Raw towns that we believe and die in; it survives,
A way of happening, a mouth.

III

Earth, receive an honoured guest:
William Yeats is laid to rest.
Let the Irish vessel lie
Emptied of its poetry.

In the nightmare of the dark
All the dogs of Europe bark,
And the living nations wait,
Each sequestered in its hate;

Intellectual disgrace
Stares from every human face,
And the seas of pity lie
Locked and frozen in each eye.

Follow, poet, follow right
To the bottom of the night,
With your unconstraining voice
Still persuade us to rejoice;

With the farming of a verse
Make a vineyard of the curse,
Sing of human unsuccess
In a rapture of distress;

In the deserts of the heart
Let the healing fountain start,
In the prison of his days
Teach the free man how to praise.

385

The Fall of Rome
(*for Cyril Connolly*)

THE piers are pummelled by the waves;
In a lonely field the rain
Lashes an abandoned train;
Outlaws fill the mountain caves.

Fantastic grow the evening gowns;
Agents of the Fisc pursue
Absconding tax-defaulters through
The sewers of provincial towns.

Private rites of magic send
The temple prostitutes to sleep;
All the literati keep
An imaginary friend.

Cerebrotonic Cato may
Extol the Ancient Disciplines,
But the muscle-bound Marines
Mutiny for food and pay.

Caesar's double-bed is warm
As an unimportant clerk
Writes *I DO NOT LIKE MY WORK*
On a pink official form.

Unendowed with wealth or pity,
Little birds with scarlet legs,
Sitting on their speckled eggs,
Eye each flu-infected city.

Altogether elsewhere, vast
Herds of reindeer move across
Miles and miles of golden moss,
Silently and very fast.

386   *Good-Bye to the Mezzogiorno*
       (*For Carlo Izzo*)

OUT of a gothic North, the pallid children
    Of a potato, beer-or-whisky
Guilt culture, we behave like our fathers and come
    Southward into a sunburnt otherwhere

Of vineyards, baroque, *la bella figura*,
    To these feminine townships where men
Are males, and siblings untrained in a ruthless
    Verbal in-fighting as it is taught

In Protestant rectories upon drizzling
    Sunday afternoons—no more as unwashed
Barbarians out for gold, nor as profiteers
    Hot for Old Masters, but for plunder

Nevertheless—some believing *amore*
    Is better down South and much cheaper
(Which is doubtful), some persuaded exposure
    To strong sunlight is lethal to germs

(Which is patently false) and others, like me,
    In middle-age hoping to twig from
What we are not what we might be next, a question
    The South seems never to raise. Perhaps

A tongue in which Nestor and Apemantus,
    Don Ottavio and Don Giovanni make
Equally beautiful sounds is unequipped
    To frame it, or perhaps in this heat

It is nonsense: the Myth of an Open Road
    Which runs past the orchard gate and beckons
Three brothers in turn to set out over the hills
    And far away, is an invention

Of a climate where it is a pleasure to walk
    And a landscape less populated
Than this one. Even so, to us it looks very odd
    Never to see an only child engrossed

In a game it has made up, a pair of friends
   Making fun in a private lingo,
Or a body sauntering by himself who is not
   Wanting, even as it perplexes

Our ears when cats are called *Cat* and dogs either
   Lupo, *Nero* or *Bobby*. Their dining
Puts us to shame: we can only envy a people
   So frugal by nature it costs them

No effort not to guzzle and swill. Yet (if I
   Read their faces rightly after ten years)
They are without hope. The Greeks used to call the Sun
   He-who-smites-from-afar, and from here, where

Shadows are dagger-edged, the daily ocean blue,
   I can see what they meant: his unwinking
Outrageous eye laughs to scorn any notion
   Of change or escape, and a silent

Ex-volcano, without a stream or a bird,
   Echoes that laugh. This could be a reason
Why they take the silencers off their Vespas,
   Turn their radios up to full volume,

And a minim saint can expect rockets—noise
   As a counter-magic, a way of saying
Boo to the Three Sisters: 'Mortal we may be,
   But we are still here!'—might cause them to hanker

After proximities—in streets packed solid
   With human flesh, their souls feel immune
To all metaphysical threats. We are rather shocked,
   But we need shocking: to accept space, to own

That surfaces need not be superficial
   Nor gestures vulgar, cannot really
Be taught within earshot of running water
   Or in sight of a cloud. As pupils

We are not bad, but hopeless as tutors: Goethe,
   Tapping homeric hexameters
On the shoulder-blade of a Roman girl, is
   (I wish it were someone else) the figure

Of all our stamp: no doubt he treated her well,
    But one would draw the line at calling
The Helena begotten on that occasion,
    Queen of his Second *Walpurgisnacht*,

Her baby: between those who mean by a life a
    Bildungsroman and those to whom living
Means to-be-visible-now, there yawns a gulf
    Embraces cannot bridge. If we try

To 'go southern', we spoil in no time, we grow
    Flabby, dingily lecherous, and
Forget to pay bills: that no one has heard of them
    Taking the Pledge or turning to Yoga

Is a comforting thought—in that case, for all
    The spiritual loot we tuck away,
We do them no harm—and entitles us, I think
    To one little scream at *A piacere*,

Not two. Go I must, but I go grateful (even
    To a certain *Monte*) and invoking
My sacred meridian names, *Vico*, *Verga*,
    Pirandello, *Bernini*, *Bellini*,

To bless this region, its vendanges, and those
    Who call it home: though one cannot always
Remember exactly why one has been happy,
    There is no forgetting that one was.

387   *Up There*

(FOR ANNE WEISS)

MEN would never have come to need an attic.
Keen collectors of glass or Roman coins build
Special cabinets for them, dote on, index
Each new specimen: only women cling to
Items out of their past they have no use for,
Can't name now what they couldn't bear to part with.

Up there, under the eaves, in bulging boxes,
Hats, veils, ribbons, galoshes, programmes, letters
Wait unworshipped (a starving spider spins for
The occasional fly): no clock recalls it
Once an hour to the household it's a part of,
No Saint's Day is devoted to its function.

All it knows of a changing world it has to
Guess from children, who conjure in its plenum,
Now an eyrie for two excited sisters,
Where, when Mother is bad, her rage can't reach them,
Now a schooner on which a lonely only
Boy sails north or approaches coral islands.

388   *On the Circuit*

AMONG Pelagian travellers,
Lost on their lewd conceited way
To Massachusetts, Michigan,
Miami or L.A.,

An airborne instrument I sit,
Predestined nightly to fulfil
Columbia-Giesen-Management's
Unfathomable will,

By whose election justified,
I bring my gospel of the Muse
To fundamentalists, to nuns,
To Gentiles and to Jews,

And daily, seven days a week,
Before a local sense has jelled,
From talking-site to talking-site
Am jet- or prop-propelled.

Though warm my welcome everywhere
I shift so frequently, so fast,
I cannot now say where I was
The evening before last,

Unless some singular event
Should intervene to save the place,
A truly asinine remark,
A soul-bewitching face,

Or blessed encounter, full of joy,
Unscheduled on the Giesen Plan,
With, here, an addict of Tolkein,
There, a Charles Williams fan.

Since Merit but a dunghill is,
I mount the rostrum unafraid:
Indeed, 'twere damnable to ask
If I am overpaid.

Spirit is willing to repeat
Without a qualm the same old talk,
But Flesh is homesick for our snug
Apartment in New York.

A sulky fifty-six, he finds
A change of mealtime utter hell,
Grown far too crotchety to like
A luxury hotel.

The Bible is a goodly book
I always can peruse with zest,
But really cannot say the same
For Hilton's *Be My Guest*,

Nor bear with equanimity
The radio in students' cars,
Musak at breakfast, or—dear God!—
Girl-organists in bars.

Then, worst of all the anxious thought,
Each time my plane begins to sink
And the No Smoking sign comes on:
What will there be to drink?

Is this a milieu where I must
How grahamgreeneish! How infra dig!
Snatch from the bottle in my bag
An analeptic swig?

425

Another morning comes: I see,
Dwindling below me on the plane,
The roofs of one more audience
I shall not see again.

God bless the lot of them, although
I don't remember which was which:
God bless the U.S.A., so large,
So friendly, and so rich.

R. N. CURREY

1907–

389 *Jersey Cattle*

IN rosy-fingered dawn they go
Beneath my window through the street
The kine that Homer used to know
With shambling gait and trailing feet.

Dappled with gold their ridged backs rise
And fall like waves; each white horn curls
Like a ship's prow; the heifers' eyes
Are brown and soft, like a young girl's.

An island in the wine-dark sea
Gave them first grazing: Jupiter
Assumed their shape; their sire was he
Who fathered golden Minotaur.

Their shambling gait and trailing feet
Raise sea-girt Ithaca again,
As they pad through the village street
With a sound like heavy rain.

390   FROM *Unseen Fire*

THIS is a damned inhuman sort of war.
I have been fighting in a dressing-gown
Most of the night; I cannot see the guns,
The sweating gun-detachments or the planes;

I sweat down here before a symbol thrown
Upon a screen, sift facts, initiate
Swift calculations and swift orders; wait
For the precise split-second to order fire.

We chant our ritual words; beyond the phones
A ghost repeats the orders to the guns:
One Fire . . . Two Fire . . . ghosts answer: the guns roar
Abruptly; and an aircraft waging war
Inhumanly from nearly five miles height
Meets our bouquet of death—and turns sharp right.

JOHN HEWITT

1907–

391   *From a Museum Man's Album*

MY trade takes me frequently into decaying houses,
house not literally in the sense of gaping roof,
although often with the damp maps of wallpaper in the attic
and the pickle of plaster on the cellar shelf:
but house usually represented by a very old woman
who bears a name once famous for trade or wealth
or skill or simply breeding,
and is the last of that name.

Take, for instance, the tall large-knuckled woman in tweeds
whose grandfather was an artist of repute,
and had his quarrel with the Academy
and wrote his angry letters, and marginal notes
on those from his friends and patrons. (O pitiful letters,
I keep your copies safely in a metal drawer.)
Her mother had been part of the caravan
he trundled through Europe, eloquent, passionate, poor.

Now she offers us a few early copies
made in his student days when Rubens hit him
like a boy's first cigar;
a badly-cracked circular head-of-a-girl
with flowers on a balcony, from his Roman days;
a thick bronze medal from the Exposition;
and a beaded chair-cover made by her grandmother.

She will die in a boarding house.

I remember, too, the small stout woman well,
her white hair brushed up in a manner
which was then out of fashion but has been in it again,
her deafness and her gentle smile,
her way of talking as if her words
were like the porcelain in her cabinets.
The substance of her conversation has gone blurred:
something of Assisi and Siena and Giotto
and the children singing at evening
and mist coming up the valley, and, I think, bells.

I remember, too, her shelves of books;
Okey, Henry James, Berenson, Vernon Lee,
and a number of popular manuals
like Chaffers on Pottery Marks;
and the maiolica plaque of a smiling head,
and the large glossy photograph of Mussolini
on the mantelpiece.

She was a widow, and I remember thinking it odd
that she displayed no photograph of her nephew
who was at that time a Cabinet Minister.

She died later at another address,
and left us her ceramics, but her books were to be
divided among the friends who used to come in
for an evening's bridge in the winter—
That is, all except the green-bound Chaffers
which came to us with the ceramics.

Another, younger, a spinster, led me up to an attic,
offering antlered heads, and a ship in a bottle,
and an ivory rickshaw model.

She panted a little after climbing the stairs,
and sat on a leather trunk to get her breath,
and pointed out a golden photograph
of her tall brother who died of a fever in Siam
after his first leave home.

She was giving up the house to go and live
in a larger one among trees, left by her aunt,
and in the family at least two hundred years.

I selected a rough-edged book in wooden covers,
watercolours on worm-holed rice paper, with unstuck silk
—a series of Chinese tortures of prisoners.

JOHN LEHMANN

1907–

392

This Excellent Machine

THIS excellent machine is neatly planned,
A child, a half-wit would not feel perplexed:
No chance to err, you simply press the button—
At once each cog in motion moves the next,
The whole revolves, and anything that lives
Is quickly sucked towards the running band,
Where, shot between the automatic knives,
It's guaranteed to finish dead as mutton.

This excellent machine will illustrate
The Modern World divided into nations:
So neatly planned, that if you merely tap it
The armaments will start their devastations,
And though we're for it, though we're all convinced
Some fool will press the button soon or late,
We stand and stare, expecting to be minced,—
And very few are asking, *Why not scrap it?*

E. J. SCOVELL
1907–

393   *The Swan's Feet*

WHO is this whose feet
Close on the water,
Like muscled leaves darker than ivy
Blown back and curved by unwearying wind?
They, that thrust back the water,
Softly crumple now and close, stream in his wake.

These dank weeds are also
Part and plumage of the magnolia-flowering swan.
He puts forth these too—
Leaves of ridged and bitter ivy
Sooted in towns, coal-bright with rain.

He is not moved by winds in air
Like the vain boats on the lake.
Lest you think him too a flower of parchment,
Scentless magnolia,
See his living feet under the water fanning.
In the leaves' self blows the efficient wind
That opens and bends closed those leaves.

394   *After Midsummer*

LOVE, we curve downwards, we are set to night
After our midsummer of longest light,
After hay harvest, though the days are warmer
And fruit is rounding on the lap of summer.

Still as in youth in this time of our fruition
Thought sifts to space through the words of definition,
But strangeness darkens now to a constant mood
Like hands shone dark with use or hafts of wood;

And over our dense days of activity
Brooding like stillness and satiety
The wonder deepens as clouds mass over corn
That here we are wakened and to this world born

That with its few colours so steeps and dyes
Our hearts, and with its runic signs implies
Meaning we doubt we read, yet love and fear
The forms more for the darkened light they bear.

It was so in youth too; now youth's spaces gone
And death of parents and our time's dark tone
Shadow our days—even children too, whose birth
And care through by-ways bring our thoughts to death;

Whose force of life speaks of the distant future,
Their helplessness of helpless animal nature;
Who, like the old in their shroud of age, close bound
In childhood, impress our natural pattern and end.

The springy twigs arch over walls and beds
Of lilac buddleia, and the long flower-heads
Run down the air like valleys. Not by force
But weight, the flowers of summer bend our course;

And whether we live or die, from this time on
We must know death better; though here as we stand upon
The rounded summit we think how softly the slope
And the sky have changed, and the further dales come up.

JOAN BARTON

1908–

395   *The Mistress*

THE short cut home lay through the cemetery—
A suburban shrubbery swallowing up old graves
Iron palings tipped with rusted fleur-de-lys
A sort of cottage orné at the gates,
Ridiculous and sad;

And lost in their laurel groves,
Eaten up by moss,
Stained marble flaking stone like hatches down,
The unloved unvisited dead.

In the no-man's-land of dusk a short cut home—
The exultant sense of life a trail of fire
Drawn into that tunnel roofed with the cypress smell
And walled with silence adding year to year:

Too far, too far: always
Under the smothering boughs in airless dark
The spirit dwindled, and the fire
Flickered then failed:

Gently implacably from the shade
The indecipherable dedications spoke
'Dear wife' . . . 'devoted mother' . . .
'Beloved child' . . .

KATHLEEN RAINE

1908–

396

The World

IT burns in the void,
Nothing upholds it.
Still it travels.

Travelling the void
Upheld by burning
Nothing is still.

Burning it travels.
The void upholds it.
Still it is nothing.

Nothing it travels
A burning void
Upheld by stillness.

397   *Two Invocations of Death*

I

DEATH, I repent
Of these hands and feet
That for forty years
Have been my own
And I repent
Of flesh and bone,
Of heart and liver,
Of hair and skin—
Rid me, death,
Of face and form,
Of all that I am.

And I repent
Of the forms of thought,
The habit of mind
And heart crippled
By long-spent pain,
The memory-traces
Faded and worn
Of vanished places
And human faces
Not rightly seen
Or understood
Rid me, death,
Of the words I have used.

Not this or that
But all is amiss,
That I have done,
And I have seen
Sin and sorrow
Befoul the world—
Release me, death,
Forgive, remove
From place and time
The trace of all
That I have been.

II

From a place I came
That was never in time,
From the beat of a heart
That was never in pain.
The sun and the moon,
The wind and the world,
The song and the bird
Travelled my thought
Time out of mind.
Shall I know at last
My lost delight?

Tell me, death,
How long must I sorrow
My own sorrow?
While I remain
The world is ending,
Forests are falling,
Suns are fading,
While I am here
Now is ending
And in my arms
The living are dying.
Shall I come at last
To the lost beginning?

MALCOLM LOWRY

1909–1957

398 *Delirium in Vera Cruz*

WHERE has tenderness gone, he asked the mirror
Of the Biltmore Hotel, cuarto 216. Alas,
Can its reflection lean against the glass
Too, wondering where I have gone, into what horror?
Is that it staring at me now with terror
Behind your frail tilted barrier? Tenderness
Was here, in this very bedroom, in this
Place, its form seen, cries heard, by you. What error

434

Is here? Am I that rashed image?
Is this the ghost of the love you reflected?
Now with a background of tequila, stubs, dirty collars,
Sodium perborate, and a scrawled page
To the dead, telephone off the hook? In rage
He smashed all the glass in the room. (Bill: $50.)

399 *He Liked the Dead*

As the poor end of each dead day drew near
he tried to count the things which he held dear.
No Rupert Brooke and no great lover, he
remembered little of simplicity:
his soul had never been empty of fear
and he would sell it thrice now for a tarot of beer.
He seemed to have known no love, to have valued dread
above all human feelings. He liked the dead.
The grass was not green not even grass to him;
nor was sun, sun; rose, rose; smoke, smoke; limb, limb.

BERNARD SPENCER

1909–1963

400 *Boat Poem*

I WISH there were a touch of these boats about my life;
so to speak, a tarring,
the touch of inspired disorder and something more than that,
something more too
than the mobility of sails or a primitive bumpy engine,
under that tiny hot-house window,
which eats up oil and benzine perhaps
but will go on beating in spite of the many strains
not needing with luck to be repaired too often,
with luck lasting years piled on years.

There must be a kind of envy which brings me peering
and nosing at the boats along the island quay
either in the hot morning
with the lace-light shaking up against their hulls from the water,
or when their mast-tops
keep on drawing lines between stars.
(I do not speak here of the private yachts from the clubs
which stalk across the harbour like magnificent white cats
but sheer off and keep mostly to themselves.)

Look for example at the Bartolomé; a deck-full
of mineral water and bottles of beer in cases
and great booming barrels of wine from the mainland,
endearing trade;
and lengths of timber and iron rods for building
and, curiously, a pig with flying ears
ramming a wet snout into whatever it explores.

Or the Virgen del Pilar, mantled and weavy with drooping nets
PM/708/3A
with starfish and pieces of cod drying on the wheel-house roof
some wine, the remains of supper on an enamel plate
and trousers and singlets 'passim';
both of these boats stinky and forgivable like some great men
both needing paint,
but both, one observes, armoured far better than us against jolts
by a belt of old motor-tyres lobbed round their sides for buffers.

And having in their swerving planks and in the point of their bows
the never-enough-to-be-praised
authority of a great tradition, the sea-shape
simple and true like a vase,
something that stays too in the carved head of an eagle
or that white-eyed wooden hound crying up beneath the bowsprit.

Qualities clearly admirable. So is their response to occasion,
how they celebrate such times
and suddenly fountain with bunting and stand like ocean maypoles
on a Saint's Day when a gun bangs from the fortifications,
and an echo-gun throws a bang back
and all the old kitchen bells start hammering from the churches.

Admirable again
how one of them, perhaps tomorrow, will have gone with no hooting
   or fuss,
simply absent from its place among the others,
occupied, without self-importance, in the thousands-of-
millions-of-sea.

ROBERT GARIOCH
(ROBERT SUTHERLAND)

1909–

401

Heard in the Cougate

'WHU'S aw thae fflag-poles ffur in Princes Street?
Chwoich! Ptt! Hechyuch! Ab-boannie cairry-on.
Seez-owre the wa'er. Whu' the deevil's thon
inaidie, heh?' 'The Queen's t'meet

The King o Norway wi his royal suite.'
'His royal wh'?' 'The hale jing-bang. It's aw in
the papur. Whaur's ma speck-sh? Aye they're gaun
t' day-cor-ate the toun. It's a fair treat,

somethin ye dinnae see jist ivry day.
foun'uns in the Gairdens, muckle spates
dancin t'music, an thir's t'be nae

chairge t'gi'in, it aw comes aff the Rates.'
'Ah ddae-ken whu' the pplace is comin tae
wi aw thae, hechyuch! fforeign po'entates.'

402

I Was Fair Beat

I SPENT a nicht amang the cognoscenti,
a hie-brou clan, ilk wi a beard on him
like Mark Twain's miners, due to hae a trim.
their years on aiverage roun three-and-twenty.

437

Of poetry and music we had plenty,
owre muckle, but ye maun be in the swim:
Kurt Schwitters' Ur-sonata that gaes 'Grimm
glimm gnimm bimmbimm,' it fairly wad hae sent ye

daft, if ye'd been there; modern jazz wi juicy
snell wud-wind chords, three new anes, I heard say
by thaim that ken't, new, that is, sen Debussy.

Man, it was awfie. I wad raither hae
a serenata sung by randy pussy,
and what a time a reel of tape can play!

JOHN PUDNEY

1909–

403 *Missing*

LESS said the better.
The bill unpaid, the dead letter,
No roses at the end
Of Smith, my friend.

Last words don't matter,
And there are none to flatter.
Words will not fill the post
Of Smith, the ghost.

For Smith, our brother,
Only son of loving mother,
The ocean lifted, stirred,
Leaving no word.

JAMES REEVES

1909–

404   *The Little Brother*

GOD! how they plague his life, the three damned sisters,
Throwing stones at him out of the cherry trees,
Pulling his hair, smudging his exercises,
Whispering. How passionately he sees
His spilt minnows flounder in the grass.

There will be sisters subtler far than these,
Balcful and dark, with slender, cared-for hands,
Who will not smirk and babble in the trees,
But feed him with sweet words and provocations,
And in his sleep practise their sorceries,
Appearing in the form of ragged clouds
And at the corners of malignant seas.

As with his wounded life he goes alone
To the world's end, where even tears freeze,
He will in bitter memory and remorse
Hear the lost sisters innocently tease.

405   *You in Anger*

YOU in your anger tried to make us new,
    To cancel all the warmth and loving-kindness
With which maturing time has joined us two,
    And re-infect love with his former blindness.

It was as if you said, 'I am a stranger;
    Unknown we face each other, woman and man.
We stand, as once we stood, in mortal danger;
    Risk everything, as I do, if you can.'

Then do not now repent your wilful scorn;
    Although in that black hour I hated you,
Yet in that hour, love, was my love re-born;
    When you in anger tried to make us new.

STEPHEN SPENDER

1909–

406

ACTS passed beyond the boundary of mere wishing
Not privy looks, hedged words, at times you saw.
These, blundering, heart-surrendered troopers were
Small presents made, and waiting for the tram.
Then once you said: 'Waiting was very kind',
And looked surprised. Surprising for me, too,
Whose every movement had been missionary,
A pleading tongue unheard. I had not thought
That you, who nothing else saw, would see this.

So 'very kind' was merest overflow
Something I had not reckoned in myself,
A chance deserter from my force. When we touched hands,
I felt the whole rebel, feared mutiny
And turned away,
Thinking, if these were tricklings through a dam,
I must have love enough to run a factory on,
Or give a city power, or drive a train.

407

Beethoven's Death Mask

I IMAGINE him still with heavy brow.
Huge, black, with bent head and falling hair,
He ploughs the landscape. His face
Is this hanging mask transfigured,
This mask of death which the white lights make stare.

I see the thick hands clasped; the scare-crow coat;
The light strike upwards at the holes for eyes;
The beast squat in that mouth, whose opening is
The hollow opening of an organ pipe:
There the wind sings and the harsh longing cries.

He moves across my vision like a ship.
What else is iron but he? The fields divide
And, heaving, are changing waters of the sea.
He is prisoned, masked, shut off from Being.
Life, like a fountain, he sees leap—outside.

Yet, in that head there twists the roaring cloud
And coils, as in a shell, the roaring wave.
The damp leaves whisper; bending to the rain
The April rises in him, chokes his lungs
And climbs the torturing passage of his brain.

Then the drums move away, the Distance shows:
Now cloud-hid peaks are bared; the mystic One
Horizons haze, as the blue incense, heaven.
Peace, peace. . . . Then splitting skull and dream, there come
Blotting our lights, the Trumpeter, the sun.

408

I THINK continually of those who were truly great.
Who, from the womb, remembered the soul's history
Through corridors of light where the hours are suns,
Endless and singing. Whose lovely ambition
Was that their lips, still touched with fire,
Should tell of the Spirit, clothed from head to foot in song.
And who hoarded from the Spring branches
The desires falling across their bodies like blossoms.

What is precious is never to forget
The essential delight of the blood drawn from ageless springs
Breaking through rocks in worlds before our earth.
Never to deny its pleasure in the morning simple light
Nor its grave evening demand for love.
Never to allow gradually the traffic to smother
With noise and fog, the flowering of the Spirit.

Near the snow, near the sun, in the highest fields,
See how these names are fêted by the waving grass
And by the streamers of white cloud
And whispers of wind in the listening sky.

The names of those who in their lives fought for life,
Who wore at their hearts the fire's centre.
Born of the sun, they travelled a short while toward the sun
And left the vivid air signed with their honour.

409   *The Landscape Near an Aerodrome*

MORE beautiful and soft than any moth
With burring furred antennae feeling its huge path
Through dusk, the air liner with shut-off engines
Glides over suburbs and the sleeves set trailing tall
To point the wind. Gently, broadly, she falls,
Scarcely disturbing charted currents of air.

Lulled by descent, the travellers across sea
And across feminine land indulging its easy limbs
In miles of softness, now let their eyes trained by watching
Penetrate through dusk the outskirts of this town
Here where industry shows a fraying edge.
Here they may see what is being done.

Beyond the winking masthead light
And the landing ground, they observe the outposts
Of work: chimneys like lank black fingers
Or figures, frightening and mad: and squat buildings
With their strange air behind trees, like women's faces
Shattered by grief. Here where few houses
Moan with faint light behind their blinds,
They remark the unhomely sense of complaint, like a dog
Shut out, and shivering at the foreign moon.

In the last sweep of love, they pass over fields
Behind the aerodrome, where boys play all day
Hacking dead grass: whose cries, like wild birds,
Settle upon the nearest roofs
But soon are hid under the loud city.

Then, as they land, they hear the tolling bell
Reaching across the landscape of hysteria,
To where, louder than all those batteries
And charcoaled towers against that dying sky,
Religion stands, the Church blocking the sun.

410 *Two Armies*

DEEP in the winter plain, two armies
Dig their machinery, to destroy each other.
Men freeze and hunger. No one is given leave
On either side, except the dead, and wounded.
These have their leave; while new battalions wait
On time at last to bring them violent peace.

All have become so nervous and so cold
That each man hates the cause and distant words
That brought him here, more terribly than bullets.
Once a boy hummed a popular marching song,
Once a novice hand flapped their salute;
The voice was choked, the lifted hand fell,
Shot through the wrist by those of his own side.

From their numb harvest, all would flee, except
For discipline drilled once in an iron school
Which holds them at the point of the revolver.
Yet when they sleep, the images of home
Ride wishing horses of escape
Which herd the plain in a mass unspoken poem.

Finally, they cease to hate: for although hate
Bursts from the air and whips the earth with hail
Or shoots it up in fountains to marvel at,
And although hundreds fall, who can connect
The inexhaustible anger of the guns
With the dumb patience of those tormented animals?

Clean silence drops at night, when a little walk
Divides the sleeping armies, each
Huddled in linen woven by remote hands.
When the machines are stilled, a common suffering
Whitens the air with breath and makes both one
As though these enemies slept in each other's arms.

Only the lucid friend to aerial raiders
The brilliant pilot moon, stares down
Upon this plain she makes a shining bone
Cut by the shadows of many thousand bones.
Where amber clouds scatter on No-Man's-Land
She regards death and time throw up
The furious words and minerals which destroy.

NORMAN MacCAIG

1910–

411 *Summer Farm*

STRAWS like tame lightnings lie about the grass
And hang zigzag on hedges. Green as glass
The water in the horse-trough shines.
Nine ducks go wobbling by in two straight lines.

A hen stares at nothing with one eye,
Then picks it up. Out of an empty sky
A swallow falls and, flickering through
The barn, dives up again into the dizzy blue.

I lie, not thinking, in the cool, soft grass,
Afraid of where a thought might take me—as
This grasshopper with plated face
Unfolds his legs and finds himself in space.

Self under self, a pile of selves I stand
Threaded on time, and with metaphysic hand
Lift the farm like a lid and see
Farm within farm, and in the centre, me.

412 *Moorings*

IN a salt ring of moonlight
The dinghy nods at nothing.
It paws the bright water
And scatters its own shadow
In a false net of light.

A ruined chain lies reptile,
Tied to the ground by grasses.
Two oars, wet with sweet water
Filched from the air, are slanted
From a wrecked lobster creel.

The cork that can't be travels—
Nose of a dog otter.
It's piped at, screamed at, sworn at
By elegant oyster catcher
On furious red legs.

With a sort of idle swaying
The tide breathes in. Harsh seaweed
Uncrackles to its kissing;
The skin of the water glistens;
Rich fat swims on the brine.

And all night in his stable
The dinghy paws bright water,
Restless steeplechaser
Longing to clear the hurdles
That ring the Point of Stoer.

413

Wild Oats

EVERY day I see from my window
pigeons, up on a roof ledge—the males
are wobbling gyroscopes of lust.

Last week a stranger joined them, a snowwhite
pouting fantail,
Mae West in the Women's Guild.
What becks, what croo-croos, what
demented pirouetting, what a lack
of moustaches to stroke.

The females—no need to be one of them
to know
exactly what they were thinking—pretended
she wasn't there
and went dowdily on with whatever
pigeons do when they're knitting.

445

ROBERT GITTINGS

1911–

414 *The Great Moth*

VISITANT to our dumbly human home,
Dull coal or shrivelled leaf, the great moth lay,
Out of storm-wet October come,
The window's lashing spray.

Strange confidant, the legs that crooked my finger
Settled like truth, though little I had to give,
Knowing how short such breath-spans linger,
How brief the creatures live.

Yet wishing to offer the slightest goodwill gesture,
Placed with free hand a bowl of honeysuckle near,
And sudden as a charm, the charred vesture
Was shed: a tremble like a tear

Shook the rose-barred body and vibrant wings,
Delight stood quivering in violent, delicate spread.
Above the sweetly-scented springs
Of life, it arose from the dead

Triumphant: and not one of us, bending over,
But felt the catch of hope and courage of heart,
As if with plumes of grace to hover
A spirit took our part.

HAL SUMMERS
1911–

415 *My Old Cat*

MY old cat is dead,
Who would butt me with his head.
He had the sleekest fur.
He had the blackest purr.
Always gentle with us
Was this black puss,
But when I found him today
Stiff and cold where he lay
His look was a lion's,
Full of rage, defiance:
Oh, he would not pretend
That what came was a friend
But met it in pure hate.
Well died, my old cat.

CHRISTOPHER HASSALL
1912–1964

416 *Santa Claus*
in a department store

WOLSEY, or possibly my John of Gaunt,
Was the best thing I did. Come over here,
Behind the Christmas crib. (I'm not supposed
To let the children see me having tea.)
To tell the truth I'm glad of this engagement.
Dozens applied, but all they said was Thank you,
We'll stick to Mr. Borthwick.
It's nice to feel one has given satisfaction.
Time was I had it all at my finger-tips,
Could plant a whisper in the back of the pit,

Or hold them breathless with the authority
Of absolute repose—a skill despised,
Not seen, in *your* day. It amounts to this:
Technique's no more than the bare bones. There are some
Unwittingly instil the faith that Man
Is greater than he knows. This I fell short of.
    You never met my wife. You are too young.
She often came with me on tour. One night
At Nottingham, got back from the show, and there
She was. I knew at once what made her do it.
She had resented me for years. No, not
Myself, but what she knew was *in* me, my
Belief in—Sir, forgive me if I say
My 'art', for I had shown, you'll understand,
Some promise. To use her word, she felt herself
'Usurped', and by degrees, unconsciously,
She managed somehow to diminish me,
Parch all my vital streams. A look would do it.
I was a kind of shrunken river-bed
Littered with tins, old tyres, and bicycle frames.

    Well, that was years ago, and by then too late
To start afresh. Yet all the while I loved her.
Explain that if you can. . . . By all means, madam,
Those clocks are very popular this year.
I'll call the man in charge. No, there's no risk
Of damage. They pack the cuckoo separately.

KENNETH ALLOTT

1912–

417   *Lament for a Cricket Eleven*

FOR S. T.

BEYOND the edge of the sepia
Rises the weak photographer
With the moist moustaches and the made-up tie.
He looked with his mechanical eye,
And the upshot was that they had to die.

Portrait of the Eleven nineteen-o-five
To show when these missing persons were last alive.
Two sit in Threadneedle Street like gnomes.
One is a careless schoolmaster
Busy with carved desks, honour and lines.
He is eaten by a wicked cancer.
They have detectives to watch their homes.

From the camera hood he looks at the faces
Like the spectral pose of the praying mantis.
Watch for the dicky-bird. But, O my dear,
That bird will not migrate this year.
Oh for a parasol, oh for a fan
To hide my weak chin from the little man.

One climbs mountains in a storm of fear,
Begs to be unroped and left alone.
One went mad by a tape-machine.
One laughed for a fortnight and went to sea.
Like a sun one follows the jeunesse dorée.

With his hand on the bulb he looks at them.
The smiles on their faces are upside down.
'I'll turn my head and spoil the plate.'
'Thank you, gentlemen.' Too late. Too late.

One greyhead was beaten in a prison riot.
He needs injections to keep him quiet.
Another was a handsome clergyman,
But mortification has long set in.
One keeps six dogs in an unlit cellar.
The last is a randy bachelor.

The photographer in the norfolk jacket
Sits upstairs in his darkroom attic.
His hand is expert at scissors and pin.
The shadows lengthen, the days draw in,
And the mice come out round the iron stove.
'What I am doing, I am doing for love.
When shall I burn this negative
And hang the receiver up on grief?'

PAUL DEHN

1912–

418 *Armistice*

IT is finished. The enormous dust-cloud over Europe
Lifts like a million swallows; and a light,
Drifting in craters, touches the quiet dead.

Now, at the bugle's hour, before the blood
Cakes in a clean wind on their marble faces,
Making them monuments; before the sun,

Hung like a medal on the smoky noon,
Whitens the bone that feeds the earth; before
Wheat-ear springs green, again, in the green spring

And they are bread in the bodies of the young:
Be strong to remember how the bread died, screaming;
Gangrene was corn, and monuments went mad.

LAWRENCE DURRELL

1912–

419 *This Unimportant Morning*

THIS unimportant morning
Something goes singing where
The capes turn over on their sides
And the warm Adriatic rides
Her blue and sun washing
At the edge of the world and its brilliant cliffs.

Day rings in the higher airs
Pure with cicadas, and slowing
Like a pulse to smoke from farms,
Extinguished in the exhausted earth,
Unclenching like a fist and going.

Trees fume, cool, pour—and overflowing
Unstretch the feathers of birds and shake
Carpets from windows, brush with dew
The up-and-doing: and young lovers now
Their little resurrections make.

And now lightly to kiss all whom sleep
Stitched up—and wake, my darling, wake.
The impatient Boatman has been waiting
Under the house, his long oars folded up
Like wings in waiting on the darkling lake.

420   *Poggio*

THE rubber penis, the wig, the false breasts . . .
The talent for entering rooms backwards
Upon a roar of laughter, with his dumb
Pained expression, wheeling there before him
That mythological great hippo's bum:

'Who should it be but Poggio?' The white face,
Comical, flat, and hairless as a cheese.
Nose like a member: something worn:
A Tuscan fig, a leather can, or else,
A phallus made of putty and slapped on.

How should you know that behind
All this the old buffoon concealed a fear—
And reasonable enough—that he might be
An artist after all? Always after this kind
Of side-splitting evening, sitting there
On a three-legged stool and writing, he

Hoped poems might form upon the paper.
But no. Dirty stories. The actress and the bishop.
The ape and the eunuch. This crapula clung
To him for many years between his dinners . . .
He sweated at them like a ham unhung.

And like the rest of us hoped for
The transfigured story of the mantic line
Of poetry free from this mortuary smell.
For years slept badly—who does not?
Took bribes, and drugs, ate far too much and dreamed.
Married unwisely, yes, but died quite well.

421   *Mythology*

ALL my favourite characters have been
Out of all pattern and proportion:
Some living in villas by railways,
Some like Katsimbalis heard but seldom seen,
And others in banks whose sunless hands
Moved like great rats on ledgers.

Tibble, Gondril, Purvis, the Duke of Puke,
Shatterblossom and Dude Bowdler
Who swelled up in Jaffa and became a tree:
Hollis who had wives killed under him like horses
And that man of destiny,

Ramon de Something who gave lectures
From an elephant, founded a society
To protect the inanimate against cruelty.
He gave asylum to aged chairs in his home,
Lampposts and crockery, everything that
Seemed to him suffering he took in
Without mockery.

The poetry was in the pity. No judgement
Disturbs people like these in their frames
O men of the Marmion class, sons of the free.

ROY FULLER

1912–

422   *Spring 1942*

ONCE as we were sitting by
The falling sun, the thickening air,
The chaplain came against the sky
And quietly took a vacant chair.

And under the tobacco smoke:
'Freedom,' he said, and 'Good' and 'Duty.'
We stared as though a savage spoke.
The scene took on a singular beauty.

And we made no reply to that
Obscure, remote communication,
But only looked out where the flat
Meadow dissolved in vegetation.

And thought: O sick, insatiable
And constant lust; O death, our future;
O revolution in the whole
Of human use of man and nature!

423   *The Image*

A SPIDER in the bath. The image noted:
Significant maybe but surely cryptic.
A creature motionless and rather bloated,
The barriers shining, vertical and white:
Passing concern, and pity mixed with spite.

Next day with some surprise one finds it there.
It seems to have moved an inch or two, perhaps.
It starts to take on that familiar air
Of prisoners for whom time is erratic:
The filthy aunt forgotten in the attic.

Quite obviously it came up through the waste,
Rejects through ignorance or apathy
That passage back. The problem must be faced;
And life go on though strange intruders stir
Among its ordinary furniture.

One jibs at murder, so a sheet of paper
Is slipped beneath the accommodating legs.
The bathroom window shows for the escaper
The lighted lanterns of laburnum hung
In copper beeches—on which scene it's flung.

We certainly would like thus easily
To cast out of the house all suffering things.
But sadness and responsibility
For our own kind lives in the image noted:
A half-loved creature, motionless and bloated.

424   *Translation*

Now that the barbarians have got as far as Picra,
And all the new music is written in the twelve-tone scale,
And I am anyway approaching my fortieth birthday,
          I will dissemble no longer.

I will stop expressing my belief in the rosy
Future of man, and accept the evidence
Of a couple of wretched wars and innumerable
          Abortive revolutions.

I will cease to blame the stupidity of the slaves
Upon their masters and nurture, and will say,
Plainly, that they are enemies to culture,
          Advancement and cleanliness.

From progressive organisations, from quarterlies
Devoted to daring verse, from membership of
Committees, from letters of various protest
          I shall withdraw forthwith.

When they call me reactionary I shall smile,
Secure in another dimension. When they say
'Cinna has ceased to matter' I shall know
    How well I reflect the times.

The ruling class will think I am on their side
And make friendly overtures, but I shall retire
To the side further from Picra and write some poems
    About the doom of the whole boiling.

Anyone happy in this age and place
Is daft or corrupt. Better to abdicate
From a material and spiritual terrain
    Fit only for barbarians.

425   *The Day*

AT the time it seemed unimportant: he was lying
In bed, off work, with a sudden pain,
And she was haloed by the morning sun,
Enquiring if he'd like the daily paper.

So idle Byzantium scarcely felt at first
The presence in her remoter provinces
Of the destructive followers of the Crescent.

But in retrospect that day of moderate health
Stood fired in solid and delightful hues,
The last of joy, the first of something else—
An inconceivable time when sex could be
Grasped for the asking with gigantic limbs,
When interest still was keen in the disasters
Of others—accident, uprising, drouth—
And the sharp mind perceived the poignancy
Of the ridiculous thoughts of dissolution.

A day remembered by a shrivelled empire
Nursed by hermaphrodites and unsustained
By tepid fluids poured in its crying mouth.

426   *Faust's Servant*

I'M quite the opposite of my clever master.
He's at his books all day. I spy on ladies
And think of naught but filth, though there's no faster
Road for a chap to Hades.

I wish I had his brains to take my mind
Off of the feminine anatomy.
He reads at Greek and Latin till he's blind,
Doesn't see the things I see.

Today the girls seem bigger there than ever:
Not that I ask for anything so young.
It's just I find it hard that I shall never
Again slip home the bung.

A widow thirtyfive or so would do—
But what's the use of dreaming when my chin
Says to my nose 'How are you?' as I chew,
And buttocks are so thin.

When bladder gets me up at four I'd give
My soul for sweeter breath and tighter pills,
And sometimes for a second really live
With magic's miracles.

427   *Metamorphoses*

THE girl in trousers wheeling a red baby
Stops to look in the window of a bread-shop.
One wants to tell her that it's all steam-
Baked muck, but really there's no chance
Of stopping her buying a bogus
Farm-house cob. Reassuring to think
That anyway it will be transformed
To wholesome milk, just as somehow she
Has gathered herself together from
The chaos of parturition and
Appears now with a lacquered bouffant
Top-knot and her old wiles unimpaired.

Why should one trouble to disguise the
Origin of the terrifying
Earth-mother, that lies in wait for men
With her odours of bergamot and
Plasma, and her soft rind filled with tripes?

DONAGH MacDONAGH

1912–

428   *Dublin Made Me*

DUBLIN made me and no little town
With the country closing in on its streets
The cattle walking proudly on its pavements
The jobbers the gombeenmen and the cheats

Devouring the fair day between them
A public-house to half a hundred men
And the teacher, the solicitor and the bank-clerk
In the hotel bar drinking for ten.

Dublin made me, not the secret poteen still
The raw and hungry hills of the West
The lean road flung over profitless bog
Where only a snipe could nest

Where the sea takes its tithe of every boat.
Bawneen and curragh have no allegiance of mine,
Nor the cute self-deceiving talkers of the South
Who look to the East for a sign.

The soft and dreary midlands with their tame canals
Wallow between sea and sea, remote from adventure,
And Northward a far and fortified province
Crouches under the lash of arid censure.

I disclaim all fertile meadows, all tilled land
The evil that grows from it and the good,
But the Dublin of old statutes, this arrogant city,
Stirs proudly and secretly in my blood.

CHARLES MADGE

1912–

429   *Solar Creation*

THE sun, of whose terrain we creatures are,
Is the director of all human love,
Unit of time, and circle round the earth

And we are the commotion born of love
And slanted rays of that illustrious star
Peregrine of the crowded fields of birth,

The crowded lanes, the market and the tower
Like sight in pictures, real at remove,
Such is our motion on dimensional earth.

Down by the river, where the ragged are,
Continuous the cries and noise of birth,
While to the muddy edge dark fishes move

And over all, like death, or sloping hill,
Is nature, which is larger and more still.

F. T. PRINCE

1912–

430   *The Token*

MORE beautiful than any gift you gave
You were, a child so beautiful as to seem
To promise ruin what no child can have,
Or woman give. And so a Roman gem
I choose to be your token: here a laurel
Springs to its young height, hangs a broken limb;
And here a group of women wanly quarrel
At a sale of Cupids. A hawk looks at them.

431   *Soldiers Bathing*

THE sea at evening moves across the sand.
Under a reddening sky I watch the freedom of a band
Of soldiers who belong to me. Stripped bare
For bathing in the sea, they shout and run in the warm air;
Their flesh worn by the trade of war, revives
And my mind towards the meaning of it strives.

All's pathos now. The body that was gross,
Rank, ravenous, disgusting in the act or in repose,
All fever, filth and sweat, its bestial strength
And bestial decay, by pain and labour grows at length
Fragile and luminous. 'Poor bare forked animal,'
Conscious of his desires and needs and flesh that rise and fall,
Stands in the soft air, tasting after toil
The sweetness of his nakedness: letting the sea-waves coil
Their frothy tongues about his feet, forgets
His hatred of the war, its terrible pressure that begets
A machinery of death and slavery,
Each being a slave and making slaves of others: finds that he
Remembers his old freedom in a game
Mocking himself, and comically mimics fear and shame.

He plays with death and animality;
And reading in the shadows of his pallid flesh, I see
The idea of Michelangelo's cartoon
Of soldiers bathing, breaking off before they were half done
At some sortie of the enemy, an episode
Of the Pisan wars with Florence. I remember how he showed
Their muscular limbs that clamber from the water,
And heads that turn across the shoulder, eager for the slaughter,
Forgetful of their bodies that are bare,
And hot to buckle on and use the weapons lying there.
—And I think too of the theme another found
When, shadowing men's bodies on a sinister red ground,
Another Florentine, Pollaiuolo,
Painted a naked battle: warriors, straddled, hacked the foe,
Dug their bare toes into the ground and slew
The brother-naked man who lay between their feet and drew
His lips back from his teeth in a grimace.

They were Italians who knew war's sorrow and disgrace
And showed the thing suspended, stripped: a theme
Born out of the experience of war's horrible extreme
Beneath a sky where even the air flows
With lacrimae Christi. For that rage, that bitterness, those blows,
That hatred of the slain, what could they be
But indirectly or directly a commentary
On the Crucifixion? And the picture burns
With indignation and pity and despair by turns,
Because it is the obverse of the scene
Where Christ hangs murdered, stripped, upon the Cross. I mean,
That is the explanation of its rage.

And we too have our bitterness and pity that engage
Blood, spirit, in this war. But night begins,
Night of the mind: who nowadays is conscious of our sins?
Though every human deed concerns our blood,
And even we must know, what nobody has understood,
That some great love is over all we do,
And that is what has driven us to this fury, for so few
Can suffer all the terror of that love:
The terror of that love has set us spinning in this groove
Greased with our blood.

                    These dry themselves and dress,
Combing their hair, forget the fear and shame of nakedness.
Because to love is frightening we prefer
The freedom of our crimes. Yet, as I drink the dusky air,
I feel a strange delight that fills me full,
Strange gratitude, as if evil itself were beautiful,
And kiss the wound in thought, while in the west
I watch a streak of red that might have issued from Christ's breast.

GEORGE BARKER

1913–

432   *To My Mother*

MOST near, most dear, most loved and most far,
Under the window where I often found her
Sitting as huge as Asia, seismic with laughter,
Gin and chicken helpless in her Irish hand,
Irresistible as Rabelais, but most tender for
The lame dogs and hurt birds that surround her,—
She is a procession no one can follow after
But be like a little dog following a brass band.

She will not glance up at the bomber, or condescend
To drop her gin and scuttle to a cellar,
But lean on the mahogany table like a mountain
Whom only faith can move, and so I send
O all my faith, and all my love to tell her
That she will move from mourning into morning.

433   *Turn on Your Side and Bear the Day to Me*

TURN on your side and bear the day to me
Beloved, sceptre-struck, immured
In the glass wall of sleep. Slowly
Uncloud the borealis of your eye
And show your iceberg secrets, your midnight prizes
To the green-eyed world and to me. Sin
Coils upward into thin air when you awaken
And again morning announces amnesty over
The serpent-kingdomed bed. Your mother
Watched with as dove an eye the unforgiveable night
Sigh backward into innocence when you
Set a bright monument in her amorous sea.
Look down, Undine, on the trident that struck
Sons from the rock of vanity. Turn in the world
Sceptre-struck, spellbound, beloved,
Turn in the world and bear the day to me.

In Memory of a Friend

THE fury this Friday broke through my wall
   With a death certificate in its hand.
Bright, bright, Elipsion, burn to-night
   Across the sky and tell the whole
Empty and insignificant world that I grieve
   For a tall Jack with the sun on his wrist
And a sky stuffed up his sleeve. Let me leave
   Love on the mantelpiece looking East
To gather together the dust that I have lost.

They walk in silence over the same spaces
   Where they once talked, and now do not,
The dumb friends with the whitewashed faces
   Who lifted a hand and died. They forget us
In the merciful amnesia of their death,
   But by us, the disremembered, they cannot
Ever be forgotten. For, always, in all places,
   They rise eloquently up to remind us
Of the unforgettable allegiances behind us.

My love, my love, why do you leave me alone?
   My love, my love, where, where are you gone?
Here the tall altitudes grieve as they gaze down
   Knowing that you, elusive their lover, are gone,
And that you will never again
   Kiss the teeth of the morning at a vivid four hundred,
Uncurling, at nine angels, the gold and splendid
   Wake on which you walk across the sky.
Grieving, like them, I cannot believe it is ended.

Remember the eye that haunts me for ever
   Wherever I am under any sky,
O completely from leaf and smiling from over
   Every horizon he looks at me.
The simple sea shall fold its sad arms
   Less long about the world
Than I shall hold him in my dreams
   Until every moment seems
To reclaim part of him.

The salt that at the lashes of
   All Seven Seas laces the shores
Grazing my weeping eye of sores,
   Engenders the more of love.
Here by the salt tide at the South
   That washes its coils along
The coast that lies behind the eyes,
   His wreck is like a rock in my mouth
With his body on my tongue.

Time with its shoving shall unsmooth
   The brightest lying lover
And in the teeth of human truth
   Prove that the heart needs more than faith
To help it to recover
   The love that took a look at death
And promised me forever:
   As, under Northern Seas, his face
Fades as the seas wash over.

My love, my love, lift up your joystick hand.
   Dismiss the dividing
Grief. Bring, bring again the kiss and the guiding
   Glory. From his hiding
Place in the cleft of the cloud, O dove of evening,
   Lead him back over that dark intervening
Day when he died. Lead him back in a loving
   Return to that room where I
Look out and watch his death glittering in the sky.

The killers shall spring into each other's arms
   And the storms subside:
The catalytical shall kiss, and the relief
   Wrap cities in mutual belief
And the dove preside.
   Then all but this tall one and the dead
Shall feel the warming of the world
   Running through every board and bed
Colder because they died.

Sleep, long and beautiful, in that bag
   Where loneliness, my tall falcon,
Shall never again cheat you with the mirage
   Of sensual satisfaction.

Look, look, the grave shakes over his head
And the red dirt stands up, as
Across existence I beg him heed:
To those that love there are no dead,
Only the long sleepers.

435 *Wild Dreams of Summer What is Your Grief*

WILD dreams of Summer, what is your grief?
Wild dreams of Winter, what is your delight?
O holy day, O holy day, so brief
O holy day, before so long a night.

My love, my love, no, there is no waking
From that long bed or that sleep.
My love, my love, the heart is here for the taking,
And we can take, but not keep.

R. S. THOMAS

1913–

436 *The Country Clergy*

I SEE them working in old rectories
By the sun's light, by candlelight,
Venerable men, their black cloth
A little dusty, a little green
With holy mildew. And yet their skulls,
Ripening over so many prayers,
Toppled into the same grave
With oafs and yokels. They left no books,
Memorial to their lonely thought
In grey parishes; rather they wrote
On men's hearts and in the minds
Of young children sublime words
Too soon forgotten. God in his time
Or out of time will correct this.

437

On the Farm

THERE was Dai Puw. He was no good.
They put him in the fields to dock swedes,
And took the knife from him, when he came home
At late evening with a grin
Like the slash of a knife on his face.

There was Llew Puw, and he was no good.
Every evening after the ploughing
With the big tractor he would sit in his chair,
And stare into the tangled fire garden,
Opening his slow lips like a snail.

There was Huw Puw, too. What shall I say?
I have heard him whistling in the hedges
On and on, as though winter
Would never again leave those fields,
And all the trees were deformed.

And lastly there was the girl:
Beauty under some spell of the beast.
Her pale face was the lantern
By which they read in life's dark book
The shrill sentence: God is love.

438

They

I TAKE their hands,
Hard hands. There is no love
For such, only a willed
Gentleness. Negligible men
From the village, from the small
Holdings, they bring their grief
Sullenly to my back door,
And are speechless. Seeing them
In the wind with the light's
Halo, watching their eyes
Blur, I know the reason
They cry, their worsting
By one whom they will fight.

Daily the sky mirrors
The water, the water the
Sky. Daily I take their side
In their quarrel, calling their faults
Mine. How do I serve so
This being they have shut out
Of their houses, their thoughts, their lives?

DYLAN THOMAS

1914–1953

439

THE force that through the green fuse drives the flower
Drives my green age; that blasts the roots of trees
Is my destroyer.
And I am dumb to tell the crooked rose
My youth is bent by the same wintry fever.

The force that drives the water through the rocks
Drives my red blood; that dries the mouthing streams
Turns mine to wax.
And I am dumb to mouth unto my veins
How at the mountain spring the same mouth sucks.

The hand that whirls the water in the pool
Stirs the quicksand; that ropes the blowing wind
Hauls my shroud sail.
And I am dumb to tell the hanging man
How of my clay is made the hangman's lime.

The lips of time leech to the fountain head;
Love drips and gathers, but the fallen blood
Shall calm her sores.
And I am dumb to tell a weather's wind
How time has ticked a heaven round the stars.

And I am dumb to tell the lover's tomb
How at my sheet goes the same crooked worm.

440

ESPECIALLY when the October wind
With frosty fingers punishes my hair,
Caught by the crabbing sun I walk on fire
And cast a shadow crab upon the land,
By the sea's side, hearing the noise of birds,
Hearing the raven cough in winter sticks,
My busy heart who shudders as she talks
Sheds the syllabic blood and drains her words.

Shut, too, in a tower of words, I mark
On the horizon walking like the trees
The wordy shapes of women, and the rows
Of the star-gestured children in the park.
Some let me make you of the vowelled beeches,
Some of the oaken voices, from the roots
Of many a thorny shire tell you notes,
Some let me make you of the water's speeches.

Behind a pot of ferns the wagging clock
Tells me the hour's word, the neural meaning
Flies on the shafted disk, declaims the morning
And tells the windy weather in the cock.
Some let me make you of the meadow's signs;
The signal grass that tells me all I know
Breaks with the wormy winter through the eye.
Some let me tell you of the raven's sins.

Especially when the October wind
(Some let me make you of autumnal spells,
The spider-tongued, and the loud hill of Wales)
With fists of turnips punishes the land,
Some let me make you of the heartless words.
The heart is drained that, spelling in the scurry
Of chemic blood, warned of the coming fury.
By the sea's side hear the dark-vowelled birds.

441

LIGHT breaks where no sun shines;
Where no sea runs, the waters of the heart
Push in their tides;
And, broken ghosts with glow-worms in their heads,
The things of light
File through the flesh where no flesh decks the bones.

A candle in the thighs
Warms youth and seed and burns the seeds of age;
Where no seed stirs,
The fruit of man unwrinkles in the stars,
Bright as a fig;
Where no wax is, the candle shows its hairs.

Dawn breaks behind the eyes;
From poles of skull and toe the windy blood
Slides like a sea;
Nor fenced, nor staked, the gushers of the sky
Spout to the rod
Divining in a smile the oil of tears.

Night in the sockets rounds,
Like some pitch moon, the limit of the globes;
Day lights the bone;
Where no cold is, the skinning gales unpin
The winter's robes;
The film of spring is hanging from the lids.

Light breaks on secret lots,
On tips of thought where thoughts smell in the rain;
When logics die,
The secret of the soil grows through the eye,
And blood jumps in the sun;
Above the waste allotments the dawn halts.

442   *The Countryman's Return*

EMBRACING low-falutin
London (said the odd man in
A country pot, his hutch in
The fields, by a motherlike henrun)
With my fishtail hands and gently
Manuring popeye or
Swelling in flea-specked linen
The rankest of the city
I spent my unwasteable
Time among walking pintables
With sprung and padded shoulders,
Tomorrow's drunk club majors
Growing their wounds already,
The last war's professional
Unclaimed dead, girls from good homes
Studying the testicle
In communal crab flats
With the Sunflowers laid on,
Old paint-stained tumblers riding
On stools to a one man show down,
Gasketted and sirensuited
Bored and viciously waiting
Nightingales of the casualty stations
In the afternoon wasters
White feathering the living.

London's arches are falling
In, in Pedro's or Wendy's
With a silverfox farmer
Trying his hand at failing
Again, a collected poet
And some dismantled women,
Razor man and belly king,
I propped humanity's weight
Against the fruit machine,
Opened my breast and into
The spongebag let them all melt.
Zip once more for a traveller

With his goods under his eyes,
Another with hers under her belt,
The black man bleached to his tide
Mark, trumpet lipped and blackhead
Eyed, while the tears drag on the tail,
The weighing-scales, of my hand.
Then into blind streets I swam
Alone with my bouncing bag,
Too full to bow to the dim
Moon with a relation's face
Or lift my hat to unseen
Brothers dodging through the fog
The affectionate pickpocket
And childish, snivelling queen.

Beggars, robbers, inveiglers,
Voices from manholes and drains,
Maternal short time pieces,
Octopuses in doorways,
Dark inviters to keyholes
And evenings with great danes,
Bedsitting girls on the beat
With nothing for the metre,
Others whose single beds hold two
Only to make two ends meet,
All the hypnotised city's
Insidious procession
Hawking for money and pity
Among the hardly possessed.
And I in the wanting sway
Caught among never enough
Conjured me to resemble
A singing Walt from the mower
And jerrystone trim villas
Of the upper of the lower half,
Beardlessly wagging in Dean Street,
Blessing and counting the bustling
Twolegged handbagged sparrows,
Flogging into the porches
My cavernous, featherbed self.

Cut. Cut the crushed streets, leaving
A hole of errands and shades;
Plug the paper-blowing tubes;
Emasculate the seedy clocks;
Rub off the scrawl of prints on
Body and air and building;
Branch and leaf the birdless roofs;
Faces of melting visions,
Magdalene prostitution,
Glamour of the bloodily bowed,
Exaltation of the blind,
That sin-embracing dripper of fun
Sweep away like a cream cloud;
Bury all rubbish and love signs
Of my week in the dirtbox
In this anachronistic scene
Where sitting in clean linen
In a hutch in a cowpatched glen
Now I delight, I suppose, in
The countryman's return
And count by birds' eggs and leaves
The rusticating minutes,
The wasteful hushes among trees.
And O to cut the green field, leaving
One rich street with hunger in it.

443

THE tombstone told when she died.
Her two surnames stopped me still.
A virgin married at rest.
She married in this pouring place,
That I struck one day by luck,
Before I heard in my mother's side
Or saw in the looking-glass shell
The rain through her cold heart speak
And the sun killed in her face.
More the thick stone cannot tell.
Before she lay on a stranger's bed
With a hand plunged through her hair,

Or that rainy tongue beat back
Through the devilish years and innocent deaths
To the room of a secret child,
Among men later I heard it said
She cried her white-dressed limbs were bare
And her red lips were kissed black,
She wept in her pain and made mouths,
Talked and tore though her eyes smiled.

I who saw in a hurried film
Death and this mad heroine
Meet once on a mortal wall
Heard her speak through the chipped beak
Of the stone bird guarding her:
I died before bedtime came
But my womb was bellowing
And I felt with my bare fall
A blazing red harsh head tear up
And the dear floods of his hair.

444

IT is the sinners' dust-tongued bell claps me to churches
When, with his torch and hourglass, like a sulphur priest,
His beast heel cleft in a sandal,
Time marks a black aisle kindle from the brand of ashes,
Grief with dishevelled hands tear out the altar ghost
And a firewind kill the candle.

Over the choir minute I hear the hour chant:
Time's coral saint and the salt grief drown a foul sepulchre
And a whirlpool drives the prayerwheel;
Moonfall and sailing emperor, pale as their tide-print,
Hear by death's accident the clocked and dashed-down spire
Strike the sea hour through bellmetal.
There is loud and dark directly under the dumb flame,
Storm, snow, and fountain in the weather of fireworks,
Cathedral calm in the pulled house;
Grief with drenched book and candle christens the cherub time
From the emerald, still bell; and from the pacing weather-cock
The voice of bird on coral prays.

Forever it is a white child in the dark-skinned summer
Out of the font of bone and plants at that stone tocsin
Scales the blue wall of spirits;
From blank and leaking winter sails the child in colour,
Shakes, in crabbed burial shawl, by sorcerer's insect woken,
Ding dong from the mute turrets.

I mean by time the cast and curfew rascal of our marriage,
At nightbreak born in the fat side, from an animal bed
In a holy room in a wave;
And all love's sinners in sweet cloth kneel to a hyleg image,
Nutmeg, civet, and sea-parsley serve the plagued groom and bride
Who have brought forth the urchin grief.

445   *A Refusal to Mourn the Death, by Fire,*
of a Child in London

NEVER until the mankind making
Bird beast and flower
Fathering and all humbling darkness
Tells with silence the last light breaking
And the still hour
Is come of the sea tumbling in harness

And I must enter again the round
Zion of the water bead
And the synagogue of the ear of corn
Shall I let pray the shadow of a sound
Or sow my salt seed
In the least valley of sackcloth to mourn

The majesty and burning of the child's death.
I shall not murder
The mankind of her going with a grave truth
Nor blaspheme down the stations of the breath
With any further
Elegy of innocence and youth.

Deep with the first dead lies London's daughter,
Robed in the long friends,
The grains beyond age, the dark veins of her mother,
Secret by the unmourning water
Of the riding Thames.
After the first death, there is no other.

446   *Do not go gentle into that good night*

Do not go gentle into that good night,
Old age should burn and rave at close of day;
Rage, rage against the dying of the light.

Though wise men at their end know dark is right,
Because their words had forked no lightning they
Do not go gentle into that good night.

Good men, the last wave by, crying how bright
Their frail deeds might have danced in a green bay,
Rage, rage against the dying of the light.

Wild men who caught and sang the sun in flight,
And learn, too late, they grieved it on its way,
Do not go gentle into that good night.

Grave men, near death, who see with blinding sight
Blind eyes could blaze like meteors and be gay,
Rage, rage against the dying of the light.

And you, my father, there on the sad height,
Curse, bless, me now with your fierce tears, I pray.
Do not go gentle into that good night.
Rage, rage against the dying of the light.

447 ## *Fern Hill*

Now as I was young and easy under the apple boughs
About the lilting house and happy as the grass was green,
  The night above the dingle starry,
   Time let me hail and climb
  Golden in the heydays of his eyes,
And honoured among wagons I was prince of the apple towns
And once below a time I lordly had the trees and leaves
  Trail with daisies and barley
  Down the rivers of the windfall light.

And as I was green and carefree, famous among the barns
About the happy yard and singing as the farm was home,
  In the sun that is young once only,
   Time let me play and be
  Golden in the mercy of his means,
And green and golden I was huntsman and herdsman, the calves
Sang to my horn, the foxes on the hills barked clear and cold,
  And the sabbath rang slowly
  In the pebbles of the holy streams.

All the sun long it was running, it was lovely, the hay
Fields high as the house, the tunes from the chimneys, it was air
  And playing, lovely and watery
   And fire green as grass.
  And nightly under the simple stars
As I rode to sleep the owls were bearing the farm away,
All the moon long I heard, blessed among stables, the nightjars
  Flying with the ricks, and the horses
  Flashing into the dark.

And then to awake, and the farm, like a wanderer white
With the dew, come back, the cock on his shoulder: it was all
  Shining, it was Adam and maiden,
   The sky gathered again
  And the sun grew round that very day.
So it must have been after the birth of the simple light
In the first, spinning place, the spellbound horses walking warm
  Out of the whinnying green stable
  On to the fields of praise.

And honoured among foxes and pheasants by the gay house
Under the new made clouds and happy as the heart was long,
   In the sun born over and over,
      I ran my heedless ways,
   My wishes raced through the house high hay
And nothing I cared, at my sky blue trades, that time allows
In all his tuneful turning so few and such morning songs
   Before the children green and golden
      Follow him out of grace,

Nothing I cared, in the lamb white days, that time would take me
Up to the swallow thronged loft by the shadow of my hand,
   In the moon that is always rising,
      Nor that riding to sleep
   I should hear him fly with the high fields
And wake to the farm forever fled from the childless land.
Oh as I was young and easy in the mercy of his means,
      Time held me green and dying
   Though I sang in my chains like the sea.

CLIFFORD DYMENT

1914–1971

448   *'As a boy with a richness of needs I wandered'*

As a boy with a richness of needs I wandered
In car parks and streets, epicure of Lagondas,
Minervas, Invictas, and Hispano Suizas;
And I sampled as roughage and amusing sauce
Little Rovers and Rileys, and the occasional funny
Trojan with chain drive, and the Morris Cowleys
With their modest bonnets, sedate Fiat
Of the nineteen-twenties, and the Alvis, middle-brow
Between the raffish sports car and the family bus.
I was tempted by aircraft too, sniffing
Over *The Aeroplane* and *Flight*—those kites,
They seem today, knocked up in a back yard
By young and oily artists who painted with rivets:

Westland Wapiti, Bristol Bulldog, and the great
De Havilland Hercules, invading the desert
And pulsing within its sleep like a troubling nerve;
And surely, I think, as I remember those feasts,
They were days of excitement and lavish surprise?
Where is the tantalizing richness and hazard
Of assertive styling, of crazy rigs,
Now that a car is unremarkably one of a million,
And an aeroplane is a tubular schedule? I wander
Still in the car parks, but now uneasily,
Thinking that engineering is a sort of evolution—
Out of the fittest come the many merely fit;
And I wonder if I am wrong, or the world, whose aspect
Is nowhere strange, but is nowhere home.

HENRY REED

1914–

449   *Chard Whitlow*

(*Mr. Eliot's Sunday Evening Postscript*)

As we get older we do not get any younger.
Seasons return, and to-day I am fifty-five,
And this time last year I was fifty-four,
And this time next year I shall be sixty-two.
And I cannot say I should care (to speak for myself)
To see my time over again—if you can call it time,
Fidgeting uneasily under a draughty stair,
Or counting sleepless nights in the crowded Tube.

There are certain precautions—though none of them very reliable—
Against the blast from bombs, or the flying splinter,
But not against the blast from Heaven, *vento dei venti*,
The wind within a wind, unable to speak for wind;
And the frigid burnings of purgatory will not be touched
By any emollient.
              I think you will find this put,
Far better than I could ever hope to express it,
In the words of Kharma: 'It is, we believe,
Idle to hope that the simple stirrup-pump
Can extinguish hell.'

477

Oh, listeners,
And you especially who have switched off the wireless,
And sit in Stoke or Basingstoke, listening appreciatively to the
    silence
(Which is also the silence of hell), pray not for yourselves but your
    souls.

And pray for me also under the draughty stair.
As we get older we do not get any younger.

And pray for Kharma under the holy mountain.

450   *Lessons of the War*

TO ALAN MICHELL

Vixi duellis nuper idoneus
Et militavi non sine gloria

I. NAMING OF PARTS

TO-DAY we have naming of parts. Yesterday,
We had daily cleaning. And to-morrow morning,
We shall have what to do after firing. But to-day,
To-day we have naming of parts. Japonica
Glistens like coral in all of the neighbour gardens,
    And to-day we have naming of parts.

This is the lower sling swivel. And this
Is the upper sling swivel, whose use you will see,
When you are given your slings. And this is the piling swivel,
Which in your case you have not got. The branches
Hold in the gardens their silent, eloquent gestures,
    Which in our case we have not got.

This is the safety-catch, which is always released
With an easy flick of the thumb. And please do not let me
See anyone using his finger. You can do it quite easy
If you have any strength in your thumb. The blossoms
Are fragile and motionless, never letting anyone see
    Any of them using their finger.

And this you can see is the bolt. The purpose of this
Is to open the breech, as you see. We can slide it
Rapidly backwards and forwards: we call this
Easing the spring. And rapidly backwards and forwards
The early bees are assaulting and fumbling the flowers:
    They call it easing the Spring.

They call it easing the Spring: it is perfectly easy
If you have any strength in your thumb: like the bolt,
And the breech, and the cocking-piece, and the point of balance,
Which in our case we have not got; and the almond blossom
Silent in all of the gardens and the bees going backwards and forwards,
    For to-day we have naming of parts.

C. H. SISSON

1914–

451   *The Temple*

WHO are they talking to in the big temple?
If there were a reply it would be a conversation:
It is because there is none that they are fascinated.
What does not reply is the answer to prayer.

JOHN CORNFORD

1915–1936

452   *To Margot Heinemann*

HEART of the heartless world,
Dear heart, the thought of you
Is the pain at my side,
The shadow that chills my view.

The wind rises in the evening,
Reminds that autumn is near.
I am afraid to lose you,
I am afraid of my fear.

On the last mile to Huesca,
The last fence for our pride,
Think so kindly, dear, that I
Sense you at my side.

And if bad luck should lay my strength
Into the shallow grave,
Remember all the good you can;
Don't forget my love.

ALUN LEWIS

1915–1944

453   *All Day it has Rained . . .*

ALL day it has rained, and we on the edge of the moors
Have sprawled in our bell-tents, moody and dull as boors,
Groundsheets and blankets spread on the muddy ground
And from the first grey wakening we have found
No refuge from the skirmishing fine rain
And the wind that made the canvas heave and flap
And the taut wet guy-ropes ravel out and snap.
All day the rain has glided, wave and mist and dream,
Drenching the gorse and heather, a gossamer stream
Too light to stir the acorns that suddenly
Snatched from their cups by the wild south-westerly
Pattered against the tent and our upturned dreaming faces.
And we stretched out, unbuttoning our braces,
Smoking a Woodbine, darning dirty socks,
Reading the Sunday papers—I saw a fox
And mentioned it in the note I scribbled home;—
And we talked of girls, and dropping bombs on Rome,
And thought of the quiet dead and the loud celebrities
Exhorting us to slaughter, and the herded refugees;
—Yet thought softly, morosely of them, and as indifferently
As of ourselves or those whom we
For years have loved, and will again
Tomorrow maybe love; but now it is the rain
Possesses us entirely, the twilight and the rain.

And I can remember nothing dearer or more to my heart
Than the child I watched in the woods on Saturday
Shaking down burning chestnuts for the schoolyard's merry play,
Or the shaggy patient dog who followed me
By Sheet and Steep and up the wooded scree
To the Shoulder o' Mutton where Edward Thomas brooded long
On death and beauty—till a bullet stopped his song.

454   *Goodbye*

So we must say Goodbye, my darling,
And go, as lovers go, for ever;
Tonight remains, to pack and fix on labels
And make an end of lying down together.

I put a final shilling in the gas,
And watch you slip your dress below your knees
And lie so still I hear your rustling comb
Modulate the autumn in the trees.

And all the countless things I shall remember
Lay mummy-cloths of silence round my head;
I fill the carafe with a drink of water;
You say 'We paid a guinea for this bed,'

And then, 'We'll leave some gas, a little warmth
For the next resident, and these dry flowers,'
And turn your face away, afraid to speak
The big word, that Eternity is ours.

Your kisses close my eyes and yet you stare
As though God struck a child with nameless fears;
Perhaps the water glitters and discloses
Time's chalice and its limpid useless tears.

Everything we renounce except our selves;
Selfishness is the last of all to go;
Our sighs are exhalations of the earth,
Our footprints leave a track across the snow.

We made the universe to be our home,
Our nostrils took the wind to be our breath,
Our hearts are massive towers of delight,
We stride across the seven seas of death.

Yet when all's done you'll keep the emerald
I placed upon your finger in the street;
And I will keep the patches that you sewed
On my old battledress tonight, my sweet.

G. S. FRASER

1915–

455   *Christmas Letter Home*
                    (*To my sister in Aberdeen*)

DRIFTING and innocent and like snow,
Now memories tease me, wherever I go,
And I think of the glitter of granite and distances
And against the blue air the lovely and bare trees,
And slippery pavements spangled with delight
Under the needles of a winter's night,
And I remember the dances, with scarf and cane,
Strolling home in the cold with the silly refrain
Of a tune by Cole Porter or Irving Berlin
Warming a naughty memory up like gin,
And Bunny and Sheila and Joyce and Rosemary
Chattering on sofas or preparing tea,
With their delicate voices and their small white hands
This is the sorrow everyone understands.
More than Rostov's artillery, more than the planes
Skirting the cyclonic islands, this remains,
The little, lovely taste of youth we had:
The guns and not our silliness were mad,
All the unloved and ugly seeking power
Were mad, and not our trivial evening hour
Of swirling taffetas and muslin girls,
Oh, not their hands, their profiles, or their curls,

Oh, not the evenings of coffee and sherry and snow,
Oh, not the music. Let us rise and go—
But then the months and oceans lie between,
And once again the dust of spring, the green
Bright beaks of buds upon the poplar trees,
And summer's strawberries, and autumn's ease,
And all the marble gestures of the dead,
Before my eyes caress again your head,
Your tiny strawberry mouth, your bell of hair,
Your blue eyes with their deep and shallow stare,
Before your hand upon my arm can still
The nerves that everything but home makes ill:
In this historic poster-world I move,
Noise, movement, emptiness, but never love.
Yet all this grief we had to have my dear,
And most who grieve have never known, I fear,
The lucky streak for which we die and live,
And to the luckless must the lucky give
All trust, all energy, whatever lies
Under the anger of democracies:
Whatever strikes the towering torturer down,
Whatever can outface the bully's frown,
Talk to the stammerer, spare a cigarette
For tramps at midnight . . . oh, defend it yet!
Some Christmas I shall meet you. Oh, and then
Though all the boys you used to like are men,
Though all my girls are married, though my verse
Has pretty steadily been growing worse,
We shall be happy: we shall smile and say,
'These years! It only seems like yesterday
I saw you sitting in that very chair.'
'You have not changed the way you do your hair.'
'These years were painful, then?' 'I hardly know.
Something lies gently over them, like snow,
A sort of numbing white forgetfulness . . .'

And so, good-night, this Christmas, and God bless!

THOMAS BLACKBURN
1916–

456   *Hospital for Defectives*

BY your unnumbered charities
A miracle disclose,
Lord of the Images, whose love,
The eyelid and the rose,
Takes for a language, and today
Tell to me what is said
By these men in a turnip field
And their unleavened bread.

For all things seem to figure out
The stirrings of your heart,
And two men pick the turnips up
And two men pull the cart;
And yet between the four of them
No word is ever said
Because the yeast was not put in
Which makes the human bread.
But three men stare on vacancy
And one man strokes his knees;
What is the meaning to be found
In such dark vowels as these?

Lord of the Images, whose love,
The eyelid and the rose,
Takes for a metaphor, today
Beneath the warder's blows,
The unleavened man did not cry out
Or turn his face away;
Through such men in a turnip field
What is it that you say?

457 *Felo Da Se*

'THIRTY,' the doctor said, 'three grains, each one,
That's quite a lot of sodium-amytol!
Five, ten more minutes, and the job was done,
Just why do you think she wished to end it all?
Ah, well, that's not my business. You've her things?
Damn lucky that I had the stomach pump—
Take them up to her if the Sister rings.'
I thanked him and agreed the night was damp,
Then flicked through Punch and waited the event;
It was, you see, no time for sentiment.
Her things, though, had been much in evidence
Back in the flatlet when I searched through drawers
To find a nightgown (blue is for romance)
And her remembered hairbrush through such tears
As in these situations must be shed—
(It is the cause, my soul, it is the cause)
I found her slippers underneath the bed
Where we had . . . where she drained her bitter cup
In solitude the night before this night;
What mattered was to pack a suitcase up,
Put out the light, 'and then put out the light'.

'So,' the nurse said, 'you've come. She may go out.'
I noticed that my shoe-lace was untied,
But though some words climbed up into my throat
Found none appropriate to suicide;
I took her arm, though, like a helpful friend
And led her downstairs to the waiting car,
Thinking, our game we do not understand
Nor who is playing it or what we are,
Her landlord came in time and that was luck.
I changed the gear. Who drives behind my back?

Her friend was waiting for us at the flat
With tea and so on. This I had arranged.
Knowing too well such passion spun the plot,
Death was its end unless the scene was changed,

What could I do but tear apart the script
Which made quite clear the end of our impasse?
As, kneading with her hands, she sat white lipped,
(There are some shadows which take long to pass)
Her friend poured tea, and slowly, drop by drop,
In solitude we drained our acid cup.

We had exhausted words as well as touch,
Therefore at half past ten I said goodbye,
Breaking the silence with a lifted latch,
To join, once more, my own identity.
That night the chilly street was not as dark
With its faint lamp as my intelligence,
And since more suited is a question mark
Than a full-stop, to human ignorance,
The blue stone I recall on her left hand;
Just what it means I do not understand.

GAVIN EWART

1916–

458 *Officers' Mess*

IT'S going to be a thick night tonight (and the night before was a
 thick one),
I've just seen the Padre disappearing into 'The Cock' for a quick one.
I don't mind telling you this, old boy, we got the Major drinking—
You probably know the amount of gin he's in the habit of sinking—
And then that new MO came in, the Jewish one, awful fellow,
And his wife, a nice little bit of stuff, dressed in a flaming yellow.
Looked a pretty warmish piece, old boy,—no, have this one with me—
They were both so blind (and so was the Major) that they could
 hardly see.
She had one of those amazing hats and a kind of silver fox fur
(I wouldn't mind betting several fellows have had a go at her).
She made a bee-line for the Major, bloody funny, old boy,
Asked him a lot about horses and India, you know, terribly coy—
And this MO fellow was mopping it up and at last he passed right out
(Some silly fool behind his back put a bottle of gin in his stout).
I've never seen a man go down so quick. Somebody drove him home.
His wife was almost as bad, old boy, said she felt all alone

And nestled up to the Major—it's a great pity you weren't there—
And the Padre was arguing about the order of morning and evening
    prayer.
Never laughed so much in all my life. We went on drinking till three.
And this bloody woman was doing her best to sit on the Major's
    knee!
Let's have the blackout boards put up and turn on the other light.
Yes, I think you can count on that, old boy—tonight'll be a thick
    night.

459   *When a Beau Goes In*

WHEN a Beau goes in,
Into the drink,
It makes you think,
Because, you see, they always sink
But nobody says 'Poor lad'
Or goes about looking sad
Because, you see, it's war,
It's the unalterable law.

Although it's perfectly certain
The pilot's gone for a Burton
And the observer too
It's nothing to do with you
And if they both should go
To a land where falls no rain nor hail
    nor driven snow—
Here, there or anywhere,
Do you suppose *they* care?

You shouldn't cry
Or say a prayer or sigh.
In the cold sea, in the dark,
It isn't a lark
But it isn't Original Sin—
It's just a Beau going in.

460   *Love Song*

YOU'VE got nice knees.
Your black shoes shine like taxis.
You are the opposite of
all farting and foulness.
Your exciting hair
is like a special moss,
on your chest are two soft medals
like pink half-crowns under your dress.
Your smell is far beyond
the perfumes at parties,
your eyes nail me
on a cross of waiting. Hard is
the way of the worshipper.
But the heart line on my hand
foretold you;
in your army of lovers
I am a private soldier.

461   *A New Poet Arrives*

A NEW man flies in from Manchester.
Frank Frittlewood.
Death to the Public Schools,
Ready to piss in the eye of the Old Universities.

A big woolly striped scarf round his neck,
The hunched antagonism of a left wing student.
How right he is!
Through immense spectacles he sees clearly

That only a New Movement can save our souls.
Wordsworth's great beak was pecking at that apple.
The tree of knowledge,
Dividing line between the past and future.

Take off those vestments, and those vested interests.
Show as a naked soul. You must admit
He's onto something.
Change, in the Arts, is nearly always good.

DAVID GASCOYNE
1916–

462   *Salvador Dali*

THE face of the precipice is black with lovers;
The sun above them is a bag of nails; the spring's
First rivers hide among their hair.
Goliath plunges his hand into the poisoned well
And bows his head and feels my feet walk through his brain.
The children chasing butterflies turn round and see him there
With his hand in the well and my body growing from his head,
And are afraid. They drop their nets and walk into the wall like smoke.

The smooth plain with its mirrors listens to the cliff
Like a basilisk eating flowers.
And the children, lost in the shadows of the catacombs,
Call to the mirrors for help:
'Strong-bow of salt, cutlass of memory,
Write on my map the name of every river.'

A flock of banners fight their way through the telescoped forest
And fly away like birds towards the sound of roasting meat.
Sand falls into the boiling rivers through the telescopes' mouths
And forms clear drops of acid with petals of whirling flame.
Heraldic animals wade through the asphyxia of planets,
Butterflies burst from their skins and grow long tongues like plants,
The plants play games with a suit of mail like a cloud.
Mirrors write Goliath's name upon my forehead,
While the children are killed in the smoke of the catacombs
And lovers float down from the cliffs like rain.

PHILIP O'CONNOR
1916–

463   *Writing in England Now*
from a commercially unsuccessful point of view

THIS poem I write to teach the reader
what I know about writing in England today,
which is a country, England, chronologically,
in no other way,
today, because it is old-fashioned, as *Les Temps Modernes* wrote
in 1964, 'emerging from Victorianism', I think it wrote, 'uneasily'.

This means:
'I' wields a muffin-density challenge
from a poxed centrality shaped like a fortress;
the terrain's abstracted to cartography
to cater for the entropy;
the people is a-Mused.

The able writer hears what he has written being said by people
who of the right sex he wouldn't mind in bed
before he writes it. It gives felicity to his writing.
It makes his challenge biting
to save his readers writing
what they hear is very true,
they pay their servant.

The able writer is a man to himself
and has proved his virility to prove this to himself,
never mind the woman.

The able writer by not agreeing
agrees more agreeably
than by disagreeing; he has a broad mind
to accommodate a changing rate of exchange
of people who said what he wrote
from time to time in bed. This bed may be spiritual. I'm not saying
his attitude is carnal, I'm not saying his attitude and I'm not
saying. But he chooses that view which they said he wrote was true.

The able ugh writer must coo. That coo must be punctuated without
its stopping.
Punctuations provide the clipped snarl to stop the too sweet.

Writing in England today is like waving the red programme of a
bullfight at a menu with roast beef on it.
It is definitely transcendental because it writes in terms of solid things
unsolidly. But it writes of transcendental things like dropping cowpats
& calls this realism.

The rudeness of the able writer in England today is bad breath not a
fart because it comes from the mouth.
The politeness of the able writer in England today is eau de cologne
from the fundament,
than which there is no greater part of respect. It is fundamental respect.

I have mangled the lavatory towel of this language as it has become
through the terrified mastications of terrorized journalists
and brilliant, shocking and disturbing novelists
until I think it was toothpaste, and my teeth are black, it was bad
toothpaste.
I have not respect. I have not money therefore. I want money.
Editor, print this and send me some when you call it a poem
to teach the reader what I know about writing in England today.

CHARLES CAUSLEY

1917–

464 *Chief Petty Officer*

HE is older than the naval side of British history,
And sits
More permanent than the spider in the enormous wall.
His barefoot, coal-burning soul
Expands, puffs like a toad, in the convict air
Of the Royal Naval Barracks at Devonport.

Here, in depôt, in his stone Nirvana:
More real than the opium-pipes,
The uninteresting relics of his Edwardian foreign-commission.
And, from his thick stone box,
He surveys with a prehistoric eye the hostilities-only ratings.

He has the face of the dinosaur
That sometimes stares from old Victorian naval photographs:
That of some elderly lieutenant
With boots and a celluloid Crippen-collar,
Brass buttons and cruel ambitious eyes of almond.

He was probably made a Freemason in Hong Kong.
He has a son (on War Work) in the Dockyard,
And an appalling daughter
In the W.R.N.S.
He writes on your draft-chit
Tobacco-permit or request-form
In a huge antique Borstal hand,
And pins notices on the board in the Chiefs' Mess
Requesting his messmates not to
Lay on the billiard table.
He is an anti-Semite, and has somewhat reactionary views,
And reads the pictures in the daily news.

And when you return from the nervous Pacific
Where the seas
Shift like sheets of plate-glass in the dazzling morning;
Or when you return
Browner than Alexander, from Malta,
Where you have leaned over the side, in harbour,
And seen in the clear water
The salmon-tins, wrecks and tiny explosions of crystal fish,
A whole war later
He will still be sitting under a pussar's clock
Waiting for tot-time,
His narrow forehead ruffled by the Jutland wind.

465   *Recruiting Drive*

UNDER the willow the willow
    I heard the butcher-bird sing,
Come out you fine young fellow
    From under your mother's wing.
I'll show you the magic garden
    That hangs in the beamy air,
The way of the lynx and the angry Sphinx
    And the fun of the freezing fair.

Lie down lie down with my daughter
    Beneath the Arabian tree,
Gaze on your face in the water
    Forget the scribbling sea.
Your pillow the nine bright shiners
    Your bed the spilling sand,
But the terrible toy of my lily-white boy
    Is the gun in his innocent hand.

You must take off your clothes for the doctor
    And stand as straight as a pin,
His hand of stone on your white breast-bone
    Where the bullets all go in.
They'll dress you in lawn and linen
    And fill you with Plymouth gin,
O the devil may wear a rose in his hair
    I'll wear my fine doe-skin.

My mother weeps as I leave her
    But I tell her it won't be long,
The murderers wail in Wandsworth Gaol
    But I shoot a more popular song.
Down in the enemy country
    Under the enemy tree
There lies a lad whose heart has gone bad
    Waiting for me, for me.

He says I have no culture
    And that when I've stormed the pass
I shall fall on the farm with a smoking arm
    And ravish his bonny lass.
Under the willow the willow
    Death spreads her dripping wings
And caught in the snare of the bleeding air
    The butcher-bird sings, sings, sings.

466   *Betjeman, 1984*

I SAW him in the Airstrip Gardens
    (Fahrenheit at 451)
Feeding automative orchids
    With a little plastic bun,
While above his brickwork cranium
    Burned the trapped and troubled sun.

'Where is Piper? Where is Pontefract?
    (Devil take my boiling pate!)
Where is Pam? And where's Myfanwy?
    Don't remind me of the date!
Can it be that I am *really*
    Knocking on for 78?

In my splendid State Apartment
    Underneath a secret lock
Finger now forbidden treasures
    (Pray for me St. Enodoc!):
T.V. plate and concrete lamp-post
    And a single nylon sock.

Take your ease, pale-haired admirer,
    As I, half the century saner,
Pour a vintage Mazawattee
    Through the Marks and Spencer strainer
In a *genuine* British Railways
    (Luton made) cardboard container.

Though they say my verse-compulsion
    Lacks an interstellar drive,
Reading Beverley and Daphne
    Keeps *my* sense of words alive.
Lord, but *how* much beauty was there
    Back in 1955!'

467 *Death of a Poet*

SUDDENLY his mouth filled with sand.
His tractor of blood stopped thumping.
He held five icicles in each hand.
His heart packed up jumping.

His face turned the colour of something forgotten in the larder.
His thirty-two teeth were expelled on the kitchen floor.
His muscles, at long last, got considerably harder.
He felt younger than he had for some time before.

Four heroes, steady as wrestlers, each carried him on a shoulder
Into a great grey church laid out like a brain.
An iron bowl sent out stiff rays of chrysanthemums. It grew colder.
The sun, as expected, failed to break through the pane.

The parson boomed like a dockyard gun at a christening.
Somebody read from the bible. It seemed hours.
I got the feeling you were curled up inside the box, listening.
There was the thud of hymn-books, the stench of flowers.

I remembered hearing your voice on a bloody foment
Of Atlantic waters. The words burned clear as a flare.
Life begins, you said, as of this moment.
A bird flew down out of the hurling air.

Over the church a bell broke like a wave upended.
The hearse left for winter with a lingering hiss.
I looked in the wet sky for a sign, but no bird descended.
I went across the road to the pub; wrote this.

ROBERT CONQUEST
1916–

468   *Horror Comic*

YOUR bottoms are not purple.
But imagine a mandrill
Come like John Mandeville
To report on this people.

He finds despisal of fur,
Respect for the false,
Hate of fleas
And love of fire;

While bishops bless
Wowsers, narks,
With snide remarks
In Sunday press.

But our mandrill marvel
Does not, like Lawrence,
Call customs tyrants
And draws no moral.

Is glad that some
Are made of wood,
Thinks 'dull the world
If all were same'.

And looking at mitre
And at blue pencil
Laughter shakes his tonsil
As at a theatre.

469 *Man and Woman*

SOBER, he thinks of her; so he gets drunk.
Drunk, he weeps for her. Drunker, he sleeps,
Waking in the small hours to absence.

The trees sway moodlessly to a blank wind;
Right communication with symbol and sensation
Frays off hotly into silence.

Certain bacilli cause worse pain,
So do the instruments of secret police torments,
Yet here's the inexplicable quag

Into which all that towers fully founded,
Deepest assured, keels over fissured,
The universe torn up like a rag.

Other tensions rasp the brain and body
Rougher, stitch the tic on eyelid or in cheek:
Desperations of money, fears

Of torn flesh, of death. More real, you say?
Yet those are not the things break bedrock, strike the springs'
Profundities: tears. Yes, why the tears?

MARTIN BELL

1918–

470 *Winter Coming On*
A caricature from Laforgue

FOR PETER PORTER

FINE feelings under blockade! Cargoes just in from Kamschatka!
Rain falling and falling the night falling
And how the wind howls . . .
Halloween, Christmas, New Year's Day
Sodden in drizzle—all my tall chimneys—
Industrial smoke through the rain!

497

No sitting down, all the park-benches are wet.
It's finished, I tell you, till next season.
Park-benches wet and all the leaves rust-eaten,
Horns and their echoes—dying, dying . . .

Rally of rain-clouds! Procession from the Channel—
You certainly spoiled our last free Sunday.

Drizzles:
And in wet woods the spiders' webs
Weigh down with rain-drops: and that's their lot.
O golden delegates from harvest festivals,
Broad suns from cattle-shows,
Where have they buried you?
This evening a sun lies, shagged, on top of the hill,
On a tramp's mattress, rags in the gorse—
A sun as white as a blob of spittle
On tap-room saw-dust, on a litter of yellow gorse,
Of yellow October gorse.
And the horns echo and call to him—
Come back! Won't you come back?
View halloo, Tally-ho . . . Gone away.
O oratorio chorus, when will you be done?
Carrying on like mad things . . .
And there he lies, like a torn-out gland on a neck,
Shivering, with no one by.
Tally-ho, then, and get on with it.
It's good old Winter coming, we know that.
By-passes empty, turnings on main roads
With no Red Riding Hood to be picked up.
Ruts from the wheels of last month's traffic—
Quixotic tram-lines to the rescue of
Cloud-patrols scurrying
Bullied by winds to transatlantic sheep-folds.
Get a move on, it's the well-known season coming, now.
And the wind last night, on top of its form,
Smashing suburban front-gardens—what a mess!
Disturbing my night's sleep with dreams of axes.

These branches, yesterday, had all their dead leaves—
Nothing but compost now, just lying about.
Dear leaves of various shapes and sizes
May a good breeze whirlpool you away
To lie on ponds, decorative,

To glow in the park-keeper's fire,
To stuff ambulance mattresses, comforts
For our soldiers overseas.

Time of year, time of year: the rust is eating,
The rust is gnawing long miles of ennui,
Telegraph-wires along main roads, deserted.

Horns, again horns . . . the echoes dying,
Dying . . .
Now changing key, going north
With the North Wind, Wagnerian,
Up to all those bloody skalds and Vikings . . .

Myself, I can't change key; too many echoes!
What beastly weather! Good-bye autumn, good-bye ripeness . . .
And here comes the rain with the diligence of an angel.
Good-bye harvest, good-bye baskets for nutting,
And Watteau picnics under the chestnut trees.
It's barrack-room coughing again,
The landlady's horrible herbal tea—
It's TB in the garden suburb,
All the sheer misery of satellite towns.

Wellingtons, long underwear, cash chemists, dreams,
Undrawn curtains over verandas, shores
Of the red-brick sea of roofs and chimney-pots,
Lamp-shades, tea and biscuits, all the picture papers—
You'll have to be my only loves!
(And known them, have you? ritual more portentous
Than the sad pianos tinkling through the dusk,
The registrar's returns of births and deaths,
In small type weekly in the press.)

No! It's the time of year, and this clown of a planet!
O please let the wind, let the high wind
Unknit the bed-socks Time is knitting herself!
Time of year, things tearing, time of year!
O let me every year, every year, just at this time
Join in the chorus, sound the right sour note.

W. S. GRAHAM
1918–

471 *Letter V*

LIE where you fell and longed
Broken to fall to from
Grace in your maidenhooded
Cage. And further fall.
Lie down where in a word
That blinding greying bard,
Earl of an armed uprising,
Lifted his head to you
And made you right of way
To the silence-felling prow.
And tonight listen under
The watch kept by the height
Sailed and its gazing host.
Winter sits on the gable.

From where these words first fell
Fall to me now. Fall through
This high browbeating night
And slowly, my dear, loving
Take breath for both of us
In this poem in this house
Awake. Your name is long
A byword on my tongue.
You long remember me.
This room. The narrow lamp
Casting the net of light
On this element. The table
Scrubbed with salt and become
For me the grave's table.
And that same voice listening
And blindly trying the latch.
And listen, my love, almost
I heard the quay night bell
Strike on the sea wall.

W. S. GRAHAM

Anyhow tonight here all
Is again almost at one
With us, and no, there's not
The least sorrow to shade
Or fear to fall. Dearly
Make haste now in the sweet
Oil-wending light keeping
Us endless for a moment
Changing becomes you. Dress
In your loved best. Put on
Your roomy cramasie
And gloves of the wild fox.
Nor fear, you've been undone
By myriads everywhere always.
And here slip on your emerald
Deeps and your frilled shallows.
The dark befrond you. The first
Of light shall know you by
Your snares of the bright dew.
Even wear your herring bells
To ring the changes and your
Jingling sea-charms along
Your tongue. To find your sea-thighs
Sail where the metaphor flies.

To find your best for me
Spring all your maiden locks.
I stand by what I see.
You blush like new. You're shy
The same. What nets and beds
We've drifted on. It's tides
And tides ago. And here,
Here's where you wept the first
Time and me with only
A few words to my name.
Lie longing down, my dear
Again. Cast in this gold
Wicklight this night within
This poem, we two go down
Roaring between the lines
To drown. Who hears? Who listens?

I entered. Enter after
Me here and encounter
Dimensions of a grave.
Sometimes night sinks its shaft
And I am crossed with light
Here where I lie in language
Braced under the immense
Weight of dumb founded silence.

I heard voices within
The empty lines and tenses.

The tiller takes my hand
In a telling grip. We drive
On in the white soaring
Meantime of fair morning.
Happy the threshold-whetted
Blade that lays us low
Each time for ever. My sweet
Sea-singer shearing the wave
Engrave us where we fall.
Under the wanderlusting
Sky of morning waked
And worded beyond itself
By me to you, who leans
Down through the fanfared lists
To listen? A day to gladden.
A sight to unperish us from
The flashing wake unwinding
Us to our end. And quick,
Take hold, the quick foam blooms
And combs to our side. And now
Rounding the Rhinns, keep hold
And watch as the fisher flies
With beaks in the netting gale
That veers to the kill, and now
As you sail here look the word's
Bright garment from your eyes.
Be for me still, steering
Here at my keeling trade
Over the white heathering
Foam of the tide-race.

Who asks to listen? And who
Do these words listen to
In some far equivalent?
Through me they read you through.
Present your world. Reply
Now at the growing end
As words rush to become
You changing at your best.
Stand by me here. The roar
Is rising. The old defender
Towers. His head soars.
He stands like downfall over
The high gables of morning
In kindling light. Under
His eye that blinds us now
We go down dazzled into
The crowded scroll of the wake.
As silence takes me back
Changed to my last word,

Reply. Present your world.
Gannet of God, strike.

JOHN HEATH-STUBBS

1918–

472   *Valse Oublieé*

AND as we came down the staircase—
Broad the balustrade, shining and bronze in the lustre
Of hanging lights, smooth and strong to the touch like your arm—
Down the grand sweep of the staircase eagerly stepping,
We two, to the lighted ballroom, the swirl of my music,
You paused and said: 'The moon is a strange questing
Creature embodied out over these wide white plains;
But whether hunter or huntress, I do not know—
But whether hunter or hunted!'
And your mouth smiled, though while your eyes were thoughtful.
I said: 'She is a maiden pursuing, or a wild white falcon
Unmewed through the skies, or she is a hind, or a hound,

Or a frightened hare—the bewitched princess who wanders
There through the snow-covered night and over the pine-trees,
Or a wild swan perhaps, or a wizened dwarf,
Back-crook'd and broken because of his burden of silver,
Who stumbles home in the cold to his cave in the mountains!
But let us go down now to the lighted ballroom
Where they are expecting us, for the dance begins.'
And we went down into the hall, alone no longer.

* * * * *

And standing by a window a girl said:
'Only once I saw one, once, once;
Far out over the snow, in a hard winter—
When I was a little girl, at our country place.
And Anya, our old nurse, said: "Look, child—
Come to the window, and I will show you a wolf."
(For often the long evenings she had told us of them)
And there it went, the lonely one, like a great dog—
But hindquarters narrow and drooping, like a cowardly dog—
Hungry nose to the snow, onward, onward.
But sometimes it paused, and scraped in its tracks, and raised
Its great head to the bitter skies, and howled.'

* * * * *

Oh curved, curved in a scroll the violin's neck and carved
With concentration of the patient hand;
And tight those strings and quick to break in the harsh
Air, and in the inclement weather;
And shrill, shrill the song of the strings when the horse-hair sweeps
Caressingly upon them. And the flutes ice-blue, and the harps
Like melting frost, and the trumpet marching, marching
Like fire above them, like fire through the frozen pine-trees.
And the dancers came, swirling, swirling past me—
Plume and swansdown waving, white plume over the gold hair,
Arms held gallantly, and silk talking—and an eye caught
In the candle-shadow, and the curve of a mouth
Going home to my heart (the folly of it!), going home to my heart!

* * * * *

And the black-browed girl by the window said, remembering:
'Always in my dreams it is thus, always in my dreams—
Snow and moonlight, snow and the dark pines moaning,
Fur over my body, and my feet small,

JOHN HEATH-STUBBS

Delicate and swift to run through the powdery snow;
And my sharp mouth to the ground, hungry, hungry,
And always onward, onward, alone, alone. . . .'
   *   *   *   *   *

   Moon, moon, cold mouth over the pine-trees,
   Or are you hunting me, or I pursuing?

473   *Epitaph*

MR. HEATH-STUBBS as you must understand
Came of a gentleman's family out of Staffordshire
Of as good blood as any in England
But he was wall-eyed and his legs too spare.

His elbows and finger-joints could bend more ways than one
And in frosty weather would creak audibly
As to delight his friends he would give demonstration
Which he might have done in public for a small fee.

Amongst the more learned persons of his time
Having had his schooling in the University of Oxford
In Anglo-Saxon Latin ornithology and crime
Yet after four years he was finally not preferred.

Orthodox in beliefs as following the English Church
Barring some heresies he would have for recreation
Yet too often left these sound principles (as I am told) in the lurch
Being troubled with idleness, lechery, pride and dissipation.

In his youth he would compose poems in prose and verse
In a classical romantic manner which was pastoral
To which the best judges of the Age were not averse
And the public also but his profit was not financial.

Now having outlived his friends and most of his reputation
He is content to take his rest under these stones and grass
Not expecting but hoping that the Resurrection
Will not catch him unawares whenever it takes place.

474 *The History of the Flood*

BANG Bang Bang
Said the nails in the Ark.

It's getting rather dark
Said the nails in the Ark.

For the rain is coming down
Said the nails in the Ark.

And you're all like to drown
Said the nails in the Ark.

Dark and black as sin
Said the nails in the Ark.

So won't you all come in
Said the nails in the Ark.

But only two by two
Said the nails in the Ark.

So they came in two by two,
The elephant, the kangaroo,
And the gnu,
And the little tiny shrew.

Then the birds
Flocked in like wingéd words:
Two racket-tailed motmots, two macaws,
Two nuthatches and two
Little bright robins.

And the reptiles: the gila monster, the slow-worm,
The green mamba, the cottonmouth and the alligator—
All squirmed in;
And after a very lengthy walk,
Two giant Galapagos tortoises.

And the insects in their hierarchies:
A queen ant, a king ant, a queen wasp, a king wasp,
A queen bee, a king bee,
And all the beetles, bugs, and mosquitoes,
Cascaded in like glittering, murmurous jewels.

But the fish had their wish;
For the rain came down.
People began to drown:
The wicked, the rich—
They gasped out bubbles of pure gold,
Which exhalations
Rose to the constellations.

So for forty days and forty nights
They were on the waste of waters
In those cramped quarters.
It was very dark, damp and lonely.
There was nothing to see, but only
The rain which continued to drop.
It did not stop.

So Noah sent forth a Raven. The raven said 'Kark!
I will not go back to the Ark.'
The raven was footloose,
He fed on the bodies of the rich—
Rich with vitamins and goo.
They had become bloated,
And everywhere they floated.
The raven's heart was black,
He did not come back.
It was not a nice thing to do:
Which is why the raven is a token of wrath,
And creaks like a rusty gate
When he crosses your path; and Fate
Will grant you no luck that day:
The raven is fey:
You were meant to have a scare.
Fortunately in England
The raven is rather rare.

Then Noah sent forth a dove
She did not want to rove.
She longed for her love—
The other turtle dove—
(For her no other dove!)
She brought back a twig from an olive-tree.
There is no more beautiful tree
Anywhere on the earth,
Even when it comes to birth
From six weeks under the sea.

She did not want to rove.
She wanted to take her rest,
And to build herself a nest
All in the olive grove.
She wanted to make love.
She thought that was the best.

The dove was not a rover;
So they knew that the rain was over.
Noah and his wife got out
(They had become rather stout)
And Japhet, Ham, and Shem.
(The same could be said of them.)
They looked up at the sky.
The earth was becoming dry.

Then the animals came ashore—
There were more of them than before:
There were two dogs and a litter of puppies;
There were a tom-cat and two tib-cats
And two litters of kittens—cats
Do not obey regulations;
And, as you might expect,
A quantity of rabbits.

God put a rainbow in the sky.
They wondered what it was for.
There had never been a rainbow before.
The rainbow was a sign;
It looked like a neon sign—
Seven colours arched in the skies:
What should it publicize?
They looked up with wondering eyes.

It advertises Mercy
Said the nails in the Ark.

Mercy Mercy Mercy.
Said the nails in the Ark.

Our God is merciful
Said the nails in the Ark.

Merciful and gracious
Bang Bang Bang Bang.

VALENTIN IREMONGER

1918–

475   *This Houre Her Vigil*

ELIZABETH, frigidly stretched,
On a spring day surprised us
With her starched dignity and the quietness
Of her hands clasping a black cross.

With book and candle and holy-water dish
She received us in the room with the blind down.
Her eyes were peculiarly closed and we knelt shyly
Noticing the blot of her hair on the white pillow.

We met that evening by the crumbling wall
In the field behind the house where I lived
And talked it over, but could find no reason
Why she had left us whom she had liked so much.

Death, yes, we understood: something to do
With age and decay, decrepit bodies;
But here was this vigorous one, aloof and prim,
Who would not answer our furtive whispers.

Next morning, hearing the priest call her name,
I fled outside, being full of certainty,
And cried my seven years against the church's stone wall.
For eighteen years I did not speak her name

Until this autumn day when, in a gale,
A sapling fell outside my window, its branches
Rebelliously blotting the lawn's green. Suddenly, I thought
Of Elizabeth, frigidly stretched.

KEITH DOUGLAS

1920–1944

476 *Russians*

How silly that soldier is pointing his gun at the wood:
he doesn't know it isn't any good.
You see, the cold and cruel northern wind
has frozen the whole battalion where they stand.

That's never a corporal: even now he's frozen
you could see he's only a commercial artist
whom they took and put those clothes on,
and told him he was one of the smartest.

Even now they're in ice it's easy to know
what a shock it was, a long shock
that's been coming home to them wherever they go,
with their mazy minds taking stock.

Walk among the innocuous parade
and touch them if you like, they're properly stayed:
keep out of their line of sight and they won't look.
Think of them as waxworks, or think they're struck

with a dumb immobile spell,
to wake in a thousand years with the sweet force
of spring upon them in the merry world. Well,
at least forget what happens when it thaws.

477   *Simplify Me When I'm Dead*

REMEMBER me when I am dead
and simplify me when I'm dead.

As the processes of earth
strip off the colour and the skin:
take the brown hair and blue eye

and leave me simpler than at birth,
when hairless I came howling in
as the moon entered the cold sky.

Of my skeleton perhaps,
so stripped, a learned man will say
'He was of such a type and intelligence,' no more.

Thus when in a year collapse
particular memories, you may
deduce, from the long pain I bore

the opinions I held, who was my foe
and what I left, even my appearance
but incidents will be no guide.

Time's wrong-way telescope will show
a minute man ten years hence
and by distance simplified.

Through that lens see if I seem
substance or nothing: of the world
deserving mention or charitable oblivion,

not by momentary spleen
or love into decision hurled,
leisurely arrive at an opinion.

Remember me when I am dead
and simplify me when I'm dead.

478   *Vergissmeinicht*

THREE weeks gone and the combatants gone,
returning over the nightmare ground
we found the place again, and found
the soldier sprawling in the sun.

The frowning barrel of his gun
overshadowing. As we came on
that day, he hit my tank with one
like the entry of a demon.

Look. Here in the gunpit spoil
the dishonoured picture of his girl
who has put: *Steffi. Vergissmeinicht*
in a copybook gothic script.

We see him almost with content
abased, and seeming to have paid
and mocked at by his own equipment
that's hard and good when he's decayed.

But she would weep to see today
how on his skin the swart flies move;
the dust upon the paper eye
and the burst stomach like a cave.

For here the lover and killer are mingled
who had one body and one heart.
And death who had the soldier singled
has done the lover mortal hurt.

479   *A Wartime Exchange*

ALEX COMFORT
1920–

and

GEORGE ORWELL
(ERIC BLAIR)
1903–1950

Letter to an American Visitor

BY OBADIAH HORNBOOKE[1]

COLUMBIAN poet, whom we've all respected
From a safe distance for a year or two,
Since first your *magnum opus* was collected—
It seems a pity no one welcomed you
Except the slippery professional few,
Whose news you've read, whose posters you've inspected;
Who gave America Halifax, and who
Pay out to scribes and painters they've selected
    Doles which exceed a fraction of the debts
    Of all our pimps in hardware coronets.

You've seen the ruins, heard the speeches, swallowed
The bombed-out hospitals and cripples' schools—
You've heard (on records) how the workers hollowed
And read in poker-work GIVE US THE TOOLS:
You know how, with the steadfastness of mules,
The Stern Determination of the People
Goes sailing through a paradise of fools
Like masons shinning up an endless steeple—
    A climb concluding after many days
    In a brass weathercock that points all ways.

---

[1] Pseudonym of Alex Comfort.

The land sprouts orators. No doubt you've heard
  How every buffer, fool and patrioteer
Applies the Power of the Spoken Word
  And shoves his loud posterior in your ear;
    So Monkey Hill competes with Berkeley Square—
The B.B.C. as bookie, pimp and vet
  Presenting Air Vice-Marshals set to cheer
Our raided towns with vengeance (though I've yet
    To hear from any man who lost his wife
    Berlin or Lubeck brought her back to life).

You've heard of fighting on the hills and beaches
  And down the rabbit holes with pikes and bows—
You've heard the Baron's bloody-minded speeches
  (Each worth a fresh Division to our foes)
    That smell so strong of murder that the crows
Perch on the Foreign Office roof and caw
  For German corpses laid in endless rows,
'A Vengeance such as Europe never saw'—
    The maniac Baron's future contribution
    To peace perpetual through retribution . . .

You've heard His Nibs decanting year by year
  The dim productions of his bulldog brain,
While homes and factories sit still to hear
  The same old drivel dished up once again—
    You heard the Churches' cartwheels to explain
That bombs are Christian when the English drop them—
  The Union bosses scrapping over gain
While no one's the temerity to stop them
    Or have the racketeers who try to bleed 'em
    Flogged, like the Indians for demanding freedom.

They found you poets—quite a decent gallery
  Of painters who don't let their chances slip;
And writers who prefer a regular salary
  To steer their writings by the Party Whip—
    Hassall's been tipped to have Laureateship:
Morton is following Goebbels, not St. Paul.
  There's Elton's squeaky pump still gives a drip,
And Priestley twists his proletarian awl
    Cobbling at shoes that Mill and Rousseau wore
    And still the wretched tool contrives to bore.

They found you critics—an astounding crowd:
  (Though since their work's living, I won't say
Who howled at Eliot, hooted Treece, were loud
    In kicking Auden when he slipped away
    Out of the looney-bin to find, they say,
A quiet place where men with minds could write:
    But since Pearl Harbour, in a single day
The same old circus chase him, black is white,
        And once again by day and night he feels
        The packs of tripehounds yelling at his heels).

I say, they found you artists, well selected,
    Whom we export to sell the British case:
We keep our allied neighbours well protected
    From those who give the thing a different face—
    One man's in jail, one in a 'medical place';
Another working at a farm with pigs on:
    We take their leisure, close their books, say grace,
And like that bus-conducting lad Geoff Grigson
        We beat up every buzzard, kite and vulture,
        And dish them out to you as English Culture.

Once in a while, to every Man and Nation,
    There comes, as Lowell said, a sort of crisis
Between the Ministry of Information
    And what your poor artistic soul advises:
    They catch the poets, straight from Cam or Isis:
'Join the brigade, or be for ever dumb—
    Either cash in your artistic lysis
Or go on land work if you won't succumb:
        Rot in the Army, sickened and unwilling':
        So you can wonder that they draw their shilling?

You met them all. You don't require a list
    Of understrapping ghosts who once were writers—
Who celebrate the size of Britain's fist,
    Write notes for sermons, dish out pep to mitres,
    Fake letters from the Men who Fly our Fighters.
Cheer when we blast some enemy bungalows—
    Think up atrocities, the artful blighters,
To keep the grindstone at the public's nose—
        Combining moral uplift and pornography,
        Produced with arty paper and typography.

They find their leisure to fulfil their promise,
   Their work is praised, *funguntur vice cotis;*
And Buddy Judas cracks up Doubting Thomas.
   Their ways are paved with favourable notice
   (Look how unanimous the Tory vote is).
They write in papers and review each other,
   You'd never guess how bloody full the boat is;
I shan't forgive MacNeice his crippled brother
     Whom just a year ago on New Year's Day
     The Germans murdered in a radio play.

O for another Dunciad—a POPE
   To purge this dump with his gigantic boot—
Drive fools to water, aspirin or rope—
   Make idle lamp-posts bear their fitting fruit:
   Private invective's far too long been mute—
O for another vast satiric comet
   To blast this wretched tinder, branch and root.
The servile stuff that makes a true man vomit—
     Suck from the works to which they cling like leeches,
     Those resurrection-puddings, Churchill's speeches.

God knows—for there is libel—I can't name
   How many clammy paws of these you've shaken,
Been told our English spirit is the same
   From Lord Vansittart back to pseudo-Bacon—
   Walked among licensed writers, and were taken
To Grub Street, Malet Street, and Portland Place,
   Where every question that you ask will waken
The same old salesman's grin on every face
     Among the squads of columbines and flunkeys,
     Set on becoming Laureate of Monkeys.

We do not ask, my friend, that you'll forget
   The squirts and toadies when you were presented,
The strength-through-joy brigades you will have met
   Whose mouths are baggy and whose hair is scented—
   Only recall we were not represented.
We wrote our own refusals, and we meant them.
   Our work is plastered and ourselves resented—
Our heads are bloody, but we have not bent them.
     Wo hold no licences, like ladies' spaniels;
     We live like lions in this den of Daniels.

O friend and writer, deafened by the howls
 That dying systems utter, mad with fear
In darkness, with a sinking of the bowels,
 Where all the devils of old conscience leer—
 Forget the gang that met you on the pier,
Grinning and stuffed with all the old excuses
 For starving Europe, and the crocodile tear
Turned on for visitors who have their uses.
 We know the capers of the simian crew.
 We send our best apologies to you.

As One Non-Combatant to Another
(A LETTER TO 'OBADIAH HORNBOOKE')

O poet strutting from the sandbagged portal
Of that small world where barkers ply their art,
And each new 'school' believes itself immortal,
Just like the horse that draws the knacker's cart:
O captain of a clique of self-advancers,
Trained in the tactics of the pamphleteer,
Where slogans serve for thoughts and sneers for answers—
You've chosen well your moment to appear
And hold your nose amid a world of horror
Like Dr. Bowdler walking through Gomorrah.

In the Left Book Club days you wisely lay low,
But when 'Stop Hitler!' lost its old attraction
You bounded forward in a Woolworth's halo
To cash in on anti-war reaction;
You waited till the Nazis ceased from frightening,
Then, picking a safe audience, shouted 'Shame!'
Like a Prometheus you defied the lightning,
But didn't have the nerve to sign your name.[1]
You're a true poet, but as saint and martyr
You're a mere fraud, like the Atlantic Charter.

---

[1] In a footnote to Orwell's reply the Editor of *Tribune* stated: 'In fairness to "Mr Hornbrooke" it should be stated that he was willing to sign his name if we insisted, but preferred a pseudonym.'

Your hands are clean, and so were Pontius Pilate's,
But as for 'bloody heads', that's just a metaphor;
The bloody heads are on Pacific islets
Or Russian steppes or Libyan sands—it's better for
The health to be a C.O. than a fighter,
To chalk a pavement doesn't need much guts,
It pays to stay at home and be a writer
While other talents wilt in Nissen huts;
'We live like lions'—yes, just like a lion,
Pensioned on scraps in a safe cage of iron.

For while you write the warships ring you round
And flights of bombers drown the nightingales,
And every bomb that drops is worth a pound
To you or someone like you, for your sales
Are swollen with those of rivals dead or silent,
Whether in Tunis or the B.B.C.,
And in the drowsy freedom of this island
You're free to shout that England isn't free;
They even chuck you cash, as bears get buns,
For crying 'Peace!' behind a screen of guns.

In 'seventeen to snub the nosing bitch
Who slipped you a white feather needed cheek,
But now, when every writer finds his niche
Within some mutual-admiration clique,
Who cares what epithets by Blimps are hurled?
Who'd give a damn if handed a white feather?
Each little mob of pansies is a world,
Cosy and warm in any kind of weather;
In such a world it's easy to 'object',
Since that's what both your friends and foes expect.

At times it's almost a more dangerous deed
Not to object; I know, for I've been bitten.
I wrote in nineteen-forty that at need
I'd fight to keep the Nazis out of Britain;
And Christ! how shocked the pinks were! Two years later
I hadn't lived it down; one had the effrontery
To write three pages calling me a 'traitor',
So black a crime it is to love one's country.
Yet where's the pink that would have thought it odd of me
To write a shelf of books in praise of sodomy?

ALEX COMFORT AND GEORGE ORWELL

Your game is easy, and its rules are plain:
Pretend the war began in 'thirty-nine,
Don't mention China, Ethiopia, Spain,
Don't mention Poles except to say they're swine;
Cry havoc when we bomb a German city,
When Czechs get killed don't worry in the least,
Give India a perfunctory squirt of pity
But don't inquire what happens further East;
Don't mention Jews—in short, pretend the war is
Simply a racket 'got up' by the Tories.

Throw in a word of 'anti-Fascist' patter
From time to time, by way of reinsurance,
And then go on to prove it makes no matter
If Blimps or Nazis hold the world in durance;
And that we others who 'support' the war
Are either crooks or sadists or flag-wavers
In love with drums and bugles, but still more
Concerned with cadging Brendan Bracken's favours;
Or fools who think that bombs bring back the dead,
A thing not even Harris ever said.

If you'd your way we'd leave the Russians to it
And sell our steel to Hitler as before;
Meanwhile you save your soul, and while you do it,
Take out a long-term mortgage on the war.
For after war there comes an ebb of passion,
The dead are sniggered at—and there you'll shine,
You'll be the very bull's-eye of the fashion,
You almost might get back to 'thirty-nine,
Back to the dear old game of scratch-my-neighbour
In sleek reviews financed by coolie labour.

But you don't hoot at Stalin—that's 'not done'—
Only at Churchill; I've no wish to praise him,
I'd gladly shoot him when the war is won,
Or now, if there was someone to replace him.
But unlike some, I'll pay him what I owe him;
There was a time when empires crashed like houses,
And many a pink who'd titter at your poem
Was glad enough to cling to Churchill's trousers.
Christ! how they huddled up to one another
Like day-old chicks about their foster-mother!

I'm not a fan for 'fighting on the beaches',
And still less for the 'breezy uplands' stuff,
I seldom listen-in to Churchill's speeches,
But I'd far sooner hear that kind of guff
Than your remark, a year or so ago,
That if the Nazis came you'd knuckle under
And peaceably 'accept the *status quo*'.
Maybe you would! But I've a right to wonder
Which will sound better in the days to come,
'Blood, toil and sweat' or 'Kiss the Nazi's bum'.

But your chief target is the radio hack,
The hired pep-talker—he's a safe objective,
Since he's unpopular and can't hit back.
It doesn't need the eye of a detective
To look down Portland Place and spot the whores,
But there are men (I grant, not the most heeded)
With twice your gifts and courage three times yours
Who do that dirty work because it's needed;
Not blindly, but for reasons they can balance,
They wear their seats out and lay waste their talents.

All propaganda's lying, yours or mine;
It's lying even when its facts are true;
That goes for Goebbels or the 'party line',
Or for the Primrose League or P.P.U.
But there are truths that smaller lies can serve,
And dirtier lies that scruples can gild over;
To waste your brains on war may need more nerve
Than to dodge facts and live in mental clover;
It's mean enough when other men are dying,
But when you lie, it's much to know you're lying.

That's thirteen stanzas, and perhaps you're puzzled
To know why I've attacked you—well, here's why:
Because your enemies all are dead or muzzled,
You've never picked on one who might reply.
You've hogged the limelight and you've aired your virtue,
While chucking sops to every dangerous faction,
The Left will cheer you and the Right won't hurt you;
What did you risk? Not even a libel action.
If you would show what saintly stuff you're made of,
Why not attack the cliques you *are* afraid of?

Denounce Joe Stalin, jeer at the Red Army,
Insult the Pope—you'll get some come-back there;
It's honourable, even if it's barmy,
To stamp on corns all round and never care.
But for the half-way saint and cautious hero,
Whose head's unbloody even if 'unbowed',
My admiration's somewhere near to zero;
So my last words would be: Come off that cloud,
Unship those wings that hardly dared to flitter,
And spout your halo for a pint of bitter.

D. J. ENRIGHT

1920–

480   *University Examinations in Egypt*

THE air is thick with nerves and smoke: pens tremble
                              in sweating hands:
Domestic police flit in and out, with smelling salts
                              and aspirin:
And servants, grave-faced but dirty, pace the aisles,
With coffee, Players and Coca-Cola.

Was it like this in my day, at my place? Memory boggles
Between the aggressive fly and curious ant—but did I really
Pause in my painful flight to light a cigarette or swallow drugs?

The nervous eye, patrolling these hot unhappy victims,
Flinches at the symptoms of a year's hard teaching—
'Falstaff indulged in drinking and sexcess', and then,
'Doolittle was a dusty man' and 'Dr. Jonson edited the Yellow Book.'

Culture and aspirin: the urgent diploma, the straining brain—
                              all in the evening fall
To tric-trac in the café, to Hollywood in the picture-house:
Behind, like tourist posters, the glamour of laws and committees,
Wars for freedom, cheap textbooks, national aspirations—

And, farther still and very faint, the foreign ghost
                              of happy Shakespeare,
Keats who really loved things, Akhenaton who adored the Sun,
And Goethe who never thought of Thought.

481 *Waiting for the Bus*

SHE hung away her years, her eyes grew young,
  And filled the dress that filled the shop;
Her figure softened into summer, though wind stung
  And rain would never stop.

A dreaming not worn out with knowing,
A moment's absence from the watch, the weather.
I threw the paper down, that carried no such story,
But roared for what it could not have, perpetual health
                and liberty and glory.
It whirled away, a lost bedraggled feather.

Then have we missed the bus? Or are we sure
                which way the wind is blowing?

482 *Unlawful Assembly*

THIS vale of teargas,
More a hospital than an inn.

Clarity begins at home,
How far does it spread?

A gathering is a mob,
Mobs are to be dispersed

Back to their homes
(Lucky to have one)

Back to their jobs
(Lucky to have one)

Why subscribe to clarity?
In this vale of teargas

Should one enter a caveat,
Or a monastery?

483 *No Offence*

IN no country
Are the disposal services more efficient.

Standardized dustbins
Fit precisely into the mouth of a large cylinder
Slung on a six-wheeled chassis.
Even the dustbin lid is raised mechanically
At the very last moment.
You could dispose of a corpse like this
Without giving the least offence.

In no country
Are the public lavatories more immaculately kept.
As neat as new pins, smelling of pine forests,
With a roar like distant Wagner
Your sins are washed away.

In no country
Do the ambulances arrive more promptly.
You are lying on the stretcher
Before the police, the driver, the bystanders and the
                                        neighbouring shopkeepers
Have finished lecturing you.

In no country
Are the burial facilities more foolproof.
A few pfennigs a week, according to age,
Will procure you a very decent funeral.
You merely sign on the dotted line
And keep your payments regular.

In no country
Are the disposal services more efficient
—I reflect—
As I am sorted out, dressed down, lined up,

Shepherded through the door,
Marshalled across the smooth-faced asphalt,
And fed into the mouth of a large cylinder
Labelled 'Lufthansa'.

HUGH POPHAM

1920–

484

THE usual exquisite boredom of patrols.
    The endless orbiting at twenty grand;
the growing pins and needles in the arse,
    the endlessness of time, the crawling clock,
and nothing to relieve monotony.
    The necessary plague of oxygen,
the routine checks of fuel, pressures, temperatures,
    oil, coolant, guns—
(as if there's any chance of using them!)—
    browned off with looking round, above, behind,
conducive to no rational thought or act
    but the conditioned reflexes of fear.

The ships below, sculling like water-beetles on a pond
    in white-tracked zig-zags, escorts on the flank.
And the careful, modulated tones
    of the directing officer: 'Steer One Fife Eight!
Bogey at fifteen miles.' Turn onto course—
    another bloody Sunderland, for sure.
And still half-an-hour to go. 'Blue two—
    open to five. And keep a good watch out.'

For eighteen months one has awaited this,
    this consummation justifying all,
the means the end, the end the means. Just this,
    to have the bastard steady in one's sight—
a spot more deflection—now. And the dulled drumming
    of the wing cannon, the ruled tracer lines,
and smoke flowering from the engines,
    and the dive away into the neutral sea.
The wild oblivion of excitement,
    mastery beyond all thought or doubt or argument.

HUGH POPHAM

Last time—an 88 it was—above the fleet;
    we picked him up at dusk at thirteen grand,
chased him as he dived into the dusk:
    somebody hit him, saw the bits come off.
Then the last light went. We lost him
    to the eastward, going like hell
right down on the drink. And can those pockers go.
    We only got a probable for him. He might
have made it home. Not the clean, concise
    explosion of the bastard that you jump,
two quick sure bursts—and there an end.

    But here, the mainland a dim shadow
in the haze, there's not much chance.
    'Blue two: we'll start going down, I think'—
blow out your ears and spiral down. Thank God,
    the bar should be open when we land.

DRUMMOND ALLISON

1921–1943

485   *No Remedy*

No remedy, my retrospective friend,
We've found no remedy;
Nor from these fields the briared and barbed wired end
Can keep our enemy,
To mend the gaps
Would take perhaps a century.
So, praise each other's poem though we may,
The day of easy speech
Succeeded soon by love and fright, and they
Made madness out of reach
Gave way in turn
To speed to learn, vain wish to teach,

Success and jealousy their unsought sons;
That day won't leap again,
As when some amateur card trickster runs
His hands through all the plain
Cards, stuns the girls
When he uncurls the royal strain;
Or as the prober of the ancient text
Years after one rare find
Discovers in the margin the great next.
But not that day. We blind
Or vexed must be,
No remedy for our split mind.

SIDNEY KEYES

1922–1943

486 *William Wordsworth*

No room for mourning: he's gone out
Into the noisy glen, or stands between the stones
Of the gaunt ridge, or you'll hear his shout
Rolling among the screes, he being a boy again.
He'll never fail nor die
And if they laid his bones
In the wet vaults or iron sarcophagi
Of fame, he'd rise at the first summer rain
And stride across the hills to seek
His rest among the broken lands and clouds.
He was a stormy day, a granite peak
Spearing the sky; and look, about its base
Words flower like crocuses in the hanging woods,
Blank though the dalehead and the bony face.

487   *Death and the Plowman*

THE RIDER   O DON'T, don't ever ask me for alms:
                  The winter way I'm riding. Beggar, shun
                  My jingling bonebag equipage, beware
                  My horse's lifted hoof, the sinewed whip.
                  I am the man started a long time since
                  To drive into the famous land some call
                  Posterity, some famine, some the valley
                  Of bones, valley of bones, valley of dry
                  Bones where a critical mind is always searching
                  The poor dried marrow for a drop of truth.
                  Better for you to ask no alms, my friend.

THE PLOWMAN   I will go with you.
                  Better plow-following, the searching wind
                  About my bones than this nonentity.

THE RIDER   Then get you up beside me, gull-brained fool.

BOTH   We're driving to the famous land some call
                  Posterity, some famine, some the valley
                  Of bones, valley of bones, valley of dry
                  Bones where there is no heat nor hope nor dwelling:
                  But cold security, the one and only
                  Right of a workless man without a home.

KINGSLEY AMIS

1922–

488   *A Bookshop Idyll*

BETWEEN the GARDENING and the COOKERY
     Comes the brief POETRY shelf;
By the Nonesuch Donne, a thin anthology
     Offers itself.

Critical, and with nothing else to do,
     I scan the Contents page,
Relieved to find the names are mostly new;
     No one my age.

Like all strangers, they divide by sex:
    Landscape near Parma
Interests a man, so does *The Double Vortex*,
    So does *Rilke and Buddha.*

'I travel, you see', 'I think' and 'I can read'
    These titles seem to say;
But *I Remember You, Love is my Creed,*
    Poem for J.,

The ladies' choice, discountenance my patter
    For several seconds;
From somewhere in this (as in any) matter
    A moral beckons.

Should poets bicycle-pump the human heart
    Or squash it flat?
Man's love is of man's life a thing apart;
    Girls aren't like that.

We men have got love well weighed up; our stuff
    Can get by without it.
Women don't seem to think that's good enough;
    They write about it,

And the awful way their poems lay them open
    Just doesn't strike them.
Women are really much nicer than men:
    No wonder we like them.

Deciding this, we can forget those times
    We sat up half the night
Chockfull of love, crammed with bright thoughts,
    names, rhymes,
    And couldn't write.

489   *After Goliath*

'What shall be done to the man
that killeth this Philistine?'
1 Sam. 17: 27.

THE first shot out of that sling
Was enough to finish the thing:
The champion laid out cold
Before half the programmes were sold.
And then, what howls of dismay
From his fans in their dense array:
From aldermen, adjutants, aunts,
Administrators of grants,
Assurance-men, auctioneers,
Advisers about careers,
And advertisers, of course,
Plus the obvious b——s in force:
The whole reprehensible throng
Ten times an alphabet strong.
But such an auspicious debut
Was a little too good to be true,
Our victor sensed; the applause
From those who supported his cause
Sounded shrill and excessive now,
And who were they, anyhow?
Academics, actors who lecture,
Apostles of architecture,
Ancient-gods-of-the-abdomen men,
Angst-pushers, adherents of Zen,
Alastors, Austenites, A-test
Abolishers—even the straightest
Of issues looks pretty oblique
When a movement turns into a clique,
The conqueror mused, as he stopped
By the sword his opponent had dropped:
Trophy, or means of attack
On the rapturous crowd at his back?
He shrugged and left it, resigned
To a new battle, fought in the mind,
For faith that his quarrel was just,
That the right man lay in the dust.

490 *New Approach Needed*

SHOULD you revisit us,
Stay a little longer,
And get to know the place.
Experience hunger,
Madness, disease and war.
You heard about them, true,
The last time you came here;
It's different having them.
And what about a go
At love, marriage, children?
All good, but bringing some
Risk of remorse and pain
And fear of an odd sort:
A sort one should, again,
Feel, not just hear about,
To be qualified as
A human-race expert.
On local life, we trust
The resident witness,
Not the royal tourist.

People have suffered worse
And more durable wrongs
Than you did on that cross
(I know—you won't get me
Up on one of those things),
Without sure prospect of
Ascending good as new
On the third day, without
'I die, but man shall live'
As a nice cheering thought.
So, next time, come off it,
And get some service in,
Jack, long before you start
Laying down the old law:
If you still want to then.
Tell your dad that from me.

491   *Aberdarcy : the Main Square*

BY the new Boot's, a tool-chest with flagpoles
Glued on, and flanges, and a dirty great
Baronial doorway, and things like portholes,
Evans met Mrs. Rhys on their first date.

Beau Nash House, that sells Clothes for Gentlemen,
Jacobethan, every beam nailed on tight—
Real wood, though, mind you—was in full view when,
Lunching at the Three Lamps, she said all right.

And he dropped her beside the grimy hunk
Of castle, that with luck might one day fall
On to the *Evening Post*, the time they slunk
Back from that lousy weekend in Porthcawl.

The journal of some bunch of architects
Named this the worst town centre they could find;
But how disparage what so well reflects
Permanent tendencies of heart and mind?

All love demands a witness: something 'there'
Which it yet makes part of itself. These two
Might find Carlton House Terrace, St. Mark's Square,
A bit on the grand side. What about you?

492   *St. Asaph's*

A CHESTNUT tree stands in the line of sight
Between the GIRLS entrance and 'Braich-y-Pwll',
Where, half past eightish, Evans shaves his face,
  Squints out the window.

Not that he really wants to get among
Schoolchildren—see, some of the stuff by there,
All bounce and flounce, rates keeping an eye on:
  Forthcoming models.

It's tough, though. Past the winter boughs he'll spot
Bunches of overcoats quite clear; come May,
Just the odd flash of well-filled gingham, and
    Stacks of rich verdure.

You can't win, Dai. Nature's got all the cards.
But bear up: you still know the bloody leaf
From bole or blossom, dancer from the dance.
    Hope for you yet, then.

DONALD DAVIE

1922–

493   *Remembering the 'Thirties*

I

HEARING one saga, we enact the next.
We please our elders when we sit enthralled;
But then they're puzzled; and at last they're vexed
To have their youth so avidly recalled.

It dawns upon the veterans after all
That what for them were agonies, for us
Are high-brow thrillers, though historical;
And all their feats quite strictly fabulous.

This novel written fifteen years ago,
Set in my boyhood and my boyhood home,
These poems about 'abandoned workings', show
Worlds more remote than Ithaca or Rome.

The Anschluss, Guernica—all the names
At which those poets thrilled or were afraid
For me mean schools and schoolmasters and games;
And in the process some-one is betrayed.

Ourselves perhaps. The Devil for a joke
Might carve his own initials on our desk,
And still we'd miss the point because he spoke
An idiom too dated, Audenesque.

Ralegh's Guiana also killed his son.
A pretty pickle if we came to see
The tallest story really packed a gun,
The Telemachiad an Odyssey.

II

Even to them the tales were not so true
As not to be ridiculous as well:
The ironmaster met his Waterloo,
But Rider Haggard rode along the fell.

'Leave for Cape Wrath to-night!' They lounged away
On Fleming's trek or Isherwood's ascent.
England expected every man that day
To show his motives were ambivalent.

They played the fool, not to appear as fools
In time's long glass. A deprecating air
Disarmed, they thought, the jeers of later schools;
Yet irony itself is doctrinaire,

And, curiously, nothing now betrays
Their type to time's derision like this coy
Insistence on the quizzical, their craze
For showing Hector was a mother's boy.

A neutral tone is nowadays preferred.
And yet it may be better, if we must,
To find the stance impressive and absurd
Than not to see the hero for the dust.

For courage is the vegetable king,
The sprig of all ontologies, the weed
That beards the slag-heap with his hectoring,
Whose green adventures is to run to seed.

494   *The Fountain*

FEATHERS up fast, and steeples; then in clods
Thuds into its first basin; thence as surf
Smokes up and hangs; irregularly slops
Into its second, tattered like a shawl;
There, chill as rain, stipples a danker green,
Where urgent tritons lob their heavy jets.

For Berkeley this was human thought, that mounts
From bland assumptions to inquiring skies,
There glints with wit, fumes into fancies, plays
With its negations, and at last descends,
As by a law of nature, to its bowl
Of thus enlightened but still common sense.

We who have no such confidence must gaze
With all the more affection on these forms,
These spires, these plumes, these calm reflections, these
Similitudes of surf and turf and shawl,
Graceful returns upon acceptances.
We ask of fountains only that they play,

Though that was not what Berkeley meant at all.

495   *Heigh-ho on a Winter Afternoon*

THERE is a heigh-ho in these glowing coals
By which I sit wrapped in my overcoat
As if for a portrait by Whistler. And there is
A heigh-ho in the bird that noiselessly
Flew just now past my window, to alight
On winter's moulding, snow; and an alas,
A heigh-ho and a desultory chip,
Chip, chip on stone from somewhere down below.

Yes I have 'mellowed', as you said I would,
And that's a heigh-ho too for any man;
Heigh-ho that means we fall short of alas
Which sprigs the grave of higher hopes than ours.

Yet heigh-ho too has its own luxuries,
And salts with courage to be jocular
Disreputable sweets of wistfulness,
By deprecation made presentable.

What should we do to rate the long alas
But skeeter down a steeper gradient?
And then some falls are still more fortunate,
The meteors spent, the tragic heroes stunned
Who go out like a light. But here the chip,
Chip, chip will flake the stone by slow degrees,
For hour on hour the fire will gutter down,
The bird will call at longer intervals.

496   FROM *The Forests of Lithuania*

BUT this, so feminine?
Can this be the place? a piano,
Sheet-music upon it, books . . .
And see, across a chair
The white gown freshly shaken.
Cross to the window. A brook
That ran through nettles once
Borders a garden plot
Of grass and mint. Those beds
Were lately rained upon:
The watering pot that stands
Half-full has felt
Just now her hand, the gate
Swings from her touch, on the sand
—Dry, white as snow—the print
Is light but clear of some
Unshod, unstockinged foot
That lately ran. His eyes
Rove, and as they rise
See her upon the wall
Balanced, in her white
And morning disarray
That will not screen,
Though crossed arms veil the breast,

Swan's throat and shoulders. Hair
In curling-papers rays
A small head, in the sun
Thus crowned, an ikon. Turning
From wall to turf, across
Stile and parterre, and up
A leaning plank, like a bird
Flying, and like a ray
Of moonlight darting through
The windowframe she gains
The very chamber. He
Blushes and bows, retires
And will not look, but hears
Cry as of a child
No one . . .

497   *Thanks to Industrial Essex*

THANKS to industrial Essex,
I have spun on the greasy axis
Of business and sociometrics;
I have come to know the structures
Of public service
As well as I know the doves
Crop-full in mildewed haycocks.
I know that what they merit
Is not scorn, sometimes scorn
And hatred, but sadness really.

Italic on chalky tussocks,
The devious lovely weasel
Snakes through a privileged annex,
An enclave of directors.
Landscapes of supertax
Record a deathful failure
As clearly as the lack
Of a grand or expansively human
Scale to the buildings of Ilford.

The scale of that deprivation
Goes down in no statistics.

PHILIP LARKIN

1922– *1985*

498   *Toads*

WHY should I let the toad *work*
        Squat on my life?
Can't I use my wit as a pitchfork
        And drive the brute off?

Six days of the week it soils
        With its sickening poison—
Just for paying a few bills!
        That's out of proportion.

Lots of folk live on their wits:
        Lecturers, lispers,
Losels, loblolly-men, louts—
        They don't end as paupers;

Lots of folk live up lanes
        With fires in a bucket,
Eat windfalls and tinned sardines—
        They seem to like it.

Their nippers have got bare feet,
        Their unspeakable wives
Are skinny as whippets—and yet
        No one actually *starves*.

Ah, were I courageous enough
        To shout *Stuff your pension!*
But I know, all too well, that's the stuff
        That dreams are made on:

For something sufficiently toad-like
        Squats in me, too;
Its hunkers are heavy as hard luck,
        And cold as snow,

And will never allow me to blarney
   My way to getting
The fame and the girl and the money
   All at one sitting.

I don't say, one bodies the other
   One's spiritual truth;
But I do say it's hard to lose either,
   When you have both.

499   *Coming*

On longer evenings,
Light, chill and yellow,
Bathes the serene
Foreheads of houses.
A thrush sings,
Laurel-surrounded
In the deep bare garden,
Its fresh-peeled voice
Astonishing the brickwork.
It will be spring soon,
It will be spring soon—
And I, whose childhood
Is a forgotten boredom,
Feel like a child
Who comes on a scene
Of adult reconciling,
And can understand nothing
But the unusual laughter,
And starts to be happy.

500   *At Grass*

The eye can hardly pick them out
From the cold shade they shelter in,
Till wind distresses tail and mane;
Then one crops grass, and moves about
—The other seeming to look on—
And stands anonymous again.

Aubade

I work all day, and get half drunk at night.
Waking at four to soundless dark, I stare.
In time the curtain-edges will grow light.
Till then I see what's really always there :
Unresting death, a whole day nearer now,
Making all thought impossible but how
And where and when I shall myself die.
Arid interrogation : yet the dread
Of dying, and being dead,
Flashes afresh to hold and horrify.

The mind blanks at the glare. Not in remorse
—The good not done, the love not given, time
Torn off unused—nor wretchedly because
An only life can take so long to climb
Clear of its wrong beginnings, and may never ;
But at the total emptiness for ever,
The sure extinction that we travel to
And shall be lost in always. Not to be here,
Not to be anywhere,
And soon ; nothing more terrible, nothing more
    true.

This is a special way of being afraid
No trick dispels. Religion used to try,
That vast moth-eaten musical brocade
Created to pretend we never die,
And specious stuff that says *No rational being
Can fear a thing it will not feel*, not seeing
That this is what we fear—no sight, no sound,
No touch or taste or smell, nothing to think with,
Nothing to love or link with,
The anaesthetic from which none come round.

And so it stays just on the edge of vision,
A small unfocused blur, a standing chill
That slows each impulse down to indecision.
Most things may never happen : this one will,
And realisation of it rages out
In furnace-fear when we are caught without
People or drink. Courage is no good :
It means not scaring others. Being brave
Lets no one off the grave.
Death is no different whined at than withstood.

Slowly light strengthens, and the room takes
    shape.
It stands plain as a wardrobe, what we know,
Have always known, know that we can't escape,
Yet can't accept. One side will have to go.
Meanwhile telephones crouch, getting ready to
    ring
In locked-up offices, and all the uncaring
Intricate rented world begins to rouse.
The sky is white as clay, with no sun.
Work has to be done.
Postmen like doctors go from house to house.

Yet fifteen years ago, perhaps
Two dozen distances sufficed
To fable them: faint afternoons
Of Cups and Stakes and Handicaps,
Whereby their names were artificed
To inlay faded, classic Junes—

Silks at the start: against the sky
Numbers and parasols: outside,
Squadrons of empty cars, and heat,
And littered grass: then the long cry
Hanging unhushed till it subside
To stop-press columns on the street.

Do memories plague their ears like flies?
They shake their heads. Dusk brims the shadows.
Summer by summer all stole away,
The starting-gates, the crowds and cries—
All but the unmolesting meadows.
Almanacked, their names live; they

Have slipped their names, and stand at ease,
Or gallop for what must be joy,
And not a fieldglass sees them home,
Or curious stop-watch prophesies:
Only the groom, and the groom's boy,
With bridles in the evening come.

501   *Take One Home for the Kiddies*

ON shallow straw, in shadeless glass,
Huddled by empty bowls, they sleep:
No dark, no dam, no earth, no grass—
Mam, get us one of them to keep.

Living toys are something novel,
But it soon wears off somehow.
Fetch the shoebox, fetch the shovel—
Mam, we're playing funerals now.

502 *Nothing to be Said*

For nations vague as weed,
For nomads among stones,
Small-statured cross-faced tribes
And cobble-close families
In mill-towns on dark mornings
Life is slow dying.

So are their separate ways
Of building, benediction,
Measuring love and money
Ways of slow dying.
The day spent hunting pig
Or holding a garden-party,

Hours giving evidence
Or birth, advance
On death equally slowly.
And saying so to some
Means nothing; others it leaves
Nothing to be said.

503 *The Whitsun Weddings*

That Whitsun, I was late getting away:
    Not till about
One-twenty on the sunlit Saturday
Did my three-quarters-empty train pull out,
All windows down, all cushions hot, all sense
Of being in a hurry gone. We ran
Behind the backs of houses, crossed a street
Of blinding windscreens, smelt the fish-dock; thence
The river's level drifting breadth began,
Where sky and Lincolnshire and water meet.

All afternoon, through the tall heat that slept
   For miles inland,
A slow and stopping curve southwards we kept.
Wide farms went by, short-shadowed cattle, and
Canals with floatings of industrial froth;
A hothouse flashed uniquely: hedges dipped
And rose: and now and then a smell of grass
Displaced the reek of buttoned carriage-cloth
Until the next town, new and nondescript,
Approached with acres of dismantled cars.

At first, I didn't notice what a noise
   The weddings made
Each station that we stopped at: sun destroys
The interest of what's happening in the shade,
And down the long cool platforms whoops and skirls
I took for porters larking with the mails,
And went on reading. Once we started, though,
We passed them, grinning and pomaded, girls
In parodies of fashion, heels and veils,
All posed irresolutely, watching us go,

As if out on the end of an event
   Waving goodbye
To something that survived it. Struck, I leant
More promptly out next time, more curiously,
And saw it all again in different terms:
The fathers with broad belts under their suits
And seamy foreheads; mothers loud and fat;
An uncle shouting smut; and then the perms,
The nylon gloves and jewellery-substitutes,
The lemons, mauves, and olive-ochres that

Marked off the girls unreally from the rest.
   Yes, from cafés
And banquet-halls up yards, and bunting-dressed
Coach-party annexes, the wedding-days
Were coming to an end. All down the line
Fresh couples climbed aboard: the rest stood round;
The last confetti and advice were thrown,
And, as we moved, each face seemed to define
Just what it saw departing: children frowned
At something dull; fathers had never known

Success so huge and wholly farcical;
  The women shared
The secret like a happy funeral;
While girls, gripping their handbags tighter, stared
At a religious wounding. Free at last,
And loaded with the sum of all they saw,
We hurried towards London, shuffling gouts of steam.
Now fields were building-plots, and poplars cast
Long shadows over major roads, and for
Some fifty minutes, that in time would seem

Just long enough to settle hats and say
  I nearly died,
A dozen marriages got under way.
They watched the landscape, sitting side by side
—An Odeon went past, a cooling tower,
And someone running up to bowl—and none
Thought of the others they would never meet
Or how their lives would all contain this hour.
I thought of London spread out in the sun,
Its postal districts packed like squares of wheat:

There we were aimed. And as we raced across
  Bright knots of rail
Past standing Pullmans, walls of blackened moss
Came close, and it was nearly done, this frail
Travelling coincidence; and what it held
Stood ready to be loosed with all the power
That being changed can give. We slowed again,
And as the tightened brakes took hold, there swelled
A sense of falling, like an arrow-shower
Sent out of sight, somewhere becoming rain.

ALAN ROSS

1922–

504

Stanley Matthews

NOT often *con brio*, but *andante, andante,*
    horseless, though jockey-like and jaunty,
Straddling the touchline, live margin
    not out of the game, nor quite in,
Made by him green and magnetic, stroller
Indifferent as a cat dissembling, rolling
A little as on deck, till the mouse, the ball,
    slides palely to him,
And shyly, almost with deprecatory cough, he is off.

Head of a Perugino, with faint flare
Of the nostrils, as though Lipizzaner-like,
    he sniffed at the air,
Finding it good beneath him, he draws
Defenders towards him, the ball a bait
They refuse like a poisoned chocolate,
    retreating, till he slows his gait
To a walk, inviting the tackle, inciting it.

At last, unrefusable, dangling the ball at the instep
He is charged—and stiffening so slowly
It is rarely perceptible, he executes with a squirm
Of the hips, a twist more suggestive than apparent,
    that lazily disdainful move *toreros* term
        a Veronica—it's enough.
Only emptiness following him, pursuing some scent
Of his own, he weaves in towards,
    not away from, fresh tacklers,
Who, turning about to gain time, are by him
    harried, pursued not pursuers.

543

Now gathers speed, nursing the ball as he cruises,
Eyes judging distance, noting the gaps, the spaces
Vital for colleagues to move to, slowing a trace,
As from Vivaldi to Dibdin, pausing,
    and leisurely, leisurely, swings
To the left upright his centre, on hips
His hands, observing the goalkeeper spring,
    heads rising vainly to the ball's curve
Just as it's plucked from them; and dispassionately
Back to his mark he trots, whistling through closed lips.

Trim as a yacht, with similar lightness
    —of keel, of reaction to surface—with salt air
Tanned, this incomparable player, in decline fair
    to look at, nor in decline either,
Improving like wine with age, has come far—
    born to one, a barber, who boxed
Not with such filial magnificence, but well.
'The greatest of all time,' *meraviglioso*, Matthews—
    Stoke City, Blackpool and England.
Expressionless enchanter, weaving as on strings
Conceptual patterns to a private music, heard
Only by him, to whose slowly emerging theme
He rehearses steps, soloist in compulsions of a dream.

VERNON SCANNELL

1922–

505   *Autumn*

I T is the football season once more
And the back pages of the Sunday papers
Again show the blurred anguish of goalkeepers.

In Maida Vale, Golders Green and Hampstead
Lamps ripen early in the surprising dusk;
They are furred like stale rinds with a fuzz of mist.

The pavements of Kensington are greasy;
The wind smells of burnt porridge in Bayswater,
And the leaves are mushed to silence in the gutter.

The big hotel like an anchored liner
Rides near the park; lit windows hammer the sky.
Like the slow swish of surf the tyres of taxis sigh.

On Ealing Broadway the cinema glows
Warm behind glass while mellow the church clock chimes
As the waiting girls stir in their delicate chains.

Their eyes are polished by the wind,
But the gleam is dumb, empty of joy or anger.
Though the lovers are long in coming the girls still linger.

We are nearing the end of the year.
Under the sombre sleeve the blood ticks faster
And in the dark ear of Autumn quick voices whisper.

It is a time of year that's to my taste,
Full of spiced rumours, sharp and velutinous flavours,
Dim with the mist that softens the cruel surfaces,
Makes mirrors vague. It is the mist that I most favour.

506   *Any Complaints?*

LAWRENCE—not the bearded one—the one
Who dressed up as a wog and crashed his bike
Doing a ton, if those old jobs could make it then,
Lawrence said something about courage: Courage is like
A bank account; you keep on writing cheques
Until the day comes when there's nothing there,
No more to draw. You're broke. What next?
They tie you to a gunwheel in the lashing air
Or blind you with a bandage and lead you out
As target for small arms.
                         If you are very rich,
Got plenty in that bank, you'll probably get hit
But by the other lot; wind up in a different ditch
But just as dead. With extraordinary luck
You might survive and get back home quite safe.

But what if all your days you've been dead broke,
Never owned a cheque-book in your life,
Nothing in the bank at all?
                    You go to jail
Or try to bluff it out, let others pay your way.
It's not an easy game, and if you fail,
Are shown up as a fraud, no matter what you say
You'll get the gunsheel or the firing-squad.
It isn't fair? All right, but don't tell me.
The Company Commander is the man to see
Or, better still, complain direct to God.

DAVID HOLBROOK

1923–

507   *Drought*

So, we're estranged again—how it goes on!
Your who-you-are dissolved: my disappointed me
Skulking in silence. Rain falls, then it is gone.
The sun's bright on wet roofs, every washed tree
Has June's hard highlights, while a rivulet
Runs down the road that has been dry a month.
And with it run the feelings that I let
Flow as I contemplate our last dry month.

We have been very close, we have been sweet,
Fresh, active, despite flaws, and our old rout
Of masked ghost predators. Perhaps tonight
Some sudden shower again will break our drought?
Both of us are, I know, in our sorrow,
Watching the same rain from our each window.

508   *Maternity Gown*

THE window insulates me from the street,
And you are gone into a cubicle.
The London crowd goes by: the shop worries the girls
Whose fits or stares would suit an undertaker's!
I notice a youth's cruel face in a blue sports car.

The day is warm, the October sunlight strong—
A balm for us, after that wreck of a summer!
Scraps of curled leaves whisk under passing feet,
And as I watch I have Kent cobs to eat.

We have come to Baker Street to buy you a gown:
Why does the soft-lit scene bite at me so?
I smell the foetid tube shelters of war-time
(A news-vendor tied with string): see willow-herb
Stretch purple in the sun, though there are now no bomb-sites.
I weep in a taxi over Waterloo Bridge, just by St. Thomas's
Where our first child was born. I recognise the moment
As when an awareness gels, and I seem to be regarding
Our life from a distant height: 'this is what happened'
Is happening now. I accept that you are pregnant:
The new life walks already where the confused crowds go,
A legacy of isolation bred between us two!
A rag of a queue of boys queueing for a film
Begins to move along, and the arrested scene is broken:
But when I turn, I am changed, as the capacity of middle age
Is filled with a young man's love, in a scalding wave.
I feel the exclusive joy that first new lovers feel,
And the need to be, and make, even where annihilation threatens.

Yet as you come back in the smock my loneliness returns:
Remote in your breeding trance, as a woman is,
You seem hardly to know me: so, it's exactly so,
As when you were first big, and you fainted in a queue,
And I stood in wonder, instead of wondering what to do,
Some sixteen years ago, on the floor of a Hampstead shop!
When your eyes first opened then, they looked as they do now:
'Who is this man?'—soft light of creative care—'Ah, yes, he'll do'
As you saw the love in mine—as you do now, say you do!

JAMES KIRKUP

1923–

509   *A Correct Compassion*

*To Mr. Philip Allison, after watching him perform a mitral
stenosis valvulotomy in the General Infirmary at Leeds.*

CLEANLY, sir, you went to the core of the matter.
Using the purest kind of wit, a balance of belief and art,
You with a curious nervous elegance laid bare
The root of life, and put your finger on its beating heart.

The glistening theatre swarms with eyes, and hands, and eyes.
On green-clothed tables, ranks of instruments transmit a sterile gleam.
The masks are on, and no unnecessary smile betrays
A certain tension, true concomitant of calm.

Here we communicate by looks, though words,
Too, are used, as in continuous historic present
You describe our observations and your deeds.
All gesture is reduced to its result, an instrument.

She who does not know she is a patient lies
Within a tent of green, and sleeps without a sound
Beneath the lamps, and the reflectors that devise
Illuminations probing the profoundest wound.

A calligraphic master, improvising, you invent
The first incision, and no poet's hesitation
Before his snow-blank page mars your intent:
The flowing stroke is drawn like an uncalculated inspiration.

A garland of flowers unfurls across the painted flesh.
With quick precision the arterial forceps click.
Yellow threads are knotted with a simple flourish.
Transfused, the blood preserves its rose, though it is sick.

Meters record the blood, measure heart-beats, control the breath.
Hieratic gesture: scalpel bares a creamy rib; with pincer knives
The bone quietly is clipped, and lifted out. Beneath,
The pink, black-mottled lung like a revolted creature heaves,

Collapses; as if by extra fingers is neatly held aside
By two ordinary egg-beaters, kitchen tools that curve
Like extraordinary hands. Heart, laid bare, silently beats. It can hide
No longer yet is not revealed.—'A local anaesthetic in the cardiac
    nerve.'

Now, in the firm hands that quiver with a careful strength,
Your knife feels through the heart's transparent skin; at first,
Inside the pericardium, slit down half its length,
The heart, black-veined, swells like a fruit about to burst,

But goes on beating, love's poignant image bleeding at the dart
Of a more grievous passion, as a bird, dreaming of flight, sleeps on
Within its leafy cage.—'It generally upsets the heart
A bit, though not unduly, when I make the first injection.'

Still, still the patient sleeps, and still the speaking heart is dumb.
The watchers breathe an air far sweeter, rarer than the room's.
The cold walls listen. Each in his own blood hears the drum
She hears, tented in green, unfathomable calms.

'I make a purse-string suture here, with a reserve
Suture, which I must make first, and deeper,
As a safeguard, should the other burst. In the cardiac nerve
I inject again a local anaesthetic. Could we have fresh towels to cover

All these adventitious ones. Now can you all see.
When I put my finger inside the valve, there may be a lot
Of blood, and it may come with quite a bang. But I let it flow,
In case there are any clots, to give the heart a good clean-out.

Now can you give me every bit of light you've got.'
We stand on the benches, peering over his shoulder.
The lamp's intensest rays are concentrated on an inmost heart.
Someone coughs. 'If you have to cough, you will do it outside this
    theatre.'—'Yes, sir.'

'How's she breathing, Doug.? Do you feel quite happy?'—'Yes, fairly
Happy.'—'Now. I am putting my finger in the opening of the valve.
I can only get the tip of my finger in.—It's gradually
Giving way.—I'm inside.—No clots.—I can feel the valve

Breathing freely now around my finger, and the heart working.
Not too much blood. It opened very nicely.
I should say that anatomically speaking
This is a perfect case.—Anatomically.

For of course, anatomy is not physiology.'
We find we breathe again, and hear the surgeon hum.
Outside, in the street, a car starts up. The heart regularly
Thunders.—'I do not stitch up the pericardium.

It is not necessary.'—For this is imagination's other place,
Where only necessary things are done, with the supreme and grave
Dexterity that ignores technique; with proper grace
Informing a correct compassion, that performs its love, and makes
   it live.

PATRICIA BEER

1924–

510   *Lion Hunts*

A LION is never a lion in a royal hunt,
Only a victory to cheer the king up.
Sometimes six men carry him upside down,
His tail stiff as a leg, though his dewlap
Must be soft still because they grasp it.
He started proudly and knew when to stop.

Sometimes he stands, shoulder high to the king,
Nearly as good as the king, almost man to man.
Only his bare genitals and the ten weapons
Growing out of his paws show he is not one.
More honour to the king who is about to kill him.
A little of the blade has already gone in.

Years later he is in colour, so is the king,
And they fight among pink rocks. A prince lies
Restfully dead, a cub watches to learn.
Magenta blood spurts from the lion's thighs
And the king's, but the curved sword is itching.
It must always be the animal who dies.

MICHAEL HAMBURGER

1924–

511   *Memory*

MY wives do not write.
Sweetly young, hair flowing,
They walk where they belong,
Riverside, lakeside,
Mountainside, hillside,
Woodland or grassy plain.

One I consoled—
Black-haired, sad
In her forest clearing—
Another I followed
From a wellspring up in the scree
To a pool's golden rushes.

Did I leave them, forsake them?
I travelled,
Remember no parting.
Ways, I recall, transitions,
The shadows, the colours turning,
Herbs acrid or heady,
Sweet wives the world over,
Sweet virgins walking where they belong—

Unchanged, unchanging regions,
And they unchanged.

But by the knee a stranger
Clawed me, held on;
I fought: my grappling hand
Slid deep into rotten flesh,
A hole behind his ear.
I knocked him down and ran,
Clegs covering me,
A grey crust;
Ran to the church, thinking
They could not enter there,
But still they clung, stinging,

And up I climbed, climbed
To the belfry, pursued
By a man half-decayed.

Sweet wives, sweet virgins
Walk still unchanged,
Do not write, do not miss me,
Never forget.
It was the sunshine, the shadows,
It was the herbs and the haze.

MICHAEL IVENS

1924–

512 *First Day at School*

FIRST day at school
the large boy
kindly
hurled my ball
with amazing skill
high over the roof

soaring out of sight
out of my prosaic life

Unstintingly
I gave him
my admiration

MICHAEL IVENS

As others have done
when their respect
money
virginity
honour hope and lives
have been hurled
triumphantly out of sight

K. W. GRANSDEN

1925–

An Interview

HAVE you lived long, sir, in these parts?
—That hill would not think so.
What are your favourite loves, your special hates?
—The things I do not know.

Have you never wanted to move on?
—I have known that despair.
Yet you haven't actually up sticks and gone?
—Perhaps next year.

Have you seen many changes since you came?
—I have seen the green branch bare.
Yet I suppose a lot of things are the same?
—Your questionnaire.

What have you been doing all this time?
—Making my will,
Committing and solving crime,
    Watching the sun over that hill.

What made you come here in the first place, sir?
—It was not the first place.
Then you have memories going back earlier?
—As a child I stole fruit, was in disgrace.

But you've done pretty well since then?
  —It was only one tree;
They say each year it drips with blood again,
  Tears for my victory.

What is the secret of your long innings, sir?
  Have you any tips to pass on to us?
—Try and grow used to the place of every star
  And forget your own dark house.

LAURENCE LERNER

1925–

514   *A Wish*

OFTEN I've wished that I'd been born a woman.
It seems the one sure way to be fully human.
Think of the trouble—keeping the children fed,
Keeping your skirt down and your lips red,
Watching the calendar and the last bus home,
Being nice to all the dozens of guests in the room;
Having to change your hairstyle and your name
At least once; learning to take the blame;
Keeping your husband faithful, and your char.
And all the things you're supposed to be grateful for
—Votes and proposals, chocolates and seats in the train—
Or expert with—typewriter, powderpuff, pen,
Diaphragm, needle, chequebook, casserole, bed.
It seems the one sure way to be driven mad.

So why would anyone want to be a woman?
Would you rather be the hero or the victim?
Would you rather win, seduce, and read the paper,
Or be beaten, pregnant, and have to lay the table?
Nothing is free. In order to pay the price
Isn't it simpler, really, to have no choice?
Only ill-health, recurring, inevitable,
Can teach the taste of what it is to be well.

No man has ever felt his daughter tear
The flesh he had earlier torn to plant her there.
Men know the pain of birth by a kind of theory:
No man has been a protagonist in the story,
Lying back bleeding, exhausted and in pain,
Waiting for stitches and sleep and to be alone,
And listened with tender breasts to the hesitant croak
At the bedside growing continuous as you wake.
That is the price. That is what love is worth.
It will go on twisting your heart like an afterbirth.
Whether you choose to or not you will pay and pay
Your whole life long. Nothing on earth is free.

JOHN WAIN

1925–

515   *Apology for Understatement*

FORGIVE me that I pitch your praise too low.
Such reticence my reverence demands,
For silence falls with laying on of hands.

Forgive me that my words come thin and slow.
This could not be a time for eloquence,
For silence falls with healing of the sense.

We only utter what we lightly know.
And it is rather that my love knows me.
It is that your perfection set me free.

Verse is dressed up that has nowhere to go.
You took away my glibness with my fear.
Forgive me that I stand in silence here.

It is not words could pay you what I owe.

516 *Au Jardin des Plantes*

THE gorilla lay on his back,
One hand cupped under his head,
Like a man.

Like a labouring man tired with work,
A strong man with his strength burnt away
In the toil of earning a living.

Only of course he was not tired out with work,
Merely with boredom; his terrible strength
All burnt away by prodigal idleness.

A thousand days, and then a thousand days,
Idleness licked away his beautiful strength,
He having no need to earn a living.

It was all laid on, free of charge.
We maintained him, not for doing anything,
But for being what he was.

And so that Sunday morning he lay on his back,
Like a man, like a worn-out man,
One hand cupped under his terrible hard head.

Like a man, like a man,
One of those we maintain, not for doing anything,
But for being what they are.

A thousand days, and then a thousand days,
With everything laid on, free of charge,
They cup their heads in prodigal idleness.

517 *A Song about Major Eatherly*

The book (Fernard Gigon's *Formula for Death—The Atom Bombs and After*) also describes how Major Claude R. Eatherly, pilot of the aircraft which carried the second bomb to Nagasaki, later started having nightmares. His wife is quoted as saying: 'He often jumps up in the middle of the night and screams out in an inhuman voice which makes me feel ill: "Release it, release it." '

Major Eatherly began to suffer brief periods of madness, says Gigon. The doctors diagnosed extreme nervous depression, and Eatherly was awarded a pension of 237 dollars a month.

This he appears to have regarded 'as a premium for murder, as a payment for what had been done to the two Japanese cities'. He never touched the money, and took to petty thievery, for which he was committed to Fort Worth prison.

Report in The Observer, August 1958.

I

GOOD news. It seems he loved them after all.
His orders were to fry their bones to ash.
He carried up the bomb and let it fall.
And then his orders were to take the cash,

A hero's pension. But he let it lie.
It was in vain to ask him for the cause.
Simply that if he touched it he would die.
He fought his own, and not his country's wars.

His orders told him he was not a man:
An instrument, fine-tempered, clear of stain,
All fears and passions closed up like a fan:
No more volition than his aeroplane.

But now he fought to win his manhood back.
Steep from the sunset of his pain he flew
Against the darkness in that last attack.
It was for love he fought, to make that true.

II

To take life is always to die a little: to stop
any feeling and moving contrivance, however ugly,
unnecessary, or hateful, is to reduce by so much the total
of life there is. And that is to die a little.

To take the life of an enemy is to help him,
a little, towards destroying your own. Indeed, that is why
we hate our enemies: because they force us to kill them.
A murderer hides the dead man in the ground:
but his crime rears up and topples on to the living,
for it is they who now must hunt the murderer,
murder him, and hide him in the ground: it is they
who now feel the touch of death cold in their bones.

Animals hate death. A trapped fox will gnaw
through his own leg: it is so important to love
that he forgives himself the agony,
consenting, for life's sake, to the desperate teeth
grating through bone and pulp, the gasping yelps.

That is the reason the trapper hates the fox.
You think the trapper doesn't hate the fox?
But he does, and the fox can tell how much.
It is not the fox's teeth that grind his bones,
It is the trapper's. It is the trapper, there,
Who keeps his head down, gnawing, hour after hour.

And the people the trapper works for, they are there too,
heads down beside the trap, gnawing away.
Why shouldn't they hate the fox? Their cheeks are smeared
with his rank blood, and on their tongues his bone
being splintered, feels uncomfortably sharp.

So once Major Eatherley hated the Japanese.

III

Hell is a furnace, so the wise men taught.
The punishment for sin is to be broiled.
A glowing coal for every sinful thought.

The heat of God's great furnace ate up sin,
Which whispered up in smoke or fell in ash:
So that each hour a new hour could begin.

So fire was holy, though it tortured souls,
The sinners' anguish never ceased, but still
Their sin was burnt from them by shining coals.

Hell fried the criminal but burnt the crime,
Purged where it punished, healed where it destroyed:
It was a stove that warmed the rooms of time.

No man begrudged the flames their appetite.
All were afraid of fire, yet none rebelled.
The wise men taught that hell was just and right.

'The soul desires its necessary dread:
Only among the thorns can patience weave
A bower where the mind can make its bed.'

Even the holy saints whose patient jaws
Chewed bitter rind and hands raised up the dead
Were chestnuts roasted at God's furnace doors.

The wise men passed. The clever men appeared.
They ruled that hell be called a pumpkin face.
They robbed the soul of what it justly feared.

Coal after coal the fires of hell went out.
Their heat no longer warmed the rooms of time,
Which glistened now with fluorescent doubt.

The chilly saints went striding up and down
To warm their blood with useful exercise.
They rolled like conkers through the draughty town.

Those emblematic flames sank down to rest,
But metaphysical fire can not go out:
Men ran from devils they had dispossessed,

And felt within their skulls the dancing heat
No longer stored in God's deep boiler-room.
Fire scorched their temples, frostbite chewed their feet.

That parasitic fire could race and climb
More swiftly than the stately flames of hell!
Its fuel gone, it licked the beams of time.

So time dried out and youngest hearts grew old.
The smoky minutes cracked and broke apart.
The world was roasting but the men were cold.

Now from this pain worse pain was brought to birth,
More hate, more anguish, till at last they cried,
'Release this fire to gnaw the crusty earth:

Make it a flame that's obvious to sight
And let us say we kindled it ourselves,
To split the skulls of men and let it light.

Since death is camped among us, wish him joy,
Invite him to our table and our games.
We cannot judge, but we can still destroy.'

And so the curtains of the mind were drawn.
Men conjured hell a first, a second time:
And Major Eatherly took off at dawn.

IV

Suppose a sea-bird,
its wings stuck down with oil, riding the waves
in no direction, under the storm-clouds, helpless,
lifted for an instant by each moving billow
to scan the meaningless horizon, helpless,
helpless, and the storms coming, and its wings dead,
its bird-nature dead:
                Imagine this castaway,
loved, perhaps, by the Creator, and yet abandoned,
mocked by the flashing scales of the fish beneath it,
who leap, twist, dive, as free of the wide sea
as formerly the bird of the wide sky,
now helpless, starving, a prisoner of the surface,
unable to dive or rise:
                this is your emblem.
Take away the bird, let it be drowned
in the steep black waves of the storm, let it be broken
against rocks in the morning light, too faint to swim:
take away the bird, but keep the emblem.

It is the emblem of Major Eatherly,
who looked round quickly from the height of each wave,
but saw no land, only the rim of the sky
into which he was not free to rise, or the silver
gleam of the mocking scales of the fish diving
where he was not free to dive.

Men have clung always to emblems,
to tokens of absolution from their sins.
Once it was the scapegoat driven out, bearing
its load of guilt under the empty sky
until its shape was lost, merged in the scrub.
Now we are civilized, there is no wild heath.
Instead of the nimble scapegoat running out
to be lost under the wild and empty sky,
the load of guilt is packed into prison walls,
and men file inward through the heavy doors.

But now that image, too, is obsolete.
The major entering prison is no scapegoat.
His penitence will not take away our guilt,
nor sort with any consoling ritual:
this is penitence for its own sake, beautiful,
uncomprehending, inconsolable, unforeseen.
He is not in prison for his penitence:
it is no outrage to our law that he wakes
with cries of pity on his parching lips.
We do not punish him for cries or nightmares.
We punish him for stealing things from stores.

O, give his pension to the storekeeper.
Tell him it is the price of all our souls.
But do not trouble to unlock the door
and bring the Major out into the sun.
Leave him: it is all one: perhaps his nightmares
grow cooler in the twilight of the prison.
Leave him; if he is sleeping, come away.
But lay a folded paper by his head,
nothing official or embossed, a page
torn from your notebook, and the words in pencil.
Say nothing of love, or thanks, or penitence:
say only 'Eatherly, we have your message.'

518 *Brooklyn Heights*

THIS is the gay cliff of the nineteenth century,
Drenched in the hopeful ozone of a new day.

Erect and brown, like retired sea-captains,
The houses gaze vigorously at the ocean.

With the hospitable eyes of retired captains
They preside over the meeting of sea and river.

On Sunday mornings the citizens revisit their beginnings.
Whole families walk in the fresh air of the past.

Their children tricycle down the nineteenth century:
America comes smiling towards them like a neighbour.

While the past on three wheels unrolls beneath them,
They hammer in the blazing forge of the future.

Brooklyn Bridge flies through the air on feathers.
The children do not know the weight of its girders.

It is the citizens carry the bridge on their shoulders:
Its overhead lights crackle in their blood-vessels.

But now it is Sunday morning, and a sky swept clean.
The citizens put down the bridge and stroll at ease.

They jingle the hopeful change in their pockets.
They forget the tripping dance of the profit motive.

The big ships glide in under the high statue,
The towers cluster like spear-grass on the famous island.

And the citizens dream themselves back in a sparkle of morning.
They ride with their children under a sky swept clean.

Dream on, citizens! Dream the true America, the healer,
Drawing the hot blood from throbbing Europe!

Dream the dark-eyed immigrants from the narrow cities:
Dream the iron steamers loaded with prayers and bundles:

Breathe the ozone older than the name of commerce:
Be the citizens of the true survival!

ELIZABETH JENNINGS
1926–

519 *Delay*

THE radiance of that star that leans on me
Was shining years ago. The light that now
Glitters up there my eye may never see,
And so the time lag teases me with how

Love that loves now may not reach me until
Its first desire is spent. The star's impulse
Must wait for eyes to claim it beautiful
And love arrived may find us somewhere else.

520 *Song at the Beginning of Autumn*

Now watch this autumn that arrives
In smells. All looks like summer still;
Colours are quite unchanged, the air
On green and white serenely thrives.
Heavy the trees with growth and full
The fields. Flowers flourish everywhere.

Proust who collected time within
A child's cake would understand
The ambiguity of this—
Summer still raging while a thin
Column of smoke stirs from the land
Proving that autumn gropes for us.

But every season is a kind
Of rich nostalgia. We give names—
Autumn and summer, winter, spring—
As though to unfasten from the mind
Our moods and give them outward forms.
We want the certain, solid thing.

But I am carried back against
My will into a childhood where
Autumn is bonfires, marbles, smoke;
I lean against my window fenced
From evocations in the air.
When I said autumn, autumn broke.

521   *Answers*

I KEPT my answers small and kept them near;
Big questions bruised my mind but still I let
Small answers be a bulwark to my fear.

The huge abstractions I kept from the light;
Small things I handled and caressed and loved.
I let the stars assume the whole of night.

But the big answers clamoured to be moved
Into my life. Their great audacity
Shouted to be acknowledged and believed.

Even when all small answers build up to
Protection of my spirit, still I hear
Big answers striving for their overthrow

And all the great conclusions coming near.

522   *The Young Ones*

THEY slip on to the bus, hair piled up high.
New styles each month, it seems to me. I look,
Not wanting to be seen, casting my eye
Above the unread pages of a book.

They are fifteen or so. When I was thus,
I huddled in school coats, my satchel hung
Lop-sided on my shoulder. Without fuss
These enter adolescence; being young

Seems good to them, a state we cannot reach,
No talk of 'awkward ages' now. I see
How childish gazes staring out of each
Unfinished face prove me incredibly

Old-fashioned. Yet at least I have the chance
To size up several stages—young yet old,
Doing the twist, mocking an 'old-time' dance:
So many ways to be unsure or bold.

523   *One Flesh*

LYING apart now, each in a separate bed,
He with a book, keeping the light on late,
She like a girl dreaming of childhood,
All men elsewhere—it is as if they wait
Some new event: the book he holds unread,
Her eyes fixed on the shadows overhead.

Tossed up like flotsam from a former passion,
How cool they lie. They hardly ever touch,
Or if they do it is like a confession
Of having little feeling—or too much.
Chastity faces them, a destination
For which their whole lives were a preparation.

Strangely apart, yet strangely close together,
Silence between them like a thread to hold
And not wind in. And time itself's a feather
Touching them gently. Do they know they're old,
These two who are my father and my mother
Whose fire from which I came, has now grown cold?

CHRISTOPHER LOGUE
1926–

524   *Epitaph*

I AM old.
Nothing interests me now.
Moreover,
I am not very intelligent,
And my ideas
Have travelled no further
Than my feet.
You ask me:
What is the greatest happiness on earth?
Two things:
Changing my mind
As I change a penny for a shilling;
And,
Listening to the sound
Of a young girl
Singing down the road
After she has asked me the way.

525   FOREWORD TO *New Numbers*

THIS book was written in order to change the world
and published at 12/- (softback), 25/- (hardback) by Cape
of 30 Bedford Square, London, WC1
(a building formerly occupied by the Czarist Embassy)
in 1969.
It is generously scattered with dirty words
particularly on pages 9, 31, 37 and 45,
and was written by © Logue
a sexy young girl living among corrupted villagers
who keeps her innocence through love;
its weight is 7·926 oz,
its burning temperature is Fahrenheit 451,
and it was printed in Great Britain by
Butler & Tanner of London and Frome.
On the day of publication its price would buy
11 cut loaves,

3 yards of drip-dry nylon,
25 gallons of boiling dishwater,
5 rounds of M1 carbine ammunition,
or a cheap critic;
what do you expect for 12/- Paradise Lost?

This book will offend a number of people,
some of them influential people;
its commercial potential is slight,
the working classes will ignore it,
the middle classes will not buy it,
the ruling class will bolt it with a smile,
for I am a Western Art Treasure!
What right do I have to complain?
Nobody asked me to write it, yet
be sure I will complain.

This book is dedicated to new men,
astronauts meter-maids Chinese Ambassadors
quizmasters disc-jockeys South Vietnamese
rocket-designers thalidomide babies
anchormen skindivers African Generals
Israelis and launderette manageresses
multi-lingual porpoises left-wing doctors
draft-dodgers brainwashers bingo-queens con-
crete poets pollsters commuters computer-
programmers panels of judges gas-chamber victims
abstract expressionist chimpanzees
surfies and self-made millionaire teenagers
skydivers aquanauts working-class playwrights
industrial spies with identikit smiles
intrusion specialists and four-minute milers
motivation researchers and systems analysts
noise abatement society members
collective farmers and war criminals
transplanted heart men and water-ski champions
the Misses World and those I love.
If this book doesn't change you
give it no house space;
if having read it you
are the same person you
were before picking it up,
then throw it away.

Not enough for me
that my poems shine in your eye;
not enough for me
that they look from your walls
or lurk on your shelves;
I want my poems to be in your mind
so you can say them when you are in love
so you can say them when the plane takes off
and death comes near;
I want my poems to come between
the raised stick and the cowering back,
I want my poems to become
a weapon in your trembling hands,
a sword whose blade both makes and mirrors change;
but most of all I want my poems sung
unthinkingly between your lips like air.

526   *Friday. Wet dusk.*

FRIDAY. Wet dusk.
Three blind men outside an Indian restaurant.
They shout at each other.
They have been drinking.

White sticks wave in the doorway.
The place is almost empty.
They feel about the tables.
Two patrons draw their curries back.
They find a table near the door.
They telescope their sticks and wait.

Their order is: two eggs and chips, one curry.
Their chins are up.
Their mouths are open.
One drums the laminated calico.
Their plates arrive.

The taller of the egg men reads his chips.
He learns their number and their average size.
The other one eats furiously.
He who chose curry stirs it, looking upwards.

The rapid eater finishes and listens to the first.
He hears a fork enter a chip,
he hears the chip approach and disappear
forever into his companion's mouth,
and as its mastication starts
his fork moves confidently out
and spears the cluster of remaining chips
securing two.

He eats them both.
Yolk coagulates on his lapel.
The one with curry yawns.
None of them have removed their overcoats.

The masticator's fork returns,
touches the plate, lifts half an inch, dips in,
lifts, hesitates, swings to and fro,
then stabs the gobbler in his face.

All three get to their feet.
The curry man supplies the waiter with his purse.
Their sticks expand.
Outside
they start to shout obscene remarks.

MOLLY HOLDEN

1927–

527   *Photograph of Haymaker, 1890*

IT is not so much the image of the man
that's moving—he pausing from his work
to whet his scythe, trousers tied
below the knee, white shirt lit by
another summer's sun, another century's—
as the sight of the grasses beyond
his last laid swathe, so living yet
upon the moment previous to death;
for as the man stooping straightened up
and bent again they died before his blade.

Sweet hay and gone some seventy years ago
And yet they stand before me in the sun,
stems damp still where their neighbours' fall
uncovered them, succulent and straight,
immediate with moon-daisies.

528   *Giant Decorative Dahlia*

IT is easy enough to love flowers but these
had never appealed to me before, so
out of proportion above my garden's
other coloured heads and steady stems.

This spring though, in warm soil, I set
an unnamed tuber, offered cheap, and,
when August came and still no sign,
assumed the slugs had eaten it.

                    Suddenly it showed;
began to grow, became a small tree.
It was a race between the dingy bud
and the elements. It has beaten
the frost, rears now three feet above
the muddled autumn bed, barbaric petals
pink quilled with tangerine, turning
its great innocent face towards me
triumphantly through the damp afternoon.

I could not deny it love if I tried.

JAMES MICHIE

1927–

529   *Dooley is a Traitor*

'So then you won't fight?'
'Yes, your Honour,' I said, 'that's right.'
'Now is it that you simply aren't willing,
Or have you a fundamental moral objection to killing?'
Says the judge, blowing his nose
And making his words stand to attention in long rows.
I stand to attention too, but with half a grin
(In my time I've done a good many in).
'No objection at all, sir,' I said.
'There's a deal of the world I'd rather see dead—
Such as Johnny Stubbs or Fred Settle or my last landlord, Mr. Syme.
Give me a gun and your blessing, your Honour, and I'll be killing them
    all the time.
But my conscience says a clear no
To killing a crowd of gentlemen I don't know.
Why, I'd as soon think of killing a worshipful judge,
High-court, like yourself (against whom, God knows, I've got no
    grudge—
So far), as murder a heap of foreign folk.
If you've got no grudge, you've got no joke
To laugh at after.'
                    Now the words never come flowing
Proper for me till I get the old pipe going.
And just as I was poking
Down baccy, the judge looks up sharp with 'No smoking,
Mr. Dooley. We're not fighting this war for fun.
And we want a clearer reason why you refuse to carry a gun.
This war is not a personal feud, it's a fight
Against wrong ideas on behalf of the Right.
Mr. Dooley, won't you help to destroy evil ideas?'
'Ah, your Honour, here's
The tragedy,' I said. 'I'm not a man of the mind.
I couldn't find it in my heart to be unkind
To an idea. I wouldn't know one if I saw one. I haven't one of my own.
So I'd best be leaving other people's alone.'

'Indeed,' he sneers at me, 'this defence is
Curious for someone with convictions in two senses.
A criminal invokes conscience to his aid
To support an individual withdrawal from a communal crusade
Sanctioned by God, led by the Church, against a godless, churchless
    nation!'
I asked his Honour for a translation.
'You talk of conscience,' he said. 'What do you know of the Christian
    creed?'
'Nothing, sir, except what I can read.
That's the most you can hope for from us jail-birds.
I just open the Book here and there and look at the words.
And I find when the Lord himself misliked an evil notion
He turned it into a pig and drove it squealing over a cliff into the ocean,
And the loony ran away
And lived to think another day.
There was a clean job done and no blood shed!
Everybody happy and forty wicked thoughts drowned dead.
A neat and Christian murder. None of your mad slaughter
Throwing away the brains with the blood and the baby with the
    bathwater.
Now I look at the war as a sportsman. It's a matter of choosing
The decentest way of losing.
Heads or tails, losers or winners,
We all lose, we're all damned sinners.
And I'd rather be with the poor cold people at the wall that's shot
Than the bloody guilty devils in the firing-line, in Hell and keeping
    hot.'
'But what right, Dooley, what right,' he cried,
'Have you to say the Lord is on your side?'
'That's a dirty crooked question,' back I roared.
'I said not the Lord was on my side, but I was on the side of the Lord.'
Then he was up at me and shouting,
But by and by he calms: 'Now we're not doubting
Your sincerity, Dooley, only your arguments,
Which don't make sense.'
('Hullo,' I thought, 'that's the wrong way round.
I may be skylarking a bit, but my brainpan's sound.')
Then biting his nail and sugaring his words sweet:
'Keep your head, Mr. Dooley. Religion is clearly not up your street.
But let me ask you as a plain patriotic fellow
Whether you'd stand there so smug and yellow

If the foe were attacking your own dear sister.'
'I'd knock their brains out, mister,
On the floor,' I said. 'There,' he says kindly, 'I knew you were no
  pacifist.
It's your straight duty as a man to enlist.
The enemy is at the door.' You could have downed
Me with a feather. 'Where?' I gasp, looking round.
'Not this door,' he says angered. 'Don't play the clown.
But they're two thousand miles away planning to do us down.
Why, the news is full of the deeds of those murderers and rapers.'
'Your Eminence,' I said, 'my father told me never to believe the papers
But to go by my eyes,
And at two thousand miles the poor things can't tell truth from lies.'
His fearful spectacles glittered like the moon: 'For the last time what
  right
Has a man like you to refuse to fight?'
'More right,' I said, 'than you.
You've never murdered a man, so you don't know what it is I won't do.
I've done it in good hot blood, so haven't I the right to make bold
To declare that I shan't do it in cold?'
Then the judge rises in a great rage
And writes DOOLEY IS A TRAITOR in black upon a page
And tells me I must die.
'What, me?' says I.
'If you still won't fight.'
'Well, yes, your Honour,' I said, 'that's right.'

CHARLES TOMLINSON

1927–

530   *Paring the Apple*

THERE are portraits and still-lifes.

And there is paring the apple.

And then? Paring it slowly,
From under cool-yellow
Cold-white emerging. And . . . ?

573

The spring of concentric peel
Unwinding off white,
The blade hidden, dividing.

There are portraits and still-lifes
And the first, because 'human'
Does not excel the second, and
Neither is less weighted
With a human gesture, than paring the apple
With a human stillness.

The cool blade
Severs between coolness, apple-rind
Compelling a recognition.

531 *Oxen : Ploughing at Fiesole*

THE heads, impenetrable
And the slow bulk
Soundless and stooping,
A white darkness—burdened
Only by sun, and not
By the matchwood yoke—
They groove in ease
The meadow through which they pace
Tractable. It is as if
Fresh from the escape,
They consent to submission,
The debris of captivity
Still clinging there
Unnoticed behind those backs:
'But we submit'—the tenor
Unambiguous in that stride
Of even confidence—
'Giving and not conceding
Your premises. Work
Is necessary, therefore—'

CHARLES TOMLINSON

(With an unsevered motion
Holding the pauses
Between stride and stride)
'We will be useful
But we will not be swift: now
Follow us for your improvement
And at our pace.' This calm
Bred from this strength, and the reality
Broaching no such discussion,
The man will follow, each
As the other's servant
Content to remain content.

THOMAS KINSELLA

1928–

532   *Scylla and Charybdis*

ABSTRACTED, sour, as he reaches across a dish
Of plaice, his hand on a tray of birds, O'Neill
Unplugs the weary fan: flat heaps of fish
Exhale. He watches Reynolds grope and pile
His window opposite with melons, fresh
Leather of cabbage, oranges . . . and smile.

Wiping his gamy hands he turns and thirsts
Abruptly for clay and fragrance, until it seems
The South in a sweet globe sinks to his lips and bursts.
And yet red-wristed Reynolds dreams and dreams
That he flies with the snipe in the sparse bracken, or thrusts
Cold muscle to the depths and dumbly screams.

I have slipped at evening through that ghostly quarrel,
Making a third, to round the simple moral.

MATTHEW MITCHELL
1928–

533 *Printing Jenny*

PRINTING Bibles is Jenny's daily chore,
Or rather, stacking wads of India paper
As the press revolves them out galore.

Today it's Genesis and all that caper—
Catch a modern girl listening to snakes!—
Still it's a job and, viewed through the vapour

Of four o'clock tea, has got what it takes,
That is, nice pay, nice hours, no coming the boss.
Only an hour before knock-off, which makes

Three-quarters really, then off to the Cross
To meet Dan with his guitar and scooter,
Who says her lips are sweet as candy-floss.

Jenny's not sure these tight jeans really suit her
But for pillions and jive they're ideal.
Dan's picked up lots of tunes without a tutor.

Silly of him last month to go and steal.
He says he got that passionate in clink!
But, as the mags say, how to know love's real?

There's Rachel, who was told she'd get a mink:
She's had the kid adopted and she's back
On Cost Accounting, but it makes you think.

Jenny chucks the last heap on the binding stack:
Scriptures for those whose faith is on the cool,
For those who burn or twist upon the rack,

For many a bell-resounding mission school,
For best-seller export to the States:
She leaves them with her mug, her only tool,

And hurls her sixteen summers through the gates.

MARTIN SEYMOUR-SMITH
1928–

534   *What Schoolmasters Say*

WHAT schoolmasters say is not always wrong.
'You're a good chap, Smiggers, but don't go to seed'
Said Pettitt in bathtime at school long ago.
He seemed so earnest that I nearly cried,
But up until now I've laughed at his warning
Of where disregard of his words might lead—
Until last night when I dreamed I had died
           And Pettitt was God.

Hank made us lay out our beds like soldiers;
After Cert 'A' he summoned me, scowling
'Vile boy, I see that you've mucked it again!'
Of course, I didn't care then: I was proud
And resigned from the Corps against his advice—
But heard Hank's voice with its military sting
As today I strode through the playground crowd:
           'Well, Smith, you've failed!'

I pity myself that now I'm a puppet
Like Hank, and Pettitt, and roaring Gubbo;
That I must answer, when asked by my friends
'If you take your pupils aside and say:
"Vile boys, this won't do, disobedience is wrong,
And if you don't know it I'll make you know!"
Do you *really* mean that those boys should obey?':
           'I may, in a way.'

They are singing this morning before me
'How wonderful' etc. 'must thy sight be'
And if their croaking cannot quite mean God
Nor can it quite mean me. I ask myself: what
Should it mean? Their heads incline: I bow
My own, until a colleague warns: 'Hey, old
Boy! Head up, and watch for talking: we're not
           Expected to pray!'

ALAN SILLITOE
1928–

535 *Picture of Loot*

CERTAIN dark underground eyes
Have been set upon
The vast emporiums of London.

Lids blink red
At glittering shops
Houses and museums

Shining at night,
Chandeliers of historic establishments
Showing interiors to Tartar eyes,

Certain dark underground eyes
Bearing bloodred sack
The wineskins of centuries

Look hungrily at London:
How many women in London?
A thousand thousand houses

Filled with the world's high living
And fabulous knick-knacks;
Each small glossy machine

By bedside or on table or in bathroom
Is the electrical soul of its owner
The finished heart responding

To needle or gentle current;
And still more houses, endlessly stacked
Asleep with people waiting

To be exploded
The world's maidenhead supine for breaking
By corpuscle Tartars

To whom a toothbrush
Is a miracle;
What vast looting

What jewels of fires
What great cries
And long convoys

Of robbed and robbers leaving
The sack of rich great London.

IAIN CRICHTON SMITH

1928–

536   *Old Woman*

AND she, being old, fed from a mashed plate
as an old mare might droop across a fence
to the dull pastures of its ignorance.
Her husband held her upright while he prayed

to God who is all-forgiving to send down
some angel somewhere who might land perhaps
in his foreign wings among the gradual crops.
She munched, half dead, blindly searching the spoon.

Outside, the grass was raging. There I sat
imprisoned in my pity and my shame
that men and women having suffered time
should sit in such a place, in such a state

and wished to be away, yes, to be far away
with athletes, heroes, Greeks or Roman men
who pushed their bitter spears into a vein
and would not spend an hour with such decay.

'Pray God,' he said, 'we ask you, God,' he said.
The bowed back was quiet. I saw the teeth
tighten their grip around a delicate death.
And nothing moved within the knotted head

but only a few poor veins as one might see
vague wishless seaweed floating on a tide
of all the salty waters where had died
too many waves to mark two more or three.

THOM GUNN

1929–

537   *Autumn Chapter in a Novel*

THROUGH woods, Mme Une Telle, a trifle ill
With idleness, but no less beautiful,
Walks with the young tutor, round their feet
Mob syllables slurred to a fine complaint,
Which in their time held off the natural heat.

The sun is distant, and they fill out space
Sweatless as watercolour under glass.
He kicks abruptly. But we may suppose
The leaves he scatters thus will settle back
In much the same position as they rose.

A tutor's indignation works on air,
Altering nothing; action bustles where,
Towards the pool by which they lately stood,
The husband comes discussing with his bailiff
Poachers, the broken fences round the wood.

Pighead! The poacher is at large, and lingers,
A dead mouse gripped between his sensitive fingers:
Fences already keep the live game out:
See how your property twists her parasol,
Hesitates in the tender trap of doubt.

Here they repair, here daily handle lightly
The brief excitements that disturb them nightly;
Sap draws back inch by inch, and to the ground
The words they uttered rustle constantly:
Silent, they watch the growing, weightless mound.

They leave at last a chosen element,
Resume the motions of their discontent;
She takes her sewing up, and he again
Names to her son the deserts on the globe,
And leaves thrust violently upon the pane.

538   *On the Move*

'Man, you gotta Go.'

THE blue jay scuffling in the bushes follows
Some hidden purpose, and the gust of birds
That spurts across the field, the wheeling swallows,
Have nested in the trees and undergrowth.
Seeking their instinct, or their poise, or both,
One moves with an uncertain violence
Under the dust thrown by a baffled sense
Or the dull thunder of approximate words.

On motorcycles, up the road, they come:
Small, black, as flies hanging in heat, the Boys,
Until the distance throws them forth, their hum
Bulges to thunder held by calf and thigh.
In goggles, donned impersonality,
In gleaming jackets trophied with the dust,
They strap in doubt—by hiding it, robust—
And almost hear a meaning in their noise.

Exact conclusion of their hardiness
Has no shape yet, but from known whereabouts
They ride, direction where the tires press.
They scare a flight of birds across the field:
Much that is natural, to the will must yield.
Men manufacture both machine and soul,
And use what they imperfectly control
To dare a future from the taken routes.

It is a part solution, after all.
One is not necessarily discord
On earth; or damned because, half animal,
One lacks direct instinct, because one wakes
Afloat on movement that divides and breaks.
One joins the movement in a valueless world,
Choosing it, till, both hurler and the hurled,
One moves as well, always toward, toward.

A minute holds them, who have come to go:
The self-defined, astride the created will
They burst away; the towns they travel through
Are home for neither bird nor holiness,
For birds and saints complete their purposes.
At worst, one is in motion; and at best,
Reaching no absolute, in which to rest,
One is always nearer by not keeping still.

539   *The Byrnies*

THE heroes paused upon the plain.
When one of them but swayed, ring mashed on ring:
   Sound of the byrnie's knitted chain,
Vague evocations of the constant Thing.

   They viewed beyond a salty hill
Barbaric forest, mesh of branch and root
   —A huge obstruction growing still,
Darkening the land, in quietness absolute.

   That dark was fearful—lack of presence—
Unless some man could chance upon or win
   Magical signs to stay the essence
Of the broad light that they adventured in.

   Elusive light of light that went
Flashing on water, edging round a mass,
   Inching across fat stems, or spent
Lay thin and shrunk among the bristling grass.

Creeping from sense to craftier sense,
Acquisitive, and loss their only fear,
These men had fashioned a defence
Against the nicker's snap, and hostile spear.

Byrnie on byrnie! as they turned
They saw light trapped between the man-made joints,
Central in every link it burned,
Reduced and steadied to a thousand points.

540   *No Speech from the Scaffold*

THERE will be no speech from
the scaffold, the scene must
be its own commentary.

The glossy chipped
surface of the block is like
something for kitchen use.

And the masked man with his
chopper: we know him: he
works in a warehouse nearby.

Last, the prisoner, he
is pale, he walks through
the dewy grass, nodding

a goodbye to acquaintances.
There will be no speech. And we
have forgotten his offence.

What he did is, now,
immaterial. It is the
execution that matters, or,

rather, it is his conduct
As he rests there, while
he is still a human.

583

PETER PORTER

1929–

541   *Metamorphosis*

THIS new Daks suit, greeny-brown,
Oyster coloured buttons, single vent, tapered
Trousers, no waistcoat, hairy tweed—my own:
A suit to show responsibility, to show
Return to life—easily got for two pounds down
Paid off in six months—the first stage in the change.
I am only the image I can force upon the town.

The town will have me: I stalk in glass,
A thin reflection in the windows, best
In jewellers' velvet backgrounds—I don't pass,
I stop, elect to look at wedding rings—
My figure filled with clothes, my putty mask,
A face fragrant with arrogance, stuffed
With recognition—I am myself at last.

I wait in the pub with my Worthington.
Then you come in—how many days did love have,
How can they be catalogued again?
We talk of how we miss each other—I tell
Some truth—you, cruel stories built of men:
'It wasn't good at first but he's improving.'
More talk about his car, his drinks, his friends.

I look to the wild mirror at the bar—
A beautiful girl smiles beside me—she's real
And her regret is real. If only I had a car,
If only—my stately self cringes, renders down;
As in a werewolf film I'm horrible, far
Below the collar—my fingers crack, my tyrant suit
Chokes me as it hugs me in its fire.

542   FROM *Annotations of Auschwitz*

LONDON is full of chickens on electric spits,
     Cooking in windows where the public pass.
This, say the chickens, is their Auschwitz,
     And all poultry eaters are psychopaths.

543   *Your Attention Please*

THE Polar DEW has just warned that
A nuclear rocket strike of
At least one thousand megatons
Has been launched by the enemy
Directly at our major cities.
This announcement will take
Two and a quarter minutes to make,
You therefore have a further
Eight and a quarter minutes
To comply with the shelter
Requirements published in the Civil
Defence Code—section Atomic Attack.
A specially shortened Mass
Will be broadcast at the end
Of this announcement—
Protestant and Jewish services
Will begin simultaneously—
Select your wavelength immediately
According to instructions
In the Defence Code. Do not
Take well-loved pets (including birds)
Into your shelter—they will consume
Fresh air. Leave the old and bed-
ridden, you can do nothing for them.
Remember to press the sealing
Switch when everyone is in
The shelter. Set the radiation
Aerial, turn on the geiger barometer.
Turn off your Television now.

Turn off your radio immediately
The Services end. At the same time
Secure explosion plugs in the ears
Of each member of your family. Take
Down your plasma flasks. Give your children
The pills marked one and two
In the C.D. green container, then put
Them to bed. Do not break
The inside airlock seals until
The radiation All Clear shows
(Watch for the cuckoo in your
perspex panel), or your District
Touring Doctor rings your bell.
If before this, your air becomes
Exhausted or if any of your family
Is critically injured, administer
The capsules marked 'Valley Forge'
(Red pocket in No. 1 Survival Kit)
For painless death. (Catholics
Will have been instructed by their priests
What to do in this eventuality.)
This announcement is ending. Our President
Has already given orders for
Massive retaliation—it will be
Decisive. Some of us may die.
Remember, statistically
It is not likely to be you.
All flags are flying fully dressed
On Government buildings—the sun is shining.
Death is the least we have to fear.
We are all in the hands of God,
Whatever happens happens by His Will.
Now go quickly to your shelters.

BRIAN HIGGINS

1930–1965

544   *The Corrupt Man in the French Pub*

'I'M corrupt' he said to me in the French,
'I think I live in corruption's stench.'
Did this mean something about pay
Or those he was about to betray?
Was he selling out for a screw with a wrench
Or selling his wife six times a day?
'I'm corrupt' is a big thing to say
Though your chair is not a park bench.
I know that I am called corrupt myself
When seen around in good health
(By journalists usually)
And also because I get away
With 'not working' and such
Soi-disant words in inverted commas.
So in the common eye my form is
Perverted. An accusation to be ignored
Only the mind can be corrupt with a word.
So I asked him what he meant by corruption.
He said he was drinking too much.

TONY CONNOR

1930–

545   *Last of the Poet's Car*

THE end came as I drove it down the road
that leads off this one.
           The chassis broke with a *clang*,
pitching the rear suspension on the near side
on to the ground, where it dragged for a moment or two
until I was able to stop.

I drove home
somehow. It stood there in the drive looking
alright—like a poem seen in a magazine
that looks alright although you read it yesterday
and know that it's crap.
                        I had to force myself
to ring the breaker, who came and towed it away,
giving in exchange five pound notes
which I took to town and spent on books of verse.

What debts are owed to Life by Art and *vice-
versa*, I thought as I placed my books upon
the shelf, remembering how I bought the car
with dollars I earned from the sale of love poems.

546   *Lancashire Winter*

THE town remembers no such plenty,
under the wind from off the moor.
The labour exchange is nearly empty;
stiletto heels on the Palais floor
move between points of patent leather.
Sheepskin coats keep out the weather.

Commerce and Further Education
won't be frozen. Dully free
in snack bars and classrooms sits the patient
centrally heated peasantry,
receiving Wimpies like the Host;
striving to get that Better Post.

Snow on the streets and Mini-Minors
thickens to drifts, and in the square
from dingy plinths, blind eyes, stone collars,
the fathers of revolution stare,
who, against pikes and burning brands,
built the future with bare hands.

TED HUGHES

1930– 1999

Pike

PIKE, three inches long, perfect
Pike in all parts, green tigering the gold.
Killers from the egg: the malevolent aged grin.
They dance on the surface among the flies.

Or move, stunned by their own grandeur,
Over a bed of emerald, silhouette
Of submarine delicacy and horror.
A hundred feet long in their world.

In ponds, under the heat-struck lily pads—
Gloom of their stillness:
Logged on last year's black leaves, watching upwards.
Or hung in an amber cavern of weeds

The jaws' hooked clamp and fangs
Not to be changed at this date;
A life subdued to its instrument;
The gills kneading quietly, and the pectorals.

Three we kept behind glass,
Jungled in weed: three inches, four,
And four and a half: fed fry to them—
Suddenly there were two. Finally one

With a sag belly and the grin it was born with.
And indeed they spare nobody.
Two, six pounds each, over two feet long,
High and dry and dead in the willow-herb—

One jammed past its gills down the other's gullet:
The outside eye stared: as a vice locks—
The same iron in this eye
Though its film shrank in death.

A pond I fished, fifty yards across,
Whose lilies and muscular tench
Had outlasted every visible stone
Of the monastery that planted them—

Stilled legendary depth:
It was as deep as England. It held
Pike too immense to stir, so immense and old
That past nightfall I dared not cast

But silently cast and fished
With the hair frozen on my head
For what might move, for what eye might move.
The still splashes on the dark pond,

Owls hushing the floating woods
Frail on my ear against the dream
Darkness beneath night's darkness had freed,
That rose slowly towards me, watching.

548   *View of a Pig*

THE pig lay on a barrow dead.
It weighed, they said, as much as three men.
Its eyes closed, pink white eyelashes.
Its trotters stuck straight out.

Such weight and thick pink bulk
Set in death seemed not just dead.
It was less than lifeless, further off.
It was like a sack of wheat.

I thumped it without feeling remorse.
One feels guilty insulting the dead,
Walking on graves. But this pig
Did not seem able to accuse.

It was too dead. Just so much
A poundage of lard and pork.
Its last dignity had entirely gone.
It was not a figure of fun.

Too dead now to pity.
To remember its life, din, stronghold
Of earthly pleasure as it had been,
Seemed a false effort, and off the point.

Too deadly factual. Its weight
Oppressed me—how could it be moved?
And the trouble of cutting it up!
The gash in its throat was shocking, but not pathetic.

Once I ran a fair in the noise
To catch a greased piglet
That was faster and nimbler than a cat,
Its squeal was the rending of metal.

Pigs must have hot blood, they feel like ovens.
Their bite is worse than a horse's—
They chop a half-moon clean out.
They eat cinders, dead cats.

Distinctions and admirations such
As this one was long finished with.
I stared at it a long time. They were going to scald it,
Scald it and scour it like a doorstep.

549 *Hawk Roosting*

I SIT in the top of the wood, my eyes closed.
Inaction, no falsifying dream
Between my hooked head and hooked feet:
Or in sleep rehearse perfect kills and eat.

The convenience of the high trees!
The air's buoyancy and the sun's ray
Are of advantage to me;
And the earth's face upward for my inspection.

My feet are locked upon the rough bark.
It took the whole of Creation
To produce my foot, my each feather:
Now I hold Creation in my foot

Or fly up, and revolve it all slowly—
I kill where I please because it is all mine.
There is no sophistry in my body:
My manners are tearing off heads—

The allotment of death.
For the one path of my flight is direct
Through the bones of the living.
No arguments assert my right:

The sun is behind me.
Nothing has changed since I began.
My eye has permitted no change.
I am going to keep things like this.

550   *Thistles*

AGAINST the rubber tongues of cows and the hoeing hands of men
Thistles spike the summer air
Or crackle open under a blue-black pressure.

Every one a revengeful burst
Of resurrection, a grasped fistful
Of splintered weapons and Icelandic frost thrust up

From the underground stain of a decayed Viking.
They are like pale hair and the gutturals of dialects.
Every one manages a plume of blood.

Then they grow grey, like men.
Mown down, it is a feud. Their sons appear,
Stiff with weapons, fighting back over the same ground.

551   *The Howling of Wolves*

Is without world.

What are they dragging up and out on their long leashes of sound

That dissolve in the mid-air silence?

Then crying of a baby, in this forest of starving silences,
Brings the wolves running.
Tuning of a violin, in this forest delicate as an owl's ear,
Brings the wolves running—brings the steel traps clashing and
    slavering,
The steel furred to keep it from cracking in the cold,
The eyes that never learn how it has come about
That they must live like this,

That they must live

Innocence crept into minerals.

The wind sweeps through and the hunched wolf shivers.
It howls you cannot say whether out of agony or joy.

The earth is under its tongue,
A dead weight of darkness, trying to see through its eyes.
The wolf is living for the earth.
But the wolf is small, it comprehends little.

It goes to and fro, trailing its haunches and whimpering horribly.

It must feed its fur.

The night snows stars and the earth creaks.

JON SILKIN

1930–

Death of a Son

(*who died in a mental hospital aged one*)

SOMETHING has ceased to come along with me.
Something like a person: something very like one.
      And there was no nobility in it
            Or anything like that.

      Something was there like a one year
Old house, dumb as stone. While the near buildings
      Sang like birds and laughed
            Understanding the pact

      They were to have with silence. But he
Neither sang nor laughed. He did not bless silence
      Like bread, with words.
            He did not forsake silence.

      But rather, like a house in mourning
Kept the eye turned in to watch the silence while
      The other houses like birds
            Sang around him.

And the breathing silence neither
Moved nor was still.

      I have seen stones: I have seen brick
But this house was made up of neither bricks nor stone
      But a house of flesh and blood
            With flesh of stone

      And bricks for blood. A house
Of stones and blood in breathing silence with the other
      Birds singing crazy on its chimneys.
            But this was silence,

This was something else, this was
Hearing and speaking though he was a house drawn
Into silence, this was
      Something religious in his silence,

Something shining in his quiet,
This was different this was altogether something else:
Though he never spoke, this
      Was something to do with death.

And then slowly the eye stopped looking
Inward. The silence rose and became still.
The look turned to the outer place and stopped,
      With the birds still shrilling around him.
      And as if he could speak

He turned over on his side with his one year
Red as a wound
He turned over as if he could be sorry for this
And out of his eyes two great tears rolled, like stones, and he died.

ANTHONY THWAITE

1930–

553   *Sunday Afternoons*

On Sunday afternoons
In winter, snow in the air,
People sit thick as birds
In the station buffet-bar.
They know one another.
Some exchange a few words
But mostly they sit and stare
At the urns and the rock buns.

Not many trains today.
Not many are waiting for trains
Or waiting for anything
Except for the time to pass.
The fug is thick on the glass
Beyond which, through honks and puffing,
An express shrugs and strains
To sidings not far away.

Here no one is saying goodbye:
Tears, promises to write,
Journeys, are not for them.
Here there are other things
To mull over, till the dark brings
Its usual burdensome
Thoughts of a place for the night,
A bit of warm and dry.

On Sunday afternoons
The loudspeaker has little to say
Of wherever the few trains go.
Not many are travellers.
But few are as still as these
Who sit here out of the snow,
Passing the time away
Till the night begins.

554   *Mr. Cooper*

Two nights in Manchester: nothing much to do,
One of them I spent partly in a pub,
Alone, quiet, listening to people who
Didn't know me. *So I told the bloody sub-*
Manager what he could do with it. . . . Mr. Payne
Covers this district—you'll have met before?
Caught short, I looked for the necessary door
And moved towards it; could hear, outside, the rain.

The usual place, with every surface smooth
To stop, I suppose, the aspirations of
The man with pencil stub and dreams of YOUTH
AGED 17. And then I saw, above
The stall, a card, a local jeweller's card
Engraved with name, JEWELLER AND WATCHMENDER
FOR FIFTY YEARS, address, telephone number.
I heard the thin rain falling in the yard.

The card was on a sort of shelf, just close
Enough to let me read this on the front.
Not, I'd have said, the sort of words to engross
Even the keenest reader, nothing to affront
The public decency of Manchester.
And yet I turned it over. On the back
Were just three words in rather smudgy black
Soft pencil: MR. COOPER—DEAD. The year

Grew weakly green outside, in blackened trees,
Wet grass by statues. It was ten to ten
In March in Manchester. Now, ill at ease
And made unsure of sense and judgement when
Three words could throw me, I walked back into
The bar, where nothing much had happened since
I'd left. A man was trying to convince
Another man that somehow someone knew

Something that someone else had somehow done.
Two women sat and drank the lagers they
Were drinking when I'd gone. If anyone
Knew I was there, or had been, or might stay,
They didn't show it. *Good night*, I almost said,
Went out to find the rain had stopped, walked back
To my hotel, and felt the night, tall, black,
Above tall roofs. And Mr. Cooper dead.

555 *Ali Ben Shufti*

YOU want coins? Roman? Greek? Nice vase? Head of god, goddess?
Look, shufti here, very cheap. Two piastres? You joke.

I poke among fallen stones, molehills, the spoil
Left by the archaeologists and carelessly sieved.
I am not above ferreting out a small piece
From the foreman's basket when his back is turned.
One or two of my choicer things were acquired
During what the museum labels call 'the disturbances
Of 1941': you may call it loot,
But I keep no records of who my vendors were—
Goatherds, Johnnies in berets, Neapolitan conscripts
Hot foot out of trouble, dropping a keepsake or two.
I know a good thing, I keep a quiet ear open when
The college bodysnatchers arrive from Chicago,
Florence, Oxford, discussing periods
And measuring everything. I've even done business with them:
You will find my anonymous presence in the excavation reports
When you get to 'Finds Locally Purchased'. Without a B.A.—
And unable to read or write—I can date and price
Any of this rubbish. Here, from my droll pantaloons
That sag in the seat, amusing you no end,
I fetch out Tanagra heads, blue Roman beads,
A Greek lamp, bronze from Byzantium,
A silver stater faced with the head of Zeus.
I know three dozen words of English, enough French
To settle a purchase, and enough Italian
To convince the austere *dottore* he's made a bargain.

As for the past, it means nothing to me but this:
A time when things were made to keep me alive.
You are the ones who go on about it: I survive
By scratching it out with my fingers. I make you laugh
By being obsequious, roguish, battered, in fact
What you like to think of as a typical Arab.
Well, Amr Ibn el-As passed this way
Some thirteen hundred years ago, and we stayed.
I pick over what he didn't smash, and you
Pay for the leavings. That is enough for me.
You take them away and put them on your shelves
And for fifty piastres I give you a past to belong to.

DEREK WALCOTT

1930–

556   *Tales of the Islands*

CHAPTER I

la rivière dorée ...

THE marl white road, the Dorée rushing cool
Through gorges of green cedars, like the sound
Of infant voices from the Mission School,
Like leaves like dim seas in the mind; ici, Choiseul.
The stone cathedral echoes like a well,
Or as a sunken sea-cave, carved, in sand.
Touring its Via Dolorosa I tried to keep
That chill flesh from my memory when I found
A Sancta Teresa in her nest of light;
The skirts of fluttered bronze, the uplifted hand,
The cherub, shaft upraised, parting her breast.
Teach our philosophy the strength to reach
Above the navel; black bodies, wet with light,
Rolled in the spray as I strolled up the beach.

CHAPTER II

'Qu'un sang impur ...'

Cosimo de Chrétien controlled a boarding house.
His maman managed him. No. 13.
Rue St. Louis. It had a court, with rails,
A perroquet, a curio-shop where you
Saw black dolls and an old French barquentine
Anchored in glass. Upstairs, the family sword,
The rusting ikon of a withered race,
Like the first angel's kept its pride of place,
Reminding the bald count to keep his word
Never to bring the lineage to disgrace.
Devouring Time, which blunts the Lion's claws,
Kept Cosimo, count of curios fairly chaste,
For Mama's sake, for hair oil, and for whist;
Peering from balconies for his tragic twist.

CHAPTER III

la belle qui fut ...

Miss Rossignol lived in the lazaretto
For Roman Catholic crones; she had white skin,
And underneath it, fine, old-fashioned bones;
She flew like bats to vespers every twilight,
The living Magdalen of Donatello;
And tipsy as a bottle when she stalked
On stilted legs to fetch the morning milk,
In a black shawl harnessed by rusty brooches.
My mother warned us how that flesh knew silk
Coursing a green estate in gilded coaches.
While Miss Rossignol, in the cathedral loft
Sang to her one dead child, a tattered saint
Whose pride had paupered beauty to this witch
Who was so fine once, whose hands were so soft.

CHAPTER IV

'Dance of death'

Outside I said, 'He's a damned epileptic
Your boy, El Greco! Goya, he don't lie.'
Doc laughed: 'Let's join the real epileptics.'
Two of the girls looked good. The Indian said
That rain affects the trade. In the queer light
We all looked green. The beer and all looked green.
One draped an arm around me like a wreath.
The next talked politics. 'Our mother earth'
I said. 'The great republic in whose womb
The dead outvote the quick.' 'Y'all too obscene'
The Indian laughed. 'Y'all college boys ain't worth
The trouble.' We entered the bare room.
In the rain, walking home was worried, but Doc said:
'Don't worry, kid, the wages of sin is birth.'

DEREK WALCOTT

CHAPTER V

'moeurs anciennes'

The fête took place one morning in the heights
For the approval of some anthropologist.
The priests objected to such savage rites
In a Catholic country; but there was a twist
As one of the fathers was himself a student
Of black customs; it was quite ironic.
They lead sheep to the rivulet with a drum,
Dancing with absolutely natural grace
Remembered from the dark past whence we come.
The whole thing was more like a bloody picnic.
Bottles of white rum and a brawling booth.
They tie the lamb up, then chop off the head,
And ritualists take turns drinking the blood.
Great stuff, old boy; sacrifice, moments of truth.

CHAPTER VI

Poopa, da' was a fête! I mean it had
Free rum free whisky and some fellars beating
Pan from one of them band in Trinidad
And everywhere you turn was people eating
And drinking and don't name me but I think
They catch his wife with two tests up the beach
While he drunk quoting Shelley with 'Each
Generation has its *angst*, but we has none'
And wouldn't let a comma in edgewise.
(Black writer chap, one of them Oxbridge guys.)
And it was round this part once that the heart
Of a young child was torn from it alive
By two practitioners of native art,
But that was long before this jump and jive.

CHAPTER VII

lotus eater ...

'Maingot', the fishermen called that pool blocked by
Increasing filth that piled between ocean
And jungle, with a sighing grove
Of dry bamboo, its roots freckled with light
Like feathers fallen from a migratory sky.

Beyond that, the village. Through urine-stunted trees
A mud path wriggled like a snake in flight.
Franklin gripped the bridge-stanchions with a hand
Trembling with fever. Each spring, memories
Of his own country where he could not die
Assaulted him. He watched the malarial light
Shiver the canes. In the tea-coloured pool, tadpoles
Seemed happy in their element. Poor, black souls.
He shook himself. Must breed, drink, rot with motion.

CHAPTER VIII

In the Hotel Miranda, 10, Grass St., who fought
The Falangists en la guerra civil, at the hour
Of bleeding light and beads of crimson dew,
This exile, with the wry face of a Jew
Lets dust powder his pamphlets; crook't
Fingers clutch a journal to his shirt.
The eye is glacial; mountainous, the hook'd
Nose down which an ant, caballo, rides. Besides
As pious fleas explore a seam of dirt
The sunwashed body, past the age of sweat
Sprawls like a hero, curiously inert.
Near him a dish of olives has turned sour.
Above the children's street cries, a girl plays
A marching song not often sung these days.

CHAPTER IX

'le loupgarou'

A curious tale that threaded through the town
Through greying women sewing under eaves,
Was how his greed had brought old Le Brun down,
Greeted by slowly shutting jalousies
When he approached them in white-linen suit,
Pink glasses, cork hat, and tap-tapping cane,
A dying man licensed to sell sick fruit,
Ruined by fiends with whom he'd made a bargain.
It seems one night, these Christian witches said,
He changed himself to an Alsatian hound,
A slavering lycanthrope hot on a scent,
But his own watchman dealt the thing a wound
Which howled and lugged its entrails, trailing wet
With blood back to its doorstep, almost dead.

CHAPTER X

'adieu foulard ...'

I watched the island narrowing the fine
Writing of foam around the precipices then
The roads as small and casual as twine
Thrown on its mountains; I watched till the plane
Turned to the final north and turned above
The open channel with the grey sea between
The fishermen's islets until all that I love
Folded in cloud; I watched the shallow green
That broke in places where there would be reef,
The silver glinting on the fuselage, each mile
Dividing us and all fidelity strained
Till space would snap it. Then, after a while
I thought of nothing, nothing, I prayed, would change;
When we set down at Seawell it had rained.

557   *A Letter from Brooklyn*

AN old lady writes me in a spidery style,
Each character trembling, and I see a veined hand
Pellucid as paper, travelling on a skein
Of such frail thoughts its thread is often broken;
Or else the filament from which a phrase is hung
Dims to my sense, but caught, it shines like steel,
As touch a line, and the whole web will feel.
She describes my father, yet I forget her face
More easily than my father's yearly dying;
Of her I remember small, buttoned boots and the place
She kept in our wooden church on those Sundays
Whenever her strength allowed;
Grey haired, thin voiced, perpetually bowed.

'I am Mable Rawlins,' she writes, 'and know both your parents;'
He is dead, Miss Rawlins, but God bless your tense:
'Your father was a dutiful, honest,
Faithful and useful person.'
For such plain praise what fame is recompense?

'A horn-painter, he painted delicately on horn,
He used to sit around the table and paint pictures.'
The peace of God needs nothing to adorn
It, nor glory nor ambition.
'He is twenty-eight years buried,' she writes, 'he was called home,
And is, I am sure, doing greater work.'

The strength of one frail hand in a dim room
Somewhere in Brooklyn, patient and assured,
Restores my sacred duty to the Word.
'Home, home,' she can write, with such short time to live,
Alone as she spins the blessings of her years;
Not withered of beauty if she can bring such tears,
Nor withdrawn from the world that breaks its lovers so;
Heaven is to her the place where painters go,
All who bring beauty on frail shell or horn,

There was all made, thence their lux-mundi drawn,
Drawn, drawn, till the thread is resilient steel,
Lost though it seems in darkening periods,
And there they return to do work that is God's.

So this old lady writes, and again I believe,
I believe it all, and for no man's death I grieve.

ALAN BROWNJOHN

1931–

558 *The Train*

THE train will come tomorrow year,
The signals clamber into signs,
The gates will open on the track
Where weeds have grown among the lines.

A murmur in the listening air
Besides the heart's emphatic beat
Will rise beyond the junction bridge
Out of the summer's static heat,

ALAN BROWNJOHN

And round the distant, anxious bend
Engine and carriages appear.
But on a sultry afternoon
Your waiting hope could turn to fear.

Confronted with achieved desires
You may see nothing more to do
Than shrink from noise and turn away
As every devil thunders through.

559   *Class Incident from Graves*

Wednesdays were guest night in the mess, when the colonel expected the
married officers, who usually dined at home, to attend. The band played
Gilbert and Sullivan music behind a curtain. . . . Afterwards the band-
master was invited to the senior officers' table for his complimentary glass of
Light or Vintage.   (*Good-bye to All That*)

AT the officers' table, for half an hour afterwards, port,
The bandmaster. He accepts, one drink long,
All the courtesy of the gentlemen. They are suave, and equal.
'I expect with your job . . . Do you find . . . Oh well. . . .'
The bandmaster edges the shining inch of port along the grain of the
    table,
Precisely covering one knot with the transparent
Base of the glass. He crouches forward over the polished wood
Towards the officers, not comfortably convivial,
Eyes always going to the face speaking next,
Deferential, very pleased.
The band put away their instruments out at the back, having
Drunk their beers, standing.
The detachable pieces of brass lie down
In the felt grooves of the cases, just as they should.
Nine-thirty strikes.
There is laughter of men together, coming from inside.
'Mitchell's still in there, hob-nobbing with the officers.'

P. J. KAVANAGH
1931–

560 *The Temperance Billiards Rooms*

THE Temperance Billiards Rooms in red and green and brown
with porridge-coloured stucco in between
and half a child's top for a dome, also green—
it's like a Protestant mosque! It'll come down;
no room for this on the Supermarket scene.
Eight years ago on a Saturday afternoon
we used to walk past it, for no particular reason,
dressed in our weekend clothes now long out of fashion.
and bump into friends, newly married, just as we were,
and go to a film, or not, or window-shop.
Eight years before that I was seventeen,
eight years from now I may be forty-one;
thirty-three salutes the Billiards Rooms alone.
Because I'm the one who's alive still, but without much enthusiasm,
for loving someone has no particular season,
just goes on, as I do too I notice; not only from fear—
though it's true I won't want to go for I've never been there—
but while you are breathing it takes a decision to stop;
and I'm vaguely pleased to see that green and brown
(something so uneconomical's sure to come down)
in all its uselessness waiting out its season:
pleased to find the Temperance Billiards Rooms still here,
and for all I know men playing billiards temperately in there.

ADRIAN HENRI

1932–

561   *Mrs Albion You've Got a Lovely Daughter*
(for ALLEN GINSBERG)

ALBION'S most lovely daughter sat on the banks of the
    Mersey dangling her landing stage in the water.

The daughters of Albion
    arriving by underground at Central Station
    eating hot ecclescakes at the Pierhead
    writing 'Billy Blake is fab' on a wall in Mathew St

    taking off their navyblue schooldrawers and
    putting on nylon panties ready for the night

The daughters of Albion
    see the moonlight beating down on them in Bebington
    throw away their chewinggum ready for the goodnight kiss
sleep in the dinnertime sunlight with old men
    looking up their skirts in St. Johns Gardens
comb their darkblonde hair in suburban bedrooms
powder their delicate little nipples/wondering if tonight will be the
      night
their bodies pressed into dresses or sweaters
lavender at The Cavern or pink at The Sink

The daughters of Albion
    wondering how to explain why they didn't go home

The daughters of Albion
    taking the dawn ferry to tomorrow
    worrying about what happened
    worrying about what hasn't happened
    lacing up blue sneakers over brown ankles
    fastening up brown stockings to blue suspenderbelts

ADRIAN HENRI

Beautiful boys with bright red guitars
in the spaces between the stars

Reelin' an' a-rockin'
Wishin' an' a-hopin'
Kissin' an' a-prayin'
Lovin' an' a-layin'

Mrs Albion you've got a lovely daughter.

GEOFFREY HILL

1932–

562   *In Memory of Jane Fraser*

An Attempted Reparation

WHEN snow like sheep lay in the fold
And winds went begging at each door
And the far hills were blue with cold
And a cold shroud lay on the moor

She kept the siege. And every day
We watched her brooding over death
Like a strong bird above its prey.
The room filled with the kettle's breath.

Damp curtains glued against the pane
Sealed time away. Her body froze
As if to freeze us all and chain
Creation to a stunned repose.

She died before the world could stir.
In March the ice unloosed the brook
And water ruffled the sun's hair.
Dead cones upon the alder shook.

PHILIP HOBSBAUM

1932–

563 *A Lesson in Love*

SITTING straightbacked, a modest Irish miss,
Knees clenched together—even then I knew
Your full mouth would open under my kiss,
The line under your eyes gave me my clue.

Now on the floor, legs thrashing your dress
Over your stocking-tops, your tight blue pants
Bursting to be off at my caress,
This is the underside of our romance.

Which is the truer? I, speaking of Donne,
Calling the act a means and not an end,
Or at your sweet pudenda, sleeking you down:
Was there no other way to be your friend?

None, none. The awkward pauses when we talk,
The literary phrases, are a lie.
It was for this your teacher ran amock:
Truth lies between your legs, and so do I.

JENNY JOSEPH

1932–

564 *Warning*

WHEN I am an old woman I shall wear purple
With a red hat which doesn't go, and doesn't suit me,
And I shall spend my pension on brandy and summer gloves
And satin sandals, and say we've no money for butter.
I shall sit down on the pavement when I'm tired
And gobble up samples in shops and press alarm bells
And run my stick along the public railings
And make up for the sobriety of my youth.
I shall go out in my slippers in the rain
And pick the flowers in other people's gardens
And learn to spit.

You can wear terrible shirts and grow more fat
And eat three pounds of sausages at a go
Or only bread and pickle for a week
And hoard pens and pencils and beermats and things in boxes.

But now we must have clothes that keep us dry
And pay our rent and not swear in the street
And set a good example for the children.
We will have friends to dinner and read the papers.

But maybe I ought to practise a little now?
So people who know me are not too shocked and surprised
When suddenly I am old and start to wear purple.

GEORGE MACBETH

1932–

565   *The Miner's Helmet*

MY father wore it working coal at Shotts
When I was one. My mother stirred his broth
And rocked my cradle with her shivering hands
While this black helmet's long-lost miner's-lamp
Showed him the road home. Through miles of coal
His fragile skull, filled even then with pit-props,
Lay in a shell, the brain's blue-printed future
Warm in its womb. From sheaves of saved brown paper,
Baring an oval into weeks of dust,
I pull it down: its laced straps move to admit
My larger brows; like an abdicated king's
Gold crown of thirty years ago, I touch it
With royal fingers, feel its image firm—
Hands grown to kings' hands calloused on the pick,
Feet slow like kings' feet on the throneward gradient
Up to the coal-face—but the image blurs
Before it settles: there were no crusades.
My father died a draughtsman, drawing plans
In an airy well-lit office above the ground
Beneath which his usurpers, other kings,
Reigned by the fallen helmet he resigned
Which I inherit as a concrete husk.
I hand it back to gather dust on the shelf.

566 *The Wasps' Nest*

ALL day to the loose tile behind the parapet
The droning bombers fled: in the wet gutter
Belly-upwards the dead were lying, numbed
By October cold. And now the bloat queen,
Sick-orange, with wings draped, and feelers trailing,
Like Helen combing her hair, posed on the ledge
Twenty feet above the traffic. I watched, just a foot
From her eyes, very glad of the hard glass parting
My pressed human nose from her angry sting
And her heavy power to warm the cold future
Sunk in unfertilized eggs. And I thought: if I reached
And inched this window open, and cut her in half
With my unclasped pen-knife, I could exterminate
An unborn generation. All next summer,
If she survives, the stepped roof will swarm
With a jam of striped fighters. Therefore, this winter
In burning sulphur in their dug-out hangars
All the bred wasps must die. Unless I kill her.
So I balanced assassination with genocide
As the queen walked on the ledge, a foot from my eyes
In the last sun of the year, the responsible man
With a cold nose, who knew that he must kill,
Coming to no sure conclusion, nor anxious to come.

567 *When I am Dead*

I DESIRE that my body be
properly clothed. In such things
as I may like at the time.

And in the pockets may there be
placed such things as I use at the time
as, pen, camera, wallet, file.

And I desire to be laid on my side
face down: since I have bad dreams
if I lie on my back.

No one shall see my face when I die.

And beside me shall lie
my stone pig
with holes in his eyes.

And the coffin shall be as big as a crate.
No thin box
for the bones only.

Let there be room for a rat to come in.

And see that my cat, if I have one then,
shall have my liver.
He will like that.

And lay in food for
a week and a day:
chocolate, meat, beans, cheese.

And let all lie in
the wind and the rain
And on the eighth day burn.

And the ash
scatter as the wind decides.
And the stone and metal be dug in the ground.

This is my will.

ADRIAN MITCHELL

1932–

568   *Remember Suez?*

ENGLAND, unlike junior nations,
Wears officers' long combinations.
So no embarrassment was felt
By the Church, the Government or the Crown.
But I saw the Thames like a grubby old belt
And England's trousers falling down.

569   *Fifteen Million Plastic Bags*

I WAS walking in a government warehouse
Where the daylight never goes.
I saw fifteen million plastic bags
Hanging in a thousand rows.

Five million bags were six feet long
Five million bags were five foot five
Five million were stamped with Mickey Mouse
And they came in a smaller size.

Were they for guns or uniforms
Or a kinky kind of party game?
Then I saw each bag had a number
And every bag bore a name.

And five million bags were six feet long
Five million were five foot five
Five million were stamped with Mickey Mouse
And they came in a smaller size

So I've taken my bag from the hanger
And I've pulled it over my head
And I'll wait for the priest to zip it
So the radiation won't spread

Now five million bags are six feet long
Five million are five foot five
Five million are stamped with Mickey Mouse
And they come in a smaller size.

PETER REDGROVE

1932–

570   *Corposant*

A GHOST of a mouldy larder is one thing: whiskery bread,
Green threads, jet dots,
Milk scabbed, the bottles choked with wool,
Shrouded cheese, ebony eggs, soft tomatoes
Cascading through their splits,
Whitewashed all around, a chalky smell,
And these parts steam their breath. The other thing
Is that to it comes the woman walking backwards
With her empty lamp playing through the empty house,
Her light sliding through her steaming breath in prayer.

Why exorcise the harmless mouldy ghost
With embodied clergymen and scalding texts?
Because she rises shrieking from the bone-dry bath
With bubbling wrists, a lamp and steaming breath,
Stretching shadows in her rooms till daybreak
The rancid larder glimmering from her corpse
Tall and wreathed like moulds or mists,
Spoiling the market value of the house.

571   *The Secretary*

AT work his arms wave like a windmill
Slapping designs on crisp pads with a thick soft pencil,
A girded grin next morning at his desk, but
No cross words once the pencil gets slapping,
Sliving out our luxury. No cross words.

Silk dressing-gowns and wine-dark coverlets,
Grey hair bushing on my shantung lap,
Remorse, and sheep-eyes spinning water,
Remorse, the cord smiles deeply in his girth.

A glass of water then; quick comfortable speech;
We step from silks; the cords hang loose and heavy;
I catch his breath. His teeth stained tawny with tobacco
It is rank and vicious, like menstrual blood.

Buffing his nose with a forefinger,
Sipping tonic-water at breakfast,
Relaxed and special out of the bath,
He twinkles, and I twinkle back,
Pantless, under a slim formal skirt,
Ready for work. He holds my stocking
Like a hoop in two fists as my foot flies in
And lays his palms flat along my thighs
And kisses me. My skirt is creased
And beard-rash twinkles on my thighs
But I sit up and catch the notes
He flings to me grinning,
Fly for files and mend my shoulder-strap.
They send him north occasionally
My beaked fingers pecking meanly at the keys,
And he sends me letters; I'm drawn naked
On wine-dark coverlets on crisp pad-paper
The letter scribbled down my whiteness
With XX at customary halts. Could I cook a meal perhaps?
Or change the coverlets to creamy candlewick—
Anger booms among the giggling dressing-gowns
And I sit beside the bed holding water
Until grey hair bushes on my lap
And a hand collects itself to sweep my buttocks;
He feels really close to me if I forgive him
Constantly; I watch for the rewinding of his spring
And arms begin to whirl like windmills.

Wine, restaurants, dancing, creased skirts, beard-rash,
Pleasure just this side of painful fun, and a look,
A finger laid along his rummaging nose,
That makes me laugh down into my note-book,
Keep us young; a money-spinner
Twenty years my senior with a body
Just the age of mine, for the moment.
The maid dies first, then the young woman,
But the secretary keeps growing all the while
Into perfection and exemplary service,

Sharp-pencilled, clean-typer, indispensibly informed,
The memoranda ticking down the page,
Footage filed away, and yellowing miles
Accumulating in the dust-proof cabinets
Signposted in her careful lettering;
I shall have to tout myself elsewhere, trim personnel.
What is sincerity anyway, flat on one's back?
It foams everywhere, and floats out one's best:
Best lover, secretary, and perfect staff.

EDWARD LUCIE-SMITH

1933–

572   *The Lesson*

'YOUR father's gone,' my bald headmaster said.
His shiny dome and brown tobacco jar
Splintered at once in tears. It wasn't grief.
I cried for knowledge which was bitterer
Than any grief. For there and then I knew
That grief has uses—that a father dead
Could bind the bully's fist a week or two;
And then I cried for shame, then for relief.

I was a month past ten when I learnt this:
I still remember how the noise was stilled
In school-assembly when my grief came in.
Some goldfish in a bowl quietly sculled
Around their shining prison on its shelf.
They were indifferent. All the other eyes
Were turned towards me. Somewhere in myself
Pride like a goldfish flashed a sudden fin.

ROSEMARY TONKS

573   *Story of a Hotel Room*

THINKING we were safe—insanity!
We went in to make love. All the same
Idiots to trust the little hotel bedroom.
Then in the gloom . . .
. . . And who does not know that pair of shutters
With the awkward hook on them
All screeching whispers? Very well then, in the gloom
We set about acquiring one another
Urgently! But on a temporary basis
Only as guests—just guests of one another's senses.

But idiots to feel so safe you hold back nothing
Because the bed of cold, electric linen
Happens to be illicit. . . .
To make love as well as that is ruinous.
Londoner, Parisian, someone should have warned us
That without permanent intentions
You have absolutely no protection
—If the act is clean, authentic, sumptuous,
The concurring deep love of the heart
Follows the naked work, profoundly moved by it.

574   *Farewell to Kurdistan*

As my new life begins, I start smiling at the people around me,
You would think I'd just been given a substantial meal,
I see all their good points.
The railway sheds are full of greenish-yellow electricity,
It's the great mid-day hour in London . . . that suddenly goes brown.
. . . My stupefying efforts to make money
And to have a life!
Well, I'm leaving; nothing can hold me.

The platforms are dense to the foot,
Rich, strong-willed travellers pace about in the dark daylight,
And how they stink of green fatty soaps, the rich.
More dirty weather . . . you can hardly see the newspaper stand
With its abominable, ludicrous papers . . . which are so touching
I ought to laugh and cry, instead of gritting my teeth.

Let me inhale the filthy air for the last time,
Good heavens, how vile it is. . . . I could take you step by step
Back among the twilight buildings, into my old life . . .

The trains come in, boiling, caked!
The station half tames them, there's the sound of blows; the uproar!
And I—I behave as though I've been starved of noise,
My intestine eats up this big music
And my new bourgeois soul promptly bursts into flames, in mid-air.

No use pouring me a few last minutes of the old life
From your tank of shadow, filled with lost and rotten people,
I admit: the same flow of gutter-sugar to the brain . . .
I admit it, London.

No one to see me off—Ah!
I would like to be seen off; it must be the same agonizing woman
Who does not want to understand me, and who exposes me in public,
So that I can turn away, choked with cold bile,
And feel myself loved absolutely; the bitch.

These carriages, that have the heavy brown and black bread
Up their sides! But look out for the moment of cowardice,
It's Charon's rowing-boat that lurches and fouls my hand
As I climb on—exile, Limboist.

. . . The way these people get on with their lives; I bow down
With my few deeds and my lotus-scars.
Last minutes . . . last greenish-yellow minutes
Of the lost and rotten hours . . . faro, and old winters dimmed,
On which the dark—Yes, the black sugar-crust is forming, London.

I'm leaving! Nothing can hold me!
The trains, watered and greased, scream to be off.
Hullo—I'm already sticking out my elbows for a piece of territory,
I occupy my place as though I can't get enough of it
—And with what casual, haughty, and specific gestures, incidentally.

Tradesmen, Pigs, regenerative trains—I shall be saved!
I shall go to the centre of Europe; gliding,
As children skate on the diamond lid of the lake
Never touching ground—Xenophile, on the blue-plated meadows.

Oh I shall live off myself, rainclothes, documents,
The great train simmers. . . . Life is large, large!
. . . I shall live off your loaf of shadows, London;
I admit it, at the last.

BARRY COLE

1936–

575 *The Men Are Coming Back!*

THEY say the men are
Coming back. An elder
Reports her daughter, out
For the morning manna,
As having seen short columns
At the foot of the hills.

There is a loosening of
Muscles and a dampness
In the palms of some hands.
Inexplicably, the children
Begin to shout. Some of the
Elder women bolt the doors.

How did she know? asks
Someone. Know they were
Men? Instinct, says a
Harridan in yellow lace.
Does it matter? There are
Few movements to defence.

Even as they watch the
Elders scent defeat. Some
Of the younger are spitting
Upon the red cloth cover
Of a book, rubbing the
Dye across their untouched lips.

ROGER McGOUGH
1937–

576   *My cat and i*

GIRLS are simply the prettiest things
My cat and i believe
And we're always saddened
When it's time for them to leave

We watch them titivating
(that often takes a while)
And though they keep us waiting
My cat & i just smile

We like to see them to the door
Say how sad it couldn't last
Then my cat and i go back inside
And talk about the past.

577   *If Life's a Lousy Picture, Why Not Leave*
Before the End

DON'T worry
One night we'll find that deserted kinema
The torches extinguished
The cornish ripples locked away in the safe
The tornoff tickets chucked
In the tornoff shotbin
the projectionist gone home to his nightmare

Don't worry
that film will still be running
(the one about the sunset)
& we'll find two horses
tethered in the front stalls
& we'll mount
& we'll ride off
                    into
                         our
                              happy
                                   ending

GAVIN BANTOCK

1939–

578 *Joy*

AND Paradise does come

Paradise comes like a breeze and like a breeze
drifts elsewhere than where we are at the time

and we have no way of following the wind
to the world's end.

579 *Dirge*

BODY lies under the ground.
Blow, winds!

Body blows in the sand-dunes.
Blow, winds!

Body drifts in the sea-roads.
Blow, winds!
Blow for the dead.

Body moves much with the farers.
Blow, winds!

Body stares in the snow-lands.
Blow, winds!

Body dooms all the born-ones.
Blow, winds!
Winds blow for the dead.

DOUGLAS DUNN

1942–

580 *The Clothes Pit*

THE young women are obsessed with beauty.
Their old fashioned sewing machines rattle in Terry Street.
They must keep up, they must keep up.

They wear teasing skirts and latest shoes,
Lush, impermanent coats, American cosmetics.
But they lack intellectual grooming.

In the culture of clothes and little philosophies,
They only have clothes. They do not need to be seen
Carrying a copy of *International Times*,

Or the Liverpool Poets, the wish to justify their looks
With things beyond themselves. They mix up colours,
And somehow they are often fat and unlovely.

They don't get high on pot, but get sick on cheap
Spanish Burgundy, or beer in rampant pubs,
And come home supported and kissed and bad-tempered.

But they have clothes, bright enough to show they dream
Of places other than this, an inarticulate paradise,
Eating exotic fowl in sunshine with courteous boys.

Three girls go down the street with the summer wind.
The litter of pop rhetoric blows down Terry Street,
Bounces past their feet, into their lives.

581 *On Roofs of Terry Street*

TELEVISION aerials, Chinese characters
In the lower sky, wave gently in the smoke.

Nest-building sparrows peck at moss,
Urban flora and fauna, soft, unscrupulous.

Rain drying on the slates shines sometimes.
A builder is repairing someone's leaking roof,

He kneels upright to rest his back,
His trowel catches the light and becomes precious.

HUGO WILLIAMS

1942–

582   *The Butcher*

THE butcher carves veal for two.
The cloudy, frail slices fall over his knife.

His face is hurt by the parting sinews
And he looks up with relief, laying it on the scales.

He is a rosy young man with white eyelashes
Like a bullock. He always serves me now.

I think he knows about my life. How we prefer
To eat in when it's cold. How someone

With a foreign accent can only cook veal.
He writes the price on the grease-proof packet

And hands it to me courteously. His smile
Is the official seal on my marriage.

BRIAN PATTEN

1946–

583   *Portrait of a Young Girl Raped*
at a Suburban Party

AND after this quick bash in the dark
You will rise and go
Thinking of how empty you have grown
And of whether all the evening's care in front of mirrors
And the younger boys disowned
Led simply to this.

Confined to what you are expected to be
By what you are
Out in this frozen garden
You shiver and vomit—
Frightened, drunk among trees,
You wonder at how those acts that called for tenderness
Were far from tender.

Now you have left your titterings about love
And your childishness behind you
Yet still far from being old
You spew up among flowers
And in the warm stale rooms
The party continues.

It seems you saw some use in moving away
From that group of drunken lives
Yet already ten minutes pregnant
In twenty thousand you might remember
This party
This dull Saturday evening
When planets rolled out of your eyes
And splashed down in suburban grasses.

584 *Ode on Celestial Music*
(OR: *It's The Girl In The Bathroom Singing*)

IT'S not celestial music it's the girl in the bathroom singing.
You can tell. Although it's winter
the trees outside her window have grown leaves,
all manner of flowers push up through the floorboards.
I think—what a filthy trick that is to play on me,
I snip them with my scissors shouting
'*I want only bona fide celestial music!*'
Hearing this she stops singing.

Out of her bath now the girl knocks on my door,
'Is my singing disturbing you?' she smiles entering,
'did you say it was licentious or sensual?
And excuse me, my bath towel's slipping.'
A warm and blonde creature
I slam the door on her breasts shouting
'*I want only bona fide celestial music!*'

Much later on in life I wear my hearing-aid.
What have I done to my body, ignoring it,
splitting things into so many pieces my hands
cannot mend anything. The stars, the buggers, remained silent.
Down in the bathroom now her daughter is singing.
Turning my hearing-aid full volume
I bend close to the floorboards hoping
for at least one flower to appear.

INDEX OF FIRST LINES

First lines of extracts are printed in italics
The numbers refer to pages

627

INDEX OF FIRST LINES

INDEX OF FIRST LINES

INDEX OF FIRST LINES

INDEX OF AUTHORS

The references are to the numbers of the poems

INDEX OF AUTHORS